MIXED METHODS IN HEALTH SCIENCES RESEARCH

SAGE Mixed Methods Research Series

Vicki Plano Clark and Nataliya V. Ivankova,
Series Editors

MIXED METHODS IN HEALTH SCIENCES RESEARCH

A Practical Primer

Leslie Curry

Yale University

Marcella Nunez-Smith

Yale University

Los Angeles | London | New Delhi
Singapore | Washington DC

Los Angeles | London | New Delhi
Singapore | Washington DC

FOR INFORMATION:

SAGE Publications, Inc.
2455 Teller Road
Thousand Oaks, California 91320
E-mail: order@sagepub.com

SAGE Publications Ltd.
1 Oliver's Yard
55 City Road
London EC1Y 1SP
United Kingdom

SAGE Publications India Pvt. Ltd.
B 1/I 1 Mohan Cooperative Industrial Area
Mathura Road, New Delhi 110 044
India

SAGE Publications Asia-Pacific Pte. Ltd.
3 Church Street
#10-04 Samsung Hub
Singapore 049483

Copyright © 2015 by SAGE Publications, Inc.

Printed in the United States of America.

Library of Congress Cataloging-in-Publication Data

Curry, Leslie, author.
Mixed methods in health sciences research : a practical primer / Leslie Curry, Marcella Nunez-Smith.

p. ; cm. — (Sage mixed methods research series ; volume 1)
Includes bibliographical references and index.

ISBN 978-1-4833-0677-3 (pbk. : alk. paper)

I. Nunez-Smith, Marcella, author. II. Title. III. Series: Sage mixed methods research series ; v. 1. [DNLM: 1. Health Services Research—methods. 2. Research Design. 3. Research Report. W 84.3] R850

610.72—dc23   2014013644

This book is printed on acid-free paper.

Acquisitions Editor: Vicki Knight
Editorial Assistant: Yvonne McDuffee
Project Editor: Bennie Clark Allen
Copy Editor: Megan Markanich
Typesetter: C&M Digitals (P) Ltd.
Proofreader: Laura Webb
Indexer: Maria Sosnowski
Cover Designer: Karine Hovsepian
Executive Marketing Manager: Nicole Elliott

MIX
Paper from
responsible sources
FSC® C014174
www.fsc.org

14 15 16 17 18 10 9 8 7 6 5 4 3 2 1

TABLE OF CONTENTS

Additional Materials

LIST OF FIGURES, TABLES, AND BOXES

Figures

Tables

Boxes

PREFACE

Mixed methods research in health sciences contributes unique and important knowledge that helps explain the most complex problems in health and health care by capturing the perspectives of patients and their families, health care providers, and health care delivery organizations. Yet guidance on mixed methods research that is focused on the unique needs and interests of health sciences researchers is not well developed or readily available. We hope this book will be such a resource. We aim to describe major mixed methods approaches with illustrations from the health sciences literature, summarize standards for the design and conduct of rigorous mixed methods studies, and present extensive practical information for investigators interested in using these methods.

OUR PERSPECTIVE

We are health sciences researchers who are diverse in our backgrounds and training, which we believe brings a valuable breadth of perspectives and experience to this effort. Leslie Curry is an internationally recognized expert in mixed methods research. For two decades, she has conducted extramurally funded studies using these methods to examine health care delivery and quality in diverse settings and the scale-up of health care innovations, with emphasis on translating her research into policy and practice. Leslie has extensive experience in teaching, mentoring, and consulting on qualitative and mixed methods with a wide range of researchers in the health sciences. She brings this experience to the book in order to include essential information needed to address the questions commonly asked by students and colleagues.

Marcella Nunez-Smith is a practicing physician and researcher who has been awarded multiple grants from the National Institutes of Health (NIH) and foundations to lead qualitative and mixed methods projects. She brings a unique vantage point as a traditionally trained health services and clinical researcher who subsequently incorporated mixed methods approaches into her established research portfolio. Marcella also regularly reviews manuscripts and grant applications utilizing these methods. She seeks to bridge her mixed methods knowledge with the pragmatic needs of health sciences researchers.

We would also like to note that there are multiple philosophical orientations regarding the pursuit of science; we consider ourselves to be pragmatists as defined by mixed methods experts (Creswell & Plano Clark, 2011; Tashakkori & Teddlie, 2010). Pragmatism seeks to use whatever research methods are best suited to address a particular question, given the nature of what is being studied; as such, this orientation is practical and applied in nature. Pragmatism places value on both quantitative and qualitative methods (or some might say objective and subjective knowledge) and maintains that the methods are secondary to the research question. Simply put, we use whatever works.

Our motivation to write this book is grounded in our experiences over the past decades, as interest in mixed methods first slowly and then more rapidly developed within the health sciences community. We have been asked to give ad hoc lectures in schools of medicine, public health, and nursing; run workshops at national professional meetings; teach courses in various fellowship training programs; and provide consultations to colleagues via countless e-mails. We hope that having the voluminous methods literature distilled, synthesized, accessible, and compiled for quick reference will be of value to our colleagues interested in mixed methods.

WHY DO WE NEED ANOTHER BOOK ABOUT MIXED METHODS?

It is a fair question! There are a number of excellent textbooks on mixed methods widely consulted by students and researchers and several peer-reviewed scientific journals dedicated exclusively to publishing methods pieces and studies using mixed methods. While these resources are extraordinarily useful for researchers seeking to learn about and apply mixed methods in their work, they generally do not address the unique challenges of using these methods in particular disciplines, such as the health sciences. We define health sciences as including three major, interrelated yet distinct fields of scientific investigation: health services research, implementation science, and clinical research.

Health services research: This multidisciplinary field of scientific investigation studies how social factors, financing systems, organizational structures, and processes affect access to health care, the quality and cost of health care, and ultimately our health and well-being.

Implementation science: Implementation science examines the level to which health interventions can fit within real-world public health and clinical service systems. A particular focus of this field is identifying barriers (e.g., social, behavioral, economic, management) that impede effective implementation or testing new approaches to improve health.

Clinical research: Clinical research examines the safety and effectiveness of medications, devices, diagnostic tools, and treatment regimens. Conducted with human subjects (or material of human origin), it includes studies on mechanisms of human disease, clinical trials, and epidemiologic and behavioral studies.

These three fields of health-related research are distinct yet share common aspects, such as their highly interdisciplinary nature, their focus on real-world complex problems, and the fact that many investigators in these fields also have extensive training as health care providers and clinicians. Existing foundational textbooks and resources on mixed methods that present discussions of philosophy and theory are essential for the field. However, these resources may not be readily accessible for this typically pragmatic-minded audience that is eager for direct application of their research in policy or practice. In addition, health sciences researchers encounter specific types of challenges in implementing mixed methods in the context of dynamic health care delivery settings, working with personal health information and voluminous, complex cost, and utilization data. Finally, as with other focal areas of social science research, health sciences researchers operate in a particular funding and publication context, for which mixed methods remains a relatively new approach. With all of this in mind, we set out to write a reference text tailored for this audience, to guide researchers in how to be precise, compelling, and credible in developing and applying mixed methods in this context.

INTENDED AUDIENCE

The primary intended audience for this book is established health sciences researchers who are interested in understanding the core principles of mixed methods, as either research consumers or producers (or both), yet have limited knowledge of these approaches. In particular, we have in mind junior and senior faculty in schools of medicine, nursing, public health, allied health sciences, and related fields as well as research scientists in organizations and agencies conducting health sciences research. In addition, the material may be useful for reviewers of grant applications in federal funding agencies and private foundations, as funding for studies using mixed methods increases and these applications become more common. Based on our experience as peer reviewers of manuscripts and on our work on editorial boards, we also believe the book provides practical, relevant, concise information to guide reviewers and journal editors in assessing the rigor and quality of mixed methods studies. Finally, a broad range of graduate students in health sciences who have some foundation in both qualitative and quantitative methods and who seek to expand their knowledge of mixed methods can use this book as a resource, including those receiving predoctoral and postdoctoral training in public health, nursing, medicine and related health fields.

MAKING IT RELEVANT, ACCESSIBLE, AND PRACTICAL

There is a large, established (and evolving) literature on mixed methods that can be invaluable for researchers seeking to use these methods. We are often asked, "What are the main three things I should read if I want to learn about mixed methods?" There are a number of excellent resources that provide important information on all aspects of mixed methods, in diverse formats and styles, sure to be of use to researchers using mixed methods in diverse settings. We have noted some of those we find especially helpful for our work in health sciences in a consolidated list of key resources.

So you may wonder, as did we when initially asked to develop this book, what can we possibly add to this rich literature? We believe there are two things we can contribute: first, we can demonstrate exactly how mixed methods are used in the health sciences. Grounding the methods in this field of research, with existing examples and real-world experience, can help readers appreciate and apply the method more effectively. Second, we can serve as "translators" in order to distill the voluminous and sometimes jargon-heavy material for readers who may not have the time

▶ See Appendix E: Quick Resource: A Short List of Readings and References.

or disciplinary background (or frankly stamina) required to master the extensive information presented in handbooks or textbooks and to adapt principles and techniques for use in health sciences. We seek to translate the theoretical to the practical.

We took our task as translators seriously and solicited extensive input from potential readers of the book about what would be most useful as well as tips and insights from seasoned researchers about the practical realm of using mixed methods. As enthusiastic qualitative researchers, we gathered data from all kinds of places—through informal interactions with colleagues, debriefing sessions with workshop participants across the globe, course evaluations from graduate students, and in-depth interviews with key informants, including senior officials from a variety of funding organizations, and established and aspiring researchers. You will see throughout the book illustrative quotations and brief narratives drawn from these interviews to describe examples, perspectives, and experiences from the field.

We have used several features in order to make the content relevant and accessible. First, we begin by defining key terms in Chapter 1 to prepare the reader for terminology that will be used throughout the book. Second, at the opening of each chapter appears a concise summary of the primary content included in order to guide the reader to needed information more effectively. Third, we present many practical tools, including tables, figures, checklists, a glossary, key references in each chapter, and end-of-chapter review questions. Based on our experience in teaching and mentoring mixed methods, we have found concise, visually appealing, easy-to-reference practical tools such as these to be most requested and regarded quite useful. We created a mixed methods test kitchen (MMTK) for ongoing feedback of these extensive new tools. The "chefs" included former students as well as junior and senior faculty from a broad range of disciplines. We encouraged them to give us direct and candid input into the utility, clarity, and accessibility of the material we floated by them periodically. There is no doubt in our minds that the MMTK has elevated the practical value of the book, and for this we are extremely grateful. Fourth, we include several features that are useful for course instructors and students, including discussion questions and exercises to facilitate learning core principles and practices of mixed methods. Finally, because one aim is to draw from and integrate real-world examples and illustrations, we include carefully selected sections, summaries, and figures from multiple sources including published texts, peer-reviewed journals, and successful grant applications prepared for the National Institutes of Health and other foundations. Because mixed methods research can apply to many types of health sciences studies, we have included examples of a wide range of studies from the peer-reviewed empirical literature in different scientific disciplines and content areas.

OVERVIEW OF THE BOOK

The book is organized into four parts. Part I: Mixed Methods 101 presents foundational definitions and study designs and then applies these concepts through illustrations from health sciences for each major design. The final chapter of this part provides guidance for researchers to determine whether a mixed methods approach is warranted and feasible. Part II: Getting Mixed Methods Research Funded describes criteria for scientific rigor in mixed methods designs, with tailored guidance for investigators, consumers of peer-reviewed literature, and reviewers of grants and manuscripts. In addition, extensive guidance is provided for how to write a scientifically sound and compelling grant proposal, followed by examples of successful grant applications using mixed methods with reflections from the grantees and highlights of best practices. Part III: Designing and Implementing a Mixed Methods Study presents principles and strategies for sampling, data collection, and analysis and addresses the realities of implementing mixed methods studies, with a focus on the many practical considerations faced by investigators. Special attention is given to the issue of managing mixed methods teams. Implementation challenges are illustrated by examples from the field, with possible strategies and solutions for addressing common challenges. Part IV: Disseminating Findings describes best practices for the dissemination and publication of mixed methods research in the health sciences.

References

Creswell, J. W., & Plano Clark, V. L. (2011). *Designing and conducting mixed methods research* (2nd ed.). Thousand Oaks, CA: Sage.

Tashakkori, A., & Teddlie, C. (2010). *SAGE handbook of mixed methods in social & behavioral research* (2nd ed.). Thousand Oaks, CA: Sage.

ACKNOWLEDGMENTS

It may be trite, but it is true: It really does take a village. We would like to convey our sincere appreciation for the extraordinary time, effort, expertise, and goodwill contributed to this project by the following individuals and groups.

First up is our team. There is literally no question that this book could not have been written without Margaret Lippitt, our extraordinary research associate, who calmly steered us from conception to completion with her considerable intellectual and organizational talents. Emily Cherlin is a mixed methods research colleague who is a master at literature searching and synthesis and a constant source of support. Our designer, Arian Schulze, not only has a gift for creating effective schematics and figures but also happens to be a doctoral candidate in medical anthropology. The team was rounded out by Rebecca Fine, Tara Rizzo, and Comfort Agaba, who helped with literature searching, reference tracking, and encouragement.

We also thank the many mixed methods experts who contributed in multiple generous ways, including participating in interviews, sharing their research materials, and providing feedback (in alphabetical order): Miriam Boeri, Giselle Corbie-Smith, Benjamin Crabtree, Jayne Cutter, Neal Dawson, Kelly Devers, Jennifer Elston Lafata, Michael Fetters, Shira Fischer, Kenneth Ginsburg, Chanita Hughes-Halbert, Holly Powell Kennedy, Andres Maiorana, Janice Morse, Madeline Murtagh, Alicia O'Cathain, Robin Pollini, Karen Schifferdecker, Jonathan Signer, Eleanor Palo Stoller, Benita Weathers, Terrie Wetle, Jonathan White, and Jennifer Pelt Wisdom.

The mixed methods test kitchen (MMTK) provided insights into the needs of our target audience and valuable feedback on figures, tables, and other tools we developed. The MMTK team included (in alphabetical order): Matthew Anstey, Susannah Bernheim, Oni Blackstock, Tasce Bongiovanni, Javier Cepeda, Zerrin Cetin, Peggy Chen, Uriyoan Colon-Ramos, Jennifer Cunningham, Amy Desai, Kumar Dharmarajan, Jess Holzer, Neel Iyer, Tish Knobf, Kelly Kyanko, Kasia Lipska, Karl Minges, Aasim Padela, Sarah Pallas, Erica Rogan, Calie Santana, Dena Schulman-Green, Jay Schurr, Lauren Taylor, and Emily Wang.

The unsuspecting but good-natured participants in a variety of workshops and lectures who were invited to critique content are as follows: the Robert Wood Johnson Clinical Scholars at Yale University, the Commonwealth Fund Harkness fellows, faculty of the Eastern Caribbean Health Outcomes Research Network, and the students at Yale College and in the schools of public health, medicine, and nursing at Yale University.

Thanks also go to leaders in funding and publishing mixed methods in the health sciences: Helen Meissner (director of the Tobacco Regulatory Science Program and former senior advisor in the Office of Behavioral and Social Sciences Research [OBSSR], National Institutes of Health [NIH]), Sankey Williams (deputy editor of the *Annals of Internal Medicine*), Anne Marie Audet (vice president for the Delivery System Reform & Breakthrough Opportunities at the Commonwealth Fund), Susan Bouregy (chief HIPAA privacy officer, former director of the Human Subjects Committee [HSC], Yale University), Jason Gerson (senior program officer for Comparative Effectiveness Research [CER] Methods and Infrastructure, Patient-Centered Outcomes Research Institute [PCORI]), Barbara Given (director of the PhD Program of the College of Nursing Michigan State University and editorial board member for *Nursing and Health, Cancer Nursing,* and the *European Journal of Cancer Nursing,* among other journals).

We thank our acquisitions editor at SAGE, Vicki Knight, and our primary editors and coaches, Vicki Plano Clark and Nataliya Ivankova, for their unwavering support and wise counsel every step of the way. The SAGE reviewers brought valuable perspectives from diverse fields including nursing, counseling, public health, and medicine and also represented a variety of institutions; we appreciate their encouraging, thoughtful, and constructive comments.

And finally, we are indebted to our longtime collaborators who have shaped our thinking and provided inspiration and support all these years (in alphabetical order): David Berg, Elizabeth Bradley, John Creswell, Harlan Krumholz, Alicia O'Cathain, and Terrie Wetle.

ABOUT THE AUTHORS

Leslie Curry, PhD, MPH, is Senior Research Scientist and Lecturer at the Yale School of Public Health, and Co-Director of the Robert Wood Johnson Foundation Clinical Scholars Program. She is core faculty at the Yale Global Health Leadership Institute and the former Director of the Braceland Center for Mental Health and Aging.

Leslie's research focuses on health care access, quality and outcomes in hospital, community and institutional settings in the United States and internationally. She is especially interested in the development and scale up of innovative, evidence-based health practices, programs, and policies, and regularly collaborates with government agencies and health care providers in these efforts. Her work has been supported by a variety of funders including NIH, AHRQ, The Commonwealth Fund, The Robert Wood Johnson Foundation, The Bill and Melinda Gates Foundation and The World Bank. Leslie is an internationally recognized expert in qualitative and mixed methods, and was appointed to a working group commissioned by the National Institutes of Health to develop Best Practices for Mixed Methods Research in the Health Sciences in 2011. She is actively engaged in conducting, studying and teaching about interdisciplinary research, bridging the methods communities through publishing qualitative and mixed methods empirical research and methodology in biomedical and health services journals. A Fellow of Branford College at Yale, Leslie teaches extensively and provides mentoring at the undergraduate, graduate, and post-graduate levels in public health and medicine.

Marcella Nunez-Smith, MD, MHS, is Associate Professor of General Internal Medicine at the Yale School of Medicine and Associate Professor of Chronic Disease Epidemiology at the Yale School of Public Health. She is Co-Director of Community Based Participatory Research in the Robert Wood Johnson Foundation Clinical Scholars Program and Research Faculty at Yale's Global Health Leadership Institute. She serves as Deputy Director for Health Equity Research and Workforce Development for the Yale Center for Clinical Investigation.

Most recently, Dr. Nunez-Smith is Founding Director of the Equity Research and Innovation Center (ERIC) at Yale School of Medicine. Within the Center, Dr. Nunez-Smith oversees the development and dissemination of evidence-based models that aim to narrow health and healthcare inequity gaps. She uses qualitative and mixed methodology to effectively study healthcare workforce diversity and inclusion, patient experiences of care, and health research strengthening to address chronic diseases in low and middle resource areas. She was awarded the David E. Rogers Jr. Faculty Workshop Award for her workshop "Beyond the themes: applying best practices in qualitative and mixed methods research from grant preparation to meaningful translation" at the 2012 Annual Meeting of the Society of General Internal Medicine. Dr. Nunez-Smith serves as a consultant on several grant applications both at Yale and beyond for her expertise in qualitative and mixed methods design and has been consistently recognized for excellence in medical education, mentoring and teaching.

INTRODUCTION

Mixed methods research is growing in acceptance and application across disciplines and the world. Because of this continued growth, the field of mixed methods research is becoming increasingly complex, nuanced, and specialized. In response to this growth, we initiated the SAGE Mixed Methods Research Series to provide researchers, reviewers, and consumers with practice-focused books that aim to help scholars navigate the field of mixed methods and develop an understanding of its contemporary issues and debates in a practical, applied way.

One mixed methods issue of great practical importance is the disciplinary context in which the use of mixed methods is considered. Disciplines develop their own culture, language, focus, and standards for research, and these disciplinary norms can directly influence the major decisions involved in the conduct of mixed methods research. As such, we view the process of designing and conducting a mixed methods study as located at the center of a dynamic system of decisions and contexts. The mixed methods decisions are dynamically shaped within personal, interpersonal, and social contexts and have particular relevance for how researchers apply mixed methods within their disciplines.

Because of the importance of disciplinary contexts for mixed methods research, we are delighted to have one of the first books of the SAGE Mixed Methods Research Series focus on the use of mixed methods within the health sciences. Despite clear signs of increasing interest in and application of mixed methods within health sciences research, there is not enough practical guidance and advice available for health science researchers wanting to use this approach. In this book, Leslie Curry and Marcella Nunez-Smith provide a practical guide that effectively situates many of the formal concepts discussed in the mixed methods literature to the culture, language, focus, and standards found within the health sciences. Their innovative approach uses extensive examples from practice, offers lessons learned from individual researchers' real-world experiences, and thoughtfully synthesizes the mixed methods literature to describe how the conduct of mixed methods research shapes and is shaped by a health sciences research context. This book provides a significant resource for health science researchers needing information about mixed methods and for scholars interested in better understanding the different ways that disciplinary contexts shape the use of mixed methods research. This applied and context-specific discussion of mixed methods research is exactly the kind of topic we wanted addressed when we envisioned the series.

Vicki L. Plano Clark and Nataliya V. Ivankova
Editors, SAGE Mixed Methods Research Series

We dedicate this book to our families:
Joe, Catherine, Elizabeth, Jessie, Chloe, Kinsen, Ria, Mom Curry,
and Mom Nunez, and our respective menageries.

AUTHORS' NOTE: We selected the cover image to convey two essential messages of this book. First, mixed methods exist along a single continuum of measurement anchored by qualitative and quantitative methods. Second, mixed methods are uniquely suited to explore the nonlinear, complex, and dynamic phenomena increasingly common in the health sciences.

PART I

MIXED METHODS 101

Part I is a basic introduction to using mixed methods in the health sciences. We define mixed methods as it is used in this text, review the basic types of mixed methods study designs, and present key considerations, including timing of components and approaches to integration. We then turn to a discussion of how mixed methods can be useful in health sciences research and provide several detailed examples. Finally, we review determining whether a mixed methods design is both appropriate and feasible for a given research question.

⚜ ONE ⚜

DEFINITION AND OVERVIEW OF MIXED METHODS DESIGNS

Information you will find in this chapter: This chapter opens with a review of the definition and characteristics of mixed methods research as it is used in health sciences. In the second section, we describe major considerations in mixed methods study design, including strategies for integration and the relative timing of when each component is carried out. The subsequent sections review the three basic types of mixed methods designs in more detail. Finally, we highlight two additional mixed methods designs increasingly common in health sciences research.

Key features in this chapter:

- Brief quotations and reflections from mixed methods researchers
- Figure synthesizing characteristics of qualitative, quantitative, and mixed methods research
- Figures depicting each of the basic types of mixed methods designs
- Brief illustrative examples from the peer-reviewed empirical literature with commentary on integration and timing

DEFINITION AND CHARACTERISTICS OF MIXED METHODS RESEARCH

Mixed methods research draws from multiple scientific traditions and disciplinary backgrounds. As applied in health sciences, using mixed methods may mean supplementing the perspectives of clinical and health services research with those of disciplines as varied as anthropology, psychology, sociology, economics, education, epidemiology, and genetics. It is perhaps then no surprise that there are many definitions of mixed methods, each reflecting different methodological assumptions and perspectives. Therefore, we propose a clear, concise definition so that readers from diverse backgrounds will share a common understanding of mixed methods as it is used in this book. Incidentally, a shared understanding is also a critical first task for mixed methods research teams, who must be able to approach their work with a unified mixed methods lens. Individuals trained in different disciplines are likely to have substantially different perspectives and professional languages. The diversity inherent in mixed methods research teams, though challenging, can be an extraordinary asset.

For our purposes, we adopt the definition of mixed methods developed by Johnson, Onwuegbuzie, and Turner (2007) based on a systematic synthesis of 19 previously published definitions:

> Mixed methods research is the type of research in which a researcher or team of researchers combines elements of qualitative and quantitative research approaches (e.g., use of qualitative and quantitative viewpoints, data collection, analysis, inference techniques) for the broad purposes of breadth and depth of understanding and corroboration. (p. 123)

▶ Strategies for facilitating effective communication and collaboration across mixed methods teams are presented in Chapter 9: Managing Mixed Methods Teams.

This definition, like many definitions of mixed methods, highlights the interplay of qualitative and quantitative methods in a single research study. Establishing a mixed methods definition is an important first step; however, even when researchers agree on a definition, diversity in disciplinary and methodological expertise can get in the way of effective communication and productive collaboration.

Individuals trained in different methodological approaches may have trouble agreeing on precise definitions and differentiating essential terms from frustrating jargon. Collaboration can be enhanced by team members having "methodological bilingualism," or a minimum competency in both methodologies to enable effective communication and successful integration of findings (Tashakkori & Teddlie, 2003). One tool to facilitate bilingualism is a glossary, which provides clear definitions of key content and methodological terms. At the end of the book you will find a glossary that includes concepts commonly used in qualitative and quantitative methods, with particular emphasis on the mixed methods terms, which are most likely to be new or unfamiliar to our readers.

We also include suggested illustrative citations or resources for further reading on each concept. Please note there are many other possible appropriate citations; these are only included

▶ See the Glossary of Key Terms and Definitions at the end of the book.

as a possible starting point. We encourage you to take a moment to scan the Glossary of Key Terms and Definitions for any terms that may be unfamiliar and to turn to the suggested resources and other published reference texts for additional information.

The definition of mixed methods that we are using captures the respective contributions of qualitative and quantitative inquiry and emphasizes the interaction of these approaches at multiple levels and stages throughout a research study. Because a central premise of this definition is that qualitative and quantitative approaches are complementary in nature, it is important to understand these complementary attributes as well as the defining features of mixed methods. In Figure 1.1, we present a schematic of key characteristics of qualitative, quantitative, and mixed methods research. We chose a Venn diagram in order to reflect the qualitative and quantitative as distinct traditions, each with essential distinguishing characteristics. Yet we also connect them with inward pointing arrows in order to convey that these scientific traditions exist on a continuum of methodologies, with mixed methods sitting in the nexus of their intersection.

Although quantitative methods have historically been the primary approach in health sciences research, many contemporary phenomena in health and health care are difficult, if not impossible, to measure using quantitative approaches alone. Examples include complex and dynamic social processes; beliefs, values, and motivations that underlie individual health behaviors; and social, political, economic, and organizational contexts relevant to health. In cases in which little is known about the research topic, an exploratory qualitative approach is warranted in order to inform further research. Qualitative methods focus on the quality, or essence, of a phenomenon, using an inductive

Figure 1.1 Characteristics of Qualitative, Quantitative, and Mixed Methods Research

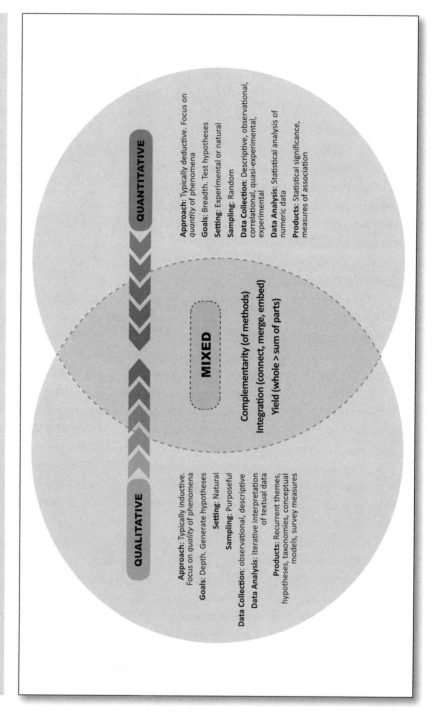

lens to gain insights from "the ground up" (Glaser & Strauss, 1967; Miles & Huberman, 1994). The goal is to produce depth of understanding, and perhaps generate hypotheses regarding a phenomenon, its precursors, and its consequences. Qualitative investigation occurs in natural (as compared to controlled or experimental) settings. Qualitative study samples are purposeful in design, with deliberate inclusion of individuals who have direct experience with or knowledge of the focal topic (sometimes called "key informants"). Data analysis involves iterative processes of data collection, coding, and interpretation. Potential products or outputs from qualitative analysis can include recurrent themes, hypotheses, taxonomies, conceptual models, or quantitative survey instruments (Bradley, Curry, & Devers, 2007).

Similarly, other phenomena in health and health care can be characterized using quantitative approaches. Examples include health care costs, utilization patterns, biologic and physiologic characteristics of patients, and prevalence and magnitude of health conditions. Quantitative methods, which are deductive in origin, focus on quantifying phenomenon, using statistical computations to establish prevalence, magnitude, causal associations, and paths (Hulley, Cummings, Browner, Grady, & Newman, 2013; Rothman, Greenland, & Lash, 2008). These methods seek to describe the breadth of phenomena, to generalize and compare across groups, and to test hypotheses. Quantitative studies can be conducted in experimental or natural settings. Random sampling approaches are necessary in order to permit generalizations or inferences to larger populations. Data analysis uses statistical approaches and often accounts for potential confounding factors that may systematically bias the results. Products are measures of statistical significance and association between variables.

When the study phenomenon of interest is multifaceted and includes dimensions that are both qualitative and quantitative in nature, a mixed methods approach is appropriate. Like other types of research, mixed methods studies require deliberate, a priori conceptualization of the phenomenon of interest, as well as its constituent parts. Where mixed methods differs from other approaches is that the phenomenon of interest involves research questions that, by their nature, require both qualitative and quantitative forms of examination, such that the design and findings of one component are central to the other. Mixed methods designs can capitalize on the respective strengths of each approach (Jick, 1979). In Box 1.1, a prominent researcher in the area of health disparities observes that pressing questions in health sciences require diverse forms of both qualitative and quantitative data.

Box 1.1　Adding Relevance to Health Sciences Research Through Mixed Methods

I think that to add to the kinds of questions that are still outstanding [in health research], you need to have both the weight of a large data set to be able to generalize the results, as well as the voices, the experiences of people that you have in qualitative research . . . . That's the only way that you can really try to tackle the problems—is to use all the data that's there.

—Giselle Corbie-Smith, MD, MSc,
Professor of Social Medicine,
University of North Carolina at Chapel Hill

The framing of the study as a single, unified undertaking is essential. Two parallel studies on the same general topic using different methods do not represent a mixed methods design (although we do see this happen in funded grants and published papers). For instance, if the overarching aim of a study is to understand adherence to a complicated nutrition and exercise regime, a mixed methods design might track compliance quantitatively over a defined period and also use qualitative interviews to uncover barriers to adherence from the patient's perspective. In mixed methods studies, the aims, sampling, data, and analysis will include characteristics of both qualitative and quantitative methods. Nevertheless, a mixed methods study is not simply a form of scientific investigation that uses both qualitative and quantitative methods. Rather, there are several fundamental defining features of mixed methods studies: complementarity (or "fit") of qualitative and quantitative components, deliberate integration of quantitative and qualitative findings, and yield to generate insights greater than what could be achieved through one method.

A core premise in mixed methods is that using complementary methods in pursuit of a

▶ We examine the complementarity and "fit" of aims and methods in Chapter 3: Determining the Appropriateness and Feasibility of Using Mixed Methods. We address integration of qualitative and quantitative data in depth in Chapter 8: Data Analysis and Integration in Mixed Methods Studies, and we also discuss yield in Chapter 6: Assessing Quality in Mixed Methods Studies.

question yields greater insight than would either method alone or both independently. As Einstein observed the limits of singular independent forms of measurement, "Not everything that can be counted counts, and not everything that counts can be counted" (Einstein, attributed). Appreciation for this reality may be one reason that mixed methods research is growing in popularity. In Box 1.2, a health services researcher with substantial experience in mixed methods reflects on the changes he has seen over the past 10 years, with increasing recognition of the value of diverse methods among senior investigators of all backgrounds.

Box 1.2 Growing Acceptability of Mixed Methods

I serve on an NIH study section and it has diverse people on it. There is no one on the section who does not think that mixed methods are appropriate . . . . Even the biostatisticians recognize the need for qualitative work. Ten years ago I saw that, but I don't see it anymore . . . . Even the real hard-core bench scientist, if you talk to them, they get it.

—Benjamin Crabtree, PhD,
Professor and Director of the Department of Family Medicine and
Community Health,
Rutgers Robert Wood Johnson
Medical School

KEY FACTORS IN MIXED METHODS RESEARCH DESIGNS

Two primary considerations in the overall design of a mixed methods study are (1) precisely how the components will be integrated and (2) the relative timing of when each component is carried out (Creswell, 2013; Creswell & Plano Clark, 2011; Guest, 2013). Although there are other important aspects of mixed methods study design, we focus on these two because they define the fundamental relationship between the various components of the study. The nature of the data required to address the research question determines how the qualitative and quantitative data will be integrated. Once the overall plan for integration is defined, the timing of each component follows naturally. By focusing first on the nature of the data and the plan for integration, researchers can avoid the kind of post hoc designs that are all too common in our experience as teachers and reviewers, in which data are collected and the research team then tries to fit the data into a design typology retrospectively. It should be noted that while some experts view the relative weight as an important defining criteria (Morse & Niehaus, 2009), others observe that the weights cannot always be determined in advance and that the relative priority of data sets is more likely to be assessed at the data analysis and writing phases (Guest, 2013). Furthermore, weighting can be perceived as a marker for valuing the data, or the amount of resources invested, or the attention devoted in a manuscript. For these reasons, we do not include weighting as a defining feature of mixed methods studies.

Integration of Data

► To read more on data integration, refer to Chapter 8: Data Analysis and Integration in Mixed Methods Studies.

Deliberate, systematic integration of the qualitative and quantitative data generated in each component is essential in order to ensure that "the whole is greater than the sum of the parts" (Barbour, 1999). Approaches to integration include merging, embedding, and connecting the data sets (Creswell, 2013; Creswell & Plano Clark, 2011; Fetters, Curry, & Creswell, 2013).

Merged integration can occur after both the qualitative and quantitative data collection and analyses are completed. The findings are then interpreted in toto and can be compared in order to identify complementarity, concordance, and discordance (or divergence) among data sets. For example, quantitative data may provide information about the accuracy and efficiency of acquiring data with a new diabetes dashboard system, while qualitative data provides information about usability and physician perceptions of the system (Koopman et al., 2011). Findings may emerge as complementary (e.g., they describe different facets of a larger phenomenon such as self-care in patients with heart failure), concordant or discordant (e.g., patient body weight measures do not appear consistently in the quantitative data while in the qualitative interviews patients report recording their body weight daily). Similarly, in a case study approach, the qualitative and quantitative data can be interpreted together in order to develop a comprehensive understanding of a specific case. For example, in a study examining implementation of a diabetes prevention program in a single community health center, qualitative data may characterize the staff experience of implementation, while quantitative data can be used to track patient-level adherence and outcomes. Taken together, the data can illustrate complementary dimensions of program success or failure (Santana et al., 2010).

Embedded integration occurs typically in studies with both primary and secondary questions, in which different methods are employed to address each question. There is lack of consensus among mixed methods experts on the topic of embedding. Interested readers can find a discussion of the debate in a recent paper by Plano Clark and colleagues (2013). In our own work, we view embedding as occurring when the secondary question (and method) is intended to support the work of the primary question (Greene, 2007) and therefore is nested, or placed, within the framework of the primary method (Creswell & Plano Clark, 2011). The secondary question, while an important part of addressing the primary aim, is not directly and explicitly related to the primary aim. Frequently in health sciences research, a qualitative component is situated within a quantitative intervention trial in order to support development of the intervention and/or to understand contextual factors that could influence the trial outcome (Lewin, Glenton, & Oxman, 2009). For example, patient interviews might be used in the formative stage of designing an electronic monitoring intervention for patients with mental health and chronic disease conditions to be tested in a clinical trial (Cohen, Chinman, Hamilton, Whelan, & Young, 2013).

Connected integration occurs when one type of data builds upon the other. This is the case when one data set is used to define the sample for another component to explain findings from another component. For example, in terms of sampling, a subset of respondents to a quantitative survey might be selected for interviews in the second phase based on their survey responses or scores. Connecting could also occur when one type of data is used to develop measurement tools for the other type of data. This form of connecting is illustrated by the survey development process for a study on the role of religion in later life, which builds upon data from qualitative interviews of older adults about religiosity to generate key constructs that are operationalized quantitatively in a survey instrument and validated psychometrically (Krause & Ellison, 2009). Some authors have also used the term *building* to describe this second mode of integration (Fetters et al., 2013).

▶ These presentation formats for mixed methods results are reviewed in detail in Chapter 11: Publishing Mixed Methods Studies in the Health Sciences.

Despite its centrality to mixed methods research, substantive integration is unfortunately not commonly described or reported in the literature. There are a variety of ways in which integrated data can be presented in journal articles. As you will see in the examples described and cited in this book, integration can be accomplished through weaving qualitative and quantitative data in the narrative, juxtaposing the data in figures or matrices, or through transforming and describing data.

Relative Timing

Relative timing of the components in a mixed methods study is determined by the relationship between them; they may be implemented at the same time or in sequence, with one following the other (Morse & Niehaus, 2009). The timing of components has important implications for resources and staffing of the study.

▶ Resource and logistical considerations are discussed in Chapter 10: Implementation Issues in Mixed Methods Research.

Designs in which all components are carried out simultaneously require sufficient staffing and resources to accomplish the core activities of data collection and analysis. Designs implemented in stages may require fewer staff that can work over the full course of the project on both components, though this depends on whether the researchers are trained in both qualitative and quantitative methods. For instance, consider a study that involves statistical analysis of a large administrative database as well as site visits and in-depth interviews with patients and providers at primary care clinics. Because both components are quite time intensive and need staff with particular training and expertise, conducting the pieces simultaneously may require a large and diverse team.

On the other hand, sequential designs may be less resource intensive at any one point in time yet can be very lengthy in duration. It is not uncommon for a sequential study to run four years or more because the first component of the study must be fully completed before the next component can be fully designed or implemented. For example, in a mixed methods study using a *positive deviance* approach to understand hospital organizational performance (Bradley et al., 2009), the first stage is to identify the best-performing organizations (the positive deviants) and study them in depth to generate hypotheses to be tested in a subsequent survey of a nationally representative sample of hospitals. The survey instrument cannot be created or administered until the qualitative stage is complete and hypotheses have been generated. The study duration has consequences for funders (who may want more rapid results than possible) and for publishing papers (since a paper integrating both sets of data may well be several years from data collected in the first stage, causing delays in publishing the first stage data).

Implications of Linkages for Methods in Each Component

The linkages across components have important implications for the sampling, data collection, and analysis methods used in each component. For instance, if the aim is to develop a survey informed by a qualitative component using focus groups, the sample for the focus groups must be purposeful on key characteristics salient to the larger population to be included in the survey component (e.g., race or ethnicity, use of long-term care services, socioeconomic status). Procedures for sound sampling and data analysis must be followed for both the quantitative and qualitative data, including cases where one component is supplementary. Ensuring that validity of each method is protected and that standards for rigor are upheld for each component is essential in mixed methods research (Morse, Wolfe, & Niehaus, 2006). On a practical level, the contingent relationship between components requires careful planning. For example, if the qualitative component follows the quantitative component with the aim of explaining quantitative findings, it is essential to allow sufficient time for quantitative data cleaning and analysis before launching the qualitative phase (Creswell, 2013; Creswell & Plano Clark, 2011; Fetters et al., 2013).

PRIMARY MIXED METHODS STUDY DESIGNS

Typologies to classify specific mixed methods designs can be useful in many ways (e.g., as tools for designing studies, establishing a common language in an emerging field, or conveying legitimacy to new audiences). A number of typologies of mixed methods have been proposed to date, although none have been able to fully accommodate the increasing complexity of approaches, particularly in large, dynamic health sciences research projects (Guest, 2013). Nevertheless, broad conceptual classification is important to guide our thinking and can be especially useful for novice mixed methods researchers (Collins & O'Cathain, 2009; Teddlie & Tashakkori, 2006). To this end, we draw upon existing typologies—particularly those proposed by Creswell and Plano Clark (Creswell & Plano Clark, 2011)—to offer a relatively simple schematic in Figure 1.2. The two columns in this figure represent independent but related decisions that a research team must make about the study design and about integrating the results of the various components. The left column presents three basic types of mixed methods designs most commonly used in health sciences research: convergent, sequential exploratory, and sequential explanatory. The right column describes study components (rather than specifying QUAL [qualitative component] and QUAN [quantitative component]) in order to show that the qualitative and quantitative components can be used in different ways. For example, in an embedded design the qualitative component could be embedded within the quantitative component or vice versa. The arrows connecting the two columns represent common paths for integration. For example, when a convergent design is used, the integration approach is most often merging or embedding.

The first of the basic design types is the convergent design. In this approach, the quantitative and qualitative components are conducted simultaneously. For example, during a community health needs assessment, researchers may determine that using a survey, interviews, and focus groups are the best way to capture the various types of information needed (e.g., prevalence of conditions, provider experiences, and community perceptions) and to collect data from different types of participants (e.g., those with differing preferences, literacy levels, or degree of comfort with research). Although the data collection for each component is done at the same time, the data may or may not be collected from the same study participants or sample. Quantitative and qualitative data are integrated either through merging the two data sets or embedding one within the other, as shown in Figure 1.2. In integrating the data from the different components, the aim is to balance the respective strengths and weaknesses of these methods in order to maximize the yield of distinct potentially complementary sources of evidence. Ongoing synthesis of information, referred to as triangulation, occurs throughout the process of data collection in order to generate a rich, multidimensional description of a case. Triangulation is a process by which a single phenomenon is examined with multiple observers, theories, methods, or data sources to generate a more comprehensive understanding of social phenomena.

Figure 1.2 Mixed Method Design and Integration Types

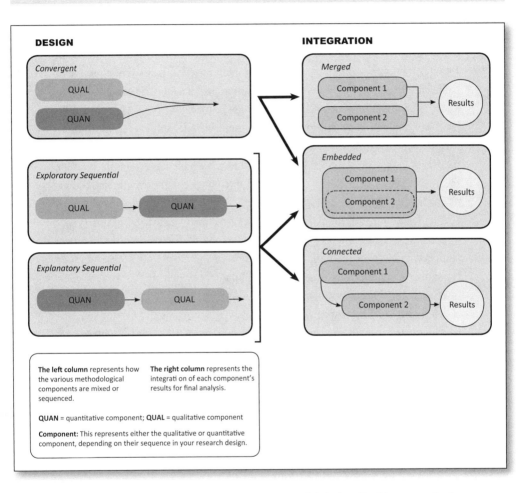

The second design is the exploratory sequential design. In this approach, the qualitative component occurs first and is followed by a quantitative component. The qualitative component may therefore generate stand-alone findings as well as inform the quantitative component, or it may simply serve a secondary function to support the primary quantitative aim. For instance, a qualitative phase with KIs from a population of interest might generate insights that inform the design of a culturally sensitive intervention. The data may be integrated through embedding or connecting, as shown in Figure 1.2.

▶ See the Glossary of Key Terms and Definitions for more information on triangulation.

The third design is the explanatory sequential design. In this design, the quantitative component is followed by a qualitative component. An explanatory design is typically chosen when the team anticipates the quantitative measures will not be wholly sufficient to address the research question. The data collection and analysis for the quantitative component is completed first, and may generate findings that are incomplete or difficult to interpret. The qualitative component is then implemented in order to generate further insights or clarification that may assist in explaining the quantitative findings. Explanatory designs may also be used when quantitative information is required in order to develop the sample for the qualitative phase. This approach often, though not always, uses a common sample (e.g., a purposeful sample is drawn from the larger sample used for the quantitative component). The data are integrated either through embedding or connecting, as shown in Figure 1.2.

At least two additional designs may not be easily classified in this typology, as they reflect one or more elements of the basic designs: intervention studies including a qualitative component and mixed methods case studies. Including a qualitative component within quantitative studies of complex interventions is becoming increasingly common (see Lewin et al., 2009) and is referred to as a concurrent embedded design. In this approach, the qualitative component can examine whether the intervention was delivered as intended, describe implementation processes, generate an understanding of why the intervention failed to work, or demonstrate how its effectiveness was promoted or limited in the real world. The qualitative component can be positioned before, during, or after the intervention study. Importantly, qualitative findings can also help mitigate publication biases against studies lacking intervention effectiveness by both explaining negative results and informing subsequent research.

A case study design using mixed methods is also valuable in health services and clinical research; a defining feature of this design is the deliberate, intense focus on a single phenomenon while understanding its real-world dynamic context (Yin, 1999). Defining the case and developing a guiding operational framework (or theory of change) are challenging yet critical first steps in this approach as they guide the specific questions to be asked through data collection. Any combination of the basic designs described previously might be used in a case study approach. Rigorous case studies employ a range of data collection methods such as the systematic review of archival or clinical data, statistical analysis of large administrative billing data sets, in-depth interviews with health care providers, and field observations of clinical encounters.

Researchers using case studies often use triangulation techniques.

> ▶ For more information on seeking funding for mixed methods projects, see Chapter 4: Writing a Scientifically Sound and Compelling Grant Proposal for a Mixed Methods Study. For tips on communicating with funders about project expectations, see Chapter 10: Implementation Issues in Mixed Methods Research.

Basic designs can also be expanded or aligned in different ways in order to create a multistage study. Multistage studies are complex, large in scope, and commonly three or more years in duration; they may include both exploratory and explanatory designs. For example, a quantitative phase might be followed by a qualitative phase, which in turn is followed by a quantitative phase. In this instance, quantitative methods may be used to identify a particular information rich subsample (e.g., emergency rooms with the highest volume of H1N1 cases in a given year) to be studied qualitatively in order to generate hypotheses to be tested in a third quantitative phase.

A final characteristic of mixed methods studies is that they may be either fixed or emergent in nature. In a fixed design, the entire study design is conceptualized at the outset, where the aims and methods for qualitative and quantitative components are explicitly defined. In an emergent design, the components are not planned in detail in advance of the study but rather emerge from the early phases of the project. Investigators proposing a study with an emergent design face several unique challenges in seeking funding and establishing project expectations with funding sources.

EXAMPLES FROM PEER-REVIEWED PUBLISHED LITERATURE

The following section presents a set of illustrative examples from mixed methods studies that have been published in peer-reviewed scientific literature in the health sciences. We feature examples of each of the three main types of mixed methods designs, including convergent, exploratory sequential and explanatory sequential as well as examples of an intervention study with a qualitative component and a case study. We deliberately selected representative papers from a range of journals and topic areas. We present the article abstract (reprinted verbatim from the published paper) as well as brief commentary regarding aspects of integration and timing for each study. We focus on describing these aspects of the studies because they are unique and critical to mixed methods designs. The integration commentary illustrates both how the data were integrated (through merging, connecting, and embedding) and presented. In addition, each example is accompanied by a figure to represent the overall design as well as integration and timing elements. We developed these figures based on information presented in the published articles as well as communication with the authors. Figures, or procedural diagrams, can be very useful tools for researchers to represent the various aims, study components, and products concisely. Readers interested in further detail are encouraged to read the primary papers.

Convergent Design

Box 1.3　Abstract From a Study That Used a Convergent Design

Maiorana, A., Steward, W. T., Koester, K. A., Pearson, C., Shade, S. B., Chakravarty, D., & Myers, J. J. (2012). Trust, confidentiality, and the acceptability of sharing HIV-related patient data: Lessons learned from a mixed methods study about health information exchanges. *Implementation Science, 7*(34).

Abstract

Background: Concerns about the confidentiality of personal health information have been identified as a potential obstacle to implementation of Health Information Exchanges (HIEs). Considering the stigma and confidentiality issues historically associated with human immunodeficiency virus (HIV) disease, we examine how trust—in technology, processes, and people—influenced the acceptability of data sharing among stakeholders prior to implementation of six HIEs intended to improve HIV care in parts of the United States. Our analyses identify the kinds of concerns expressed by stakeholders about electronic data sharing and focus on the factors that ultimately facilitated acceptability of the new exchanges.

Methods: We conducted 549 surveys with patients and 66 semi-structured interviews with providers and other stakeholders prior to implementation of the HIEs to assess concerns about confidentiality in the electronic sharing of patient data. The patient quantitative data were analyzed using SAS 9.2 to yield sample descriptive statistics. The analysis of the qualitative interviews with providers and other stakeholders followed an open-coding process, and convergent and divergent perspectives emerging from those data were examined within and across the HIEs.

Results: We found widespread acceptability for electronic sharing of HIV-related patient data through HIEs. This acceptability appeared to be driven by growing comfort with information technologies, confidence in the security protocols utilized to protect data, trust in the providers and institutions who use the technologies, belief in the benefits to the patients, and awareness that electronic exchange represents an enhancement of data sharing already taking place by other means. HIE acceptability depended both on preexisting trust among patients, providers, and institutions and on building consensus and trust in the HIEs as part of preparation for implementation. The process of HIE development also resulted in forging shared vision among institutions.

Conclusions: Patients and providers are willing to accept the electronic sharing of HIV patient data to improve care for a disease historically seen as highly stigmatized. Acceptability depends on the effort expended to understand and address potential concerns related to data sharing and confidentiality, and on the trust established among stakeholders in terms of the nature of the systems and how they will be used.

As described in Box 1.3, Maiorana and colleagues (2012) explored how patient trust in technology, processes, and people might influence the acceptability of patient data sharing in the context of health information exchanges (HIEs). Quantitative data from patients ($n = 549$) describe willingness to share their data with a range of interested parties, while semi-structured interviews with stakeholders ($n = 66$) explore potential barriers and facilitators to implementation of HIEs. Shown in Figure 1.3, the two primary defining characteristics of this convergent design—integration and timing—are summarized next.

Integration

The patient survey, administered using an audio computer-assisted self-interview method, measured patient willingness to share information using

Figure 1.3   Example Study Design: Convergent Design With Merged
Integration

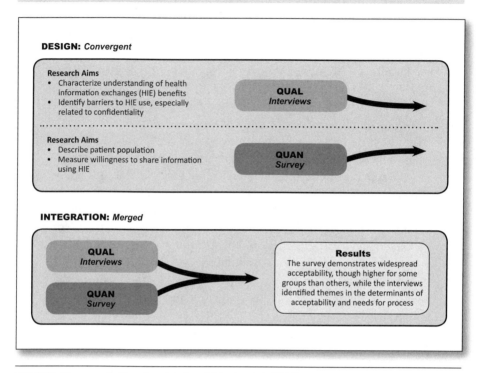

SOURCE: Figure created based on data from Maiorana et al. (2012).

NOTE: QUAL = qualitative component; QUAN = quantitative component.

HIE with a diverse set of potential care providers and insurers (for example, "I am willing to allow my personal health information to be shared with my private health insurers using a secure electronic network"), on a 5-point scale ranging from strong disagreement to strong agreement. The qualitative interviews, conducted in person or over the phone, explored the views of three stakeholder groups: project staff/IT specialists, staff from community-based organizations and public health agencies, and medical providers/staff in clinical settings. The interviews explored technological, attitudinal and structural barriers, and facilitators to acceptability of data sharing, including the issues of trust and confidentiality. Patient and stakeholder views both were considered to provide essential perspectives about acceptability and feasibility of data sharing in this context.

The researchers initially conducted separate analyses of the quantitative patient data and the qualitative stakeholder data. In a subsequent step, they merged the two sets of findings, using the quantitative patient findings to inform and frame the qualitative stakeholder findings. For instance, the patient data revealed few concerns regarding data sharing, while the qualitative data suggested potential factors that mitigate or address such concerns, including familiarity with the use of electronic technology; trust in the institutions; and in the staff providing services, and the expected benefit of HIE. In the paper, the authors presented the quantitative findings in a bar chart rating acceptability on the 5-point scale, then summarized the qualitative findings in a table, and provided detailed explanatory text with illustrative quotes for each.

Timing

The two components were implemented simultaneously across the six participating sites, in advance of HIE implementation. Data collection occurred over a 20-month period as the sites prepared to implement the intervention.

Exploratory Sequential Design

Box 1.4 Abstract From a Study That Used an Exploratory Sequential Design

Ginsburg, K. R., Howe, C. J., Jawad, A. F., Buzby, M., Ayala, J. M., Tuttle, A., & Murphy, K. (2005). Parents' perceptions of factors that affect successful diabetes management for their children. *Pediatrics, 116,* 1095–1104.

Abstract

Objective: To learn which factors parents perceive to be most influential in determining successful type 1 diabetes management.

Methods: A 4-stage mixed qualitative-quantitative method that consists of a series of focus groups, a survey, and in-depth interviews was used to ensure that parents generated, prioritized, and

(Continued)

(Continued)

explained their own ideas. In each stage, parents offered a new level of insight into their perception of how children achieve good metabolic control while living as normal a life as possible. The survey responses were divided into statistically different ranks, and the Kruskal-Wallis test was used to compare the results between subgroups.

Results: A total of 149 parents participated in the formative qualitative phases, 799 families (66%) responded to the parent-generated survey, and 67 explanatory interviews were conducted. The families who responded to the survey had children of varied ages (mean: 11.9 years; SD: 4.44) and diabetes control (mean hemoglobin A1c: 8.22%; SD: 1.65); 84.1% of respondents were white, 12.3% were black, and 89% were privately insured. The 30 survey items were statistically discriminated into 8 ranks. The items cover a wide range of categories, including concrete ways of achieving better control, families' or children's traits that affect coping ability, actions of the health care team that support versus undermine families' efforts, and the availability of community supports. No clear pattern emerged regarding 1 category that parents perceived to matter most.

Conclusions: Clinicians can affect many of the factors that parents perceive to make a difference in whether they can successfully raise a resilient child in good diabetes control. Future research needs to determine whether health care teams that address the concerns that parents raised in this study are more effective in guiding children to cope well with diabetes, to incorporate healthier lifestyles, and ultimately to achieve better metabolic control.

As described in Box 1.4, Ginsburg and colleagues (2005) examined parental views on successful management of diabetes for their children. The researchers developed a multistage mixed methods design to ensure parents' perspectives were accurately represented throughout the study from the conceptualization and development of the survey through the interpretation of survey findings. This method was previously utilized by the researchers to capture the perspectives of teens (Ginsburg, 1996; Ginsburg et al., 2002) and has been modified in this case to focus on the unique views of parents.

Figure 1.4 Example Study Design: Exploratory Sequential Design With Multistage Connected Integration

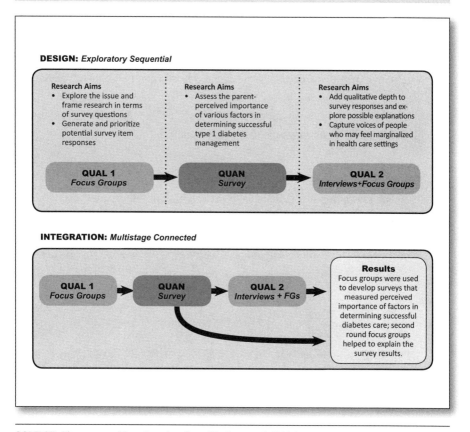

SOURCE: Figure created based on data from Ginsburg et al. (2005).

NOTE: QUAL = qualitative component; QUAN = quantitative component.

Integration

Integration occurred at the data collection and interpretation phases of the study. The results from the first set of focus groups (QUAL 1 in Figure 1.4) were used to develop the survey items in the QUAN phase. The quantitative survey data examine a broad range of dimensions of the parents' experiences, including factors that impact their ability to manage his or her child's diabetes resilience skills, sources of support, and family dynamics. The second set of qualitative data (QUAL 2 in Figure 1.4) was collected after the quantitative survey and used to provide insight into the meaning and interpretation of specific survey items. For example, one item rated how important it was for the extended family to be able to support the family. Parents described experiencing struggles in balancing competing demands and feelings of burden, as they could not turn to trained and willing family members or other caregivers for respite. Parents also expressed exasperation when clinicians did not understand "that families live with diabetes 24 hours a day and 7 days a week." The qualitative data revealed this item reflected frustration that clinicians are condescending and dismissive of parents' expertise, as well as resentment that clinicians did not understand parents' full scope of competing responsibilities and the implications for diabetes management.

Timing

The four components included a survey, in-depth interviews, and two sets of focus groups. Table 1.1 is taken from the article as a useful example of a summary table describing the stages of data collection, the specific method, the objective, and the sample size for each. These types of summary tables are very useful in grant applications, human investigations committee applications, and

Table 1.1   Study Method Explanation Example

Stage	Method	Objective	*N*
1	Open focus groups	Explore the issue, and frame a question that will generate a wide array of responses.	44 in 7 groups
2	Nominal group technique (NGT)	Generate and prioritize responses. The highest responses are to be included in survey.	105 in 16 groups
3	Parent-developed survey	Assess the importance of each response for the total population and for subgroups.	799
4	Semistructured interviews	Add qualitative depth to the responses and explore solutions.	67
	Explanatory focus groups	Allow people who may feel marginalized in health care settings to express concerns in the safety of a group.	3 groups

SOURCE: Ginsburg et al. (2005).

publications. The table concisely outlines the various data sources and their corresponding sample sizes but perhaps the most important element is the distinct objective of each component. The objectives show the respective contributions of each component and provide a justification for the timing by indicating how the components relate to each other.

Each component built upon findings of the prior component to develop a comprehensive representation of parents' perspectives on successful diabetes management in their families. The design moved from exploratory focus groups to the construction of the survey and back to interviews and focus groups to add insights to the analysis of survey data and to generate potential solutions to challenges faced by parents. While the design is exploratory sequential at the beginning, the final interviews and focus groups also provide some explanatory input. In this way, this design could also be classified as a multistage study.

Explanatory Sequential Design

Box 1.5 Abstract From a Study That Used an Explanatory Sequential Design

Cutter, J., & Jordan, S. (2012). Inter-professional differences in compliance with standard precautions in operating theatres: A multi-site, mixed methods study. *International Journal of Nursing Studies,* *49*(8): 953–968. doi: 10.1016/j.ijnurstu.2012.03.001

Abstract

   Background: Occupational acquisition of blood-borne infections has been reported following exposure to blood or body fluids. Consistent adherence to standard precautions will reduce the risk of infection.

   Objectives: To identify: the frequency of self-reported adverse exposure to blood and body fluids among surgeons and scrub nurses during surgical procedures; contributory factors to such injuries; the extent of compliance with standard precautions; and factors influencing compliance with precautions.

(Continued)

(Continued)

Design: A multi-site mixed methods study incorporating a cross-sectional survey and interviews.

Settings: Six NHS [National Health Service] trusts in Wales between January 2006 and August 2008.

Participants: Surgeons and scrub nurses and Senior Infection Control Nurses.

Methods: A postal survey to all surgeons and scrub nurses, who engaged in exposure prone procedures, followed by face-to-face interviews with surgeons and scrub nurses, and telephone interviews with Senior Infection Control Nurses.

Results: Response rate was 51.47% (315/612). Most 219/315 (69.5%) respondents reported sustaining an inoculation injury in the last five years: 183/315 (58.1%) reported sharps' injuries and 40/315 (12.7%) splashes. Being a surgeon and believing injuries to be an occupational hazard were significantly associated with increased risk of sharps' injuries (adjusted odds ratio 1.73, 95% confidence interval 1.04–2.88 and adjusted odds ratio 2.0, 1.11–3.5, respectively). Compliance was incomplete: 31/315 (10%) respondents always complied with all available precautions, 1/315 (0.003%) claimed never to comply with any precautions; 64/293 (21.8%) always used safety devices, 141/310 (45.5%) eye protection, 72 (23.2%) double gloves, and 259/307 (84.4%) avoided passing sharps from hand to hand. Others selected precautions according to their own assessment of risk. Surgeons were less likely to adopt eye protection (adjusted odds ratio 0.28, 0.11–0.71) and to attend training sessions (odds ratio 0.111, 0.061–0.19). The professions viewed the risks associated with their roles differently, with nurses being more willing to follow protocols.

Conclusion: Inter-professional differences in experiencing adverse exposures must be addressed to improve safety and reduce infection risks. This requires new training initiatives to alter risk perception and promote compliance with policies and procedures.

In the sequential explanatory study (see Figure 1.5) summarized in Box 1.5, Cutter and Jordan (2012) sought to assess multiple aspects of

Figure 1.5 Example Study Design: Explanatory Sequential Design With Connected Integration

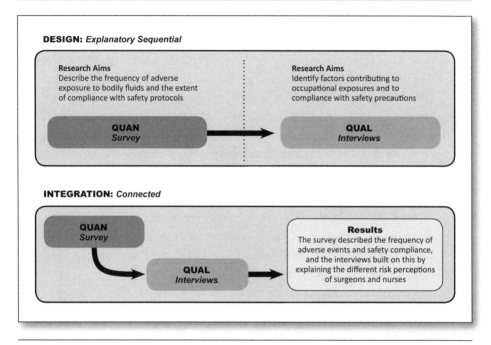

SOURCE: Figure created based on data from Cutter and Jordan (2012).

NOTE: QUAN = quantitative component; QUAL = qualitative component.

compliance with standard precautions in surgery with a focus on examining differences between surgeons and nurses in this area. Prevalence of self-reported adverse exposure events and compliance with precautions was measured quantitatively via a survey ($n = 315$). Individual provider motivations and behaviors regarding precautions were assessed qualitatively using interviews with surgeons and nurses who had responded to the survey ($n = 16$).

Integration

Quantitative findings, such as the greater number of surgeons who believed that inoculation injuries are an expected occupational hazard, were connected to and further illuminated by the qualitative data to offer possible explanations for the diversity in views. For example, qualitative data suggested personality differences such as arrogance and a tendency to take risks among surgeons, as noted in the article: "There is some innate arrogance in anybody who wants to become a surgeon that's just the type of people we are. We all think we are invincible" (p. 959). Another participant similarly explained, "You need to be a risk taker to cut someone open and remove an organ, nurses don't need to take these risks" (p. 959). The researchers reported that findings from the survey and interview data were consistent and complementary. In the paper, quantitative findings are reported in a series of tables comparing results from surgeons and nurses. The qualitative data are presented in the context of the quantitative data to provide additional insights into the findings of the quantitative data.

Timing

The study was implemented in sequence, beginning with a mail survey of scrub nurses and surgeons who routinely performed exposure-prone procedures. The survey was then followed by interviews with purposefully selected participants and a telephone survey of senior infection control nurses from each participating organization. Selection of interviewees was based on their responses to the survey and comprised those with the most extreme views or an excessive number of self-reported inoculation injuries. Infection control nurses from each participating organization were interviewed by telephone to comment on selected aspects of the data, such as availability of training.

Concurrent Embedded Design

Box 1.6   Abstract From a Study That Used a Concurrent Embedded Design

Murtagh, M. J., Thomson, R. G., May, C. R., Rapley, T., Heaven, B. R., Graham, R. H., . . . Eccles, M. P. (2007). Qualitative methods in a randomized controlled trial: The role of an integrated qualitative process evaluation in providing evidence to discontinue the intervention in one arm of a trial of a decision support tool. *Quality & Safety in Health Care, 16*(3), 224–229.

Abstract

Objective: To understand participants' experiences and under-standings of the interventions in the trial of a computerised decision support tool in patients with atrial fibrillation being considered for anti-coagulation treatment.

Design: Qualitative process evaluation carried out alongside the trial: non-participant observation and semi-structured interviews.

Participants: 30 participants aged > 60 years taking part in the trial of a computerised decision support tool.

Results: Qualitative evidence provided the rationale to under-take a decision to discontinue one arm of the trial on the basis that the intervention in that arm, a standard gamble values elicitation exercise was causing confusion and was unlikely to produce valid data on participant values.

Conclusions: Qualitative methods used alongside a trial allow an understanding of the process and progress of a trial, and provide evidence to intervene in the trial if necessary, including evidence for the rationale to discontinue an intervention arm of the trial.

As shown in Box 1.6, a study by Murtagh and colleagues (2007) involved behavioral intervention—a randomized controlled trial of a decision support tool to guide patients with atrial fibrillation in making a choice about antico-agulation treatment. Because the intervention was complex, the researchers built in a qualitative process evaluation to assess participant experiences with the tool and with participation in the trial itself.

Integration

In this study, the qualitative data were not integrated into the findings of the trial per se but rather informed the design of the trial itself. These data ultimately provided sufficient evidence to terminate one arm of the trial (see Figure 1.6). The qualitative findings were reviewed by the full team, which decided on the basis of these data to discontinue an arm of the trial. In the published paper, the qualitative data are presented in a brief case format, with excerpts from the interviews to demonstrate participants'

Figure 1.6   Example Study Design: Concurrent Embedded Study With Embedded Integration

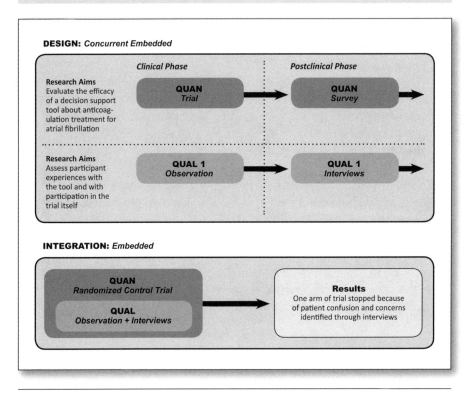

SOURCE: Figure created based on data from Murtagh et al. (2007).

NOTE: QUAN = quantitative component; QUAL = qualitative component.

inability to understand and carry out a key aspect of the study (the hypothetical scenarios gamble exercise).

Timing

Qualitative methods may be employed in pretrial development, during implementation, and subsequent to the trial. In this study, the qualitative and quantitative components were run concurrently, where the qualitative component was a "thematic observational analysis" of the trial. The first thirty participants in the trial were invited to complete interviews and videotaped consultations. The qualitative arm was specifically designed to generate real-time insights into the participants' experiences in order to characterize the process of implementing the trial and the evidence to discontinue if warranted.

Case Study Using a Convergent Design

> **Box 1.7 Abstract From a Case Study That Used a Convergent Design**
>
> Crabtree, B. F., Miller, W. L., Tallia, A. F., Cohen, D. J., DiCicco-Bloom, B., McIlvain, H. E., . . . McDaniel, R. R., Jr. (2005). Delivery of clinical preventive services in family medicine offices. *Annals of Family Medicine, 3*(5), 430–435.
>
> *Abstract*
>
> **Background:** This study aimed to elucidate how clinical preventive services are delivered in family practices and how this information might inform improvement efforts.
>
> **Methods:** We used a comparative case study design to observe clinical preventive service delivery in 18 purposefully selected Midwestern family medicine offices from 1997 to 1999. Medical records, observation of outpatient encounters, and patient exit cards were used to calculate practice-level rates of delivery of clinical preventive services. Field notes from direct observation of clinical encounters and prolonged observation of the practice and transcripts from in-depth interviews of practice staff and physicians were systematically examined to identify approaches to delivering clinical preventive services recommended by the U.S. Preventive Services Task Force (USPSTF).
>
> **Results:** Practices developed individualized approaches for delivering clinical preventive services, with no one approach being successful across practices. Clinicians acknowledged a 3-fold mission of providing acute care, managing chronic problems, and prevention, but only some made prevention a priority. The clinical encounter was a central focus for preventive service delivery in all practices. Preventive services delivery rates often appeared to be influenced by competing demands within the clinical encounter (including between different preventive services), having a physician champion who prioritized prevention, and economic concerns.
>
> **Conclusions:** Practice quality improvement efforts that assume there is an optimal approach for delivering clinical preventive services fail to account for practices' propensity to optimize care processes to meet local contexts. Interventions to enhance clinical preventive service delivery should be tailored to meet the local needs of practices and their patient populations.

Figure 1.7 Example Study Design: Case Study Design With Merged
Integration

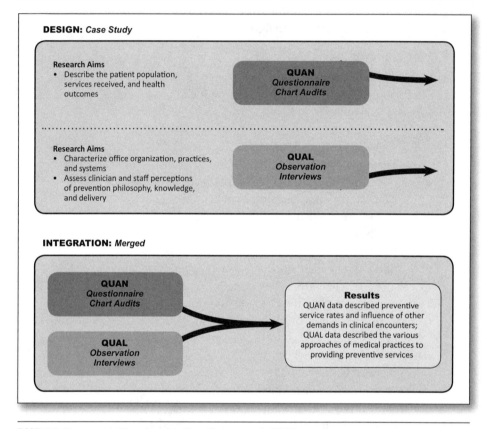

SOURCE: Figure created based on data from Crabtree et al. (2005).

NOTE: QUAN = quantitative component; QUAL = qualitative component.

In the large, observational comparative case study (using a convergent design) described in Box 1.7 and Figure 1.7, Crabtree and colleagues (2005) sought to understand the organizational features of primary care practice, with a focus on provision of clinical preventive services in this setting. Qualitative methods including interviews with clinicians ($n = 57$) and staff ($n = 71$) and observations of both the practice environment and of 30 or more patient encounters with each clinician were used to generate insights into prevention philosophy, knowledge, and delivery in these diverse practice sites (see Figure 1.7). Analyses focused on describing and understanding differences in rates of clinical preventive service delivery across the practices. Quantitative methods were used to calculate practice rates for three types of services (screening, counseling, and immunization) based on chart reviews, encounter descriptions, and patient exit card responses for 1,637 patients. These data were used selectively to enrich the qualitative data.

Integration

Quantitative and qualitative data from all sources at each practice site were merged to create a descriptive summary of each practice's key characteristics and overall strategy for delivering preventive services. In the paper, service delivery rates are woven into narrative reports from the qualitative and observational data, organized within three overarching themes: competing demands of care, variation in approaches for preventive service delivery, and organizational features that support clinical preventive services.

Timing

As is characteristic in case studies, data collection occurred simultaneously and iteratively at each of 18 purposefully selected practice sites that were diverse with regard to practice size, geographic location, and ownership.

Summary and Key Points

- We use the following definition of mixed methods research: Research in which a researcher or team of researchers combines elements of qualitative and quantitative research approaches (e.g., use of qualitative and quantitative viewpoints, data collection, analysis, and inference techniques) for the broad purposes of breadth and depth of understanding and corroboration.
- Primary factors to consider in mixed methods design are strategies for integration and relative timing of the components.
- Three core designs are convergent, explanatory sequential, and exploratory sequential; additional designs common in health sciences are qualitative methods in intervention trials and case studies.

Review Questions and Exercises

1. Think about a topic of interest to you that would be impossible to carry out successfully using only qualitative or quantitative approaches. What are the limitations of using each method independently, and how could a mixed methods study address those limitations?

2. Suppose you are reviewing the literature related to lack of adherence to HIV treatment in low-income settings. How might an embedded mixed methods design be used to study this topic?

3. Select two or three published articles that use a mixed methods design. First, create a diagram to illustrate the study design. Discuss the timing of collecting the qualitative and quantitative data. Finally, describe how the data are integrated.

References

Barbour, R. S. (1999). The case for combining qualitative and quantitative approaches in health services research. *Journal of Health Services Research and Policy, 4*(1), 39–43.

Bradley, E. H., Curry, L. A., & Devers, K. J. (2007). Qualitative data analysis for health services research: developing taxonomy, themes, and theory. *Health Services Research, 42*(4), 1758–1772. doi: 10.1111/j.1475–6773.2006.00684.x

Bradley, E. H., Curry, L. A., Ramanadhan, S., Rowe, L., Nembhard, I. M., & Krumholz, H. M. (2009). Research in action: Using positive deviance to improve quality of health care. *Implementation Science, 4,* 25. doi: 10.1186/1748–5908–4–25

Cohen, A. N., Chinman, M. J., Hamilton, A. B., Whelan, F., & Young, A. S. (2013). Using patient-facing kiosks to support quality improvement at mental health clinics. *Medical Care, 51*(3 Suppl. 1), S13–20. doi: 10.1097/MLR.0b013e31827da859

Collins, K., & O'Cathain, A. (2009). Ten points about mixed methods research to be considered by the novice researcher. *International Journal of Multiple Research Approaches, 3,* 2–7.

Crabtree, B. F., Miller, W. L., Tallia, A. F., Cohen, D. J., DiCicco-Bloom, B., McIlvain, H. E., . . . McDaniel, R. R., Jr. (2005). Delivery of clinical preventive services in family medicine offices. *Annals of Family Medicine, 3*(5), 430–435. doi: 10.1370/afm.345

Creswell, J. W. (2013). *Research design: Qualitative, quantitative, and mixed methods approaches* (4th ed.). Thousand Oaks, CA: Sage.

Creswell, J. W., & Plano Clark, V. L. (2011). *Designing and conducting mixed methods research* (2nd ed.). Thousand Oaks, CA: Sage.

Cutter, J., & Jordan, S. (2012). Inter-professional differences in compliance with standard precautions in operating theatres: A multi-site, mixed methods study. *International Journal of Nursing Studies, 49*(8), 953–968. doi: 10.1016/j. ijnurstu.2012.03.001

Einstein, A. Available at: http://www.quotationspage.com/quote/26950.html. Accessed September 17, 2007.

Fetters, M., Curry, L. A., & Creswell, J. (2013). Achieving integration in mixed methods designs: principles and practices. *Health Services Research, 48* (6 Pt. 2), 2134–2156. doi: 2110.1111/1475–6773.12117.

Ginsburg, K. R. (1996). Searching for solutions: The importance of including teenagers in the research process. *Journal of Developmental and Behavioral Pediatrics, 17*(4), 255–257.

Ginsburg, K. R., Alexander, P. M., Hunt, J., Sullivan, M., Zhao, H., & Cnaan, A. (2002). Enhancing their likelihood for a positive future: The perspective of inner-city youth. *Pediatrics, 109*(6), 1136–1142.

Ginsburg, K. R., Howe, C. J., Jawad, A. F., Buzby, M., Ayala, J. M., Tuttle, A., & Murphy, K. (2005). Parents' perceptions of factors that affect successful diabetes management for their children. *Pediatrics, 116*(5), 1095–1104. doi: 10.1542/ peds.2004–1981

Glaser, B. G., & Strauss, A. L. (1967). *The discovery of grounded theory: Strategies for qualitative research.* Chicago, IL: Aldine.

Greene, J. C. (2007). *Mixed methods in social inquiry* (1st ed.). San Francisco, CA: Jossey-Bass.

Guest, G. (2013). Describing mixed methods research: An alternative to typologies. *Journal of Mixed Methods Research, 7*(2), 141–151.

Hulley, S. B., Cummings, S. R., Browner, W. S., Grady, D. G., & Newman, T. B. (2013). *Designing clinical research* (4th ed.). Philadelphia, PA: Wolters Kluwer/ Lippincott Williams & Wilkins.

Jick, T. (1979). Mixing qualitative and quantitative methods: Triangulation in action. *Administrative Science Quarterly, 24*(4), 602–610.

Johnson, R. B., Onwuegbuzie, A. J., & Turner, L. A. (2007). Toward a definition of mixed methods research. *Journal of Mixed Methods Research, 1*(2), 112–133.

Koopman, R. J., Kochendorfer, K. M., Moore, J. L., Mehr, D. R., Wakefield, D. S., Yadamsuren, B., . . . Belden, J. L. (2011). A diabetes dashboard and physician efficiency and accuracy in accessing data needed for high-quality diabetes care. *Annals of Family Medicine, 9*(5), 398–405. doi: 10.1370/afm.1286

Krause, N., & Ellison, C. G. (2009). The doubting process: A longitudinal study of the precipitants and consequences of religious doubt. *Journal of the Scientific Study of Religion, 48*(2),   293–312. doi: 10.1111/j.1468–5906.2009.01448.x

Lewin, S., Glenton, C., & Oxman, A. D. (2009). Use of qualitative methods alongside randomised controlled trials of complex healthcare interventions: Methodological study. *BMJ, 339*(b3496). doi: 10.1136/bmj.b3496

Maiorana, A., Steward, W. T., Koester, K. A., Pearson, C., Shade, S. B., Chakravarty, D., & Myers, J. J. (2012). Trust, confidentiality, and the acceptability of sharing HIV-related patient data: Lessons learned from a mixed methods study about health information exchanges. *Implementation Science, 7*(34). doi: 10.1186/1748–5908-7–34

Miles, M. B., & Huberman, A. M. (1994). *Qualitative data analysis: An expanded sourcebook* (2nd ed.). Thousand Oaks, CA: Sage.

Morse, J. M., & Niehaus, L. (2009). *Mixed method design: Principles and procedures.* Walnut Creek, CA: Left Coast Press.

Morse, J. M., Wolfe, R. R., & Niehaus, L. (2006). Principles and procedures of maintaining validity for mixed-method design. In L. Curry, R. Shield, & T. T. Wetle (Eds.), *Improving aging and public health research: Qualitative and mixed methods* (pp. 65–78). Washington, DC: American Public Health Association.

Murtagh, M. J., Thomson, R. G., May, C. R., Rapley, T., Heaven, B. R., Graham, R. H., . . . Eccles, M. P. (2007). Qualitative methods in a randomised controlled trial: The role of an integrated qualitative process evaluation in providing evidence to discontinue the intervention in one arm of a trial of a decision support tool. *Quality & Safety in Health Care, 16*(3), 224–229. doi: 10.1136/qshc.2006.018499

Plano Clark, V. L., Schumacher, K., West, C., Edrington, J., Dunn, L. B., Harzstark, A., . . . Miaskowski, C. (2013). Practices for embedding an interpretive qualitative approach within a randomized clinical trial. *Journal of Mixed Methods Research, 7*(3), 219–242.

Rothman, K. J., Greenland, S., & Lash, T. L. (2008). *Modern epidemiology* (3rd ed.). Philadelphia, PA: Wolters Kluwer.

Santana, C., Nunez-Smith, M., Camp, A., Ruppe, E., Berg, D., & Curry, L. (2010). Quality improvement in community health centres: The role of microsystem characteristics in the implementation of a diabetes prevention initiative. *Quality and Safety in Health Care, 19*(4), 290–294. doi: 10.1136/qshc.2009.033530.

Teddlie, C., & Tashakkori, A. (2006). A general typology of research designs featuring mixed methods. *Research in the Schools, 13,* 12–28.

Yin, R. K. (1999). Enhancing the quality of case studies in health services research. *Health Services Research, 34*(5 Pt. 2), 1209–1224.

❖ Two ❖

APPLICATIONS AND ILLUSTRATIONS OF MIXED METHODS HEALTH SCIENCES RESEARCH

Information you will find in this chapter: We begin with a discussion of the increasing relevance of mixed methods research in health sciences, including specific applications in clinical research, health services research, and implementation science. In the remaining sections, we review each of the primary designs using illustrations from published peer-reviewed literature. For each illustration, we describe the broad orientation that framed the research question and present several key elements of each study, including the project abstract, overview, timeline, and design depiction. This material is followed by the researchers' biographies and excerpts from original interviews with them about their studies.

Key features in this chapter:

- Brief quotations and reflections from mixed methods researchers
- Schematic with examples of mixed methods contributions to health sciences
- Detailed illustrations from three published mixed methods studies
- Figures depicting key elements of each study, including project overview, timeline, and design
- Question and answer (Q&A) excerpts from original interviews with the study investigators

RELEVANCE OF MIXED METHODS RESEARCH IN THE HEALTH SCIENCES

The use of mixed methods in health sciences research has increased steadily over the past decade. Several factors may contribute to this growing interest. Health sciences researchers seek to understand the vast and inherent complexity of health and health care outcomes, which requires the capacity to measure multifaceted phenomena. Health sciences researchers are also solution-focused and motivated to generate knowledge of practical benefit in the real world. Mixed methods approaches therefore have substantial potential to advance health sciences research agenda because they are well suited to measuring multifaceted phenomena and are (as we perceive them) highly pragmatic in nature.

While there are good reasons why health sciences researchers are using mixed methods in general, articulating a clear and compelling rationale for using a mixed methods approach is key at the outset of any given project. The rationale for a mixed methods design provides clarity in purpose from the study's inception and can serve as a unifying goal for the highly diverse researchers who make up a mixed methods team. It is also important to recognize that the reasons to use mixed methods approaches may evolve over the course of a project as the team gathers new insights. We would note that study rationale is not synonymous with study motivation per se. The motivation to carry out a particular study may be informed by strategic considerations (e.g., funder seeks mixed methods proposals) but does not override the need for methodological justification.

▶ Additional discussion of the critical issue of study design rationale is presented in Chapter 3: Determining the Appropriateness and Feasibility of Using Mixed Methods.

There are several key justifications for choosing a mixed methods approach. The first is to offset vulnerabilities in various methods by minimizing the respective limitations of single-method qualitative or quantitative approaches (Bryman, 2006). Another reason is to use one method for the purpose of enhancing the development of design features or measures in the other method. For example, it is increasingly common for health sciences researchers to employ qualitative methods as an initial phase in development of quantitative instruments.

A third possible justification is completeness, where collecting data using diverse methods may generate a more complete picture. Multiple methods may reveal patterns that would otherwise go unnoticed and may also uncover novel relationships between variables and concepts. In the interview excerpt in Box 2.1, a surgeon and health services researcher reflects on the complementarity of qualitative and quantitative methods and invites colleagues to consider expanding their approach to research.

▶ When using multiple methods to increase the overall rigor of a study, it is important to adhere to established standards for each component. For more information, refer to Chapter 6: Assessing Quality in Mixed Methods Studies.

Box 2.1 Reflecting on the Value of Mixed Methods in Health Sciences Research

I trained and still practice as a surgeon, but I also did a master's degree in medical education and I took a module on qualitative methodologies. That's what really opened my eyes to the idea that you can ask questions through quantitative means and you can get a fairly exact answer too, but sometimes those answers aren't very interesting or informative. When you add qualitative methods or combine the methods, you can get much more information. The quantitative side tells you what most people think about a certain question and then in the qualitative piece, you start to understand what that answer really meant to different people—and it might surprise you . . . . If I could encourage researchers to do anything, I'd encourage them to do more qualitative work and look at the problem in a different way. This can get you more satisfying answers in the end than just the numbers do.

—Jonathan White, MD, PhD, FRCS, MSc,
Tom Williams Endowed Chair in Surgical Education,
University of Alberta

In addition to these methodological reasons for using mixed methods, there are two trends in health sciences that are extraordinarily compelling motivations for mixed methods: the increasing complexity of issues in health and health care and the focus on ensuring that research has demonstrable impact on practice and policy. These trends are reflected in comments from a senior official at the Commonwealth Fund, a major grant-making organization in the United States that invests heavily in health research, noted in Box 2.2.

Box 2.2   The Need for Mixed Methods in Health Research

I've been working at the Commonwealth Fund for 10 years and I've seen lots of changes with regard to mixed methods . . . . From the perspective of a grant-making organization and an organization that is very focused on communicating results to affect change, I quickly came to the understanding that with the complexity of the issues we are addressing in health care, that it's just no longer possible to address those questions through pure quantitative methods . . . . We're in a phase of health care where we're looking at complex interventions. It's no longer the traditional drug research; it's multiple, complicated interventions. Not everything can be studied in randomized trials, and not everything can be answered through traditional methods. What's really important is to start with the questions you are asking and go from there to decide what is the best way of answering those questions. Sometimes it could be that it's a randomized controlled trial, and sometimes it could be that this question is much better answered through mixed methods. The other thing is that we know there are multiple ways of understanding information. If you only tell stories or you only give numbers, you may not be able to really talk about the nuances of the questions that we're trying to answer. Something we've seen over and over again in the last ten years is that increasingly we are trying to evaluate the impact of very complex interventions such as the medical home models or complex campaigns to reduce readmissions (which involve more than one component in the intervention packet). Studies that only use quantitative methods often have been disappointing—inconclusive or no impact because of lack of power or lack of appropriate methods to control for confounders or other contextual factors. We may really be doing ourselves a disservice in these cases by relying on one analytic approach or one study design.

—Anne Marie Audet, MD, MSc, Vice President for
the Delivery System Reform & Breakthrough
Opportunities, The Commonwealth Fund

As noted in the preface, our definition of health sciences research includes clinical research, health services research, and implementation science. In the following section, we offer several examples to demonstrate the role of mixed methods in advancing the knowledge base in each of these health sciences arenas (see Figure 2.1). Of course, the list of potential applications within each arena is far from exhaustive. We sought to provide a sense of the broad range within health sciences.

Clinical Research

There is increasing appreciation for the value of qualitative data in the design, conduct, and interpretation of behavioral intervention trials in clinical research (see Box 2.3). For example, Menon and colleagues (2008) used an exploratory sequential approach in a randomized clinical trial to develop and test a culturally sensitive intervention to increase colorectal cancer (CRC) screening. The qualitative component included focus groups to provide critical insights about the design of the interactive computer-based educational tool.

Figure 2.1   Examples of Mixed Methods Contributions to Advancing Clinical, Health Services, and Implementation Science Research

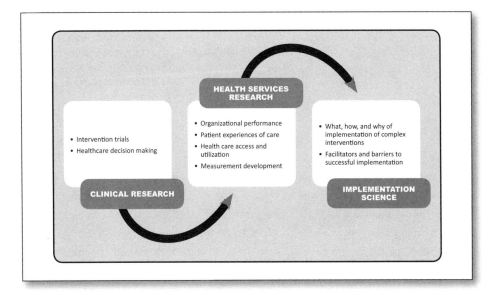

The findings guided the researchers in tailoring the tool in terms of navigation, comprehensibility, and culturally sensitive content. Identifying these potential limitations in the qualitative phase and addressing them in advance strengthened the intervention design. In another example, a randomized controlled trial of a facilitated, team-based approach to improving CRC screening rates in primary care settings included a qualitative analysis of field observation notes and recordings of interactions between providers and patients (Shaw et al., 2013). The qualitative data provided lessons about the context and application of the approach that can be used for future research. An embedded qualitative component that runs throughout the study can provide useful insights into how the study protocol was carried out, flag any unintended consequences of the intervention, or help to explain the context of null results.

Box 2.3   Using Mixed Methods in Intervention Trials

A lot of people are doing clinical trials or group-randomized trials of interventions, using specific intervention practices and measuring the outcomes. But at the same time you need to be able to understand what happened, what are people thinking, why did some things work and some things didn't work—and all that requires qualitative data. So even with a fundamentally quantitative design, you need qualitative methods to understand what's really going on.

—Benjamin Crabtree, PhD,
Professor and Director, Department of Family
Medicine and Community Health,
Rutgers Robert Wood Johnson Medical School

An additional example in clinical research is health care decision making, where the combination of qualitative and quantitative data can enhance understanding of patient and physician perspectives. For example, a study by Berman and colleagues examined the quality of informed consent for abdominal aortic aneurysm surgery. This study used in-depth interviews with patients who had undergone surgery to learn about their experiences of the consent process, paired with a national survey of surgeons to describe the content of informed consent discussions (Berman, Curry, Gusberg, Dardik, & Fraenkel,

2008; Berman, Dardik, Bradley, Gusberg, & Fraenkel, 2008). These complementary sets of findings were used in the development of a decision tool for patients with abdominal aortic aneurysms that was customized to adapt content to varied patient preferences (Berman, Curry, Goldberg, Gusberg, & Fraenkel, 2011).

Health Services Research

There is similar opportunity for contributions of mixed methods to generate new evidence in health services research. When studying health care organizational performance, quantitative metrics of performance or changes in performance on defined metrics are essential. However, we are often also interested in understanding *why* organizations perform well or poorly and what diverse types of factors might influence performance, which necessitates a qualitative approach. Schraagen and colleagues (2011) examined the relationship between teamwork, nonroutine events, and postoperative patient outcomes in pediatric cardiac surgery, using structured observations of a single surgical team, surveys of team members, documentation of nonroutine events, and patient outcomes (level of complications). These data were integrated in order to generate a teamwork quality score to relate this score with outcomes and identify deficiencies in the system.

Access to care and health care utilization are currently at the forefront of the health services research and policy agenda. Focusing on insurance coverage, a study by Kyanko and colleagues (Kyanko, Curry, & Busch, 2013; Kyanko, Pong, Bahan, & Curry, 2013; Murtagh et al., 2007) used a mixed methods approach to document the prevalence of involuntary out-of-network charges (quantitative web-based self-administered survey of a nationally representative sample of $n = 7,812$), followed by in-depth interviews with a purposeful sample of consumers who reported having had this experience in order to document its impact ($n = 26$). Together, the results paint a picture of both the magnitude and the nature of unanticipated charges incurred by insured individuals who receive services outside of their insurance network.

Health services researchers frequently face challenges in developing measurement tools, particularly for multifaceted and subjective constructs such as patient-centered outcomes. In one mixed methods study to develop a patient-centered outcome measure of treatment for prostate cancer, a qualitative component using focus groups (n = 48 participants in 7 groups) identified essential facets of outcomes including quality of life from the patients' perspective. This data was used to develop quantitative items and scales validated through psychometric testing ($n = 349$ prostate cancer patients and $n = 393$ in a comparison group) (Clark, Bokhour, Inui, Silliman, & Talcott, 2003). This particular use of a mixed methods approach is becoming widely endorsed as the optimal design for creation of complete, precise, and patient-centered measures.

Implementation Science

Implementation science investigates how best to integrate and translate research evidence into health care policy and practice (Madon, Hofman, Kupfer, & Glass, 2007). Implementation science examines the adoption, adaptation, and scale-up of health interventions in diverse settings and, because of this focus, implementation science studies are often designed to include data from multiple types of sources. In an informal search of journals in health services, medicine, nursing, and public health, we found the journal that has published the most mixed methods articles in recent years was *Implementation Science.* For example, Sax and colleagues (2013) designed a mixed methods study protocol to address the *how* and *why* of best practice implementation in the area of catheter-related bloodstream infection prevention in intensive care units of six purposefully selected hospitals. The qualitative component (InDepth) is a longitudinal case study (or cohort study or prospective study) embedded within a large randomized controlled intervention trial in Europe (Prevention of Hospital Infections by Intervention and Training, or PROHIBIT). The qualitative data examine why some hospitals are more successful at implementing the practices than others as well as identify facilitators and barriers to best practice in the institutional context. The quantitative data from the trial track multiple process and performance outcome measures; quantitative and qualitative data will be integrated at the conclusion of the trial in order to characterize the implementation and impact of the intervention.

In one study evaluating a primary care-based intervention to improve blood pressure control (Bosworth et al., 2010), the researchers developed four interdependent yet discrete aims. The initial aim, to assess organizational factors associated with the successful implementation of the intervention, included collection of both qualitative and quantitative data including interviews and standardized surveys of diverse types of clinicians (e.g., Assessment of Chronic Illness Care and Organizational Readiness to Change). The quantitative and qualitative data are aggregated to the organizational level and analyzed using a pattern-matching logic approach to explore relationships across the data (e.g., do clinics with high readiness to change scores experience fewer barriers to implementation?).

ILLUSTRATIONS FROM MIXED METHODS STUDIES IN THE HEALTH SCIENCES

In this section, we present illustrations from three mixed methods studies in health sciences, one for each of the primary types of designs: convergent, exploratory sequential, and explanatory sequential. Because the successful application of mixed methods in health sciences is still somewhat limited and the field is still in early stages of development, colleagues with experience in conducting mixed methods studies are extraordinary resources for learning about mixed methods.

Increasingly, health sciences researchers are applying three broad orientations as they explore complex issues through a practical lens; these orientations lend themselves nicely to mixed methods. They include community-based participatory research (CBPR), patient-centered outcomes research (PCOR), and implementation science (both a focal content area in health sciences and a research orientation). Major funding agencies in the United States, such as the National Institutes of Health (NIH), the Medical Research Council, the Patient-Centered Outcomes Research Institute (PCORI), the Agency for Healthcare Research and Quality (AHRQ), and others have endorsed use of these orientations, often directly citing mixed methods as central to addressing the complex and pressing research questions in health and health care. These three orientations characterize a sizable and growing proportion of health sciences research. We also believe they are in large part responsible for the steadily growing interest in mixed methods across the health sciences. Each of these broad orientations is described next more fully with the corresponding study example.

We conducted interviews with the lead researchers, who offered reflections based on their experience in developing a mixed methods project. We present an overview of each study using several figures to convey key project elements. Following the overview, excerpts from the interviews provide insights regarding early design decisions made by researchers beyond information typically available in a manuscript.

Example of a Convergent Design With a CBPR Orientation

CBPR involves partnerships between academicians and community members to ensure the integration of non-researcher expertise in all stages of research (Israel, Schulz, Parker, & Becker, 1998). Core principles include identifying health priorities specific to historically marginalized or vulnerable populations and engaging community members as equal partners toward the goal of eliminating health disparities and improving health outcomes (Horowitz, Robinson, & Seifer, 2009). Much of the health sciences research community has embraced CBPR as central to understanding the social determinants of health, health outcomes, and health equity. Although single method research approaches (either qualitative or quantitative) can be appropriate within CBPR projects, mixed methods are frequently the design choice of CBPR research teams. Qualitative methods are particularly useful in capturing rich data about the experiences and perceptions of marginalized communities, while quantitative methods can provide generalizable results that are critical for policymaking. Closely related to CBPR is a genre within mixed methods known as transformative research. Transformative research focuses on multiple dimensions of diversity and power differentials with the overarching aim of promoting social justice, including in the context of health (Mertens, 2007). An example of a study that uses a convergent design for a study with a CBPR orientation is described in Box 2.4 and Figure 2.2.

▶ For more information on how example articles for this book were chosen, see Appendix A: Biographies of Contributing Experts. To read more about implementation challenges and mechanics, refer to Chapter 10: Implementation Issues in Mixed Methods Research.

Box 2.4　Abstract From a Study That Used a Convergent Design

Weathers, B., Barg, F. K., Bowman, M., Briggs, V., Delmoor, E., Kumanyika, S., . . . Halbert, C. H. (2011). Using a mixed-methods approach to identify health concerns in an African American community. *American Journal of Public Health, 101*(11), 2087–2092. doi: 10.2105/AJPH.2010.191775

Abstract

Objectives: We used qualitative and quantitative data collection methods to identify the health concerns of African American residents in an urban community and analyzed the extent to which there were consistencies across methods in the concerns identified.

Methods: We completed nine focus groups with 51 residents, 27 KI interviews, and 201 community health surveys with a random sample of community residents to identify the health issues participants considered of greatest importance. We then compared the issues identified through these methods.

Results: Focus group participants and key informants gave priority to cancer and cardiovascular diseases, but most respondents in the community health survey indicated that sexually transmitted diseases, substance abuse, and obesity were conditions in need of intervention. How respondents ranked their concerns varied in the qualitative versus the quantitative methods.

Conclusions: Using qualitative and quantitative approaches simultaneously is useful in determining community health concerns. Although quantitative approaches yield concrete evidence of community needs, qualitative approaches provide a context for how these issues can be addressed. Researchers should develop creative ways to address multiple issues that arise when using a mixed methods approach.

As described in Box 2.4 and shown in Figure 2.2, Weathers and colleagues (2011) used a convergent design to identify research priorities for a historically underserved community in West Philadelphia neighborhoods. The ultimate project objective was "to conduct collaborative research to address disparities in chronic diseases that disproportionately affect African Americans in terms of morbidity and mortality using a community-based participatory framework" (Weathers et al., 2011, p. 2087). Applying the principles of CBPR, the leadership of four community-based organizations were intimately involved in the research design process with University of Pennsylvania researchers and staff. This academic-community partnership, the West Philadelphia Consortium to Address Disparities, decided on a mixed methods approach for their first research effort. They intended to collect information on the perspectives of community members to inform the partnership's long-term research agenda. The team used the findings from the mixed methods project

Figure 2.2   Project Overview for Example Study: Weathers et al., 2011

PROJECT TITLE	Using a Mixed Methods Approach to Identify Health Concerns in an African American Community
TEAM MEMBERS	Chanita Hughes-Halbert,[1] Benita Weathers,[2] Frances Barg,[2] Marjorie Bowman,[3] Vanessa Briggs,[4] Ernestine Delmoor,[5] Shiriki Kumanyika,[6] Jerry C.Johnson,[7] Joseph Purnell,[8] Rodney Rogers[9] [1]Department of Psychiatry and Behavioral Sciences, Medical University of South Carolina [2]Department of Family Medicine and Community Health, University of Pennsylvania Perelman School of Medicine [3]Boonshoft School of Medicine, Wright State University [4]Managing Director of Health Promotion, Public Health Management Corporation [5]President, National Black Leadership Initiative on Cancer, Philadelphia Chapter [6]Department of Biostatistics and Epidemiology, University of Pennsylvania Perelman School of Medicine [7]Division of Geriatric Medicine, University of Pennsylvania Perelman School of Medicine [8]Executive Director, Neighborhoods United Against Drugs [9]Executive Director, Christ of Calvary Community Development Corporation
PROJECT AIMS	I. Identify the health concerns of African American residents in an urban community II. Analyze the extent to which there were consistencies across methods in the concerns identified
MIXED METHODS DESIGN	Convergent parallel
PROJECT PERIOD	January 2006–present
FUNDING	The National Center on Minority Health and Health Disparties, the National Cancer Institute(NCI), and the National Center for Research Resources
MANUSCRIPTS TO DATE	1

SOURCE: Adapted from Weathers et al. (2011).

described here to design several pilot interventions. Ultimately, the team was successfully awarded additional funding to conduct the interventions grounded in their mixed methods work. See Figure 2.3 for a full timeline of the project.

As shown in Figure 2.4, this research team designed three study components to collect narrative and numeric data prior to data analysis and interpretation. Two qualitative components, focus groups ($n = 51$ participants in nine groups) and in-depth interviews ($n = 27$) both queried participants on "the most important health issues that needed to be addressed in the community" (Weathers et al., 2011, p. 2088). Although the research questions and interview guides were similar for both qualitative components, the sampling approaches were intentionally different in order to solicit views from different kinds of community representatives. The sampling frame for the focus groups was the general community in West Philadelphia, and participants were recruited through self-referrals in response to newspaper advertisements. The sampling frame for the in-depth interviews was stakeholder status as a recognized community leader; key informants (KIs) were identified by the executive council of the academic–community partnership. The team agreed focus groups were needed in addition to in-depth interviews with KIs because people participating in the latter "are typically selected for their stakeholder status within the community. This status may not be indicative of their awareness of community priorities as a whole but rather of the segment of the community with which they typically interact" (Weathers et al., 2011, p. 2091). A single quantitative component, an interviewer-administered survey questionnaire ($n = 201$), asked respondents to select the one health issue in their community that should be addressed from a list of conditions determined independently by the research team. To populate this list, the research team relied on objective reports of the leading diagnoses and diseases disproportionately affecting African Americans defined by increased prevalence or mortality compared to other demographic populations.

The data were integrated through a merging approach. The team first analyzed data from each component independently, then combined focus group and KI interview findings into a unified qualitative category, and finally interpreted the qualitative and quantitative data together. Notably, they used a participant confirmatory approach through a community forum setting to help resolve discordance in findings across the components and to finalize the two topic areas for further development as pilot interventions. Here, we present excerpts from an interview we conducted with the lead researchers on this project related to study rationale and design decisions. Biographies for the authors interviewed about this study are included in Box 2.5.

Figure 2.3 Timeline for Example Study: Weathers et al., 2011

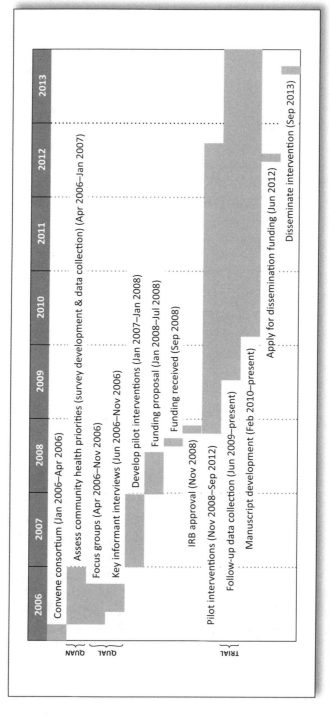

SOURCE: Adapted from Weathers et al. (2011).

NOTE: QUAL = qualitative component; QUAN = quantitative component; IRB = institutional review board.

Figure 2.4 Design Summary for Example Study: Weathers et al., 2011

Component	Methods	Objective	n
I.	Focus group discussions	Understand how residents conceptualized health, and identify the conditions in their community that they believed were more important to address	51 in 9 groups
II.	Key informant interviews	Identify the most important health issues in the community that participants felt needed to be addressed	27
III.	Surveys	Identify the heath issues participants considered of greatest importance	201

SOURCE: Adapted from Weathers et al. (2011).

Box 2.5 Biographies for Authors Interviewed About Weathers, et al., 2011

Chanita Hughes-Halbert, PhD. Dr. Hughes-Halbert is professor and endowed chair in the Department of Psychiatry and Behavioral Sciences and the Hollings Cancer Center at the Medical University of South Carolina. Previously, she was founding director of the Center for Community-Based Research and Health Disparities and associate professor in the Department of Psychiatry at the University of Pennsylvania. The goal of Dr. Hughes-Halbert's research program is to identify sociocultural, psychological, and environmental determinants of minority health and health care and to translate this information into sustainable interventions in clinic and community-based settings to improve health outcomes in these populations. Dr. Hughes-Halbert is a nationally recognized expert in minority health and health disparities.

Benita Weathers, MPH. Ms. Weathers has over 20 years of public health research experience with an emphasis on community-based participatory and health disparities research and was the senior project manager at the Center for Community-Based Research and Health Disparities. She is currently a senior research project manager in the Department of Family Medicine at the University of Pennsylvania.

Q: What was the rationale, or justification, for using a mixed methods design?

A: It was important to use quantitative methods in the form of population-based random surveys along with qualitative approaches, the focus groups, and interviews to ensure that the health priorities and concerns identified during the formative phase of our academic–community partnership were representative of most of the community. In addition, limited empirical data existed on the congruence of data obtained using different methods and that presented an opportunity for us to offer suggestions in the manuscript for managing inconsistencies that may arise when using a mixed methods approach.

Q: Please tell us about your decision to use a mixed methods approach in this study. What were the advantages of using three different methods with three unique samples, as compared to a single method such as a survey of a single sample?

A: The purpose of our academic–community partnership was to develop interventions to reduce racial disparities and improve health outcomes among African Americans in the Philadelphia, Pennsylvania, metropolitan area. A fundamental value of our partnership was that the interventions we conducted would be of value to community residents and would address their needs and priorities. We used a mixed methods approach to identify the priorities and concerns of community residents for a number of reasons. First, we recognized that there are several strengths to qualitative methods for identifying community priorities; the most important of these is that it allows investigators to elicit these issues from the residents' perspectives using their own words, phrases, and descriptions. We believed that this was important to our partnership and would ensure that we developed interventions that would be of value to community residents. Second, while we ultimately wanted to develop interventions that would be of value to community residents, we recognized that there were multiple stakeholders who were involved in efforts to address racial disparities and improve health outcomes among African Americans in our catchment area. Therefore, we conducted focus groups with community residents and in-depth key informant (KI) interviews with other stakeholders who were involved in efforts to address racial disparities and minority health. Third, the two qualitative strategies had different purposes. The individual interviews were useful to generate the widest possible range of topics and ideas. By contrast, the focus groups were useful to observe, in real time, issues around which there was consensus as well as topics that generated disagreement. We also realized that the methods we used to recruit participants for focus groups (e.g., self-referral from newspaper advertisements) and KIs (e.g., nomination by the executive council) have limitations that include limited generalizability. We believed that a random-digit survey of West Philadelphia residents would ensure that the priorities identified through the qualitative methods would be representative of our community. The community health survey would also allow us to identify psychological and behavioral factors that contribute to poor health outcomes among African Americans in our target community. We believed that the community health survey would enable us to develop a better understanding of barriers and facilitators to primary and secondary prevention behaviors that could be targeted as part of the interventions that were developed by the partnership. Collectively, the focus groups, in-depth KI interviews, and community health survey were part of the first phase of building our partnership.

Q: We classify your study design as convergent because it appears you waited until all data were collected before analyzing and interpreting the findings. In the traditional definition of a convergent design, all data components are collected simultaneously. Can you tell us more about this design decision?

A: Our study fits the description of a convergent design for two main reasons. We expected our different data components to provide different types of information. The samples for the focus groups and individual interviews were purposefully selected to reflect the perspectives identified by our consortium. We wanted to understand what they thought and why they thought it in order to tailor our subsequent interventions to their perceived needs. The survey data was designed to serve as a population-based assessment of health priorities. These data also allowed us to understand perceptions and priorities among subgroups within the population. Integrating these perspectives at the end allowed us to understand how our stakeholders' (KI interviewees) views are distributed in the wider population. Our second reason is more pragmatic. The work described in our manuscript was funded for a three-year period; we originally designed the data collection component for the first phase of developing our academic–community partnership to occur in a sequential fashion: first, focus groups; second, KI interviews; and third, the community health survey in order to have the results of each inform the next step. However, we modified this procedure for several reasons—the most important of which was the limited amount of time that was available for the project period to accomplish all of our aims. We also planned to develop and evaluate pilot interventions that were based on the priorities identified by community residents. After starting recruitment for the focus groups, we realized that there were going to be challenges with meeting our accrual goals. We also realized that additional time would be needed to complete the community health survey. In addition to developing the content for the survey, it would need pilot testing, revision, and approval by regulatory affairs prior to administration. We were not able to complete these activities until after the focus groups and KI interviews were completed. A primary goal for our partnership was to develop interventions that would address the priorities and concerns of African American community residents. We conceptualized the focus groups, KI interviews, and the community health survey as preliminary data to develop these interventions.

Q: Team composition is a critical decision at the earliest state of the project. Can you tell us how you went about developing the team?

A: In developing the partnership, we considered a number of different issues, the first of which was the overall geographic area for our research and how we could develop effective infrastructure for improving health behaviors and outcomes among African Americans in the Philadelphia metropolitan area. For instance, Philadelphia is a city of neighborhoods with multiple grassroots, government, nonprofit, and faith-based organizations that target discrete yet overlapping needs. Likewise, research units at the University of Pennsylvania have forged relationships and established multiple community advisory boards that are specific to related projects. We recognized a need to forge a collective that can bring these elements together to form a cohesive voice for intervention research on health disparities in a targeted population. The challenge of meeting this need is to identify partners who are representative of the community, who are interested or have experience in health care and the health status of the community, and who are willing to work together to foster collaborative research. In selecting the members of our partnership, we recognized an inevitable trade-off between the number of partners and the effectiveness of the working relationship. These factors led us to choose a grassroots organization that had already forged a small collective of organizations, a faith-based group that is a consortium of eight churches in West Philadelphia with a health education mission, a nonprofit organization with substantial experience in working in underserved minority populations, the school system, and a grassroots nonprofit organization with expertise in community outreach and education about cancer. Thus, members of the research group were part of a research collaborative developed to implement research interventions using a community-based participatory approach. Members consisted of a multidisciplinary group of academic and community investigators that responded to a request for applications (RFAs) by the National Center on Minority Health and Health Disparities; therefore, it was a fixed group of investigators. No one left nor did anyone join the team after the project started.

Example of an Exploratory Sequential Design Using a Patient-Centered Outcomes Research Orientation

PCOR seeks to promote the effectiveness and value of health care with a results-based orientation, focusing on what matters to patients and the public. Patients and other stakeholders are involved as partners in research to make the questions both patient-centered and actionable (Krumholz, Selby, & PCORI, 2012). By asking patients and stakeholders to prioritize the outcomes of greatest importance to them (e.g., quality of life, minimization of side effects, functional status, patient satisfaction), PCOR calls for a "reshuffling" of our historic tendency to focus solely on clinical parameters and to broaden what we capture to incorporate patient-reported preferences and experiences. PCOR provides the ultimate end users of health sciences research—patients and their caregivers— with the tools necessary to join with providers in clinical decision making. In the United States, PCORI is now a major funder of health sciences research (with more than $273.5 million as of November 2013). As described in Box 2.6, mixed methods provide a foundation for the patient experience to be more fully understood, in this instance within evaluating the efficacy of an intervention.

Box 2.6 Understanding the Full Patient Experience With Mixed Methods

My work has looked at customer perceptions of services and how you improve services. These are really complex issues. When you deal with customers' perceptions of the services they receive or staff perceptions of a new intervention, that gets into some complex issues. In the past, that work had pretty much been limited to mainly quantitative approaches that didn't provide enough solid evidence. Mixed methods provides a way to move forward and be able to capture both the really rich perceptions that can tell you their experiences of the situation, and also capture the quantitative portion of whether your intervention worked.

—Dr. Jennifer Wisdom, PhD, MPH, Professor of
Health Policy and Associate Vice President for Research,
George Washington University

As described in Box 2.7 and Figure 2.5, Stoller and colleagues (2009) used an exploratory sequential design for a study with a PCOR orientation. Specifically, this study looked at the drinking decisions of individuals diagnosed with chronic hepatitis C virus (HCV) infection classified as "non-abusing alcohol users," low-risk drinkers whose alcohol intake would not be classified as problematic in the absence of an HCV diagnosis. Given that alcohol is relatively contraindicated in HCV infection and that much of the research to date "on alcohol consumption decisions . . . focused on patients with alcohol abuse or dependence" (Stoller et al., 2009, p. 2), the team was ultimately interested in contributing to a knowledge base specific for non-alcohol related conditions for which drinking is contraindicated. They used chronic HCV infection as a prototype for this larger category of medical condition.

Box 2.7   Abstract From a Study That Used an Exploratory Sequential Design

Stoller, E. P., Webster, N. J., Blixen, C. E., McCormick, R. A., Hund, A. J., Perzynski, A. T., . . . Dawson, N. V. (2009). Alcohol consumption decisions among nonabusing drinkers diagnosed with hepatitis C: An exploratory sequential mixed methods study. *Journal of Mixed Methods Research, 3*(1), 65–86.

Abstract

Most studies of decisions to curtail alcohol consumption reflect experiences of abusing drinkers. We employ an exploratory sequential research design to explore the applicability of this research to the experience of non-abusing drinkers advised to curtail alcohol consumption after a hepatitis C diagnosis. A qualitative component identified 17 new decision factors not reflected in an inventory of factors based on synthesis of existing scales. We triangulated qualitative data by supplementing semi-structured interviews with Internet postings. A quantitative component estimated prevalence and association with current drinking of these new decision factors. Patients who quit drinking tended to attribute post-diagnosis drinking to occasional triggers, whereas patients who were still drinking were more likely to endorse rationales not tied to specific triggers.

Figure 2.5   Project Overview for Example Study: Stoller et al., 2009

PROJECT TITLE	Alcohol Consumption Decisions Among Nonabusing Drinkers Diagnosed With Hepatitis C: An Exploratory Sequential Mixed Methods Study
TEAM MEMBERS	Eleanor Palo Stoller,[1] Noah J. Webster,[1] Carol E. Blixen,[2] Richard A. McCormick,[3] Andrew J. Hund,[1] Adam T. Perzynski,[1] Charles L. Thomas ,[4] Kyle Kercher,[1] Neal V. Dawson,[5] Douglas Einstadler,[5] Kevin Mullen,[5] Yossef Ben-Porath,[6] Stephanie Wolfie,[7] Joshua Tercher[1]
	[1]Department of Sociology, Case Western Reserve University
	[2]Cleveland Clinic Foundation
	[3]Department of Psychology, Case Western Reserve University
	[4]Center for Health Care Research and Policy, Case Western Reserve University
	[5]School of Medicine, Case Western Reserve University
	[6]Department of Psychology, Kent State University
	[7]MetroHealth Medical Center
PROJECT AIMS	I. Explore the alcohol consumption experience of non-abusing drinkers diagnosed with HCV in order to identify factors not previously documented in research with abusing drinkers
	II. Elaborate existing instruments assessing consumption decisions to incorporate these additional factors experienced by HCV+ non-abusing drinkers
	III. Use indicators of these new factors to assess their prevalence and association with alcohol consumption among these drinkers
MIXED METHODS DESIGN	Exploratory sequential
PROJECT PERIOD	September 2002–August 2008
FUNDING	National Institute on Alcohol Abuse and Alcoholism
MANUSCRIPTS TO DATE	5

SOURCE: Adapted from Stoller et al. (2009).

NOTE: HCV = hepatitis C virus; HCV+ = hepatitis C virus seropositive.

The study's objective was to aggregate known and novel factors that influence the decision to reduce alcohol consumption among non-abusing hepatitis C virus seropositive (HCV+) patients. The authors cite a mixed methods rationale, Instrument Fidelity, borrowed from the education literature (Collins, Onwuegbuzie, & Sutton, 2006). "Although we are not designing a new instrument, our findings suggest areas in which existing instruments could be modified for use with non-abusing drinkers told to curtail alcohol consumption for medical reasons not related to alcohol" (Stoller et al., 2009, p. 3). This study fit within the patient-centered outcomes paradigm because the team sought to incorporate the experiences of a previously understudied group into the clinical decision making and management of alcohol consumption after HCV diagnosis. Identifying novel decision factors and describing their prevalence helped prioritize the outcomes of greatest importance to non-abusing drinkers with HCV.

The qualitative component included three data sources intended "to understand factors affecting post-diagnosis alcohol consumption among non-abusing drinkers with HCV" (Stoller et al., 2009, p. 4). The team completed semi-structured interviews ($n = 42$) with HCV+ patients at an urban teaching hospital; participants were recruited from a gastroenterology clinic and from the emergency department. A sampling grid was used to track representation across gender, race/ethnicity, and level of alcohol use. The interview data were supplemented with illness narratives and threaded discussions from eight English-language websites in order to "minimize the reactivity that can emerge when people are interviewed in clinical settings in which they are also patients and to tap experiences of people not being treated in a teaching hospital affiliated with a medical center" (Stoller et al., 2009, p. 5). To understand how these components were coordinated logistically, see the timeline in Figure 2.6.

The purpose of the qualitative data analysis was to compare findings with items related to alcohol decision making on existing instruments that were identified prior to starting data collection. Existing instruments were designed for abusers; the team did not find any scales for non-abusing drinkers in their literature review. They identified existing items that were supported in their qualitative analysis and introduced a catalog of new decision factors not found in existing instruments. Based upon the list of newly identified decision factors, the team developed and cognitively tested de novo questionnaire items before using them to collect quantitative data on the prevalence of new decision factors through structured telephone interviews ($n = 577$). Patients were drawn from a randomized list of almost 3,000 patients until adequate racial/ethnic group representation was achieved (see Figure 2.7).

Figure 2.6 Timeline for Example Study: Stoller et al., 2009

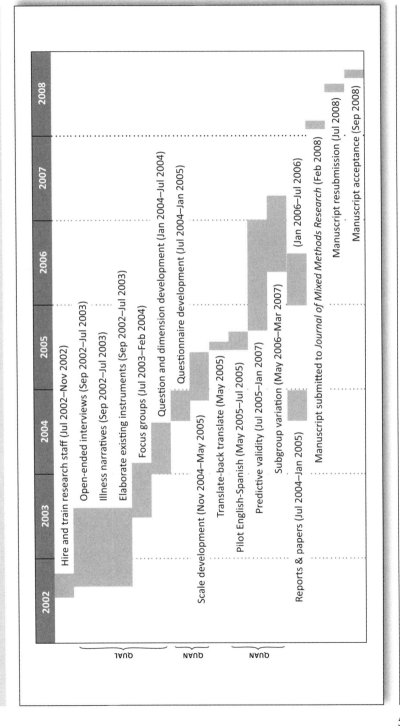

SOURCE: Adapted from Stoller et al. (2009).

NOTE: QUAL = qualitative component; QUAN = quantitative component.

Figure 2.7   Design Summary for Example Study: Stoller et al., 2009

Component	Methods	Objective	n
I.	Semi-structured interviews; Illness narratives; Threaded discussions	Assess the applicability of decision factors identified in existing instruments to postdiagnosis non-abusing alcohol drinkers with hepatitis C	42 interviews 307 narratives (8 sites) 264 threads
II.	Structured telephone interviews	Estimate prevalence and association of postdiagnosis alcohol consumption with new decision factors identified in the qualitative phase	577

SOURCE: Adapted from Stoller et al. (2009).

The data were integrated through a connecting approach. The team first analyzed data from the qualitative component, then built the quantitative component to describe a new construct further (e.g., factors influencing the initiation of decisions to curtail alcohol consumption among non-abusing HCV+ patients not reflected in existing literature), and interpreted the qualitative and quantitative data together after independently analyzing each component. Here, we present excerpts from an interview we conducted with the lead researcher on this project related to study rationale and design decisions. Biographies for the authors interviewed about this study are included in Box 2.8.

Box 2.8   Biographies for Authors Interviewed About Stoller et al., 2009

Dr. Eleanor Palo Stoller, PhD, AM. Dr. Stoller is research professor of sociology and gerontology at Wake Forest University, Winston-Salem, North Carolina. She was previously the Selah Chamberlain Professor of Sociology at Case Western Reserve University (Cleveland, Ohio) and professor of health policy at the University of Florida (Gainesville). Her research, which focuses on the ways older people and their families cope with health challenges, has been supported by the National Institute on Aging and the Administration on Aging. She served on the editorial boards of *The Gerontologist, Journal of Gerontology: Social Sciences, Research on Aging, Journal of Applied Gerontology,* the *Journal of Aging Studies,* and the *Journal of Family Issues.* She is a fellow of the Gerontological Society of America and has been a member of the Neuroscience, Behavior, and Sociology of Aging Study Section of the National Institute on Aging.

Neal V. Dawson, MD. Dr. Dawson is professor of medicine, epidemiology, and biostatistics at Case Western Reserve University and section head of the Medical Decision Making Division of the Center for Health Care Research and Policy at MetroHealth Medical Center (all in Cleveland, Ohio). His nationally funded research has covered a variety of topics (e.g., end-of-life decision making, alcohol-related issues in primary care, improving outcomes of patients with both diabetes and serious mental illness), which have been examined using methodologies from medical decision making, clinical epidemiology, and health services research. He has served as a manuscript reviewer for many clinical journals, is associate editor emeritus for the journal *Medical Decision Making,* and has served as a grant application reviewer for the National Institutes of Health (NIH), National Science Foundation (NSF), national foundations, and international funding agencies. He currently serves in numerous capacities in a postgraduate multidisciplinary research training program (the NIH-funded Case Clinical Translational Science Award).

Q: What was your rationale or justification for using a mixed methods design?

A: Our overall goal was to understand why people who don't have an alcohol disorder do or don't stop drinking after being diagnosed with the hepatitis C virus (HCV). Our review of available instruments assessing alcohol consumption revealed limited attention to these non-problematic drinkers. Before addressing our overall goal, we believed it necessary to examine the extent of overlap in the drinking decisions problematic or dependent and nondependent drinkers make when facing HCV diagnoses. This need dictated a qualitative, exploratory research component to identify factors not captured in prior research or in standardized instruments based on the experience of abusing drinkers.

Q: Why and how did you decide on an exploratory sequential approach? Did you consider other approaches? If yes, what were the other approaches, and why were those ultimately rejected?

A: Our choice of an exploratory sequential approach was based on our research goals (1) to explore the alcohol consumption experience of non-abusing drinkers diagnosed with HCV in order to identify factors not previously documented in research with abusing drinkers (qualitative component), (2) to elaborate existing instruments assessing consumption decisions to incorporate these additional factors' experience by hepatitis C virus seropositive (HCV+) non-abusing drinkers (quantitative component), and (3) to use indicators of these new factors to assess their prevalence and association with alcohol consumption among these drinkers (quantitative component).

Q: How and why did you decide to create the sample for the qualitative component (interviews) independent of the quantitative component (surveys)?

A: The two samples addressed different goals. The sample for the qualitative interviews was designed to tap a broad range of experiences; we were not concerned with identifying "typical" decision factors or assessing prevalence or distribution. In selecting the sample for the quantitative component, however, we did want to assess prevalence and distribution of emergent items. We therefore wanted to minimize overlap and maximize independence between the two samples.

Q: Did you and the team delineate any a priori processes for resolving conflicting findings across components should those arise?

A: We interpreted differences in findings across components of the design as part of our results. In terms of looking at differences among the three sources of qualitative data, our goal in identifying the three sources was to cast a broad net in capturing drinking experiences. If we had expected each source to yield the same findings, we would not have felt it necessary to include all three sources. Discrepant findings confirmed our decision to look beyond any one source. When considering differences between the qualitative and quantitative components, we focused on the goal of the quantitative component: to estimate the prevalence and distribution of decision factors emerging from the qualitative analysis. A relatively low (or high) prevalence of one of these decision factors provided additional evidence, not a conflict.

Example of an Explanatory Sequential Design
Using an Implementation Science Orientation

Implementation science investigates how best to integrate and translate research evidence into real-world public health and service delivery systems (Madon et al., 2007). Focal areas include identifying barriers (e.g., social, behavioral, economic, management) that impede effective uptake of interventions, programs, and policies in diverse settings as well as assets and facilitators of success. Because understanding these multifaceted phenomena frequently requires multiple forms of measurement, there is substantial interest in mixed methods among implementation science researchers. Quantitative methods can measure certain key elements of a particular intervention or program, such as adoption and adherence, rates of utilization, and impact on clinical outcomes. A qualitative component can be used to examine whether an intervention was delivered as intended, describe implementation processes, generate an understanding of why an intervention failed to work, or explore how its effectiveness was promoted or limited in the real world. In addition, qualitative findings can help mitigate publication biases against studies lacking intervention effectiveness by both explaining negative results and informing subsequent research. Box 2.9 provides an example of an implementation science study that uses an explanatory sequential design.

Box 2.9 Abstract From a Study That Used an Explanatory Sequential Design

Schifferdecker, K. E., Berman, N. B., Fall, L. H., & Fischer, M. R. (2012). Adoption of computer-assisted learning in medical education: The educators' perspective. *Medical Education, 46*(11), 1063–1073. doi: 10.1111/j.1365–2923.2012.04350.x

Abstract

Context: Computer-assisted learning (CAL) in medical education has been shown to be effective in the achievement of learning outcomes, but requires the input of significant resources and

(Continued)

(Continued)

development time. This study examines the key elements and processes that led to the widespread adoption of a CAL program in undergraduate medical education, the Computer-Assisted Learning in Pediatrics Program (CLIPP). It then considers the relative importance of elements drawn from existing theories and models for technology adoption and other studies on CAL in medical education to inform the future development, implementation and testing of CAL programs in medical education.

Methods: The study used a mixed methods explanatory design. All pediatric clerkship directors (CDs) using CLIPP were recruited to participate in a self-administered, online questionnaire. Semi-structured interviews were then conducted with a random sample of CDs to further explore the quantitative results.

Results: Factors that facilitated adoption included CLIPP's ability to fill gaps in exposure to core clinical problems, the use of a national curriculum, development by CDs, and the meeting of CDs' desires to improve teaching and student learning. An additional facilitating factor was that little time and effort were needed to implement CLIPP within a clerkship. The quantitative findings were mostly corroborated by the qualitative findings.

Conclusions: This study indicates issues that are important in the consideration and future exploration of the development and implementation of CAL programs in medical education. The promise of CAL as a method of enhancing the process and outcomes of medical education, and its cost, increase the need for future CAL funders and developers to pay equal attention to the needs of potential adopters and the development process as they do to the content and tools in the CAL program. Important questions that remain on the optimal design, use and integration of CAL should be addressed in order to adequately inform future development. Support is needed for studies that address these critical areas.

As described in Box 2.9 and Figure 2.8, Schifferdecker, Berman, Fall, and Fischer (2012) examined the uptake of a curricular innovation in undergraduate medical education: computer-assisted learning (CAL). This study identified the lack of understanding of the educators' perspective on widespread CAL uptake as an important knowledge gap best addressed through a mixed

Figure 2.8 Project Overview for Example Study: Schifferdecker et al., 2012

PROJECT TITLE	Adoption of Computer-Assisted Learning in Medical Education: The Educators' Perspective
TEAM MEMBERS	Karen E. Schifferdecker,[1] Norm B. Berman,[2] Leslie H. Fall,[2] Martin R. Fischer[3] [1]Department of Community and Family Medicine, Geisel School of Medicine at Dartmouth [2]Department of Paediatrics, Geisel School of Medicine at Dartmouth [3]Department of Medical Education, University Hospital, Ludwig Maximilian University, Germany
PROJECT AIMS	I. Identify the key processes and factors that led to the widespread adoption of a virtual patient CAL program in UME, the Computer-Assisted Learning in Pediatrics Program (CLIPP) II. Explore these findings in light of existing theories of and models for the adoption of technology and in relation to others studies on the use of CAL in medical education to inform the future development, implementation, and testing of CAL programs in medical education
MIXED METHODS DESIGN	Sequential explanatory
PROJECT PERIOD	August 2006–June 2012
FUNDING	Institute for Innovative Technology in Medical Education and the Office of Community-Based Education and Research at Geisel School of Medicine at Dartmouth
MANUSCRIPTS TO DATE	1

SOURCE: Adapted from Schifferdecker et al. (2012).

NOTE: CAL = computer-assisted learning; UME = undergraduate medical education.

methods approach. The project's goal was classic implementation science to identify "key processes and factors that led to the widespread adoption of a virtual patient CAL program in undergraduate medical education" (Schifferdecker et al., 2012, p. 1064). The study focused on the implementation of the Computer-Assisted Learning in Pediatrics Program (CLIPP), which is a "web-based series of 31 virtual patient cases designed to comprehensively cover a . . . pediatrics clerkship curriculum" (Schifferdecker et al., 2012, p. 1064) approved by U.S. and Canadian medical schools. First distributed in 2003 and 2004, CLIPP was in use by the majority of medical schools (80% of U.S. medical schools and 53% of Canadian medical schools) at the time of the study's publication.

The team recruited pediatric clerkship directors to assist in the development and piloting of a 23-item web-based questionnaire "to assess reasons for adopting CLIPP, time spent on incorporating CLIPP, methods of implementing CLIPP, and the characteristics of respondents and their clerkships" (Schifferdecker et al., 2012, p. 1065). The sample for the questionnaire included all 90 pediatric clerkship directors with a known CLIPP subscription. Data from this initial quantitative component (n = 64; 71% of pediatric clerkship directors using CLIPP during 2005 and 2006) were collected and analyzed prior to the development of qualitative component (see Figure 2.9).

The goal of the semi-structured interviews was "to expand, further understand, and cross-check data obtained from the questionnaire results" (Schifferdecker et al., 2012, p. 1065). In addition, the team included questions on the interview guide to explore topics that were not covered on the questionnaire. The sampling frame for the qualitative component included pediatric clerkship directors who had CLIPP subscriptions during 2006 and 2007 (n = 100), including many of the clerkship directors who used CLIPP during 2005 and 2006 (the sampling frame for the quantitative component) (see Figure 2.10). Interview participants were selected using a random table generator (n = 15) and 11 interviews were conducted by telephone. Participants in the two-study components were "fairly well-distributed in terms of the length of time they had served as clerkship directors and the sizes of their Year 3 classes" (Schifferdecker et al., 2012, p. 1066). However, interviewees "placed less reliance on the cases as learning tools within their clerkships" (Schifferdecker et al., 2012, p. 1066) compared with survey respondents as reflected by the number of cases used by clerkship directors in each group.

The data were integrated through a connecting approach. They first analyzed data from the quantitative phase, then built the qualitative phase to characterize a common domain (e.g., key processes in the adoption of CAL), and finally interpreted the qualitative and quantitative data together. "When the result from both study phases were examined and compared to explore factors facilitating the adoption and use of CLIPP, questionnaire results were often

Figure 2.9 Timeline for Example Study: Schifferdecker et al., 2012

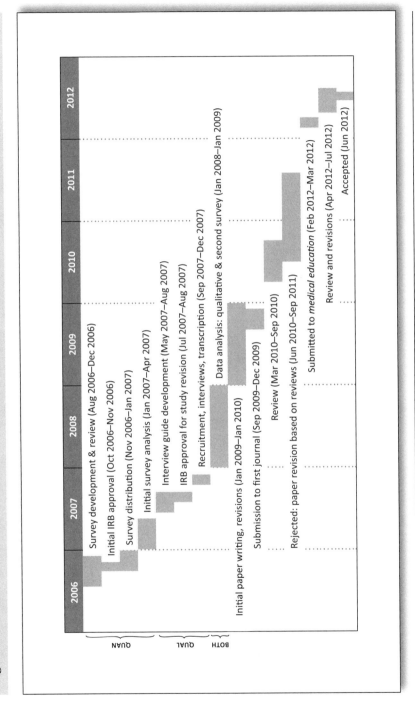

SOURCE: Adapted from Schifferdecker et al. (2012).

NOTE: QUAN = qualitative component; QUAL = qualitative component; IRB = institutional review board.

Figure 2.10 Design Summary for Example Study: Schifferdecker et al., 2012

Component	Methods	Objective	n
I.	Self-administered questionnaires	Assess reasons for adopting CLIPP, time spent on incorporating CLIPP, methods of implementing CLIPP, and the characteristics of respondents and their clerkships	47
II.	Semi-structured interviews	Expand, further understand, and cross-check data obtained from the questionnaire results	11

SOURCE: Adapted from Schifferdecker et al. (2012).

NOTE: CLIPP = Computer-Assisted Learning in Pediatrics Program.

corroborated by results from the interviews" (Schifferdecker et al., 2012, p. 1068). Here, we present excerpts from an interview we conducted with the lead researcher on this project related to study rationale and design decisions. A biography for the author interviewed about this study is included in Box 2.10.

Box 2.10   Biography for Author Interviewed About Schifferdecker et al., 2012

Karen Schifferdecker, PhD, MPH. Dr. Schifferdecker is assistant professor of community and family medicine at the Geisel School of Medicine at Dartmouth and associate director of the Center for Program Design and Evaluation at Dartmouth. A medical anthropologist with public health expertise, she has extensive experience overseeing and conducting community- and practice-based research and medical education studies and evaluation using quantitative, qualitative, and mixed research methods. Her recent work involving mixed methods approaches includes an evaluation of the Multi-Specialty MOC Portfolio Approval Pilot Program, a study of the implementation of patient-reported measures in several clinical sites nationwide, and a randomized, matched-pairs study of child welfare offices in the state of New Hampshire to improve trauma screening and well-being for children and youth served by the system.

Q: What was the rationale, or justification, for using a mixed methods design?

A: Given the nature of our questions resulting from the survey results, it was clear to us that conversations (interviews) with pediatric course directors was the logical way to better interpret the answers and to learn more about their experiences adopting the Computer-Assisted Learning in Pediatrics Program (CLIPP) cases for use in their clerkships. There were more questions than answers about particular pieces of the adoption process, and qualitative methods would allow the best exploration of these pieces.

Q: How and why did you decide to create the sample for the qualitative component independent of the quantitative component?

A: This was due to both an issue of timing (Phase I was completed a year before Phase II began, and there was turnover and new clerkship directors using CLIPP) and the rationale that there was no particular reason to target only those who had answered the survey since our interview questions did not explicitly refer to the Phase I findings or require that someone had participated in this phase of the study.

Q: How did the quantitative component inform the development of the interview guide? How did you choose which questionnaire responses to follow up on in your interviews?

A: The interview guide was informed by the quantitative component in three ways: one in deciding that we really wanted to get a better understanding of the adoption process. The survey focused a bit more on the current use of CLIPP cases, and the questions from the results we had were mostly about the adoption process and reasons for adopting CLIPP. So that is why the interview guide starts with these questions. Second, the questions were constructed to make sure that we covered some of the questions from the survey, such as defining what *quality* meant as a reason for adopting CLIPP. The third way, which relates to the second, was using the results to define probing questions, which are not included in the paper. For instance, when I asked, "What would you say are all the reasons that you ended up using CLIPP?" and they talked about the "quality," then I had a probing question to follow up on this, asking them to tell me more about what they meant by quality.

Q: Did you and the team delineate any a priori processes for resolving conflicting findings across components should those arise?

A: No, we did not define a process a priori. We had a process for resolving differences in the analysis and coding but not a process specifically for conflicting findings in the triangulation of the findings. The process we did use was to identify those areas (which were very few) and to then discuss them between us to come to some agreement on how we would report the conflict.

Summary and Key Points

- Three broad research approaches are increasingly common in the health sciences and readily lend themselves to mixed methods: CBPR, PCOR, and implementation science.
- There are many reasons to employ mixed methods, including producing a more comprehensive account, using findings from one component to explain the other and generating hypotheses and testing them quantitatively within a single project, "offsetting" the limitations of each method, developing rigorous quantitative measurement tools, and uncovering relationships among variables and concepts.
- Because the successful application of mixed methods in health sciences is still rather limited and the field is still in early stages of development, colleagues with experience in conducting mixed methods studies are a valuable resource for learning about mixed methods.

Review Questions and Exercises

1. Think about the three orientations to research in health sciences research described in this chapter: CBPR, PCOR, and implementation science. Do you see these frameworks being used in your focal area of research? How might one or more of these approaches address a need in moving your research agenda forward?

2. Read three to five published articles in your field, and describe the researchers' rationale or justification for using a mixed methods approach in each article. If no rationale was provided, develop one rationale that would be appropriate for the study.

3. Think of a research question that you might like to answer. Using a diagram like the ones provided in Figures 2.4, 2.7, and 2.10, try to show what study components might be needed to answer that question.

References

Berman, L., Curry, L., Goldberg, C., Gusberg, R., & Fraenkel, L. (2011). Pilot testing of a decision support tool for patients with abdominal aortic aneurysms. *Journal of Vascular Surgery, 53*(2), 285–292. doi: 10.1016/j.jvs.2010.08.075

Berman, L., Curry, L., Gusberg, R., Dardik, A., & Fraenkel, L. (2008). Informed consent for abdominal aortic aneurysm repair: The patient's perspective. *Journal of Vascular Surgery, 48*(2), 296–302. doi: 10.1016/j.jvs.2008.03.037

Berman, L., Dardik, A., Bradley, E. H., Gusberg, R. J., & Fraenkel, L. (2008). Informed consent for abdominal aortic aneurysm repair: Assessing variations in surgeon opinion through a national survey. *Journal of Vascular Surgery, 47*(2), 287–295. doi: 10.1016/j.jvs.2007.10.050

Bosworth, H. B., Almirall, D., Weiner, B. J., Maciejewski, M., Kaufman, M. A., Powers, B. J., . . . Jackson, G. L. (2010). The implementation of a translational study involving a primary care based behavioral program to improve blood pressure control: The HTN-IMPROVE study protocol (01295). *Implementation Science, 5,* 54. doi: 10.1186/1748–5908–5–54

Bryman, A. (2006). Integrating quantitative and qualitative research: How is it done? *Qualitative Research, 6,* 97–113.

Clark, J. A., Bokhour, B. G., Inui, T. S., Silliman, R. A., & Talcott, J. A. (2003). Measuring patients' perceptions of the outcomes of treatment for early prostate cancer. *Medical Care, 41*(8), 923–936. doi: 10.1097/01.MLR.0000078147.80071.78

Collins, K. M. T., Onwuegbuzie, A. J., & Sutton, I. L. (2006). A model incorporating the rationale and purpose for conducting mixed-methods research in special education and beyond. *Learning Disabilities: A Contemporary Journal, 4*(1), 67–100.

Horowitz, C. R., Robinson, M., & Seifer, S. (2009). Community-based participatory research from the margin to the mainstream: Are researchers prepared? *Circulation, 119*(19), 2633–2642. doi: 10.1161/CIRCULATIONAHA.107.729863

Israel, B. A., Schulz, A. J., Parker, E. A., & Becker, A. B. (1998). Review of community-based research: Assessing partnership approaches to improve public health. *Annual Review of Public Health, 19,* 173–202. doi: 10.1146/annurev.publhealth.19.1.173

Krumholz, H. M., Selby, J. V., & Patient-Centered Outcomes Research Institute. (2012). Seeing through the eyes of patients: The Patient-Centered Outcomes Research Institute funding announcements. *Annals of Internal Medicine, 157*(6), 446–447. doi: 10.7326/0003–4819–157–6–201209180–00519

Kyanko, K. A., Curry, L. A., & Busch, S. H. (2013). Out-of-network physicians: How prevalent are involuntary use and cost transparency? *Health Services Research, 48*(3), 1154–1172. doi: 10.1111/1475–6773.12007

Kyanko, K. A., Pong, D. D., Bahan, K., & Curry, L. A. (2013). Patient experiences with involuntary out-of-network charges. *Health Services Research, 48*(5), 1704–1718. doi: 10.1111/1475–6773.12071

Madon, T., Hofman, K. J., Kupfer, L., & Glass, R. I. (2007). Public health: Implementation science. *Science, 318*(5857), 1728–1729. doi: 10.1126/science.1150009

Menon, U., Szalacha, L. A., Belue, R., Rugen, K., Martin, K. R., & Kinney, A. Y. (2008). Interactive, culturally sensitive education on colorectal cancer screening. *Medical Care, 46*(9 Suppl. 1), S44–50. doi: 10.1097/MLR.0b013e31818105a0

Mertens, D. M. (2007). Transformative paradigm: Mixed methods and social justice. *Journal of Mixed Methods Research, 1*(3), 212–225.

Murtagh, M. J., Thomson, R. G., May, C. R., Rapley, T., Heaven, B. R., Graham, R. H., . . . Eccles, M. P. (2007). Qualitative methods in a randomised controlled trial: the role of an integrated qualitative process evaluation in providing evidence to discontinue the intervention in one arm of a trial of a decision support tool. *Quality & Safety in Health Care, 16*(3), 224–229. doi: 10.1136/qshc.2006.018499

Sax, H., Clack, L., Touveneau, S., da Liberdade Jantarada, F., Pittet, D., Zingg, W., & PROHIBIT Study Group. (2013). Implementation of infection control best practice in intensive care units throughout Europe: A mixed-method evaluation study. *Implementation Science, 8,* 24. doi: 10.1186/1748–5908–8–24

Schifferdecker, K. E., Berman, N. B., Fall, L. H., & Fischer, M. R. (2012). Adoption of computer-assisted learning in medical education: The educators' perspective. *Medical Education, 46*(11), 1063–1073. doi: 10.1111/j.1365–2923.2012.04350.x

Schraagen, J. M., Schouten, T., Smit, M., Haas, F., van der Beek, D., van de Ven, J., & Barach, P. (2011). A prospective study of paediatric cardiac surgical microsystems: Assessing the relationships between non-routine events, teamwork and patient outcomes. *BMJ Quality & Safety, 20*(7), 599–603. doi: 10.1136/bmjqs.2010.048983

Shaw, E. K., Ohman-Strickland, P. A., Piasecki, A., Hudson, S. V., Ferrante, J. M., McDaniel, R. R., Jr., . . . Crabtree, B. F. (2013). Effects of facilitated team meetings and learning collaboratives on colorectal cancer screening rates in primary care practices: A cluster randomized trial. *Annals of Family Medicine, 11*(3), 220–228, S221–228. doi: 10.1370/afm.1505

Stoller, E. P., Webster, N. J., Blixen, C. E., McCormick, R. A., Hund, A. J., Perzynski, A. T., . . . Dawson, N. V. (2009). Alcohol consumption decisions among nonabusing drinkers diagnosed with hepatitis C: An exploratory sequential mixed methods study. *Journal of Mixed Methods Research, 3*(1), 65–86. doi: 10.1177/155868980 8326119

Weathers, B., Barg, F. K., Bowman, M., Briggs, V., Delmoor, E., Kumanyika, S., . . . Halbert, C. H. (2011). Using a mixed-methods approach to identify health concerns in an African American community. *American Journal of Public Health, 101*(11), 2087–2092. doi: 10.2105/AJPH.2010.191775

❧ THREE ❧

DETERMINING THE APPROPRIATENESS AND FEASIBILITY OF USING MIXED METHODS

Information you will find in this chapter: This chapter addresses how to determine whether a mixed methods approach is appropriate for your research question. In the first section, we explore the fundamental task of defining the research question, which drives the choice of methodology. The second section addresses developing a compelling rationale and aims for a mixed methods study. Once you have determined that a mixed methods approach is appropriate and have defined the study aims, it is critical to decide whether the study is in fact feasible. The chapter closes with key considerations in the planning stage of a project to determine feasibility and to evaluate the capacity of your team to successfully carry out the study.

Key features in this chapter:

- Brief quotations and reflections from mixed methods expert researchers
- Examples of mixed methods designs and aims from the empirical literature
- Tips on crafting clear and appropriate study aims
- Strategies for addressing common pitfalls during the planning stage of a study
- Tips for finding collaborators and using consultants effectively
- Research team capacity inventory template

DEFINING THE NATURE OF THE RESEARCH QUESTION

Clearly defining the research question may seem to be an obvious and straightforward first step, yet this fundamental task is often quite challenging and requires a substantial investment of time and effort. In developing a research question, the team must conceptualize the phenomenon of interest with as much precision as possible and define its relevant constituent components. Only after the nature of the phenomenon is described in this way can the study methodology and appropriate forms of measurement be considered. As described in Box 3.1, an informed and appropriate decision about methodology cannot be made until the research question is clearly articulated.

Box 3.1   Aligning Methods to the Research Question

I look at the research question and then try to identify the methods that you need for that research question. And sometimes it's a single method . . . . I don't force mixed methods in but I use them when they're appropriate.

—Benjamin Crabtree, PhD,
Professor and Director, Department of Family Medicine and Community
Health,
Rutgers Robert Wood Johnson
Medical School

Mixed methods research questions should clearly define the particular role of the quantitative and qualitative components and the anticipated yield from integrating them in a mixed methods design. Insufficient attention to this deliberate process is common. Trainees or colleagues frequently approach us to say, "I want to do a qualitative study" or "I want to do a mixed methods study" rather than beginning with a substantive question that may warrant using mixed methods. As shown in Figure 3.1, the strategy for conceptualizing a study should be built from a clear understanding of the knowledge gap or research problem to be addressed. The study's purpose, or objective, is

Figure 3.1 Focusing a Study From the Research Gap to the Aims

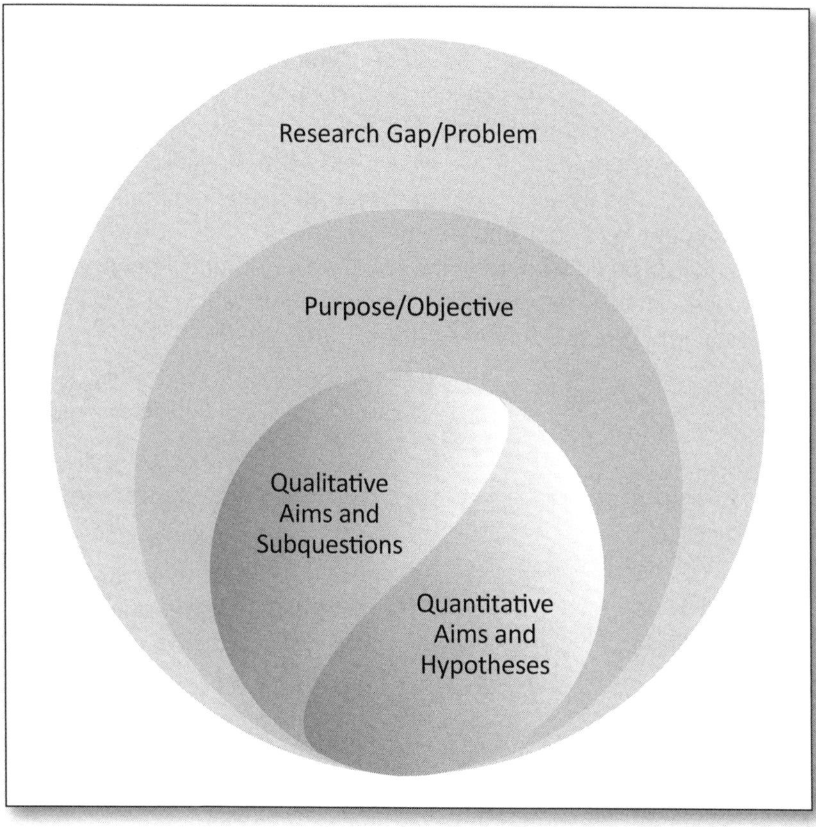

Research Gap/Problem

Purpose/Objective

Qualitative
Aims and
Subquestions

Quantitative
Aims and
Hypotheses

SOURCE: Adapted from Plano Clark & Badiee, 2010.

then developed in order to meet the defined gap. Once the objective is set, the specific research aims and corresponding quantitative and qualitative methods can be established, including identification of various data sources. In constructing a mixed methods design (which can sometimes be ambitious in scope), there is a risk of adding a method or form of data collection on to a study without thinking intently about the aim of that component and how the different components will be integrated to answer the research questions (see Box 3.2).

Box 3.2   Planning Methods From the Outset

I think the most important thing in mixed methods research is that people are extremely mindful of the research design from the beginning . . . . Too often is that people will come to us—people with expertise in qualitative methods—and say, "We did this study and in the end we asked people these questions, and we want to analyze them." But there's no forethought ahead of time about how that informs the whole study. It's just a tack-on . . . . If you do it up front and you have a carefully thought out process about what you are doing in the different arms, you're going to have a much better study.

—Holly Kennedy, CNM, PhD, FACNM, FAAN,
Executive Deputy Dean & Helen Varney
Professor of Midwifery, Yale School of Nursing

Mixed methods are well suited to answering research questions that examine a phenomenon that is both qualitative and quantitative in nature.

◀ Refer back to Chapter 1: Definition and Overview of Mixed Methods Designs, for more information on the respective characteristics of qualitative and quantitative inquiry.

There are many types of such multidimensional phenomena in health sciences research—clinical or quality of care issues, health care system performance, individual and group behavioral interventions, implementation of evidence-based guidelines, and patient and provider decision making just to name a few. In addition to these particular focal topics and as mentioned in Chapter 2, there is growing emphasis on conducting timely patient-centered, research in the real world, which requires attention to context and complexity that can sometimes be best understood through multiple forms of measurement.

Table 3.1 presents illustrative examples from published, empirical literature. These examples show how qualitative and quantitative components fit together in order to generate a comprehensive set of data that addresses the research aims. For example, a study on barriers and facilitators of self-care behaviors for patients with heart failure had a convergent design. (Riegel,

Dickson, Kuhn, Page, & Worrall-Carter, 2010). Survey data quantified the prevalence of known self-care behaviors and influencing factors, such as mood and social support, and medical records were reviewed to determine clinical diagnoses and outcomes. The analysis of qualitative data, collected simultaneously, was used to generate hypotheses that informed the subsequent quantitative analysis. In a second example, researchers sought to develop a quantitative instrument that would accurately measure a complex construct: patient-centered outcomes of prostate cancer treatment. Using an exploratory sequential design, the team first conducted qualitative interviews with patients to inform a subsequent phase of survey development and psychometric testing (Clark, Bokhour, Inui, Silliman, & Talcott, 2003).

In another study examining surrogate decision makers' interpretations of prognosis, an explanatory sequential approach was used. The characteristics of surrogate decision makers in terms of their interpretations of standardized prognostic statements were described quantitatively, followed by qualitative data to understand the factors that may lead respondents to interpret the statements in a way very different from the intended meaning (Zier, Sottile, Hong, Weissfield, & White, 2012). In each of these studies, researchers drew on the particular complementary strengths of each form of measurement and in carefully matching method to purpose developed a comprehensive response to a multifaceted research question.

DEVELOPING THE RATIONALE AND AIMS FOR A MIXED METHODS STUDY

Once you have determined that the nature of the research question requires a mixed methods approach, the next step is to construct a compelling case for the fit of methods to the overall question, as well as to each component. A clear project rationale can be useful in multiple ways: assembling and motivating a team committed to mixed methods, writing a competitive grant application, managing the study to ensure time and attention to all components, and presenting findings (especially to audiences unfamiliar with mixed methods). Despite the importance of a clear justification for a mixed methods design, few researchers are explicit on this point. A systematic review of published mixed methods health services studies found only one third of articles provided justification for a mixed methods design (Wisdom, Cavaleri, Onwuegbuzie, & Green, 2012).

Table 3.1 Illustrative Mixed Methods, Studies, Designs, and Aims

Illustrative Research Area	Illustrative Study Topic	Study Design	Qualitative Component Aim	Quantitative Component Aim	Source
Capture individual experiences (e.g., patient, provider, policymaker).	Self-care behaviors after heart failure, by gender	Convergent	Identify gender-specific barriers and facilitators influencing self-care after heart failure.	Describe self-care behaviors and health outcomes of men and women after heart failure.	Riegel, B., Dickson, V. V., Kuhn, L., Page, K., & Worrall-Carter, L. (2010). Gender-specific barriers and facilitators to heart failure self-care: A mixed methods study. *International Journal of Nursing Studies, 47*(7), 888–895. doi: 10.1016/j.ijnurstu.2009.12
Develop quantitative measurement of a complex construct.	Patient-centered measures of outcomes of treatment for prostate cancer	Exploratory sequential	Identify core facets of the phenomenon from patients' perspective.	Develop and validate items and scales through psychometric testing.	Clark, J. A., Bokhour, B. G., Inui, T. S., Silliman, R. A., & Talcott, J. A. (2003). Measuring patients' perceptions of the outcomes of treatment for early prostate cancer. *Medical Care, 41*(8), 923–936. doi: 10.1097/01.MLR.0000078147.80071.78
Understand medical decision making.	Surrogate decision makers' interpretation of prognosis	Explanatory sequential	Following quantitative data collection, explore factors that contribute to interpretation in a subset of questionnaire participants with interpretations different than actual meaning.	Determine how surrogates interpret standardized prognostic statements.	Zier, L. S., Sottile, P. D., Hong, S. Y., Weissfield, L. A., & White, D. B. (2012). Surrogate decision makers' interpretation of prognostic information: A mixed-methods study. *Annals of Internal Medicine, 156*(5), 360–366.

Illustrative Research Area	Illustrative Study Topic	Study Design	Qualitative Component Aim	Quantitative Component Aim	Source
Evaluate complex intervention trials and randomized controlled trials.	Screening for a chronic condition	Intervention study with embedded qualitative component	Explore patient experiences with type 2 diabetes screening.	Evaluate the cost effectiveness of diabetes screening and intensive treatment of screen-detected cases.	Eborall, H., Davies, R., Kinmonth, A. L., Griffin, S., & Lawton, J. (2007). Patients' experiences of screening for type 2 diabetes: Prospective qualitative study embedded in the ADDITION (Cambridge) randomised controlled trial. *BMJ, 335*(7618), 490. doi: 10.1136/bmj.39308.392176.BE
Describe health systems change.	Adoption of a shared electronic summary record in a national health system	Case study	Understand the perspectives of various stakeholders on shared electronic summary records, and identify barriers to creation of the summaries.	Describe the access to and availability of shared electronic summary records in different settings, and measure the proportion of patients with these types of records.	Greenhalgh, T., Stramer, K., Bratan, T., Byrne, E., Russell, J., & Potts, H. W. (2010). Adoption and non-adoption of a shared electronic summary record in England: A mixed-method case study. *BMJ, 340*, c3111. doi: 10.1136/bmj.c3111

There are many possible justifications for a mixed methods approach. Common reasons include pursuing a topic about which little is known and hence using a qualitative component to inform hypothesis generation, producing a comprehensive account of the nature and magnitude of a phenomenon, seeking to both understand context and to produce generalizable findings, aiming to describe both processes and outcomes, and seeking increased confidence in findings by addressing threats to validity by either approach alone (Creswell, Klassen, Plano Clark, & Smith for the Office of Behavioral and Social Sciences Research [OBSSR], 2011; O'Cathain, Murphy, & Nicholl, 2007; Padgett, 2012; Plano Clark, 2010). In the context of health sciences, mixed methods may be a fit for studying the following types of topics, among others: clinical or quality improvement issues (Crabtree et al., 2011; Dean, Hutchinson, Escoto, & Lawson, 2007; Ginsburg et al., 2009; Koppel et al., 2005), health care organizational performance (Groene et al., 2010), behavioral interventions (Clark, Mundy, Catto, & MacIntyre, 2011; Lewin, Glenton, & Oxman, 2009), processes of implementation of innovations (Riley et al., 2009; Robertson et al., 2010), health care decision making (Berman, Curry, Gusberg, Dardik, & Fraenkel, 2008), and measurement development for complex constructs in patient-centered treatment preferences and outcomes (Garavalia, Garavalia, Spertus, & Decker, 2011; Krause, 2002).

▶ For more information on developing study aims, see Chapter 4: Writing a Technically Sound and Compelling Grant Proposal for a Mixed Method Study, which includes examples of study aims in grant application format.

When developing the study aims, begin with stating the overarching goal or intent of the project. The specific aims should follow logically and directly from this unifying goal, with the methodological approach explicitly stated in each aim. Note that each specific aim in a mixed methods study should be substantive, rather than instrumental, in nature (e.g., "to explore patient experiences of discrimination in emergency departments through focus groups" rather than "to conduct patient focus groups"). At this early point in study development it is also important to consider all available data sources and to determine the optimal sources for each respective study component, with an eye toward how they will be effectively integrated. Box 3.3 provides some tips on crafting aims for a mixed methods study (Plano Clark & Badiee, 2010).

Box 3.3   Tips for Crafting Research Aims for a Mixed Methods Study

- State an overall goal that addresses the overarching research problem or question.
- State study aims that identify discrete components of the goal to be achieved.
- For each aim, identify the methodological approach to be used to accomplish the aim (which may be quantitative, qualitative, or mixed methods) to tie together the goals of the study with the methods.
- Aims that call for a qualitative approach may be inductive in nature. They may emphasize exploration; contextualize individual behavior, group behavior, organizational dynamics, and cultural influences; and convey the researchers' openness for learning from participants and data sources.
- Aims that call for a quantitative approach may be deductive in nature. They may emphasize measurable constructs, test theorized associations, and demonstrate probable causality or generalizability.
- Aims that call for a mixed methods approach require: the integration of qualitative and quantitative data and results to yield multi-dimensional, synergistic understandings of the phenomena of interest; the use of qualitative methods to explain and elaborate quantitative findings; or the use of quantitative methods to generalize, test, or confirm qualitative findings.
- Use consistent and precise terms to refer to variables or phenomena examined across multiple questions.
- State a mixed methods question that directs and foreshadows how and why the components will be integrated.
- Determine whether the study is best addressed with predetermined or emergent questions or both.

Adapted from Creswell et al. (2011); Plano Clark and Badiee (2010).

KEY CONSIDERATIONS AT THE PLANNING STAGE OF A PROJECT TO DETERMINE FEASIBILITY

Once the research question is defined, there are a number of key considerations that must be addressed in the planning phase of a project. While there are challenges common to all research endeavors, mixed methods studies are vulnerable to a number of potential pitfalls that are unique to this approach. At the earliest stages of a project, while the study aims and methods are being defined, it is also helpful to consider the capacity of the team and feasibility of the project. Identifying vulnerabilities at this point can help with refining the scope or design in order to ensure the study can be successfully carried out to address the overall research objective. You may also determine that it is just not possible to do with available resources, which is also a good thing to learn sooner rather than later. While it may seem premature for us to jump into feasibility at this early point in this book, in our mentoring and consultations with researchers developing mixed methods studies we address team capacity and project feasibility immediately following the discussion of study aims.

We focus on aspects of feasibility that are relatively unique to mixed methods studies, which are typically large in scale, have many moving parts, and are hence complex to implement and manage. In our experience, considerations regarding feasibility are underappreciated by health sciences researchers who are new to mixed methods. Potential funders informed about mixed methods are especially attuned to the potential for research teams to overpromise within a grant application. In Box 3.4, a senior program officer at the Patient-Centered Outcomes Research Institute (PCORI), a major funder of health research in the United States, stresses the importance of balancing ambitious research goals with available resources.

Box 3.4   Maintaining Feasibility and Realistic Scope of Project

Some people submit very ambitious mixed methods proposals, but our Methods program awards have a limited dollar value [$750,000 in direct costs over 3 years]. And when you're putting together a proposal you have to think about the balance between what's feasible with the amount of money available and what your research agenda is. Having those lofty research goals is worthwhile, but it's important to appropriately calibrate the research plan for the resource request.

—Jason Gerson, PhD,
Senior Program Officer, CER Methods and Infrastructure,
Patient-Centered Outcomes Research Institute (PCORI)

Table 3.2 summarizes the challenges that can arise throughout a mixed methods project in assembling and managing the research team, securing and allocating resources, implementing the research, and disseminating the findings in response to a mixed methods research question. We have experienced many of these challenges in our own work and also helped support colleagues who struggle on these fronts. We draw on this collective experience to suggest strategies for avoiding or addressing these potential pitfalls. Thinking about these issues during the design and planning phases can help you preempt potential problems and increase the likelihood of accomplishing your research aims.

Team Composition

The feasibility of a particular research design in addressing a given research question depends in large part on the capacity and skills of the research team. Because building a qualified team may be the biggest obstacle to conducting successful mixed methods research, attention should be devoted to team composition at the earliest possible point in the planning stage. A diverse and qualified team will enhance the richness of study findings and interpretation. While quantitative methods and subject matter expertise are typically present on mixed methods research teams in the health sciences, qualitative and mixed methods expertise is often underrepresented. And even in cases where the full complement of necessary expertise is intact, team members may not be available as needed to carry out their commitments on the project. In our experience, this is a special risk for the qualitative and mixed methods experts, who are often in high demand given the limited number of such researchers presently working in the health sciences.

The question of team leadership is, in our view, the most critical consideration in deciding whether a mixed methods study can be successfully conducted. Because mixed methods are relatively new in the health sciences, there are few researchers with the range of training and depth of experience required to serve in a leadership role. Leading a mixed methods team requires several unique abilities that may not be as relevant in other types of single method research. These include recognizing the strengths, limitations, and complementarity of different methods; valuing the respective contributions of team members; maintaining open and candid communication among team members; and valuing the investment in education and training for different team members as needed.

Table 3.2 Addressing Common Pitfalls at the Planning Stage of a Study

Project Element	Common Pitfalls	Strategies for Avoiding Common Pitfalls
Team composition	Inadequate staff expertise in relevant methods (e.g., statistics, qualitative methods, mixed methods)	• Identify required content and methods expertise for each component of the study, and indicate corresponding names of team members, including consultants. • Develop justification of staffing loads for each component or task, based on prior experience or guidance from colleagues who have done similar studies. • Ensure that the principal investigator(s) have experience in mixed methods or explicitly value the mixed methods design and secure deep and regular participation of a consultant. • Provide formal and informal training and capacity building for team members as needed (e.g., apprenticing a lead member of a mixed methods project).
	Insufficient time or availability of team members	• Develop realistic estimates for percentage effort required for each role and major responsibility/task throughout the entire project (all components). • Reassess effort budgeted and expended by all team members at regular intervals and adjust as needed.
Team collaboration	Lack of shared goal and valuing of mixed methods	• Foster common understanding of and agreement on the conceptual framework or theoretical orientation of the project. • Regularly discuss the particular contributions of each component of the study, reinforcing the complementarity of the methods.
	Ineffective communication	• Deliberately minimize the use of jargon, and define clearly when needed. • Establish regular meeting schedule for full team, core leadership team, and workgroups as applicable. • Clearly define decision-making authority and the locus for particular decisions to facilitate efficient and effective communication.

Project Element	Common Pitfalls	Strategies for Avoiding Common Pitfalls
		• Develop consensus on communication methods (in-person, phone, e-mail, videoconference) and types of topics suited for each forum; periodically evaluate and adjust as needed.
		• Create online space for communication using web-based platforms and virtual workspaces.
		• Create a glossary of research terminology from the disciplines represented in the study, and practice using the terms so that they become the norm.
		• Assign one person to be responsible for coordinating research meetings and tracking progress against the timeline.
	Siloing of project components	• Involve team members from different fields in parts of the study other than the one where they have primary expertise, in order to build understanding and generate new interpretations of results.
		• Include members from different components as coauthors on papers using methods other than their predominant expertise.
		• Include updates and reports on each component in full team meetings.
Resources	Insufficient financial resources	• In budget development, ensure adequate funding for all components, particularly the qualitative analysis, which tends to be underestimated.
		• Explicitly describe and budget for activities unique to mixed methods, such as data access, sharing, and integration.
	Insufficient electronic resources	• Obtain access to software for qualitative and quantitative data for all team members involved in analysis.
		• Consider options and plan for data sharing among analysts, particularly with qualitative software.
		• Secure funding and expertise to establish and maintain virtual workspaces.
	Insufficient or inflexible human resources	• Create detailed workflow plans to allow flexibility in staffing support (e.g., determine diverse skills sets, anticipate variable workloads over project period).

(Continued)

Table 3.2 (Continued)

Project Element	Common Pitfalls	Strategies for Avoiding Common Pitfalls
Timeline	Unrealistic expectations of team members and funding source(s)	• Create a comprehensive and realistic timeline specifying all components and activities (e.g., integration of data, implications of sequential designs, analysis between components). • Develop a strategy for managing potential delays associated with sequential designs.
Dissemination	Fragmentation of the study across manuscripts and other outputs	• Build agreement among team leads at project initiation on what the key manuscripts/outputs are and how they will be coordinated. • Plan for the ways in which collaboration and integration will occur during manuscript development (e.g., a single lead author for articles or multiple authors writing pieces about their part of the study).
	Poor reception of methods by publication venues	• Consider targeting journals that are receptive to mixed methods (e.g., sufficient word limits, reviewers and editors with expertise). • Identify potential journals from multiple disciplines relevant to the study.
	Lack of understanding of methods used and rationale for methods by readers	• Seek out and comply with guidelines for reporting methods, especially related to describing justification, design, sampling, study implementation, integration of results, limitations, and insights gained through integration.

SOURCES: O'Cathain, Murphy, and Nicholl (2008); Wisdom et al. (2012).

The concept of leadership in mixed methods teams is complex. Some teams will have a single principal investigator and others will have coprincipal investigators with responsibility for different components; still others will build a leadership team consisting of several senior researchers. Ideally, the principal investigator(s) will have training and experience in qualitative, quantitative, and mixed methods. Because senior researchers rarely have expertise in all domains (qualitative, quantitative, and mixed methods), the leadership structure of mixed methods teams commonly includes multiple principal investigators. Regardless of the size of the leadership team or the background of its members, authentic, demonstrable appreciation for diverse methods and disciplines is essential in order to establish and sustain a common vision of the relevance of mixed methods in pursuing the research aims.

Several strategies can help address the problem of inadequate team composition. Very early in the process of assembling the team to address the study's research questions, the lead researcher should devote deliberate attention to defining all key roles and corresponding team members as well as the scope of involvement for each. Note that this same level of attention should be devoted to replacing a team member who leaves during the project, even though it may be tempting to find a replacement quickly regardless of fit. Explicit agreement on deliverables and transparency across the team can help ensure sufficient expertise is available to support the project. Building in informal or formal training for team members who will assume responsibility for certain aspects of the project, such as the data collection, qualitative analysis, or data integration phase, can be very helpful. The capacity for training health sciences researchers in mixed methods is growing steadily, with investments in formal training programs in graduate schools such as nursing, public health, and medicine sponsored within the National Institutes of Health (NIH; Department of Health and Human Services, 2013). Researchers may also need to think creatively about how to develop the capacity of staff from within the team or find local informal resources such as apprenticing on an ongoing mixed methods study at the home institution. Some tips on identifying mixed methods collaborators are provided in Box 3.5.

> ▶ Additional information on managing and leading mixed methods teams is provided in Chapter 9: Managing Mixed Methods Teams.

Box 3.5   Tips on Finding Mixed Methods Collaborators

- **Look for local collaborators across departments and disciplines (if in an academic setting).** If you are based in a school of medicine, nursing, or public health, explore whether there are collaborators with health-related mixed methods experience in other schools or departments such as anthropology, sociology, economics, business, or education.
- **Reach out to mixed methods researchers with published literature relevant to your topic.** Even if those researchers are not available to work with you, they may be able to connect you with other researchers.
- **Leverage professional networks.** Talk with colleagues that you respect and trust who may be able to link you to their collaborators who have mixed methods experience.
- **Attend conferences featuring mixed methods research.** Professional conferences may be within a particular discipline that welcomes mixed methods empirical research within their focal topic area or those that are specifically designed as mixed methods conferences to support and build capacity in researchers using these methods. These meetings provide excellent opportunities to make connections with others in the field.
- **Join mixed methods professional groups.** Many associations have mechanisms that you can use to find collaborators on a specific project. Examples of mixed methods professional groups include the Mixed Methods International Research Association (MMIRA) and the Mixed Methods Network for Behavioral, Social and Health Sciences. Also, some universities have their own mixed methods networks.
- **Consider engaging a consultant as a last resort.** While it is always preferable to have sufficient mixed methods expertise among the full collaborators on the project, sometimes it may be necessary to use a short-term consultant for one component of the project.

Ideally, the necessary mixed methods expertise will be embedded within the research team, with members who have a history of successful and productive collaboration and strong working relationships. Nevertheless, it is common for new mixed methods investigators to add a consultant to a project. A consultant might be someone from another department in the same institution or from an outside institution or organization. The individual may have no prior work in the content area but may have methodological expertise (ideally she or he will have both). Box 3.6 contains an excerpt from our interview with an emergency medicine physician and health services researcher who described challenges in assembling his research team and his creative solution.

Box 3.6   Assembling a Qualified Mixed Methods Team

The challenge is that we are faced with finding the right group of collaborators. I had to put together a team, and qualitative researchers are in demand. Even in a situation where I had funding, finding someone who had both the qualitative experience and some conceptual knowledge about acute health care delivery was helpful. In terms of finding a partner, I went a nontraditional route. Instead of finding someone at the medical school who was on the assistant or associate professor track, I found a consultant who had experience doing qualitative analysis. She ultimately had a lot more time, and I was able to pay by the hour and engage her as a consultant. She was able to devote more time than the other consultants I could have found within the medical school.

—Jeremiah Schuur, MD, MHS,
Assistant Professor of Medicine,
Brigham and Women's Hospital

The team should be thoughtful about whether, when, and how to involve consultants with expertise in mixed methods. In our experience, consultants are frequently brought on board late in the process (e.g., when writing the methods section of a grant application or responding to reviews in a resubmission) or when challenges emerge. Rather, they should be involved as early as possible in the project conception, formulation, and construction of research aims and proposal development. A consultant, often working remotely from another location, or travelling in for periodic team meetings may not be regarded as (or in fact function as) a legitimate member of the team. An important potential consequence of fragmented participation by consultants is that the attention to integration of data, which should run throughout the entire project, may be disrupted. In order to avoid this scenario, the anticipated role of the consultant as well as the expected deliverables must be clearly defined and understood by the full team. More broadly, the project should be designed with structures and supports that will facilitate integration of the consultant. How, where, and when will the consultant do their work? How will the consultant access information needed to perform their role? How will they communicate with the other members of the team? How often will in-person meetings take place? See Box 3.7 for tips from an expert who includes consultants on many of his mixed methods projects.

Box 3.7   Tips on Using Consultants Effectively

- **Engage the consultant at the earliest possible point in the process.** If the purpose of the consultant is to provide mixed methods expertise, input should be taken into account in the study design phase.
- **Agree on clearly defined roles and expected deliverables before the work begins.** This may also include a discussion of publication authorship or giving the consultant ownership of a subset of the data so they may publish from the project. A good mixed methods project should generate many manuscripts.
- **Ensure that the role of the consultant is clear to other members of the team.** Role clarity and shared expectations can facilitate effective collaboration with other team members.
- **Consider the logistical aspects of the consultant's work.** Outline the expected process for communication and information sharing. If applicable, determine the consultant's ability to work efficiently remotely.
- **Plan a face-to-face meeting early in the project.** Develop strong relationships among team members, including consultants. Ensure all members are familiar with the entire project (as opposed to only their particular area of expertise).
- **Have an abundance mentality.** While mixed methods projects generally generate a lot of data, much of this is never used

because the project leadership and team members tend to have a "scarcity" mentality and do not share the data widely. Ask the consultants if they have a particular interest that might require additional data collection so that they have more investment in the project.

The tips in Box 3.7 were developed with input from Benjamin Crabtree, PhD, professor and director of the Department of Family Medicine and Community Health, Rutgers Robert Wood Johnson Medical School.

Realistic allocation of staff time for both the core research team and any consultants is essential. Because the time needed for certain components of the study may be more or less than expected, drawing upon prior experience from similar studies can be a very useful guide. For instance, in a multiphase mixed methods approach our team uses regularly, the qualitative exploratory component is often substantial in scope, requiring site visits to many organizations by multidisciplinary teams (Bradley et al., 2009). After underestimating the time and resources required in a prior project, we now base resource estimates on this prior experience, which has improved our human resource and budget planning. If your team has not done a project similar in scope or structure previously, it is worth the time and effort to consult with colleagues about their experience. Analysis of qualitative data is another area in which effort is often underestimated; be sure to seek the input of an experienced qualitative researcher on preparing the time and effort estimates for this work. Even with the most careful up-front planning, staffing in mixed methods projects can be challenging—in part due to the fluidity and interdependence of the components and associated staff. It is useful to plan for regular reassessments of team member roles and time allocations and to be flexible and prepared to make adjustments accordingly.

Team Collaboration

Even when the team composition is appropriate, the dynamics within highly diverse teams may present challenges to effective collaboration (Curry et al., 2012; O'Cathain et al., 2008).

▶ Challenges in managing the dynamics of mixed methods teams are discussed further in Chapter 9: Managing Mixed Methods Teams.

Collaboration can be constrained by lack of shared goal and valuing of mixed methods, ineffective communication, and *siloing* of project components. Anticipating and addressing these issues early in the project can prevent problems later in the study implementation process.

Cultivating a shared goal at a project launch meeting and revisiting the goal regularly throughout the study is critical to reinforcing the cohesion of the team. These discussions should reinforce the importance of each component in addressing the limitations of the other. The need for diverse methods in order to fully answer the research question should be highlighted frequently by team leadership. Taking advantage of opportunities to point out the relationship between the qualitative and quantitative data in various team meetings (such as those focused on data collection or analysis) can help team members appreciate the respective contributions of each and develop a common view that the mixed methods design is optimal for the project. Also, reviewing relevant empirical literature using both qualitative and quantitative studies can help demonstrate the contributions of both methods to the existing knowledge base.

Effective communication is critical for teams addressing mixed methods research questions, and strategies to support and sustain effective communication should be considered during the initial planning stage. Effective communication can be supported and sustained in several ways. Structural supports include regular meetings for the full team and workgroups made transparent to all, clarity and agreement over decision-making authority and the locus of specific decisions, and consensus on communication methods and the types of topics suited for each forum. In addition, because there are relatively few mixed methods experts in health sciences, these team members are likely to be based in different institutions and locations. Consequently it may be more important than in mono-method projects to ensure access to and training in the use of online and virtual workspaces that can support the sharing of files (e.g., Google Docs, Box, Dropbox, Mendeley) or videoconferencing for meetings (e.g., GoToMeeting, FaceTime, Skype). Other strategies are behavioral in nature, such as encouraging team members to develop understanding of relevant terminology that may be unfamiliar and regularly using these words and concepts in communications (referred to as "methodological bilingualism"). At the same time, it is important for team members to be mindful of relying too heavily on jargon, which may be off-putting or prevent engagement and participation of others.

Fragmentation can occur with siloing of project components. This can be minimized at the planning phase by actively involving team members from different fields in different parts of the study (such as having a statistician on the qualitative data collection team). Encouraging team members to stretch in this way can help foster new understandings and also spur novel ways of thinking about data collection or interpretations of results, which is the ultimate goal of mixed methods work. Similarly, team members can be invited to participate in writing papers using the data set that is not their predominant expertise, enhancing their research capacity, and bringing important diversity to the process. Finally, the team leadership can include updates and reports of each component within the full team meetings. This can provide regular space for questions and discussion among the team and opportunities for informal learning and reinforce the interconnectedness of the components.

Resources

At the planning stage, it is essential to determine what resources will be needed in order to complete the study and to construct a comprehensive budget and credible budget justification for funders. Resources can be a challenge in all research efforts and are also a persistent challenge in mixed methods studies. As noted previously, the time needed for the qualitative component is often underestimated, which has implications for financial and human resources. Similarly, researchers often underestimate the time and funding needed to support procedures for data access, sharing, and integration. One expert describes her experiences with resource allocation and planning in Box 3.8.

Box 3.8   Allocating Resources Rationally for Mixed Methods Studies

One concern . . . is that . . . people will say that there's value in the qualitative research, but they think you can get it done very quickly and cheaply. When push comes to shove in the project budget, they want to keep more of the resources for expensive quantitative data collection and/or analysis or programming to clean up secondary quantitative data and analysis with programmers.

—Kelly Devers, PhD, Senior Fellow in
the Health Policy Center, Urban Institute

Electronic resources required to address mixed methods research questions include software for both qualitative and quantitative data analysis. Sharing of qualitative data can be complicated because many health researchers may not already have access to qualitative analysis software, such as ATLAS.ti or NVivo. Ideally, the license will be sufficient for each analyst to have access to the software and data sets, but when that is not possible, some alternative arrangements must be made for purchasing a multiuser license, sharing computers, or using software that is accessible to all. As noted previously, secure virtual workspaces can greatly facilitate collaboration. Finally, several human resource considerations require attention in the planning phase. The ability to deploy a team member for multiple roles in the project is dependent on individual skill sets. Creating a skill inventory for the members of the team will allow for flexibility as possible across the components. Table 3.3 contains an example of a research skill inventory we use in our projects. Mixed methods designs often have variable workloads over the course of the study. For instance, the quantitative analyst will be very busy during the first phase of an explanatory study, then much less so as the project moves into the qualitative phase. And then the analysis may be brought back into the fold for data integration stage. Planning for the ebb and flow of these staff demands can help improve efficiency of the project staffing and resources.

Timeline

By their nature, mixed methods studies are frequently larger in scope, lengthier, and more complex than single method designs. Consequently, the timeline and project implementation plan must be comprehensive, realistic, and detailed. In addition to the types of activities common to all research, mixed methods studies require planning for integration of data and interdependencies across components. Most important, the team must plan for managing potential delays that can occur in sequential designs, where a delay in the first phase can prevent timely implementation of the second. For example, in an exploratory sequential design where the first component is qualitative, it may take longer than expected to recruit participants or conduct data analysis, meaning that work on the subsequent quantitative component cannot begin as scheduled. In implementation science studies, which are grounded in the realities of real-world interventions and programs and in which mixed methods are commonly used, flexibility and contingency planning is important. Aside from having contingency plans in place, it is also important to consider

Table 3.3 Research Team Capacity Inventory

Research Area	Skill or Competency	Team Member 1	2	3	4	5	6	Total
Study design	**Quantitative** (randomized controlled trials, observations, case control, cohort)							
	Qualitative (focus groups, interviews, observation)							
	Mixed (basic, multiphase, case studies)							
	Program evaluation (formative, summative/ outcomes, process evaluations)							
Data collection and measurement	**Quantitative** (cognitive and pilot testing, validation, web survey design)							
	Qualitative (interview guides, observational checklists)							
Data analysis	**Basic quantitative** (descriptive statistics; linear, multiple, and logistic regression)							
	Advanced quantitative (survey analysis, hierarchical linear modeling, structural equation modeling, meta-analysis)							
	Qualitative (phenomenologic, constant comparative method)							
	Mixed (data integration, data display)							
Specific software	**Excel**							
	Access							
	SAS							
	SPSS							
	AMOS							
	ATLAS.ti							
	Sequel							

(Continued)

Table 3.3 (Continued)

Research Area	Skill or Competency	Team Member						Total
		1	2	3	4	5	6	
Research team and project management	Project timelines							
	Resource mapping							
	Training supervision							
	Human research protection programs and protocols							
Manuscript preparation and submission	Manuscript drafting							
	Article formatting							
	Submission process							

communicating with any funders clearly in grant writing and from the outset of the study about the nature of and rationale for your expected timeline.

Dissemination

Finally, there are several major challenges to be anticipated at the start of the study regarding plans for the dissemination of mixed methods research in peer-reviewed empirical literature and in other forms of products (such as conference presentations and grant reports).

▶ Additional details on dissemination are provided in Chapter 11: Publishing Mixed Methods Studies in the Health Sciences.

First, fragmentation of the study into multiple discrete research articles is commonplace. Pressures from both funders and home academic institutions to publish scientific papers quickly may have the unintended effect of pushing ahead to publish the first component perhaps prematurely, in advance of integrating the full quantitative and qualitative data. It may also be that the qualitative and quantitative components of the study are led by two different members of the team who are not incentivized to write collaboratively, or who identify different high-impact journals from their disciplines to target for publication. Another factor that influences researchers to publish independent papers on components of a mixed methods study are word limits in the top-tier health sciences journals. Many word limits are in the range of 3,000 to 5,000 words, which may be too little space to allow for a comprehensive presentation of a mixed methods study. A related challenge is that few journals in the health sciences have editors and reviewers who are familiar with mixed methods or have guidance in how to assess rigor of submitted research and may therefore be less receptive. Finally, even if the researchers are successful in publishing a comprehensive mixed methods article, many readers may be wary of the study because of a lack of awareness of the methodology.

Strategies to address these challenges are clear agreement—at the outset of the project—among the principal investigators regarding the primary papers from the study and the plan for coordination of publications. It is also helpful to plan for data integration during manuscript development. For instance, will the lead author be responsible for this solely, or will multiple authors write pieces about their part of the study? If so, how will the overall fitting and writing be accomplished smoothly? There are a handful of journals in health sciences that publish mixed methods; it can sometimes be strategic to target one of these, since they likely allow sufficient space and have qualified editors and reviewers.

Summary and Key Points

- The nature of the research question of interest is critical for determining the methods that should be used. When the research question of interest is multifaceted and includes dimensions that are both qualitative and quantitative in nature, a mixed methods approach is warranted.
- Developing a clear rationale for using mixed methods is an essential step in the planning process and will facilitate other steps such as assembling and motivating a team committed to mixed methods, writing a competitive grant application, managing the study to ensure time and attention to all components, and presenting findings.
- Mixed methods studies are vulnerable to challenges related to team composition, collaboration, resources, project timeline, methods and implementation, and dissemination. We include these topics in this chapter because these common challenges often can be avoided or overcome with the use of strategic planning at the earliest design phase of the project and, throughout, communication and team management.

- Before embarking on a mixed methods study, ensuring that the appropriate methodological and content expertise is represented on the research team is key. When gaps in expertise exist, many teams engage outside consultants to support the research; however, this solution to problems of team composition may not always be an adequate substitute for adequate team composition.

Review Questions and Exercises

1. Write two sets of research aims: one for an exploratory sequential project and the other for an explanatory sequential project.

2. Select and read a qualitative study from one of the following journals: *Qualitative Health Research, Journal of Mixed Methods Research,* or *Social Science and Medicine.* Discuss the justification for the study design. Do you think the researcher provided a clear justification? If not, how do you think it could be improved?

3. In a group, discuss key pitfalls that might arise in a mixed methods approach and strategies you would use to resolve them.

4. You are asked to form a research team for a mixed methods project. What are some of the considerations of a good team?

References

Berman, L., Curry, L., Gusberg, R., Dardik, A., & Fraenkel, L. (2008). Informed consent for abdominal aortic aneurysm repair: The patient's perspective. *Journal of Vascular Surgery, 48*(2), 296–302. doi: 10.1016/j.jvs.2008.03.037

Bradley, E. H., Curry, L. A., Ramanadhan, S., Rowe, L., Nembhard, I. M., & Krumholz, H. M. (2009). Research in action: Using positive deviance to improve quality of health care. *Implementation Science, 4,* 25. doi: 10.1186/1748–5908-4-25

Clark, A. M., Mundy, C., Catto, S., & MacIntyre, P. D. (2011). Participation in community-based exercise maintenance programs after completion of hospital-based cardiac rehabilitation: A mixed-method study. *Journal of Cardiopulmonary Rehabilitation and Prevention, 31*(1), 42–46. doi: 10.1097/HCR.0b013e3181f68aa6

Clark, J. A., Bokhour, B. G., Inui, T. S., Silliman, R. A., & Talcott, J. A. (2003). Measuring patients' perceptions of the outcomes of treatment for early prostate cancer. *Medical Care, 41*(8), 923–936. doi: 10.1097/01.MLR.0000078147.80071.78

Crabtree, B. F., Chase, S. M., Wise, C. G., Schiff, G. D., Schmidt, L. A., Goyzueta, J. R., . . . Jaen, C. R. (2011). Evaluation of patient centered medical home practice transformation initiatives. *Medical Care, 49*(1), 10–16. doi: 10.1097/MLR.0b013e 3181f80766

Creswell, J. W., Klassen, A. C., Plano Clark, V. L., & Smith, K. C. for the Office of Behavioral and Social Sciences Research. (2011). *Best practices for mixed methods research in the health sciences.* Bethesda, MD: National Institutes of Health. Retrieved from http://obssr.od.nih.gov/mixed_methods_research

Curry, L. A., O'Cathain, A., Plano Clark, V. L., Aroni, R., Fetters, M., & Berg, D. (2012). The role of group dynamics in mixed methods health sciences research teams. *Journal of Mixed Methods Research, 6*(1), 5–20.

Dean, J. E., Hutchinson, A., Escoto, K. H., & Lawson, R. (2007). Using a multi-method, user centred, prospective hazard analysis to assess care quality and patient safety in a care pathway. *BMC Health Services Research, 7,* 89. doi: 10 .1186/1472–6963-7-89

Department of Health and Human Services. (2013). *Short courses on innovative methodologies in the behavioral and social sciences (R25).* Retrieved July 24, 2013, from http://grants.nih.gov/grants/guide/rfa-files/RFA-OD-13–009.html

Eborall, H., Davies, R., Kinmonth, A. L., Griffin, S., & Lawton, J. (2007). Patients' experiences of screening for type 2 diabetes: Prospective qualitative study embedded in the ADDITION (Cambridge) randomised controlled trial. *BMJ, 335*(7618), 490. doi: 10.1136/bmj.39308.392176.BE

Garavalia, L., Garavalia, B., Spertus, J. A., & Decker, C. (2011). Medication Discussion Questions (MedDQ): Developing a guide to facilitate patient-clinician communication about heart medications. *Journal of Cardiovascular Nursing, 26*(4), E12–E19. doi: 10.1097/JCN.0b013e3181efea94

Ginsburg, L. R., Chuang, Y. T., Norton, P. G., Berta, W., Tregunno, D., Ng, P., & Richardson, J. (2009). Development of a measure of patient safety event learning responses. *Health Services Research, 44*(6), 2123–2147. doi: 10.1111/j.1475–6773 .2009.01021.x

Greenhalgh, T., Stramer, K., Bratan, T., Byrne, E., Russell, J., & Potts, H. W. (2010). Adoption and non-adoption of a shared electronic summary record in England: A mixed-method case study. *BMJ, 340,* c3111. doi: 10.1136/bmj.c3111

Groene, O., Klazinga, N., Wagner, C., Arah, O. A., Thompson, A., Bruneau, C., . . . DUQuE Research Project. (2010). Investigating organizational quality improvement systems, patient empowerment, organizational culture, professional involvement and the quality of care in European hospitals: the 'Deepening our Understanding of Quality Improvement in Europe (DUQuE)' project. *BMC Health Services Research, 10,* 281. doi: 10.1186/1472–6963–10–281

Koppel, R., Metlay, J. P., Cohen, A., Abaluck, B., Localio, A. R., Kimmel, S. E., & Strom, B. L. (2005). Role of computerized physician order entry systems in facilitating medication errors. *JAMA, 293*(10), 1197–1203. doi: 10.1001/jama.293 .10.1197

Krause, N. (2002). A comprehensive strategy for developing closed-ended survey items for use in studies of older adults. *Journals of Gerontology. Series B, Psychological Sciences and Social Sciences, 57*(5), S263–274.

Lewin, S., Glenton, C., & Oxman, A. D. (2009). Use of qualitative methods alongside randomised controlled trials of complex healthcare interventions: Methodological study. *BMJ, 339,* b3496. doi: 10.1136/bmj.b3496

O'Cathain, A., Murphy, E., & Nicholl, J. (2007). Why, and how, mixed methods research is undertaken in health services research in England: A mixed methods study. *BMC Health Services Research, 7,* 85. doi: 10.1186/1472–6963-7-85

O'Cathain, A., Murphy, E., & Nicholl, J. (2008). The quality of mixed methods studies in health services research. *Journal of Health Services Research and Policy, 13*(2), 92–98. doi: 10.1258/jhsrp.2007.007074

Padgett, D. (2012). *Qualitative and mixed methods in public health.* Thousand Oaks, CA: Sage.

Plano Clark, V. L. (2010). The adoption and practice of mixed methods: U.S. trends in federally funded health-related research. *Qualitative Inquiry, 16*(6), 428–440.

Plano Clark, V. L., & Badiee, M. (2010). Research questions in mixed methods research. In A. Tashakkori & C. Teddlie (Eds.), *SAGE handbook of mixed methods social and behavioral research* (2nd ed., pp. 275–304). Thousand Oaks, CA: Sage.

Riegel, B., Dickson, V. V., Kuhn, L., Page, K., & Worrall-Carter, L. (2010). Gender-specific barriers and facilitators to heart failure self-care: a mixed methods study. *International Journal of Nursing Studies, 47*(7), 888–895. doi: 10.1016/j.ijnurstu .2009.12.011

Riley, D. L., Krepostman, S., Stewart, D. E., Suskin, N., Arthur, H. M., & Grace, S. L. (2009). A mixed methods study of continuity of care from cardiac rehabilitation to primary care physicians. *Canadian Journal of Cardiology, 25*(6), e187–192.

Robertson, A., Cresswell, K., Takian, A., Petrakaki, D., Crowe, S., Cornford, T., . . . Sheikh, A. (2010). Implementation and adoption of nationwide electronic health records in secondary care in England: Qualitative analysis of interim results from a prospective national evaluation. *BMJ, 341,* c4564. doi: 10.1136/bmj.c4564

Wisdom, J. P., Cavaleri, M. A., Onwuegbuzie, A. J., & Green, C. A. (2012). Methodological reporting in qualitative, quantitative, and mixed methods health services research articles. *Health Services Research, 47*(2), 721–745. doi: 10 .1111/j.1475–6773.2011.01344.x

Zier, L. S., Sottile, P. D., Hong, S. Y., Weissfield, L. A., & White, D. B. (2012). Surrogate decision makers' interpretation of prognostic information: A mixed-methods study. *Annals of Internal Medicine, 156*(5), 360–366.

≈ PART II ≈

GETTING MIXED METHODS RESEARCH FUNDED

Part II provides guidance on how to write high-quality mixed methods proposals and how to be an informed consumer of research using these methods. We begin with writing strong grant proposals and offer suggestions and tools to support the writing process. This is followed by a detailed review of three examples of extramurally funded research. We then turn to the critical issue of ensuring quality in mixed methods studies. We present and discuss standards for quality in designing and conducting mixed methods in health sciences research.

❧ FOUR ❧

WRITING A SCIENTIFICALLY SOUND AND COMPELLING GRANT PROPOSAL FOR A MIXED METHODS STUDY

Information you will find in this chapter: This chapter discusses how to develop a scientifically sound and compelling grant application for a mixed methods study. We begin with the strategic question of identifying a potential funding source and present recent data on trends and patterns of a major funder of health sciences research in the United States, the National Institutes of Health (NIH). Next, we provide extensive practical guidance on planning for and preparing a competitive grant application, highlighting the importance of alignment in a proposal. We use the general NIH application format as a guide, although the principles are transferable to other funding sources. In the final section, we provide guidance for satisfying grant review criteria for mixed methods studies.

Key features in this chapter:

- Brief quotations and reflections from mixed methods researchers
- Planning checklist for mixed methods grant writing
- Selected funders of mixed methods health sciences research and examples of funded projects
- Data on NIH institutes receptive to mixed methods study proposals
- Suggestions for writing a strong mixed methods research proposal
- Outline for organizing the methods section of an application
- Example rationales for using mixed methods for different design types
- Illustrative research aims for mixed methods studies in grant application format

- Example table for presenting study components
- Example figure for presenting study components
- Example table for presenting data collection activities
- Checklist for optimizing the representation of your mixed methods team
- Table of review criteria and strategies for satisfying these criteria in a grant application

BEFORE YOU WRITE

Before you begin writing a grant application, it is critical to invest the time in thinking strategically about a potential funder for the project and learning as much as you can about that funder so that you can write with your target audience in mind. Thinking strategically can help you maximize the likelihood that your time in preparing the application is well spent and that the project will be favorably reviewed. There is a dizzying array of resources (of varying quality) available on how to pursue and secure extramural research funding in health sciences. Rather than duplicate this voluminous information, we focus on the aspects of competitive grant writing that are especially relevant to mixed methods. The tips that are described in this section are summarized in Box 4.1.

Box 4.1   Planning Checklist

✓ Choose a funding institution that is appropriate for your topic and mixed methods design
✓ Communicate with representatives from the funding institutions to ensure that your study topic and approach aligns with their interests
✓ Develop a realistic timeline for grant writing that allows for collaborative writing

---

Choosing a Funding Institution

As a first step, assess the potential fit of your study for a given funder not only in terms of the research topic but also with regard to the mixed methods approach. Review the stated interests of the funder in their requests for proposals as well as general information about their mission and funding initiatives. Take advantage of resources that can help identify a funding institution that may be interested in your focal area, as well as in multidisciplinary mixed methods research. Sources of information include publicly available resources describing the types of funded research, searches of previously funded grants, and exploratory conversations with a program officer in the funding institution. Pay attention to the extent to which the target institution has historically supported mixed methods research and also try to determine whether there may be new or growing receptivity among funders who have not funded mixed methods in the past. We spoke with a senior program officer at the Patient-Centered Outcomes Research Institute (PCORI) in the United States, who described their interest in mixed methods (see Box 4.2).

Box 4.2 Research Funders' Interest in Supporting Mixed Methods Research

A significant number of our projects have mixed methods components. Some of those are randomized controlled trials with nested qualitative methods and many other types of designs. One of our fundamental jumping off points is that a lot of health services research has historically not taken the approach of integrating the patient voice or other stakeholder voices in the data collection process. So from the start there was a recognition that purely quantitative approaches will yield some evidence of import for our purposes but not all of it. Taking a mixed methods approach will improve the overall quality of the research and the relevance of the findings to patients.

—Jason Gerson, PhD, Senior Program Officer,
Comparative Effectiveness Research (CER) Methods and Infrastructure,
Patient-Centered Outcomes Research Institute (PCORI)

The funding landscape for mixed methods is complex and rapidly evolving. To provide a sense of the current funding landscape for mixed methods, we present a list of institutions that have funded mixed methods work, along with examples of studies that they have supported, in Box 4.3. We would note that given the steadily growing interest in mixed methods among funders of health sciences research, the list of potential agencies and organizations is likely to be quite dynamic. Of course, you are not limited to institutions that have previously funded mixed methods; you can also introduce these methods to new funders. In this case, we suggest you pay particular attention to citing seminal methods literature and any relevant empirical literature using mixed methods. Be sure to make a compelling case for mixed methods early in the application, indicating other major funders' support of mixed methods studies. At least in the current climate, it is safe to assume the review panels may have limited familiarity with mixed methods. Therefore, limiting jargon and defining necessary terminology and concepts can increase the likelihood your proposal will be understood and given an informed review.

Box 4.3   Selected Funders of Mixed Methods Health Sciences Research and Illustrative Examples

- **Agency for Healthcare Research and Quality (AHRQ; United States),** "Mixed Method Analysis for Medical Error Event Reports: A Report From the ASIPS Collaborative" (Harris et al., 2005)
- **The Commonwealth Fund (United States),** "Evaluation of Patient Centered Medical Home Practice Transformation Initiatives" (Crabtree et al., 2011)
- **National Patient Safety Agency (NPSA; United Kingdom),** "Large Scale Organisational Intervention to Improve Patient Safety in Four UK Hospitals: Mixed Method Evaluation" (Benning et al., 2011)
- **Max Planck Institute for Demographic Research (MPIDR; Germany),** "Social Influences on Fertility: A Comparative Mixed Methods Study in Eastern and Western Germany" (Bernardi, 2007)
- **National Institute of Mental Health (NIMH; United States),** "The Development of Valid Subtypes for Depression in Primary Care Settings: A Preliminary Study Using an Explanatory Model Approach" (Karasz, 2008)
- **National Institute of Nursing Research (NINR; United States),** "Neurocognitive and Family Functioning and Quality of Life Among Young Adult Survivors of Childhood Brain Tumors" (Hocking et al., 2011)

- **New Zealand Foundation for Research, Science and Technology (New Zealand),** "A Mixed Methods Approach: Using Cultural Modeling and Consensus Analysis to Better Understand New Zealand's International Innovation Performance" (Rinne & Fairweather, 2012)
- **Patient-Centered Outcomes Research Institute (PCORI; United States),** *Developing and Testing a Personalized, Evidence-Based, Shared Decision-Making Tool for Stent Selection in PCI* (Spertus, 2012; note that because PCORI was only founded in 2012, no publications have resulted from their mixed methods studies.)
- **Plan (Netherlands),** "Developing a Function Impairment Measure for Children Affected by Political Violence: A Mixed Methods Approach in Indonesia" (Tol, Komproe, Jordans, Susanty, & de Jong, 2011)
- **Robert Wood Johnson Foundation (United States),** "A Mixed-Methods Evaluation of School-Based Active Living Programs" (McCreary et al., 2012)
- **National Institute for Health Research (NIHR; United Kingdom),** "Adoption and Non-Adoption of a Shared Electronic Summary Record in England: A Mixed-Method Case Study" (Greenhalgh et al., 2010)
- **Women's Health Research Institute of the BC (British Columbia) Women's Hospital & Health Centre (Canada),** "Barriers to Rural Induced Abortion Services in Canada: Findings of the British Columbia Abortion Providers Survey" (Norman, Soon, Maughn, & Dressler, 2013)

Communicating With Funders

Once you have identified a possible funder, it can be very helpful to communicate with the program officer or appropriate person at the funding institution to discuss whether the study is a good fit with the institution's interests. Funders typically welcome inquiries from researchers prior to the submission of a grant application. Although many people choose not to take advantage of this opportunity, these discussions can be very helpful—especially when the application includes innovative and perhaps unfamiliar approaches such as the use of mixed methods. As described by Dr. Helen Meissner, a longtime scientific officer from the NIH, a conversation with scientific or program staff can help you determine whether your research proposal is likely to be responsive to the interests of the funder (see Box 4.4).

Box 4.4   Determining Whether Your Proposal Fits the Funders' Interests

Contact the program official at the institute where your application is going before you submit it. Talk to them and say, "This is what I'm thinking of doing . . . ." Get their feedback. You can also ask the program official at the institute their opinion of how your application will be received because they listen to discussion at different study sections, and they can tell you, "This section is a lot more open to mixed methods than others . . . ." So the best thing is to develop that relationship with the program person, and they can make recommendations . . . .I would highly recommend contacting the funding agency—whether it's NIH or some other funder—to ask if the direction you're going in is something that is feasible or of interest for them.

—Helen Meissner, ScM, PhD, Director,
Tobacco Regulatory Science Program and
Former Senior Advisor in the Office of Behavioral and Social Sciences
Research (OBSSR), National Institutes of Health (NIH)

While the administrative procedures vary by funding organization, if you are applying to a specific request for applications the materials will provide contact information for a scientific or programmatic staff person. Rather than call unannounced, it can be helpful to send a concise e-mail summarizing the project (e.g., one sentence each on the knowledge gap, aims, and rationale for mixed methods) and request an opportunity to speak briefly by telephone. Questions to ask in a conversation with a program officer might include the following: Has the funder supported mixed methods research in the past, and if so, to what degree? Do the funder's review panels include members with expertise in mixed methods, or should you assume limited knowledge and therefore tailor the writing accordingly? Is it advantageous (or not advisable) to suggest potential qualified mixed methods experts for the review panel? Are there specific suggestions as to how a grant application should be structured or written in order to communicate effectively to reviewers, such as using schematics or other tools?

Developing a Realistic Timeline

Pay attention to submission deadlines and be sure they are feasible. Writing grant applications always takes more time than you expect, and mixed methods applications can require even more preparation. Start early! As described previously, make contact with a program official as early as possible in the process in order to give your team time to address any feedback or suggestions. Some funders require a letter of intent be submitted by a given deadline. In some cases these letters are simply perfunctory placeholders, yet in other cases letters of intent can provide an opportunity to highlight (and market) the unique nature of your study in terms of mixed methods approach. You might use the letter to note the funder's prior support of mixed methods as being innovative or leading the field in health sciences, refer to a prior funded mixed methods study as demonstrating the relevance of this method for the particular topic, or convey your research team's strengths in using mixed methods to investigate focal areas of interest to this funder.

Proposals for mixed methods studies may be even more time intensive for researchers new to the methods. Several aspects of the process may require additional time. First, it is important to develop skills in writing about mixed methods, using appropriate terminology and citations. Second, sections of the application are often written by several team members who are each responsible for the qualitative and quantitative components. Coordinating writing activities and ensuring coherence and consistency across the components requires substantial time and effective communication strategies. Finally, the methods section in a mixed methods application can often be more complex than for single method studies. Preparing clear, comprehensive, and well-organized descriptions of the various methods, including describing the integration of study components, is also a time-intensive aspect of the grant writing process.

TRENDS IN FUNDING FOR MIXED METHODS STUDIES

Understanding an institution's track record of supporting mixed methods research is key to selecting an appropriate funder. The primary funding institution for U.S.-based health sciences research is the NIH. It is important to note, however, that there are many other foundations in the United States and internationally that are interested in studies using mixed methods (see Box 4.3). An analysis of trends in health-related mixed methods projects funded by the NIH through U.S. fiscal year (FY) 2008 (Plano Clark, 2010) showed that the numbers of mixed methods studies were increasing, although proportion of mixed methods studies as a percentage of all NIH grants remained relatively low. We replicated and extended this previous analysis to generate a more current view of trends through the end of FY 2013 using the NIH Research Portfolio Online Reporting Tools (RePORTER) Database. We searched for studies that included terms such as *mixed methods, mixed methodology,* or *multi-methods* in their titles and abstracts and then read the available materials to confirm that they met our definition of mixed methods. The methods for this search and analysis are described in detail in Appendix B: Methodology for National Institutes of Health RePORTER Analysis of Trends in Funding for Mixed Methods Research.

Our NIH RePORTER search revealed continued growth in the popularity of mixed methods, beyond the trend that was previously reported by Plano Clark (2010) (see Figure 4.1). The highest number of mixed methods grants to be approved in one year was 101 grants in 2012. Although mixed methods research continues to represent a small percentage of the total grants approved, this percentage has increased. Between 1997 and 2008, mixed methods studies were only 0.04% of the total grants approved; and from 2009 to 2013, they represented 0.16% of the total.

Because this search only included studies that used mixed methods terminology in their applications, it is possible that institutional funding for mixed methods is not necessarily growing but rather researchers may be more consistently using mixed methods terminology that would cause their studies to appear in the search. As the language of mixed methods becomes more prevalent, researchers may more commonly refer to their work using these terms. We have had participants in our mixed methods workshops remark the following: "I have been combining qualitative and quantitative approaches in my studies for years, now I know what to call it—mixed methods!" Researchers are increasingly identifying their work as mixed methods in grants and publications, and consequently, mixed methods research is developing a stronger presence in the health sciences.

Levels of support for mixed methods studies are not uniform across NIH institutes; this might be a result of varying levels of interest within the institute

Figure 4.1 Trend in Number of National Institutes of Health-Funded Mixed Methods Studies by Fiscal Year of Award

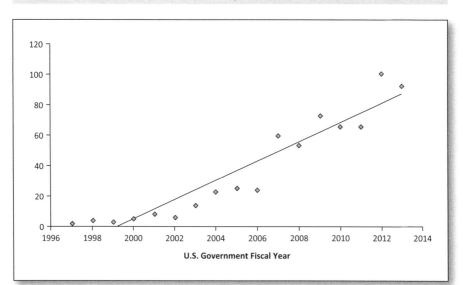

U.S. Government Fiscal Year

or varying degrees of interest among the applicants proposing projects to these institutes. The largest number of grants was approved by the NIMH ($n = 134$ since 1997). Other institutes that have approved more than 50 mixed methods grants are included in Figure 4.2.

It is worth noting that while several of the institutes are disease specific (e.g., mental health, cancer, drug abuse) and require expertise and focus in these target areas, others (e.g., National Institute of Nursing Research [NINR], Agency for Healthcare Research and Quality [AHRQ], National Institute of Child Health and Human Development [NICHD]) are broader in mission and may be a fit for a wide range of topics, populations, and disciplines. It is also true that while these institutes are the most common funders of mixed methods, there are many others with increasing interest in these designs, including the Robert Wood Johnson Foundation, the Commonwealth Fund, and PCORI. The support of mixed methods by various kinds of funding organizations is highly dynamic, and you should not be discouraged from approaching other organizations with a mixed methods proposal that includes a compelling rationale and rigorously designed study.

Figure 4.2   Number of National Institutes of Health-Funded Mixed Methods Studies by Awarding Institute, 1996–2013

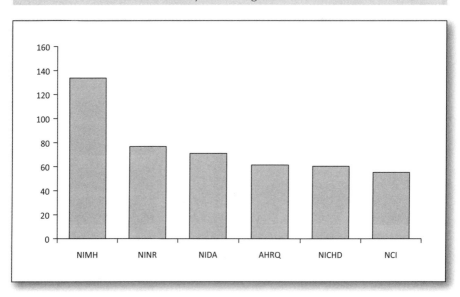

NOTE: NIMH = National Institute of Mental Health; NINR = National Institute of Nursing Research; NIDA = National Institute on Drug Abuse; AHRQ = Agency for Healthcare Research and Quality (included in the search database although not technically within NIH); NICHD = National Institute of Child Health and Human Development; NCI = National Cancer Institute.

WRITING A MIXED METHODS PROPOSAL

In this section, we begin with the critical issue of *alignment* across the components of the grant application. We then turn to a discussion of each of the major application components, including title, background or significance, specific aims, research plan or methods, investigative team and environment, and cover letter. Box 4.5 provides a summary of suggestions for writing a clear, credible, and convincing mixed methods proposal in the health sciences.

Alignment Across Components of the Grant

As you set about developing a grant proposal, carefully consider how the application will be aligned across all components. By *aligned* we mean that there is a clear and logical flow from the identified gap and problem to be

---

Box 4.5   Summary of Suggestions for Writing a Strong Mixed Methods Proposal

✓ Develop a clear conceptualization of the mixed methods research design.
✓ Provide a compelling rationale for using mixed methods.
✓ Specify aims using established techniques.
✓ Use figures and schematics to describe the methods and how they work together to achieve the study aims.
✓ Reduce the use of unnecessary jargon.
✓ Define all terms, especially those that are particular to one methodological area.
✓ Use citations heavily to support the methods section.
✓ Include citations for studies that have successfully employed a similar mixed methods design for a related topic to illustrate the feasibility and applicability of the approach.
✓ Do not underestimate the importance of having a strong title and cover letter to accompany your proposal.

---

solved through the study aims, respective methods for each, resources, and team capacity. In addition, the need for a mixed methods approach must be conveyed across each of these sections. Because a lack of alignment is common in research proposals, we recommend devoting ongoing attention to this fundamental concept as you develop each part of the application. Best practice guidelines for mixed methods grants highlight the importance of alignment and provide several useful suggestions for accomplishing this in an application (Creswell, Klassen, Plano Clark, & Smith for the Office of Behavioral and Social Sciences Research [OBSSR], 2011).

First, the mixed methods design should be embedded in all elements of the proposal. The mixed methods nature of the study should be reflected in the title, background and aims, methods, and team composition. Although you will describe the methodology in detail in the methods section, every other part of the proposal should also signal the mixed methods approach. Imagine running a thread throughout the entire document to guide the reader and demonstrate that mixed methods are the optimal approach for addressing the aims.

Second, the respective roles of each component in the proposal should be clearly delineated, including the relationship across components. For instance, if the study is an embedded design where qualitative data collection is embedded in a clinical trial in a supportive or supplementary role, then it is appropriate to place more emphasis on the quantitative and clinical aspects of the study. Note that even in this case reviewers will want to see detailed information about the sample, data collection, and analysis for the qualitative component. However, if the study components are equally weighted, then the depth of detail and type of information provided about all elements of each component (e.g., sampling, data collection, analysis) should be equal and balanced. If you choose to have different team members writing the qualitative and quantitative sections of the proposal, pay attention to achieving balance as you pull the information together into a coherent proposal. Smooth out any unevenness in the voice and style that may arise when there are multiple authors of a document. Pay particular attention whether the study's specific aims are refined along the way. Checking for consistency is essential, since the entire proposal must map clearly to the aims and they are repeated more than once in the proposal. In our experience, collaborative writing enriches the quality of a proposal but also presents challenges when several team members are writing simultaneously.

◀ For more on the alignment of research components and logistics, see Chapter 3: Determining the Appropriateness and Feasibility of Using Mixed Methods.

Finally, decisions about the structure and ordering of the methods section of the proposal should be based on the type of mixed methods design. As we have described previously, it is imperative that the evidence gap, research question, approach, and budget follow logically and are explicitly connected. This is true for all research applications regardless of methodology, although perhaps more difficult for mixed methods designs because of the multiple study components.

Title

The title is the first description of your study that the funding institution staff and reviewers will see; therefore, it influences the way they will read the rest of your proposal. As we emphasized previously, consider how to align all components of the proposal—beginning with the title. The scope of the topic is both bounded and framed in the title, setting the stage for what evidence must be addressed in the background and significance and subsequently the proposed methods particularly in terms of sampling and measurement. The title should be precise and concise. In crafting the title, pay attention to language. Certain terms are closely associated either with qualitative or quantitative methods (and therefore might trigger a bias in a reviewer) (Creswell & Plano Clark, 2011). For example, words such as *explore, characterize,* and *perspectives* tend to be associated with qualitative methods while words such as *predict, association,* and *measure* tend to be associated with quantitative methods. Therefore, consider using neutral language if possible and make sure that your language is balanced in the use of qualitative and quantitative terms. The first example here uses neutral terminology, and the second example balances the use of qualitative and quantitative terms:

"Addressing Social Determinants to Reduce Refugee Mental Health Disparities" (Goodkind, 2013)

"Disparities in HPV Vaccine Completion: Identifying and quantifying the barriers" (Niccolai, 2012)

Background and Significance

The goals of the background section are to document the nature and importance of the problem, establish the knowledge gap, and demonstrate how your proposed study will make contributions to addressing this gap. For a mixed methods study, a strong background section must not only achieve those goals but also make a compelling case for why a mixed methods approach is needed. Because mixed methods studies can be more resource and time intensive than single methods studies, you must provide a clear justification for why these methods can advance the field in a significant way. Table 4.1 provides examples of how you might describe the need for particular types of mixed methods study designs.

Study Aims

In a previous chapter we described developing aims for mixed methods studies in the context of determining whether a mixed methods approach is warranted for a given topic.

Table 4.1   Gaps in the Literature That Demand Different Types of Mixed Methods

Major Types of Mixed Methods Designs	A Need Exists in the Literature for the Following:
Convergent design	Developing a complete understanding by collecting both qualitative and quantitative data, because each provides a partial view
Exploratory sequential design	Exploring a topic because variables are unknown and assessing the extent to which the findings from a purposeful sample of study participants generalize to a population
Explanatory sequential design	Not only obtaining quantitative results but explaining such results in greater detail, especially through voices and perspectives from participants
Intervention with qualitative component	Examining intervention outcomes through experimental methods and understanding participant experiences of the intervention by obtaining qualitative data

SOURCE: Adapted from Creswell and Plano Clark (2011).

◄ For more tips on developing research aims, see Chapter 3: Determining the Appropriateness and Feasibility of Using Mixed Methods.

While these general guidelines for defining aims are useful at a conceptual level, equally important is an understanding of how to script aims in a grant application format. The specific aims page carries the grant; if it does not engage the reviewer, his or her attention may wane for the remainder of the application. Carefully craft the aims page to convey the aims, methods, and significance precisely and concisely. Share it with colleagues not connected with the project for input, and review it among the team throughout the grant writing process. Plan to revisit the aims page a dozen times or more. In Box 4.6, we present a set of draft research aims for each of the three basic design types most common in health sciences, in a style and format suited for grant applications. Each set includes an overarching research objective that, by its multifaceted nature, requires a mixed methods approach, followed by specific aims that articulate the focal topic and associated method. It is important to specify the plan for integration.

Box 4.6   Grant Application Specific Aim Examples

Example 1—Primary Care Access in Low-Income Urban Settings Among African American Male Adults

- *Overarching objective:* Describe access to key primary care services among African American male adults with Medicaid in low-income urban settings. Using a convergent mixed methods design, we propose the following aims:
- *Aim 1:* Document utilization of key primary care services using Medicaid administrative claims data in three low-income urban settings purposefully selected for diversity in geographic region and size (quantitative).
- *Aim 2:* Describe patient perceptions of unmet needs and expectations for key primary care services (qualitative interviews).
- *Aim 3:* Generate a comprehensive understanding of primary care access in these settings (merging the qualitative and quantitative data to assess complementarity, concordance, and discordance among data sets, using a mixed methods approach).

Example 2—Delayed Clinical Presentation of Young Women With Breast Cancer Symptoms

- *Overarching objective:* Understand the perceived barriers to clinical presentation of young women with breast cancer symptoms through improved measurement instruments. Using a sequential exploratory mixed methods design, we propose the following aims:
- *Aim 1:* Explore the factors that may contribute to delayed presentation of young women after onset of symptoms of breast cancer in order to generate content domains and item constructs (qualitative interviews).
- *Aim 2:* Develop and validate a novel survey instrument (connecting the qualitative and quantitative data to develop the survey using a mixed methods approach).

(Continued)

(Continued)

Example 3 — Feasibility of Mobile Technology to Support Self-Management of Diabetes Among Teens

- *Overarching objective:* Implement a novel text-messaging program to support self-management of diabetes among teens and explore the potential barriers and facilitators to use of this technology. Using a sequential explanatory mixed methods design, we propose the following aims:
- *Aim 1:* Implement a novel text-messaging program for diabetes clinic patients aged 13 to 18 and monitor usage, user satisfaction, and glycemic control over a six-month period (quantitative).
- *Aim 2:* Understand the experiences and perspectives of low and high utilizers of the text-messaging program selected from the quantitative data collected in the pilot period (qualitative focus groups).
- *Aim 3:* Assess feasibility of the text-messaging program to support self-management of diabetes in terms of adherence and glycemic control (merging the quantitative and qualitative data using a mixed methods approach).

Research Plan or Methods

◀ For detailed guidance on the development of a grant application, also see the NIH OBSSR report: *Best Practices for Mixed Methods Research in the Health Sciences* (Creswell et al., 2011). Although the best practices were prepared for NIH, they are broadly transferrable to many other funding sources including those noted in Box 4.2.

The research plan should first describe the overall design, followed by detailed information about the sampling, data collection, and analysis methods for each component. There are extensive resources available to researchers regarding techniques for developing strong grant applications (refer to various institutes within the NIH, or foundations; Foundation Center, n.d.; National Institute of Allergy and Infectious Diseases [NIAID], n.d.). Throughout this book, we focus on key recommendations that are particularly relevant to writing mixed methods applications.

First, the methods section of mixed methods is often the most challenging to organize. The outline of information should be easy for reviewers to follow and should reduce the duplication in content. Box 4.7 provides suggested outlines for proposals of different types that roughly follow the chronology of the research.

If data collection occurs at the same time for multiple components, the proposal may be best structured to describe data collection for each component, followed by data analysis and integration for each component. On the other hand,

---

Box 4.7   Suggested Outlines for Methods Sections Based on Study Design

Convergent or Embedded Designs

I. Sampling approaches

  a. Quantitative sampling

  b. Qualitative sampling

II. Data collection

  a. Quantitative data collection

  b. Qualitative data collection

III. Data analysis and integration

  a. Quantitative data analysis

  b. Qualitative data analysis

  c. Integration or merging procedures

Sequential or Multiphase Designs

I. Component 1 (qualitative or quantitative)

  a. Sampling

  b. Data collection

  c. Data analysis

II. Integration through building or connecting

III. Component 2 (qualitative or quantitative)

  a. Sampling

  b. Data collection

  c. Data analysis

IV. Integration through interpretation and reporting

SOURCE: Adapted from Creswell et al. (2011).

if data collection and analysis for the first component takes place before data collection for the other component begins, it will help the reviewer to follow the flow if you structure your proposal in the same way. Integration appears in two places in the outline (in Box 4.7) to reflect the way in which integration should occur at multiple stages of the study. The connecting form of integration (where you build on the first component to create the second component) should be described in the chronological order that it occurs in the study. At the same time, integration must also occur in the reporting and interpretation stage of the study.

Second, provide definitions for key methodological terms. The current reality is that there are relatively few established researchers with expertise and experience in conducting mixed methods research in the health sciences. It is likely that your mixed methods proposal will be reviewed by individuals with primary expertise in either qualitative or quantitative methods, and with limited understanding of mixed methods generally or the specific approach you are proposing. Furthermore, while we regard the multidisciplinary nature of mixed methods research as a great strength, this diversity also presents challenges. Keep in mind that reviewers of mixed methods proposals are more likely to have a range of disciplinary backgrounds as well as diverse content and methods expertise (and remind yourself of this throughout writing the proposal). As is the case in effectively managing mixed methods teams, deliberate attention must be invested in order to communicate effectively across disciplinary boundaries.

► For more information on fostering interdisciplinary team collaboration, refer to Chapter 9: Managing Mixed Methods Teams.

Most often in the health sciences the predominant orientation and expertise on review panels is in quantitative methods, although this varies by funding source. Consequently, terminology central to qualitative research (such as purposeful sampling, theoretical saturation, constant comparative method, and grounded theory) may be unfamiliar or frustrating for reviewers. Use concise, precise definitions and credible citations to help readers understand the methods.

A related caution is to reduce the use of jargon or language that is used by a particular profession or group and is difficult for others to understand. This is often easier said than done, since we are each fairly immune to the terminology we use in our daily work. One way to reduce jargon is to make a short list of the types of experts that may be reviewing your proposal (e.g., mixed, qualitative and quantitative experts, subject areas experts). Identify colleagues outside of your research team with similar backgrounds to review key sections of your proposal with an eye toward identifying confusing language and concepts.

Provide them with definitions and citations, and ask for feedback as to whether your clarifications are helpful.

Third, include as many key citations for the methods as feasible. This is particularly important in the case of qualitative and mixed methods, which may be relatively or even completely new to reviewers. Providing citations from credible sources (e.g., textbooks by reputable publishers, method articles in peer-reviewed scientific journals preferably in health sciences, seminal works by senior methodologists) can demonstrate that your methods are grounded in scientific literature and that your team has expertise in these methods. Include citations throughout the research plan, from the sampling approach to data collection and analysis and plans for integration methods. Nearly all aspects of a proposal can be strengthened by including appropriate citations.

▶ See the Glossary of Key Terms and Definitions in this book for key definitions and suggested citations or resources for more reading.

Fourth, not only should the methods be supported with citations but they should also include sufficient detail about all components. In our experience, the absence of detail is a particular concern in relation to qualitative methods, especially regarding sample size and data analysis. As noted in Box 4.8, some researchers offer a limited description of the data collection plan without addressing the other essential aspects of a study design.

Box 4.8   Failing to Describe Qualitative Methods With Sufficient Detail

I've reviewed many qualitative manuscripts and proposals, and there's a lot of crappy work out there where people sort of thought, "Well I'll just go talk to a few people and that's qualitative methods." Or "My mixed methods will include a few interviews or a focus group." You can tell that there was no or very little attention paid to how the sample was selected or how the interview guide was developed. What is the strategy for doing the analysis, and how will you determine the reliability of coding? How will you track the decisions you were making in that process? Will you use software to assist you in the analysis? All that should go into applications, but it's often missing.

—Terrie Wetle, PhD, Professor of Health Services, Policy and Practice, Brown University

◄ See Figures 2.4, 2.7, and 2.10 in Chapter 2: Applications and Illustrations of Mixed Methods Health Sciences Research for other examples of how the components of a study could be presented in a table or figure.

Fifth, it is strategic—and in our view essential—to include a visual diagram to help reviewers follow the mixed methods design and related methodological procedures. We strongly recommend the use of tables and figures to represent a comprehensive view of the design and how the components fit together. Next, we present two examples of visual diagrams from successful mixed methods grant applications.

An overall project figure can help effectively communicate your proposed methodological approach to reviewers. We highlight an example from *Measuring Racial/Ethnic Discrimination in Healthcare Settings,* an R21 funded by the NIH (Nunez-Smith, 2010). Although patient-reported experiences of health care discrimination are important correlates of negative health outcomes, inconsistencies in measurement approaches hinder progress in this emerging field. The team proposed a mixed methods study to develop and test items for potential inclusion on a standardized measure of health care discrimination. The aims of this multistage study were to do the following:

- Develop a comprehensive set of candidate items for a measure of patient assessments of health care discrimination in acute care hospitals.
- Conduct field testing and preliminary psychometric analyses of finalized candidate items.

In order to achieve these aims, the NIH-funded study included five separate components. Figure 4.3 demonstrates how information about the study components was presented in the grant application.

Alternatively, a simple table can go a long way in eliminating confusion. As an example, we present a study designed by researchers from the Pacific Institute for Research and Evaluation (PIRE) and funded by the NIH to investigate *OTC Syringe Sales to Prevent HIV in Underserved Areas of Inland California* (Pollini, 2011). Sterile syringe access plays a critical role in efforts to prevent HIV among injection drug users (IDUs). This team planned a mixed methods study to assess the effectiveness of a new law in California designed to reduce HIV transmission by allowing pharmacies to sell up to 30 syringes without a prescription. The application proposed a multistage design to generate a comprehensive understanding of the factors that facilitate and

Figure 4.3   Example Figure Outlining Study Components

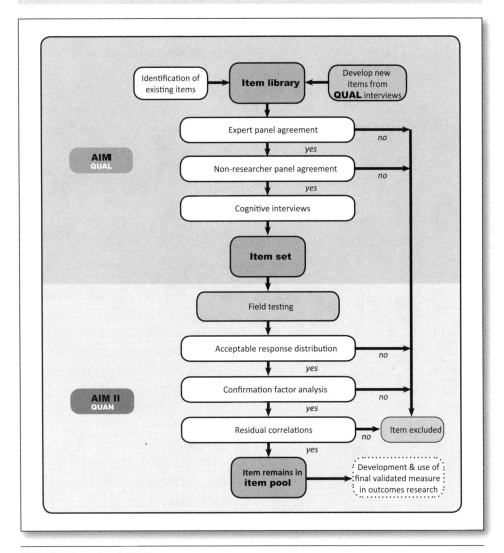

SOURCE: Nunez-Smith (2010).

impede the implementation of this new law. The aims of this study were to do the following:

- Assess the implementation of California's new OTC syringe purchase law in two geographically and ethnically diverse inland California counties, and characterize barriers and facilitators to implementation.

- Quantify IDU utilization of pharmacy-based syringe purchase under the new law, and elucidate barriers and facilitators to utilization.
- Examine structural factors related to pharmacy implementation and IDU utilization of the new OTC syringe law, including geographic, sociodemographic, and law enforcement characteristics in these two diverse inland California counties.

In order to achieve these aims, the funded study included five separate data collection strategies. Table 4.2 demonstrates how information about the data collection strategies and their corresponding objectives, samples, and analysis plans might be presented in a grant application.

Finally, a mixed methods proposal should describe how you plan to integrate the qualitative and quantitative components (Barbour, 1999; Creswell et al., 2011). Integration of qualitative and quantitative data is a hallmark of a mixed methods study. We have described various types of integration in several sections of the book.

▶ Strategies for integration are introduced in Chapter 1: Definition and Overview of Mixed Methods Designs and described in more detail in Chapter 7: Sampling and Data Collection in Mixed Methods Studies and Chapter 8: Data Analysis and Integration in Mixed Methods Studies.

For merged or embedded integration, the proposal should describe how results from the various components will be compared or synthesized and how potentially divergent results will be managed or interpreted. Because divergence can only be assessed once all data analyses are complete, this content typically would be presented in the last part of the data analysis section, after the qualitative and quantitative data analyses are described. For connected integration, the proposal should describe how the results from one component will be used to inform the other component and how the final results will be fully integrated. This information might appear in the data collection and measures section (regarding measurement development) and again in the data analysis section.

Investigative Team and Environment

Although the importance of building a strong mixed methods team has been addressed previously, we revisit the issue here.

Table 4.2   Example Table Summarizing Data Collection Strategies

Strategy	Objective	Sample	Analysis
I. Syringe purchase trial	Obtain an objective measure of pharmacy implementation of the new over-the counter (OTC) syringe law.	298 retail pharmacies	Descriptive statistics
II. Brief pharmacy survey	Assess barriers and facilitators to OTC syringe sales.	596 (one pharmacist and one staff member at 298 pharmacies)	Descriptive statistics and correlations
IIIa. Qualitative professional key informant (KI) interviews	Characterize the impact of important social agents on OTC law implementation.	16 KIs from pharmacies, law enforcement, and government	Constant comparative method
IIIb. Qualitative IDU [injection drug user] KI interviews	Formative research to inform IDU recruitment and survey development.	16 IDU KIs	Constant comparative method
IV. IDU survey	Characterize pharmacy-based syringe purchase among IDUs and elucidate related barriers and facilitators.	550 IDUs	Descriptive statistics and correlations
V. Geospatial/ contextual modeling	Examine structural factors associated with both pharmacy implementation and IDU utilization of OTC syringe sales.	Data collected in purchase trial and surveys, geographic information, U.S. census data, arrest data	Mapping and statistical modeling

SOURCE: Printed with permission from Robin Pollini, senior research scientist at the Pacific Institute for Research and Evaluation (PIRE).

It is essential to convey that the proposed team has the capacity to successfully carry out the proposed study—both to ensure that reviewers will have confidence in your capacity to succeed and to address any potential skepticism about the methods. In an interview for this book, a senior official

◀ See Chapter 3:
Determining the
Appropriateness and
Feasibility of Using
Mixed Methods.

at a major U.S. funding organization described encouraging applicants to think carefully about the full complement of content and methods expertise required to address complex research questions (see Box 4.9).

Box 4.9   Getting the Most Out of Mixed Methods

We've worked with groups that are proposing to do a quantitative study only, and we've gone back to them to say that we think that because of the complexity of the intervention a mixed methods study would be more appropriate. What's interesting is that it's often not easy for groups. They will say, "Okay, but we don't have expertise on our group." So we try to encourage collaboration between different groups that have that perspective or a group will recruit someone from another department or even another institution that can work on the qualitative piece of a grant. One example is that we had an evaluation of the alternative quality contract, which is a new payment program that Blue Cross Blue Shield is doing in the state of Massachusetts, and the group wanted to know the impact on costs. Obviously that's important, but between the alternative quality contract and costs, there are a whole lot of other intervening factors such as physician practices, frontline physicians, group practices . . . all these factors in the macro environment. So if that project only looked at the quantitative aspects of the program, the study really wouldn't tell you anything. The team was very strong quantitatively, but they said they couldn't do the qualitative part, so they recruited another colleague to work with them. And the integrated study was much stronger than it would have been if it were two studies separately.

—Anne Marie Audet, MD, MSc, Vice President
for the Delivery System Reform & Breakthrough
Opportunities, The Commonwealth Fund

Box 4.10 includes a checklist of questions that you can use to prepare information that will be beneficial for reviewers. Team members should consider whether there is additional relevant experience or expertise that may not be included in their standard biography. It is especially important to highlight relevant mixed methods skills in team members' biosketches, including participation in mixed methods projects in health sciences, teaching and invited presentations on mixed methods, and peer-reviewed empirical and methodological publications.

Box 4.10 Checklist for Optimizing the Presentation of Your Team

✓ Does your team (or members of your team) have a history of working together to write grants, conduct research, publish articles or carry out any other professional function?

✓ Have any members of your team worked on and/or published other mixed methods or multidisciplinary projects?

✓ Do(es) the leader(s) of the project have demonstrated experience in conducting mixed methods research? In managing interdisciplinary groups?

✓ Have any members of your team completed coursework or training related to mixed methods?

✓ Do any members of the team hold multiple positions or roles in different department or disciplines?

An ideal team is a well-balanced multidisciplinary group that has a history of working together on similar projects. In the absence of such a history, you can demonstrate the team's strengths through the complementary experiences of individual members. For example, indicate whether members of your team have worked effectively on other interdisciplinary teams, citing an example such as a coauthored publication, participation on a scientific panel, coteaching, or other form of collaboration. Describing prior accomplishments can indicate to reviewers that the team members have the ability to work effectively in a diverse team.

It is also useful to present the institutional environment as conducive to mixed methods research. There are a number of indicators of a supportive research environment. They include faculty who are independent investigators with extramural funding in mixed methods research, established and ad hoc forums for interdisciplinary collaboration across departments and schools, formal and informal curricula on mixed methods, and institutionally supported workshops and training opportunities in mixed methods research. Examples of these kinds of activities can be briefly summarized to demonstrate the organization's track record and capacity for successful interdisciplinary mixed methods research.

Cover Letter

Be careful not to underestimate the importance of the application's cover letter. This is your chance to make key points to influence how your proposal will be managed and reviewed. Even when the cover letter is optional, we recommend that you include one. For NIH grants, the cover letter may be the only part of the proposal that the NIH staff reads when they are assigning reviewers for your proposal. As described in Box 4.11, highlighting the mixed methods design of your study in the cover letter is one way to encourage the funder to seek out reviewers with expertise in and knowledge of mixed methods designs, which can lead to a better-informed review.

Box 4.11   Highlighting Mixed Methods Design in a Cover Letter

The Scientific Review Officers at NIH have huge databases of reviewers and their expertise, and they try to invite reviewers with expertise to match the application. But often it happens that they may focus on getting disease experts rather than focus on the actual methods that are being used. I would recommend that applicants put something in their cover letter to try to tip them off that this study is using mixed methods . . . and would require that expertise in review. You can even say in your cover letter which study section your application would be most appropriately assigned, so if it's going to a standing committee, you can look online and see the roster of who's on that committee and their area of expertise.

—Helen Meissner, ScM, PhD, Director,
Tobacco Regulatory Science Program and
Former Senior Advisor in the Office of Behavioral
and Social Sciences Research (OBSSR),
National Institutes of Health (NIH)

Think Like a Reviewer

The final step of the writing process is to review your work—and to have it reviewed by colleagues. Leave as much time as possible to address feedback and make revisions. Try to think like a reviewer and critically assess proposals based on the specific review criteria of the funder. Table 4.3 includes a list of the criteria that are used by reviewers of NIH proposals (although these are for NIH, they are broadly applicable to most funders). In the right-hand column are suggested strategies for how to best meet these criteria when proposing a mixed methods study.

One of the best ways to learn to think like a reviewer is to gain the experience of conducting scientific reviews. Reviewing grant proposals written by

Table 4.3 Review Criteria and Strategies for Satisfying Them

Criterion	Strategies for Satisfying the Criterion in Mixed Methods Proposals
Significance	Make a convincing case that the problem is relevant and that the work will improve knowledge or practice.
	Explain why the problem will be best studied through mixed methods research.
Investigators	Include evidence of the skills of each investigator to conduct all proposed methods (prior publications and/or grants related to proposed qualitative, quantitative, and mixed methods).
	Demonstrate that the project leadership is committed to mixed methods research (address each component sufficiently and consistently throughout the application; include references to current, relevant literature on mixed methods; and describe professional development or training of investigators in mixed methods).
	Describe the approach to collaboration (frequency of meetings and management of differences between leaders of different components).
Innovation	Explain how the use of mixed methods provides insights not possible with a single method.
	Describe how a combination of methods or the way in which they are integrative is innovative.

(Continued)

Table 4.3   (Continued)

Criterion	Strategies for Satisfying the Criterion in Mixed Methods Proposals
Approach	Describe the philosophy or theory informing the research and the ways this philosophy or theory shapes the investigation.
	Justify why mixed methods research is needed to address the study aims and what value is added by using this approach compared to alternative designs.
	Provide a clear description of the full study design, including where integration occurs, using a comprehensive figure or matrix.
	Describe the integration of methods, including the timing, techniques, and responsibilities for integration.
	Ensure alignment between the design and the study aims.
	Adhere to standards of rigor for quantitative and qualitative data collection and analysis and provide appropriate citations.
	Plan for the use of appropriate computer software for each analytical component (or provide a convincing rationale for why this is not planned).
	Provide a feasible budget and time frame that fully accounts for data integration needs.
Environment	Provide evidence that the associated institutions support mixed methods research (forums for multidisciplinary collaborations, training in mixed methods, or other faculty with funding for mixed methods research).

SOURCE: Adapted from Creswell et al. (2011).

others—either as a formal reviewer or as a favor to colleagues—can train your eyes to recognize weaknesses and discrepancies as well as strengths in design and presentation. These insights can help improve your own writing. Consider creating informal peer review groups or research-in-progress venues focused on mixed methods applications at your institution. Finally, serving as a well-informed reviewer of mixed methods proposals can also help to elevate the quality of mixed methods research in general and move the field forward in the health sciences. As described in Box 4.12, funding agencies may not always be able to recruit highly qualified reviewers for mixed methods proposals. One consequence of the lack of informed reviewers is that the quality of research that is approved for funding is variable, consequently some poor quality work gets funded while some high-quality proposals are rejected.

Box 4.12 Being a Good Citizen in Research: Participating in Peer Review

The reviewers are scientists who are selected for their expertise in the field. At NIH, program officials can sit in on reviews but are not allowed to speak up. When applicants complain about the reviews, they should understand that it's really their peers that are critiquing them . . . .A lot of times it isn't that [NIH] didn't try to get people with the appropriate expertise, it's that people say no. They're not willing to take the time to be a peer reviewer. So if you are asked to serve on a peer-review committee, do it. It's kind of your civic duty as a researcher to do that because the system is only as good as you make it. And oftentimes review officers have trouble getting people with the expertise they need because scientists just aren't making themselves available.

—Helen Meissner, ScM, PhD, Director,
Tobacco Regulatory Science Program
and Former Senior Advisor in the Office
of Behavioral and Social Sciences Research (OBSSR),
National Institutes of Health (NIH)

Summary and Key Points

- Before you begin writing your proposal, explore whether your targeted institutions and agencies have a history of support for mixed methods research. Contact staff from that institution or agency to present your ideas and get feedback on the appropriateness of your design to meet the institutions needs.
- Analyses of NIH funding trends indicate that the use of mixed methods in competitively funded grants is becoming increasingly common. This trend is important to many U.S.-based health researchers since the NIH is a major funder of health research.
- Your grant review committee is likely to be as diverse as your team, topic, and methods. Aim to reduce jargon, define terms, and use citations to reduce confusion and criticism from reviewers who may not be familiar with particular methods in your study.
- Be vigilant about ensuring alignment across all sections of the application.

Review Questions and Exercises

1. Think about a research topic that might be a good fit for a mixed methods approach. Conduct a targeted search to identify potential funders. Discuss why you think the funding institution you selected is appropriate.

2. Develop a title for the mixed methods study that you would like to propose. What factors are important in creating a title that will help your proposal stand out?

3. Create a visual diagram (e.g., a table) that would illustrate how you would plan to align the components in a proposal.

4. Refer to Table 4.2 and indicate the strategy, objective, sample, and type of analytic approach for the study you propose.

5. In a group, imagine you are a research team developing a proposal. Discuss how you might represent your research team composition. Refer back to Box 4.10 to be sure you use strategies for optimizing the presentation of your team.

References

Barbour, R. S. (1999). The case for combining qualitative and quantitative approaches in health services research. *Journal of Health Services Research and Policy, 4*(1), 39–43.

Benning, A., Ghaleb, M., Suokas, A., Dixon-Woods, M., Dawson, J., Barber, N., . . . Lilford, R. (2011). Large scale organisational intervention to improve patient safety in four UK hospitals: Mixed method evaluation. *BMJ, 342,* d195. doi: 10.1136/bmj.d195

Bernardi, L. (2007). Social influences on fertility: A comparative mixed methods study in Eastern and Western Germany. *Journal of Mixed Methods Research, 1*(1), 23–47.

Crabtree, B. F., Chase, S. M., Wise, C. G., Schiff, G. D., Schmidt, L. A., Goyzueta, J. R., . . . Jaen, C. R. (2011). Evaluation of patient centered medical home practice transformation initiatives. *Medical Care, 49*(1), 10–16. doi: 10.1097/MLR.0b013e 3181f80766

Creswell, J. W., Klassen, A. C., Plano Clark, V. L., & Smith, K. C. for the Office of Behavioral and Social Sciences Research. (2011). *Best practices for mixed methods research in the health sciences.* Bethesda, MD: National Institutes of Health. Retrieved from http://obssr.od.nih.gov/mixed_methods_research

Creswell, J. W., & Plano Clark, V. L. (2011). *Designing and conducting mixed methods research* (2nd ed.). Thousand Oaks, CA: Sage.

Foundation Center. (n.d.). *Strengthening the social sector by advancing knowledge and philanthropy.* Retrieved February 27, 2014, from http://www.foundationcenter.org

Goodkind, J. R. (2013). *Addressing social determinants to reduce refugee mental health disparities* (1R01MD007712–01). Retrieved October 21, 2013, from http://projectreporter.nih.gov/project_info_description.cfm?aid=8719694

Greenhalgh, T., Stramer, K., Bratan, T., Byrne, E., Russell, J., & Potts, H. W. (2010). Adoption and non-adoption of a shared electronic summary record in England: A mixed-method case study. *BMJ, 340,* c3111. doi: 10.1136/bmj.c3111

Harris, D. M., Westfall, J. M., Fernald, D. H., Duclos, C. W., West, D. R., Niebauer, L., . . . Main, D. S. (2005). Mixed method analysis for medical error event reports: A report from the ASIPS Collaborative. In K. Henrikson, J. B. Battles, E. S. Marks, & D. I. Lewin (Eds.), *Advances in patient safety: From research to implementation (Volume 2: Concepts and methodology).* Rockville, MD: Agency for Healthcare Research and Quality.

Hocking, M. C., Hobbie, W. L., Deatrick, J. A., Lucas, M. S., Szabo, M. M., Volpe, E. M., & Barakat, L. P. (2011). Neurocognitive and family functioning and quality of life among young adult survivors of childhood brain tumors. *Clinical Neuropathology, 25*(6), 942–962. doi: 10.1080/13854046.2011.580284

Karasz, A. (2008). The development of valid subtypes for depression in primary care settings: A preliminary study using an explanatory model approach. *Journal of Nervous and Mental Disease, 196*(4), 289–296. doi: 10.1097/NMD.0b013e31816a496e

McCreary, L. L., Park, C. G., Gomez, L., Peterson, S., Pino, D., & McElmurry, B. J. (2012). A mixed-methods evaluation of school-based active living programs. *American Journal of Preventive Medicine, 43*(5 Suppl. 4), S395–398. doi: 10.1016/j.amepre.2012.06.030

National Institute of Allergy and Infectious Diseases. (n.d.). *All about grants: Tutorials and samples.* Retrieved February 27, 2014, from http://www.niaid.nih.gov/researchfunding/grant/pages/aag.aspx

Niccolai, L. M. (2012). *Disparities in HPV vaccine completion: Identifying and quantifying the barriers* (1R21CA163160–01A1). Retrieved October 21, 2013, from http://projectreporter.nih.gov/project_info_details.cfm?aid=8411362

Norman, W. V., Soon, J. A., Maughn, N., & Dressler, J. (2013). Barriers to rural induced abortion services in Canada: Findings of the British Columbia Abortion Providers Survey (BCAPS). *PLoS One, 8*(6), e67023. doi: 10.1371/journal.pone.0067023

Nunez-Smith, M. (2010). *Validating the Patient-Reported Experiences of Discrimination in Care Tool (PREDICT)* (5R01CA169103–02). Retrieved March 2, 2014, from http://projectreporter.nih.gov/project_info_description.cfm?aid=8517055&icde=19494454&ddparam=&ddvalue=&ddsub=&cr=1&csb=default&cs=ASC

Plano Clark, V. L. (2010). The adoption and practice of mixed methods: U.S. trends in federally funded health-related research. *Qualitative Inquiry, 16*(6), 428–440.

Pollini, R. A. (2011). *OTC syringe sales to prevent HIV in underserved areas of inland California* (1R01DA035098–01). Retrieved October 21, 2013, from http://projectreporter.nih.gov/project_info_description.cfm?aid=8466903&icde=18074495&d dparam=&ddvalue=&ddsub=&cr=2&csb=default&cs=ASC

Rinne, T., & Fairweather, J. (2012). A mixed methods approach: Using cultural modeling and consensus analysis to better understand New Zealand's international innovation performance. *Journal of Mixed Methods Research, 6*(3), 166–183.

Spertus, J. (2012). *Developing and testing a personalized, evidence-based, shared decision-making tool for stent selection in PCI.* Manuscript in preparation. Retrieved April 18, 2014, from http://www.pcori.org/pfaawards/developing-and-testing-a-personalized-evidence-based-shared-decision-making-tool-for-stent-selection-in-pci

Tol, W. A., Komproe, I. H., Jordans, M. J., Susanty, D., & de Jong, J. T. (2011). Developing a function impairment measure for children affected by political violence: A mixed methods approach in Indonesia. *International Journal for Quality in Health Care, 23*(4), 375–383. doi: 10.1093/intqhc/mzr032

⁂ FIVE ⁂

EXAMPLES OF FUNDED GRANT APPLICATIONS USING MIXED METHODS

Information you will find in this chapter: This chapter presents examples of funded grant applications using mixed methods, including original grant material and excerpts from interviews with principal investigators who have successfully obtained funding from the National Institutes of Health (NIH) for mixed methods research. We feature an example from each of three NIH funding mechanisms that commonly support health sciences research (R21, R01, K23). Taken directly from the funded NIH grant applications, each example includes the application's specific aims and a summary of key elements of the research strategy. The chapter ends with a list of suggestions to consider when developing your mixed methods grant proposal, based on interviews with the researchers featured in these examples.

Key features in this chapter:

- Detailed examples of three funded mixed methods NIH grant applications
- Interviews with NIH-funded mixed methods principal investigators
- Overall study flow templates for three common mixed methods designs
- Funding strategy template

REAL-WORLD EXAMPLES OF NATIONAL
INSTITUTES OF HEALTH GRANT APPLICATIONS

In order to provide readers with a real-world window into the grant writing experience, we interviewed three mixed methods researchers who have successfully obtained NIH funding and reviewed their complete grant applications. Using the NIH Research Portfolio Online Reporting Tools (RePORTER) Database (a public database of all NIH-supported research projects and programs), we searched for funded mixed methods studies across multiple funding programs across all institutes and targeted researchers from diverse clinical disciplines. For each of the three featured grant awards, we present a brief overview of the funding mechanism, a description of the funded project, and excerpts from interviews with the principal investigators who generously agreed to share their work. From the submitted grant applications, we share specific aims as they are not publicly available through NIH RePORTER. Commentaries from their interviews provide useful and practical insights into the process of getting mixed methods research proposals successfully reviewed and funded.

We profile NIH-funded projects because the NIH is the largest funder of biomedical research in the United States; however, many of the elements of these examples extrapolate to other funding settings across the globe. In general, there are three categories of funding for mixed methods projects in the NIH programs. Major research grants, such as the NIH R01 mechanism, provide multiyear project support and the budgets can typically cover costs associated with both components of a mixed methods project. Small research grants, such as the NIH R21 mechanism, provide limited financial resources but can be critical at specific junctures along the trajectory of your mixed methods work. Distinct from these project-driven funding opportunities, you can also explore mechanisms that primarily support the researcher's development, such as career development awards (CDAs) that may be available for early or mid-career researchers. These awards provide protected time for investigators to develop their methodological skills in addition to conducting a specific research project. In the next section, we provide a brief overview of each of these categories of funding as an introduction to each example in the next section. There are many excellent resources available for those interested in more detailed information about grant writing (see, for example, National Institute of Allergy and Infectious Diseases [NIAID; 2012] or http://www.foundationcenter.org).

Major Research Funding

Most mixed methods researchers will seek research funding at some point in their careers. In the United States, the NIH supports the vast majority (85%) of all university-based health research. Most of this funding is awarded through the R01 grant mechanism, the oldest and most common funding opportunity announcement (FOA) by the NIH. An investigator-initiated R01 application can be prepared in response to program announcements that allow for research in any specific area, or in broadly defined areas within institutes. Institutes can also solicit research through a request for applications (RFAs), which is meant to stimulate research in the areas of highest priority to the institute by allocating funding for those topic areas at the beginning of each fiscal year (FY). Because RFAs are usually reviewed by a single panel assembled specifically for that RFA, applicants do not have the option of requesting a particular study section for review. A notable advantage of responding to an RFA is that, if the application is not successful, you can submit the same project again as a new investigator-initiated application. R01 awards do not have a dollar cap, so the budget must be proposed and justified by the applicant. They are generally awarded for roughly one to five years and can be renewed through a competitive application process. In general, R01s are the best option if you already have preliminary data to demonstrate the importance of the research question and feasibility of the proposed study. We recommend that this level of major support—both time and money—is needed in order to complete a full mixed methods project, disseminate results, and begin writing the next grant application with enough time to reduce the chance of having a funding lapse. In general, because the NIH is committed to developing new investigators as the innovators of the future, and to supporting their early transition to independence, new investigators have an advantage when applying for their first R01 over established researchers.

It is possible to identify funders that may be interested in your mixed methods project by doing some background work to understand their funding priorities.

All institutes at NIH have a transparent and ongoing process to define their funding priorities, which is described in publicly available documents. By reviewing these documents, you

◀ See Chapter 4: Writing a Scientifically Sound and Compelling Grant Proposal for a Mixed Methods Study for a list of funders with a history of funding mixed methods and information about contacting funding program officials before applying.

can get a sense of the main areas of interest that may be developed into FOAs. The process of developing FOAs is roughly two years in duration, allowing you an opportunity to draft ideas in advance of any official announcement. While not all concepts become institute initiatives, they reflect the institute's interests and are good topics to consider for investigator-initiated applications. Similar to this process at the NIH, most funding agencies release an annual report referencing their funding priorities that can provide you with insights into their interests.

With this brief overview of the R01 as background, we now present an example of a mixed methods study that was funded through an institute-specific program announcement for an R01. Dr. Jennifer Elston Lafata is a professor in the Department of Social and Behavioral Health, School of Medicine, Virginia Commonwealth University (VCU) and senior research scientist for the Henry Ford Health System (HFHS). She and her team responded to a program announcement titled "Colorectal Cancer Screening in Primary Care Practice" and the FOA stated objective was "to encourage health services, social and behavioral, and outcomes researchers to develop innovative research projects to increase the knowledge base for enhanced translation of effective colorectal cancer screening techniques into community practice." The overall goal of Dr. Elston Lafata's proposed project was to understand "how the patient-physician communication process and content contribute to adherence to physician recommendations for CRC screening use." Dr. Elston Lafata and her team proposed a sequential exploratory mixed methods design to accomplish this objective. The initial qualitative component (Aim 1) included content analysis of field notes from direct observation and transcripts of audio-recorded physician–patient conversations about colorectal cancer (CRC) screening. They planned to use the qualitative data to develop a quantitative measure to characterize elements of shared decision making (Aim 1) and then to correlate the score derived using that measure of whether or not study participants had a CRC screening as indicated within the 12-month post-visit period per administrative data (Aim 2). They also included a third distinct aim to evaluate whether concordances between patient preferences and care received were associated with subsequent use of CRC screening. Their application was reviewed by a special emphasis panel (an ad hoc review panel assembled exclusively for a particular funding opportunity) (ZCA1-SRB-4) and awarded for a four-year study period and a total budget of approximately $1.7 million dollars. The project is described in Box 5.1.

Box 5.1   Example of a Funded Mixed Methods National Institutes of Health Investigator-Initiated R01 Award

Title: Physician Recommendation and Colorectal Cancer Screening

Program announcement number: PAR-04–036

Institute: National Cancer Institute (NCI)

Project number: 1R01CA112379–01A1

Principal investigator: Jennifer Elston Lafata, PhD

Specific Aims

Studies addressing the factors associated with CRC screening repeatedly highlight the importance of physician recommendation in the receipt of care. Data from our own efforts and those of others indicate that physicians discuss cancer screening differently. The contributions patients make to these discussions as well as the dynamics of the discussions also vary. Furthermore, there is growing evidence that many patients do not adhere to physician recommendations for CRC screening. The U.S. Preventive Services Task Force (USPSTF), while not endorsing a specific style of physician–patient interaction, recently advocated for the use of shared decision making when making preventive service recommendations to individual patients. As part of this recommendation, they outline five elements of conversation content that should be discussed when a physician is recommending screening. Yet, as pointed out by the task force and others, although the use of a shared decision-making process and the five content elements can be recommended on a number of ethical and other grounds—whether their use leads to improved adherence, or ultimately improved health—remains debated. A unique opportunity therefore exists to understand how the physician–patient communication process and content contribute to adherence to physician recommendations for CRC screening use. We propose to use audio recording of physician–patient interactions together with patient surveys and the

(Continued)

(Continued)

comprehensive automated data systems afforded by the Henry Ford Health System (HFHS), a large integrated delivery system serving Detroit and its surrounding suburbs, to address the following specific aims and hypotheses:

Aim 1: To characterize the frequency, process, and content of CRC screening discussions in primary care. The USPSTF "5 As" (assess, advise, agree, assist, and arrange) and elements of shared decision making will be used as an initial guiding framework for this assessment.

Aim 2: To determine the characteristics of the physician–patient CRC screening communication process and content, which enhance a patient's adherence to physician recommended CRC screening. Of particular interest is the testing of the following hypotheses:

> *Hypothesis 2.1:* Screening use is associated with the amount or type of information ("advice" regarding risks and benefits) the physician provides during the discussion.
>
> *Hypothesis 2.2:* Discussions that offer the patient a choice from among multiple screening modalities ("advice" regarding alternatives) are associated with more CRC screening use.
>
> *Hypothesis 2.3:* Discussions that solicit and discuss patient's preferences ("agree") are associated with more CRC screening use.
>
> *Hypothesis 2.4:* Discussions that include a plan for result follow-up ("arrange") are associated with more CRC screening use.
>
> *Hypothesis 2.5:* Discussions that are more reflective of a shared decision-making process are more likely to result in CRC screening use.

Aim 3: To use survey-derived measures of patient preferences to determine how adherence to physician recommendations for CRC screening is affected by the concordance between patient preferences and the CRC screening recommendation received.

Hypothesis 3.1: Physician–patient interactions that are consistent with patient preferences for shared decision making result in increased CRC screening use.

Hypothesis 3.2: Physician–patient interactions that are consistent with patient preferences for information provision result in increased CRC screening use.

Hypothesis 3.3: A physician recommendation for a screening modality, which is consistent with patient preferences for test attributes (e.g., frequency of testing, discomfort, possible complications), is associated with more CRC screening use.

Results from these efforts will allow us to discern with which patients physicians have CRC screening discussions as well as how patients and physicians discuss CRC screening in primary care. By linking detail on these CRC screening discussions derived from audio recordings of physician–patient interactions with patient preference information from surveys and CRC screening utilization from claims and laboratory data bases, we will be in the novel position of being able to determine what aspects of the discussions result in CRC screening use for what types of patients. In particular, the racial diversity of the HFHS-insured patient population combined with the racial and gender diversity of the HFHS physician population will enable explorations into the role of race and gender as well as race and gender concordance in the translation of physician–patient discussions into CRC screening use. By focusing on the details of the patient–physician communication process as the vehicle for CRC screening decision making, our findings will allow us to identify previously unexplored elements in the CRC screening process and enable the grounding of the future interventions in an in-depth understanding of CRC screening decision making in the real world of primary care.

We asked Dr. Elston Lafata to reflect on her experience with developing this grant application, taking us through the process from start to finish. She began with describing how she identified a potential funding opportunity through a colleague and went on to share challenges and successes in the preparation and review of her application. We present excerpts from our conversation here:

Q: How did you identify a funding agency and mechanism for the project? Did you already have a project idea in mind, or did you develop your ideas after seeing the FOA?

A: I have had a diversity of funding sources throughout my career, and I knew it was time to go for an R01. I did not necessarily set out to do a mixed methods project. I was not a qualitative researcher at all. I had received some internal pilot monies to conduct a mailed patient survey to understand how patients perceived physician communication about CRC screening and whether or not those patient-reported communication processes were associated with CRC screening use. I didn't imagine in a million years—when we got the pilot monies—that we would end up conducting a study that used audio recordings of physician office visits. It was after we got the results of the survey that we knew we had to do more to figure out how the conversation about CRC screening was going between patients and their physicians. At that point, I identified collaborators who had done observational research in primary care settings, and one of them forwarded this program announcement to me. It seemed perfect for us. We submitted this application twice, and it was funded on resubmission.

Q: What was your experience with the reviewers? Were there any concerns raised about the proposed methods?

A: I leaned heavily on presenting preliminary data—both to make the case for why this was the methodological approach that was needed to answer our questions as well as to show evidence of feasibility and that we had the know-how to carry out this project. Thankfully, we—as a team—could show our experience in using automated data and in analyzing audio recordings of office visits. And I think that helped. After our first submission, one early question was why the need for the Case Western team, which was where all of the experience with content analysis of audio data was. But we had equal concerns raised about feasibility for the collection of the qualitative and quantitative data. My gut instinct is that this study was not reviewed by people who would consider themselves methodologists; they probably had expertise in cancer screening. This maybe took some methodological critique out of the process. But we made a seamless connection between the qualitative and quantitative pieces in this application. In some other mixed methods applications we've put in since this one, you can see the expertise—and biases—of the reviewers coming through. You get one person saying, "I don't see the need for the qualitative piece" and another person saying, "I don't see the need for the quantitative piece." In these subsequent applications, we have sometimes been forced to divide the quantitative and the qualitative segments, but that doesn't work well. In the CRC screening study, the integration of the qualitative and quantitative approaches was really seamless.

Q: What advice would you offer to researchers who are considering applying for funding to support mixed methods health sciences research?

A: Make sure team experience and skill match the methods you're proposing. Make sure you write the application in a way that a reviewer can't pick it apart and say there is a disconnect between the qualitative and quantitative components. That link has to be explicit and seamless. Your preliminary data needs to point to the need for mixed methods and to the ability of your team to get the job done well. Most importantly, your approach needs to match the problem.

Small Research Grants

If you do not have the necessary preliminary data to submit an application for a major grant, such as an R01, consider seeking a smaller award. For example, the NIH has two mechanisms within its exploratory–development research grant program (the R21 or R03). Although frequently viewed as perfect for a junior investigator's first NIH application, these two-year awards are primarily intended for established principal investigators who want to conduct pilot or feasibility research. Unlike the CDAs (described later in the chapter), they are not intended to help establish a principal investigator's research career and the NIH does not view these mechanisms as paths to independent investigator status. The R03 mechanism grants up to $50,000 a year in direct costs but is often insufficient as a sole source of support to complete a project and may actually hinder future R01 success, because investigators may not have adequate resources to complete their aims and generate strong preliminary data for the R01. Because the R03 is "the right mechanism" for very few investigators, here we focus on the R21.

The R21 is intended to support investigators as they introduce new ideas, models, tools, and technologies that have the potential to move their field forward considerably. They are often used by investigators as a "mini-R01" mechanism, when the project is smaller in scope than an R01 but essentially contains the same elements as an R01. R21s are also viewed as one approach to collect preliminary data prior to applying to an R01. The latter rationale is sometimes the most difficult to execute as the majority of successful R21 applications are already based on some preliminary data. Obtaining a small nonfederal project grant or an institutional award to collect foundational data may position you well in applying for an R21.

There are some potential limitations with this mechanism, particularly when used to support both components of a mixed methods project. First, the R21 research strategy section is limited to 6 pages, in contrast to the maximum of 12 pages allowed for R01s; these space constraints can pose a challenge when trying to adequately describe a complex mixed methods project. Second, both the allowable grant period (two years, nonrenewable) and budget (maximum of $275,000 in annual direct costs) are much more limited than what is permitted for an R01 application, possibly making it difficult to accomplish the aims of multiple study components, especially when using a sequential design. Also, the relatively limited funding in an R21 can mean that the support ends before you have secured an R01 or other gap funding (and before you complete your stated aims). Third, you may put yourself at risk for missing the new or early investigator eligibility window if you do not pay attention to the timing of the applications. Finally, at some institutes, the success rate for R01 applications is actually higher than for R21s. Consider these potential limitations as you decide on the best mechanism for your application. Nevertheless, the R21 can be the perfect mechanism for your mixed methods project, particularly if you are seeking funding for only one component or if the time and budgetary needs are otherwise limited in scope.

Dr. Miriam Boeri, associate professor of sociology and criminal justice at Kennesaw State University when the grant was submitted, identified the R21 program as appropriate for her mixed methods project because she sought to develop new models (e.g., mathematical models of drug use trajectories) that could benefit the field if the project were successful. The overall objective of the application was to provide insights into the life course of older drug users and develop trajectory models that could be used in future research on prevention, intervention, and treatment for drug use and abuse in this population. Dr. Boeri and her team proposed a variation of a convergent embedded design (e.g., both qualitative and quantitative methods were embedded together within a larger procedure). The larger procedure described in the application was the completion of the life roles and drug history (LRDH) matrix. In one session, participants would complete a researcher-administered quantitative questionnaire on drug history and participate in an in-depth qualitative interview to further explore life histories. Integrated data from both components would then be used to create dynamic Bayesian networks (DBNs), a new modeling framework for assessing variables associated with drug use over time. The project is described in Box 5.2.

Box 5.2   Example of a Funded Mixed Methods National Institutes of Health Investigator-Initiated R21 Award

Title: Older Drug Users: A Life Course Study of Turning Points in Drug Use and Injection

Program announcement number: PA-06–181

Institute: National Institute on Drug Abuse (NIDA)

Project number: 1R21DA025298–01A1

Principal investigator: Miriam Boeri, PhD

Specific Aims

The goal of this exploratory R21 proposal is twofold: to gain a better understanding of illicit drug use among older adults and to use this knowledge to build mathematical models of diverse drug use trajectories and turning points in use and risk behaviors over the life course. In this mixed methods study we use quantitative methods to identify turning points in drug use and risk behaviors, qualitative methods to explore these turning points more thoroughly, and mathematical analysis to build models depicting drug trajectories. These innovative models can be tested and further developed using existing large-sample data sets. The insights from this study will inform treatment and interventions aimed at older drug users and lead to future large-scale studies aimed to further develop the models started here.

While the cohort of today's older adults has been studied extensively in drug research on adolescent and young adults, the same cohort is understudied as older drug users. Life histories of older

(Continued)

(Continued)

adults provide retrospective data on the diversity of paths taken throughout the life course and changes in drug histories over time. Older users have a long history of drug use, cessation, and relapse. They also have experienced historical events that affect drug use behaviors, such as wars, recessions, and policy changes. The immediate objective of this study is to learn more regarding drug use among current older adults, and the long-term objective is to develop models that lead to a larger research grant. The R21 mechanism is used because this study is exploratory and developmental in scope.

First, this study explores drug use among an older population of drug users since research shows they are creating overwhelming demand for health services. National trend data show that adults who are 45 and older comprise the fastest growing age group of drug users as well as the largest population of new drug treatment admissions and new AIDS cases. The recent "graying of the AIDS epidemic" is a public health concern and calls for a greater focus on the older adult population of drug users and their risk behaviors. We know that transmission of HIV/AIDS is highly correlated with drug use through sexual behaviors and routes of administration. In this study we collect life history data from older drug users to examine risk behaviors based on the literature. The lives of older adult drug users allow an in-depth exploration of how these known risk factors are influenced by social roles and social context over the life course as well as provide the data needed to effectively discover turning points in the drug trajectory.

Second, this study is unique and innovative in its application of new mathematical techniques to build models that provide a greater understanding of drug trajectories that lead to health-related risk behaviors. We aim to provide a mathematical analysis of the evolution of the variables and the relations between them. The relationships expressed in the models will include the static relations between the variables, the evolution through time of the variables, and the evolution through time of the relations between the variables, as explained next. The mathematical models we build have the potential to lead to the development of new hypotheses for further research and eventually to prediction models that can be used in treatment by identifying significant turning points throughout the drug career. By applying what we learn from the lives of older drug users in this sample, the findings will inform research and health initiatives for older as well as younger users.

The community-based sample will consist of active users ($n = 50$) and former users ($n = 50$) of heroin, cocaine, and methamphetamine, ages 45 and older. The inclusion of former users allows for an investigation of life events and social circumstances surrounding cessation. Data are collected through a quantitative matrix on drug history and social roles and a qualitative in-depth interview. The study site is the metropolitan statistical area (MSA) of Atlanta that includes urban, suburban, and rural areas. We propose three specific aims:

Aim 1: To identify turning points in the onset, continuation, and cessation of drug use throughout the life course of a sample of older users—specifically how social roles, race, gender, age, social contexts, policies, and historical events influence turning points in drug use and drug-related HIV risk behaviors.

Aim 2: To thoroughly explore these turning points and transitions over the life course, specifically changes in drug availability, risk behaviors, routes of administration, social roles, networks, support, policies, settings, and geographic locations, embedded in a life course perspective.

Aim 3: To build dynamic Bayesian networks (DBNs) that best model the static and dynamic aspects found in our quantitative and qualitative data. In so doing, we are able to identify not only statistical relationships between the variables but also the influence and progression of these through time.

Together, these aims provide needed in-depth details on the lives of older drug users as well as trajectory models that can be used to target treatment strategies on specific turning points in drug use trajectories. The information and models provided by this study can be used in future research to develop better prevention, intervention, and treatment programs by focusing on turning points in drug careers. We propose that by identifying specific turning points in the diverse trajectories of older users we also provide more focused aims in future research on policy and services for all drug users.

We spoke with Dr. Boeri about her decision to apply for an R21 and her approach to preparing for submission a grant application using mixed methods. She described several strategies that she felt contributed to her success in obtaining funding. We include selected reflections from our conversation:

Q: How did you identify a funding agency and mechanism for the project? Did you already have a project idea in mind, or did you develop your ideas after seeing the FOA?

A: I knew the priority areas of the institute and the R21 were perfect for what we were doing. My mentor pointed me in that direction. We didn't have any papers written yet, and we knew we needed that before we could apply for an R01. Our primary reason for seeking the R21 support was to introduce this new way of looking at drug use using math and mathematical models. But we also saw it as an opportunity to disseminate some of our work and establish ourselves more before writing an R01.

Q: What was your communication with program staff before and during the application process?

A: Yes, I spoke with one program officer. It was very helpful. I submitted this application twice, and I spoke with him before the second submission. The first submission was not mixed methods. It was all qualitative, and that was the major problem. He advised that adding a quantitative component would help it go further. So that's when I added a mathematician to the team. And the program officer was right because we ultimately developed a stronger application and got funded. So it really was that conversation with the program officer that turned this project into a mixed methods application.

Q: Did you request a particular study section or specify reviewers?

A: I did request a particular study section. I typically do, but it's not always given to the study section I request. For this project, I wanted more people who knew about qualitative research so that is how I identified the study section. During the second review, the comments were really focused on questions about my hypothesis and seemed like they weren't familiar with qualitative research and not needing a hypothesis in that setting. That is why I asked for a specific study section—one that I saw had reviewers with qualitative expertise. That is going to be a big problem with mixed methods, quite frankly. It will be hard to know who has what expertise without asking around. But I still think you should do research on who is on the group. Even with my research, I only found two or three members on the study section with qualitative experience—not that many when you consider there are 20 to 30 members on a study section.

Q: What tools or strategies did you use to communicate the details of the research design to reviewers?

A: I included a completed LRDH matrix for an example participant, which saved a lot of space so I didn't need sentences. Looking at the application now, I would actually include many more graphics. I use a program called Creately, which produces beautiful flowcharts, but those take up room too. And I have to think about whether to include those in an appendix or in the actual application.

Q: What were the challenges you faced unique to preparing a mixed methods grant application for NIH review?

A: Not having as much space as an R01 made it difficult to describe the project. The mathematician needed so much room to write his part, and I was critiqued for not including as much information on background on the baby boomers. I had to cut out about 50% of the background to include more on the qualitative approach. I ended up including lots of references for the methods, and reviewers don't really like that—it was raised in the reviewer summary statement—but there just isn't enough room. Finding someone with whom I could write who understands qualitative methods was another challenge. Finding a statistician who understands and respects qualitative methods can be hard. I worked with a mathematician who was very open to innovative methods, and that was easy. Talking across the disciplines is hard. You have to show the reviewers your team can do that well.

Q: What was your experience with the reviewers? Were there any concerns raised about the proposed methods?

A: They liked the team we proposed. They commented on its multidisciplinary nature. One of the main challenges was using retrospective data collection and the big problem with recall. Two reviewers thought it was innovative and one did not. One reviewer actually went and read my papers and raised that in the review. That was impressive! And there were lots of positive comments too. Well, we were funded so I guess it was more positive than not. One reviewer specifically asked what we would do if the quantitative and qualitative data disagreed, so that is an important area to address in the application.

Q: How have you modified your project since being funded? Has NIH made any requests or modifications?

A: We were funded through the American Recovery and Reinvestment Act (ARRA), an economic stimulus bill enacted by the U.S. Congress, so that had to be a shovel-ready project. We had to do a few things specific to that mechanism. But we made a lot of changes over the course of resubmitting. It was a process of several years to get funding, and we wouldn't have gotten funded without the ARRA. We were funded at the last minute. But the technology changed over time, and we moved from planning to do data collection by hand to using computer programs. We added several additional variables. We added memory cues and timelines. We found it best when collecting life history data—a less expensive approach than prospective data sets—that we used two people to do the interviewing. So the process of resubmitting actually improved our application and science.

Q: What advice would you offer to researchers who are considering applying for funding to support mixed methods health sciences research?

A: There are so many ways of doing mixed methods research, so it's hard to give advice. I think each study section should have some members who understand mixed methods or who have both quantitative and qualitative expertise. I was in a non-NIH review one time and the person who was running the review specifically said they picked me because I was a qualitative researcher. They sent me the qualitative applications, and I was the only qualitative researcher in the entire section of 20 people. So I commented on any proposal that had a qualitative component. For example, explaining that much of it is exploratory and that there isn't a need for a hypothesis. Reviewers have to be educated that everything can't fit in the space and need to think about space limits for mixed methods. Use every margin you can use; use the smallest font you can use. Writing succinctly is a great skill, and it takes a lot of practice to do that . . . which is why you need to start the proposal early so that you can read it and reread it and keep editing it all the time. Don't get discouraged by reviewer comments. They really are trying to help. Just everyone has their own way of doing research, and they want to see it done that way. We integrated the entire process though. You have to be sure to do that. There aren't two separate studies but one integrated project.

Career Development Awards

The CDA is often the first grant application many postdoctoral fellows and junior faculty will submit. Distinct from other types of grant mechanisms, CDAs typically provide equal weight to the investigator's potential for future research independence and to a specific research question and methods. Evidence of institutional support is a key element of the application and should reflect both commitment to the candidate's professional development and demonstrate the resources necessary for proposal success are available and accessible. NIH offers several types of CDAs (also known as "K awards"); the Career Award Wizard is an NIH web-based tool to help you decide on the right CDA mechanism for your work and will connect you with a program officer for follow-up questions (NIH, n.d.). Some CDAs have a formal mentoring component, while others do not.

Junior researchers applying to NIH for a mentored CDA (several foundations and the Department of Veterans Affairs (VA) also have CDA-funding mechanisms for health sciences researchers) with an interest in mixed methods frequently apply for a K23. The K23, or Mentored Patient-Oriented Research Career Development Award, provides support for up to five years of supervised learning and research to clinically trained professionals committed to careers in patient-oriented research. There is a parent (cross-institute) K23 funding mechanism reissued annually and each participating NIH institute and center has different requirements and priority areas that define responsiveness. In addition, several institutes have K23 mechanisms targeted at specific diseases (e.g., muscular dystrophy research) or specific researchers (e.g., awards to promote diversity). The K awards require recipients to devote at least 75% of a full-time equivalent position to research and provide salary support up to around $100,000. The award typically provides $30,000 in funds to directly support the research project. Candidates sometimes simultaneously submit applications for additional research project support to NIH (e.g., R21 or R03) or other funding agencies. Importantly, K awards include support (time and money) for professional development, which enables the awardee to include faculty members and/or mentors to provide training and coaching in various methodologies, including mixed methods.

Dr. Jonathan Singer, assistant professor in residence at the Division of Pulmonary, Critical Care, Allergy, and Sleep Medicine in the Department of Medicine at the University of California at San Francisco, proposed a mixed methods CDA as a first step toward his long-term career goal of "improving

◄ See Chapter 2: Applications and Illustrations of Mixed Methods Health Sciences Research for a brief review of health sciences research paradigms well aligned with mixed methods approaches.

health-related quality of life (HRQL) in lung transplant recipients." As with all of the examples provided here, Dr. Singer's application fit within a patient-centered outcomes research (PCOR) paradigm.

He sought to investigate predictors of disability and HRQL among a cohort of lung transplant recipients over time. Using a convergent design, he proposed a quantitative component including a battery of health status instruments, a disability instrument, and measures of functional status. The qualitative component consisted of interviews with a subset of the cohort to explore the effect of psychosocial factors on HRQL. The analyses from both components would be integrated to identify a comprehensive set of predictors of disability and HRQL after lung transplantation. The project is described in Box 5.3.

Box 5.3   Example of a Funded Mixed Methods National Institutes of Health Career Development Award Application

Title: The Effects of Lung Transplant on Disability and Health-Related Quality of Life

Program announcement number: PA-11–194

Institute: National Heart, Lung, and Blood Institute (NHLBI)

Project number: 5K23HL111115

Principal investigator: Jonathan Singer, MD

Specific Aims

For patients suffering from end-stage lung disease, lung transplantation aims to extend survival and improve health-related quality of life (HRQL). While lung transplant can be lifesaving, posttransplant deficits in HRQL may limit the effectiveness of this intervention. Limited studies have shown that while HRQL scores improve after transplant, these scores remain below those of the general population.

HRQL research in lung transplant remains in its early phases, hindering our ability to address this key patient-oriented outcome. Studies focused on the mechanisms by which deficits in HRQL persist or emerge after lung transplant have generally examined single risk factors considered in isolation. Lung transplant and the medications necessary to preserve graft function, however, cause a constellation of morbidities, including myopathy, life-threatening infections, cancer, diabetes, osteoporosis, and chronic allograft rejection. Also, psychosocial factors related to being a transplant recipient affect HRQL. To date, studies have examined the impact of either isolated physiologic or psychosocial factors on HRQL but not both. Therefore, the *cumulative effect* of these factors on HRQL remains unknown but is likely profound. Further, in 2005, the system of organ allocation (lung allocation score [LAS]) was overhauled, dramatically increasing the medical acuity of patients undergoing lung transplant. Assessments of the impact of lung transplant on HRQL, a measure not considered in the LAS, have *not* been published since this overhaul. Thus, prior studies of HRQL may no longer be valid. To help fulfill the primary aims of lung transplant to improve both survival *and* HRQL requires a contemporary and comprehensive understanding of the determinants of lung transplant's impact on HRQL.

My long-term research goal is to improve HRQL in lung transplant recipients. Informing this goal is a conceptual model of disablement. In this model, limitations in *functioning and disability are precursors to and, ultimately, determinants of HRQL.* Thus, the overarching hypothesis underpinning this project is that extrapulmonary limitations in functioning as well as psychosocial factors are pivotal determinants of disability and, therefore, HRQL in lung transplant recipients. The objectives of this application are to (1) determine the effects of lung transplant on disability and HRQL in the era of the LAS and to (2) identify the risk factors affecting change in disability and HRQL over time in lung transplant recipients.

To achieve these objectives, a mixed methods analytic approach is proposed in which I will leverage ongoing efforts to address the aims below. In total, 105 subjects with end-stage lung disease will

(Continued)

(Continued)

be enrolled and prospectively followed after lung transplant. *Quantitative* measures of pulmonary and extrapulmonary functioning, comorbidities, disability, and HRQL will be assessed before transplant and longitudinally in repeated assessments up to three years post-transplant (Aims 1 and 2). Also, semistructured interviews will be conducted longitudinally in a subset of lung transplant recipients enrolled within the larger overall cohort. *Qualitative* methods of inquiry and analysis will be employed to explore processes by which psychosocial factors mediate the effects of pulmonary and extrapulmonary impairments on HRQL in lung transplant recipients (Aim 3).

Aim 1: Determine changes in disability and HRQL over time among lung transplant recipients.

> *Hypothesis 1.1:* Disability and HRQL will *improve* from before transplant to the end of Year 1 post-transplant.

> *Hypothesis 1.2:* Disability and HRQL will *plateau* by the end of Year 3 post-transplant.

Aim 2: Identify pulmonary and extrapulmonary physiological predictors of change in disability and HRQL among lung transplant recipients.

> *Hypothesis 2:* Extrapulmonary impairments in functioning and comorbidities will *increase* the likelihood of disability and impaired HRQL after lung transplant.

Aim 3: Estimate the effects of psychosocial factors on HRQL among lung transplant recipients.

> *Hypothesis 3:* Psychosocial factors (especially the extent of perceived helplessness) will *attenuate* or *increase* the risk of disability and impaired HRQL after accounting for quantifiable physiologic impairments.

The mentorship, didactic training, and hands-on experiences supported by this K23 will help me develop into a successful

independent investigator focused on studying how lung transplantation reduces disability and improves HRQL in the era of the
LAS. This area has *important clinical and scientific relevance.*
Clinically, evidence-based estimates of the magnitude and trajectory of change in disability and HRQL following transplant may
inform decision making; identifying novel risk factors for disability and poor HRQL could lead to modifications in pre-transplant
preparation and post-transplant care. Scientifically, data generated from this proposal may inform several goals. They will help
investigators seeking to improve HRQL focus on high-yield targets
for interventions. Further, while the goal of lung transplant is to
improve survival *and* HRQL, currently, success is assessed on the
basis of survival alone. Future policy may seek to incorporate
HRQL instruments to more holistically measure the net-benefit of
a lung transplant. These data may provide information for future
modeling of organ allocation schema that weigh both HRQL and
survival.

Dr. Singer spoke with us about his experience preparing and submitting a
CDA to NIH. We asked him to share his experiences in developing the study
and preparing an application for a mixed methods project, including the process of resubmission. Here, we include excerpts from our conversation with
Dr. Singer:

Q: What was your communication with program staff before and during the
application process?

A: I had a series of conversations with my program officer. It was invaluable
at every stage in the process and particularly during the process of resubmission. Interestingly enough, my program officer wasn't familiar with mixed
methods but really took the time and interest to discuss my project and help
me flesh out my ideas. She actually helped me communicate in the grant in a
way that would be understood by reviewers.

Q: What tools or strategies did you use to communicate the details of the
research design to readers?

A: Repetition! Say it, say it again, say it a third time, and then say it again.
Mixed methods applications to NIH are still rare so I tried to highlight the

value of the methods in the aims and throughout the research proposal. I stressed the point that a pure qualitative or pure quantitative approach would not answer my research question. I have to say this: It is definitely worth the space to justify why you're using mixed methods. My case was that the quantitative approaches to measuring quality of life had not been tested in transplant populations and that group was not reflected in existing conceptual frameworks. Therefore, we had to include a qualitative component to define the problem in this new context.

Q: What were the challenges unique to preparing a mixed methods grant application for NIH review?

A: This was the first application I prepared for NIH, but I gather it was different from submitting grant applications that aren't mixed methods. I had three aims—two quantitative and one qualitative. I used the third aim to inform the first two. There was limited space to describe what were really distinct studies and teams. That was very challenging. I had to have different sections on recruitment, instrument, data storage, and analysis for qualitative and quantitative studies. That took up most of the space. And I had to decide how much of the methods to explain. Finding the balance between satisfying reviewers that the proposal was rigorous without losing anyone in all of the methods was tricky.

Q: What was your experience with the reviewers? Were there any concerns raised about the proposed methods?

A: Their response was very enthusiastic. There weren't any critiques on the qualitative component content at all. The reason it wasn't funded on its first submission was because we didn't properly address how we would handle missing quantitative data and questions about the quantitative sample size and timeline.

Q: What advice would you offer to researchers who are considering applying for NIH funding for a CDA including mixed methods research?

A: Make sure you have really good mentors in qualitative and quantitative research who believe in the benefit of the other. That is the key. The most interesting part of mixed methods work is the overlap and intersection between the components—how they inform each other. I have benefited tremendously from having mentors that talk to each other. If they didn't value what the other one was doing, those conversations wouldn't be as fruitful. Get examples of successful projects. Talk to other junior faculty. Make sure your methods fit the study question. And the question has to be clinically important to the field. Emphasize you can't do the work without the qualitative arm. It's a necessary method and scientifically relevant. I think that resonates with reviewers. The work just can't be done without it.

TIPS FROM THE FIELD

We want to express our sincere thanks to our extraordinarily generous colleagues for sharing so freely both their intellectual property and their personal experiences. In this book, we have devoted several chapters to the conceptual foundations and core principles of mixed methods and an entire chapter to grant writing. Yet when it comes to writing grant applications, there is no question that learning from the real-world experiences of colleagues is at least equally as valuable. In this last section, we draw from the extensive materials provided by Drs. Elston Lafata, Boeri, and Singer to share several tips to consider as you set about writing your grant application. These suggestions address a diverse range of issues; we believe that attention to each one can help strengthen your application.

   ✓ **Explicitly identify the potential pitfalls and solutions associated with mixed methods designs.**

As with grant applications for all studies, regardless of method, it is essential to include a concise section at the conclusion that summarizes anticipated study limitations, challenges, and strategies to address them. Identifying potential vulnerabilities in the proposed approach and describing plans to minimize negative consequences can preempt questions or concerns from reviewers. For example, in applications proposing quantitative studies, we frequently address issues of missing data or response rates by explaining how we will handle these challenges. When preparing an application for a mixed methods study, it is important to also note any unique pitfalls that are associated with this approach. These include

◀ For a detailed discussion on avoiding common pitfalls in mixed methods studies, see Chapter 3: Determining the Appropriateness and Feasibility of Using Mixed Methods.

assembling and managing a qualified research team, securing and allocating resources efficiently, implementing the study, and disseminating the findings.

✓ Include schematic representations of key components of the study design and methods.

A picture really can be worth a thousand words—especially in an application proposing a mixed methods study—which, by its nature, has many interdependent parts. We spend lots of time teaching and coaching on how to make schematic representations and concise tables to convey essential elements of the study effectively to reviewers. Consider using schematics in order to demonstrate the flow of work across the overall study and its components, or to summarize concisely the various types of data collection and analysis that will occur in each component. Throughout the book, we have presented examples of various kinds of schematics that can be used to convey essential information efficiently for a reviewer. General design displays for convergent, sequential exploratory, sequential explanatory, concurrent embedded, and case studies approaches appear in Chapter 1. Examples of tabular or matrix presentations that summarize stages of the study, sample, and data collection are included in both Chapters 1 and 2. Illustrations of high-level project timelines are presented in Chapter 2. In Chapter 4, on grant writing, we include a schematic that demonstrates the relationship of the various study components. Finally, displays depicting various approaches to data integration and presentation of findings can be found in Chapter 8. Figures 5.1, 5.2, and 5.3 are templates for overall study flow that can be used in grant applications, or even simply as organizing and communication tools for internal use by the research team in the project plan.

✓ Appropriately account for all tasks in budget and timelines.

Grant reviewers—especially those familiar with mixed methods—will be looking closely at the timeline and budget to determine whether you have adequately planned for the activities and tasks that are unique to mixed methods studies. There are several important elements of project implementation to keep in mind. First, synchronizing activities across the study components in all phases of the project is essential. Consider the additional time needed to ensure alignment and be sure to build in sufficient time and resources for completion of this exercise. For instance, because data analysis in a mixed

Figure 5.1   Convergent Study Design Template

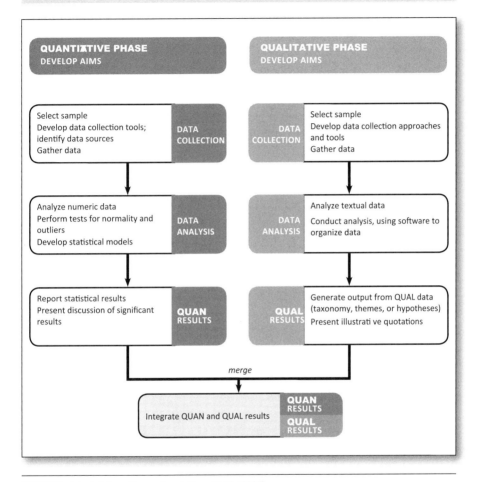

SOURCE: Adapted from Creswell and Plano Clark (2007).

NOTE: QUAN = quantitative component; QUAL = qualitative component.

methods study typically requires more time than in mono-method studies because of the need to integrate the various components, the project plan should include time explicitly allocated for data integration activities. Also keep in mind that, regardless of whether the study is a convergent or sequential design, delays in one component can have implications for the entire project. A second element of project implementation to address is human resources

Figure 5.2 Exploratory Sequential Study Design Template

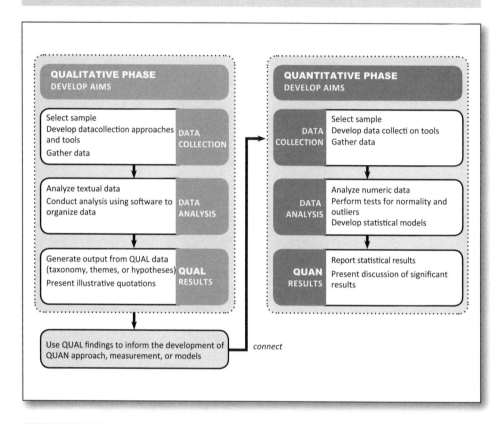

SOURCE: Adapted from Creswell and Plano Clark, 2007.

management, given the need for project staff and analysts with specific skills during different phases of the study. For instance, if you need a qualitative data analyst for an exploratory design, the position might be part-time or limited in duration. Or if you budget for one full-time research associate to extend throughout the entire study, that individual must have the necessary skills in data collection and analysis for both qualitative and quantitative components. One line item that may not typically appear in mono-method applications but, based on our experience, can be valuable in mixed methods studies is an expert in organizational dynamics and group facilitation to conduct regular check-ins with the team. Given the tensions that are inherent in mixed methods

Figure 5.3 Explanatory Sequential Study Design Template

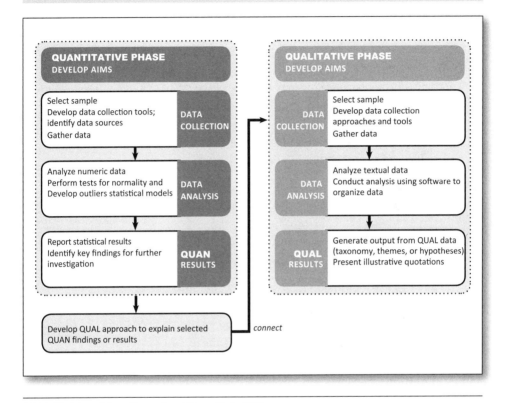

SOURCE: Adapted from Creswell and Plano Clark, 2007.

NOTE: QUAN = quantitative component; QUAL = qualitative component.

study, planning for facilitation of open discussions can strengthen the credibility and effectiveness of the team.

✓ Develop a funding strategy.

As described briefly in this chapter, there are many different possible sources of funding for mixed methods, both within the NIH and across the highly diverse grant-making organizations that support health sciences research. The defining features of mixed methods studies—the complexity, the moving and interdependent parts, the time required,

▶ For a detailed discussion on understanding group dynamics and strategies to facilitate collaboration, see Chapter 9: Managing Mixed Methods Teams.

the scope of work—make securing adequate funding a challenging undertaking. As you contemplate developing a mixed methods study or embarking on a career devoted to this field, we strongly suggest developing a funding road map (see Box 5.4). For instance, you may need to seek smaller project funding to test feasibility issues and assemble a capable and fully staffed team before moving on to larger awards. It may also be that you will need overlapping awards to fund all components of a study (beware of the complexities here). As with all research regardless of methods, you should have a clear direction for what comes next after the project. Is it designing an intervention? An evaluation? The future application or direction of the research will determine in large part potential sources of funding. It is useful to think strategically about the mid- to long-term funding plan at the outset of a project.

Box 5.4 Creating a Funding Strategy for Mixed Methods Health Sciences Research

- *Detail a comprehensive project budget.* Project your expenses for the life of the project, including start-up and dissemination phases. Be sure to build in a buffer to account for unanticipated costs. Align potential funders with the project stage for which they would have the greatest interest.
- *Chart the landscape for both federal and nonfederal funding sources.* Learn what types of mixed methods projects your target funders have funded in the past. Understand the funding cycle (when and how grants are funded). Check eligibility. Research funders' current and future priorities.
- *Look local first.* Explore funding opportunities at your institution for pilot projects. Meet with your Office of Development or equivalent. Philanthropic giving, or seed funding, can be enough to generate preliminary data, demonstrate feasibility, or supplement expenses not allowed on federal or foundation grants.
- *Create research interest.* Present at conferences, post on social media, explore crowd-sourced funding sites, discuss your ideas with funders, and otherwise generate academic interest in your research question.
- *Plan early to prevent interruption in project funding.* Begin the application process at least one to two years before your current

funding ends. Propose a consortium approach, and apply to multiple funders simultaneously.

- *Build partnerships with other researchers and other projects.* Embedding all or part of your mixed methods project within funding applications for other research initiatives is one strategy to support your research effort.

✓ **Demonstrate that the team has all the necessary skills and experience to implement all proposed methods.**

As we have noted previously, based on our experience as well as the wisdom of the experts quoted in this book, it is critical to clearly and convincingly convey that the team has the full complement of necessary expertise in qualitative, quantitative, and mixed methods.

◀ We encourage you to use the research team capacity inventory presented in Chapter 3: Determining the Appropriateness and Feasibility of Using Mixed Methods to identify and address any possible gaps in team composition.

Once you have assembled members who collectively have all of the needed skills for a mixed methods project, there are several specific things you can do to communicate the strengths of your team. First, include references to all relevant prior funded research and publications using qualitative, quantitative, and mixed methods. This can be done in multiple places—within the background and significance section where you report prior related research, in the individual biographical sketches and letters of support, and in the investigators' qualifications section. If the application format allows for a brief summary of professional expertise ("personal statement"), include evidence of accomplishment in mixed methods, such as grant or manuscript reviewer roles where you are included for your mixed methods expertise. Second, ensure there are established senior investigators with the proper expertise available to lead each component of the study (this can be one or more individuals as long as they have the credentials). Do not indicate these individuals will donate time; be sure there is a reasonable and credible amount of support allocated to them in the budget, and clearly define their roles in the budget justification. Third, use mixed methods terminology precisely, and include appropriate references to mixed methods

◄ See Chapter 4: Writing a Scientifically Sound and Compelling Grant Proposal for a Mixed Methods Study for further discussion of how to optimize the presentation of the team capacity.

methodological literature throughout the application (not only in the methods section).

The critical importance of team capacity is described by a senior program official at a major grant-making organization in the United States that has a strong track record in funding mixed methods research, the Commonwealth Fund (see Box 5.5).

Box 5.5   Describing the Importance of Team Capacity

One of the main weaknesses that we see [in grant applications] is that researchers are not well trained in mixed methods research. And when you read a proposal you can really tell that in the strength of the methods section. The other area that comes across my radar is that the mixed methods proposed can be really strong, but sometimes the execution of the research methods isn't easy. For example, in mixed methods you will likely conduct a number of interviews with different stakeholders and it's one thing to have a plan for how you select people for your interviews but how you conduct those interviews, collect the information, and analyze the results is another thing altogether. It's really an art and a science and takes a lot of experience before one can use qualitative methods well and master them. There is a saying about data analyses: garbage in, garbage out. The same applies for qualitative information gathered from an interview. If you do not ask the right question and listen keenly, you will not gather quality data. So in proposals people will say, "We'll do these interviews and record them and analyze them using software such as ATLAS.ti." The challenge is to assess the team's expertise in how to use the software. It's not just that you input the transcripts in the software, and the software is going to come out with all of the analysis and themes. The research team has to have a strong conceptual model and create a sound framework to analyze results. So this is one area where I can often see that people haven't thought through that process.

—Anne Marie Audet, MD, MSC, Vice President
for the Delivery System & Reform Breakthrough
Opportunities, The Commonwealth Fund

✓ **Provide evidence of commitment by project leadership to mixed methods research.**

Reviewers familiar with mixed methods are also aware of the many challenges inherent in leading research teams. They will be looking for evidence that the project leadership (whether a single principal investigator or several coinvestigators) recognizes these challenges and has the experience to manage them effectively. This experience can be conveyed in multiple ways. You might highlight evidence of a professional commitment to mixed methods (e.g., service on editorial boards or journals that publish mixed methods research, study sections for funding agencies that support mixed methods, membership or leadership in mixed methods professional societies, or invited lectures related to mixed methods). It can also be helpful to describe the structures and processes that will facilitate collaboration across the team (e.g, define the frequency of meetings, communication media, opportunities for in-person full team meetings). As noted previously, one strategy is to include a person with training in group dynamics on the project team whose role includes supporting and coaching throughout the project. This explicit investment can reflect recognition of the unique aspects of mixed methods work as well as authentic valuing of necessary expertise to manage them.

✓ **Consult available resources.**

Our final tip is to encourage you to carefully consult available resources on mixed methods research in the health sciences. Seek out a variety of sources of information and support for your professional development as a mixed methods researcher. These include, for example, organizations such as the Mixed Methods International Research Association (MMIRA), training workshops such as those sponsored by the NIH Office of Behavioral and Social Sciences Research (Creswell, Klassen, Plano Clark, & Smith for the OBSSR, 2011) Agency for Healthcare Research and Quality (AHRQ), professional associations, and formal and informal interest groups on university campuses.

The NIH *Best Practices for Mixed Methods Research in the Health Sciences* (Creswell et al.,

◀ For detailed information on preparing your mixed methods grant application including review criteria and strategies for meeting them, refer to Chapter 4: Writing a Scientifically Sound and Compelling Grant Proposal for a Mixed Methods Study.

2011b) is an excellent resource for researchers interested in pursuing mixed methods. Focused on the unique elements of a mixed methods research proposal, these guidelines were developed by an appointed working group of mixed methods researchers from diverse backgrounds. The document presents "best practices" and is intended to assist researchers in preparing competitive and rigorous research proposals, as well as peer reviewers and program staff who evaluate grant applications.

Summary and Key Points

- Major research funding is typically necessary to complete a mixed methods project in its entirety, but small research grants and CDAs are other potential avenues to support essential elements of mixed methods research.
- The real-world experiences of funded mixed methods health sciences researchers provide a critical complement to the conceptual foundations and core principles of these methods for those seeking to understand mixed methods in the health sciences.
- Investigate grant opportunities fully, and make informed decisions about the where, when, what, and how of grant submission to maximize your chances of funding success for your mixed methods application.
- Developing a funding road map for your mixed methods project is an important tool for project success.

Review Questions and Exercises

1. Using a research question that would be best answered by mixed methods, create an outline of a study design that could be used to answer the question in a figure like Figure 5.1, 5.2, or 5.3. This could be based on a research question that you are interested in answering or on an article that you have read.

2. Try to identify a researcher who has been successful in getting a mixed methods grant, and ask them if they would be willing to give you a chance to ask them some questions about their experiences. You can use

the questions that were used with the principal investigators in this chapter, and add some of your own. It may be most helpful if you can find a researcher who applied through the funding institution that you plan to target.

3. Develop a funding road map for your mixed methods project, using the template in Box 5.4 as a guide.

References

Agency for Healthcare Research and Quality. *Opportunities for advancing delivery system research.* Retrieved January 30, 2014, from http://www.ahrq.gov/professionals/systems/system/delivery-system-initiative/index.html

Boeri, M. (2010). *Older drug users: A life course study of turning points in drug use and injection* (1R21DA0252908-01A1). Retrieved April 26, 2007, from http://projectreporter.nih.gov/project_info_description.cfm?projectnumber=5R21DA025298-02

Creswell, J. W., Klassen, A. C., Plano Clark, V. L., & Smith, K. C. for the Office of Behavioral and Social Sciences Research. (2011). *Best practices for mixed methods research in the health sciences.* Bethesda, MD: National Institutes of Health. Retrieved January 30, 2014, from http://obssr.od.nih.gov/mixed_methods_research

Creswell, J. W., & Plano Clark, V. L. (2007). *Designing and conducting mixed methods research.* Thousand Oaks, CA: Sage.

Elston Lafata, J. (2009). *Physician recommendation and colorectal cancer screening* (1R01CA112379-01A1). Retrieved April 25, 2014, from http://projectreporter.nih.gov/project_info_description.cfm?projectnumber=3R01CA112379-04S1

National Institute of Allergy and Infectious Disease. (2012, March 16). *All about grants: Tutorials and samples.* Retrieved February 27, 2014, from http://www.niaid.nih.gov/researchfunding/grant/pages/aag.aspx

National Institutes of Health. (n.d.). *Career Award Wizard.* Retrieved January 30, 2014, from http://grants2.nih.gov/training/kwizard

Singer, J. (2011). *The effects of lung transplant on disability and health-related quality of life* (5K23H111115). Retrieved April 25, 2014, from, http://projectreporter.nih.gov/project_info_description.cfm?projectnumber=1F32HL107003-01

❊ SIX ❊

ASSESSING QUALITY IN MIXED METHODS STUDIES

Information you will find in this chapter: This chapter discusses issues of quality (or scientific rigor) in mixed methods research. In the first section, we summarize common standards of quality and appraisal criteria that apply in both qualitative and quantitative studies. The next section presents a critical appraisal framework for quality that is uniquely relevant to designing and conducting mixed methods research. Finally, we describe potential methodological threats to quality that arise from decisions related to sampling, data collection, analysis, interpretation, and presentation in mixed methods studies.

Key features in this chapter:

- Brief quotations and reflections from mixed methods researchers
- Figure of key stakeholders with an interest in quality in mixed methods
- Brief list of resources on assessing quality of qualitative research
- Table summarizing standards of quality and appraisal criteria for qualitative and quantitative studies
- Critical appraisal framework for quality in mixed methods studies in the health sciences
- Examples of justifications for using mixed methods
- Examples of design decisions and threats to quality

THE IMPORTANCE OF RESEARCH QUALITY FOR DIFFERENT AUDIENCES

In this chapter we address scientific rigor, which we also refer to as quality, in mixed methods research. Many texts present this topic as a concluding chapter; however, we have deliberately placed it in Part II: Getting Mixed Methods Research Funded because we believe it is important for researchers to be familiar with the standards of quality and to apply them actively in the development of their research. We would also note that the quality of evidence generated through mixed methods is of interest to a wide range of potential audiences (see Figure 6.1). These audiences include research affiliates (e.g., members of the research team, research participants), research reviewers (e.g., funders, peer reviewers, instructors, research colleagues), and research users (e.g., policymakers, the public, practitioners, advocates).

▶ Researchers can find more specific and practical guidance on addressing domains of quality when developing grant applications and manuscripts for publication in Chapter 4: Writing a Scientifically Sound and Compelling Grant Proposal for a Mixed Methods Study and in Chapter 11: Publishing Mixed Methods Studies in the Health Sciences.

While the issue of research quality is relevant for each of these audiences, in this chapter we generally tailor the discussion for reviewers of grant applications or manuscripts. We seek to provide those in a position of evaluating mixed methods studies with an informed understanding of essential principles and concepts relevant to scientific rigor. Of course, researchers who are planning or conducting a mixed methods study must also be familiar with and apply these principles and concepts in their work. In addition, when designing a study and writing a proposal, it is important to keep these audiences in mind, especially in terms of how they will assess the quality of your research.

COMMON STANDARDS OF QUALITY IN QUALITATIVE AND QUANTITATIVE RESEARCH

There is a large universe of robust and dynamic literature addressing issues of scientific rigor for both quantitative and qualitative research. Mastery of this literature is surely a daunting task for methodologists whose careers are devoted to improving processes of scientific discovery, let alone busy health

Figure 6.1   Audiences With an Interest in the Quality of Mixed Methods
Research

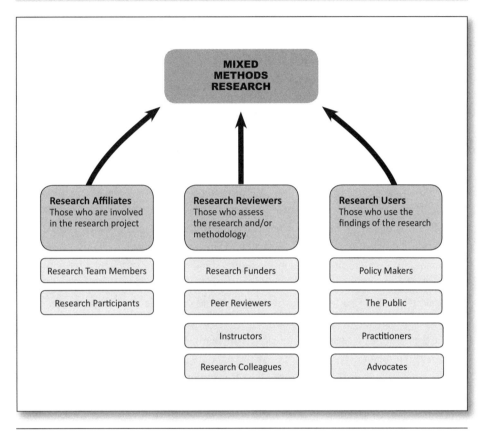

SOURCE: Adapted from O'Cathain (2010b).

sciences researchers embarking on a path to use mixed methods in their work. Using mixed methods requires turning an eye toward three sets of standards: those for qualitative methods, those for quantitative methods, and those for mixed methods. Reading across these voluminous sets of standards is no small task, especially given the varied orientations, terminology, and practices that characterize each. While there is a very well-developed science around conducting systematic reviews of quantitative studies, systematic reviews have increasingly begun to include qualitative and mixed methods studies. The literature around appraising the quality of several methods in a single review is emerging accordingly (Pluye, Grad, Levine, & Nicolau, 2009).

We presume that many readers of this text will be familiar with established criteria for quality in quantitative studies. Exponential growth in big data and increasing access to large data sets of all types has given rise to exciting innovations in advanced analytic techniques that are evolving rapidly. Nevertheless, quantitative research sits firmly upon a foundational set of principles for scientific rigor for which there is clear consensus in the field (e.g., Aschengrau & Seage, 2008; Cook & Campbell, 1979; Gordis, 2009; Hulley, Cummings, Browner, Grady, & Newman, 2013). On the other hand, qualitative research has highly diverse roots, with origins in anthropology, sociology, philosophy, and other disciplines and has been introduced into the health sciences comparatively recently (Crabtree & Miller, 1999; Glaser & Strauss, 1967; Miles & Huberman, 1994; Patton, 2002; Strauss & Corbin, 1998). This disciplinary diversity brings richness to the methods yet presents challenges to achieving consensus on how to most appropriately describe and assess the quality of qualitative research as used in health sciences. The central question is whether to ground the standards in concepts and terminology from quantitative research or to apply unique standards created exclusively for qualitative methods. Multiple sets of standards for qualitative research exist that reflect these varied scientific traditions and orientations. While essential, they are sometimes inconsistent and often overwhelming for researchers new to the method. Researchers interested in learning more about standards of quality in qualitative research *per se* are encouraged to turn to resources such as those in Box 6.1. This is just a small sampling; there are many excellent resources available in textbook form, journal articles, and on the Internet.

Box 6.1   Resources on Assessing Quality in Qualitative Research

We expect that many of the readers of this text may be somewhat new to qualitative research. For more information on this topic, we suggest these selected resources:

- Denzin, N. K., & Lincoln, Y. (Eds.). (2000). *Handbook of qualitative research* (2nd ed.). Thousand Oaks, CA: Sage.
- Glaser, B., & Strauss, A. (1967). *The discovery of grounded theory: Strategies for qualitative research.* Chicago: Aldine.

- Horsburgh, D. (2003). Evaluation of qualitative research. *Journal of Clinical Nursing, 12*(2), 307–312.
- Mays, N., & Pope, C. (2000). Qualitative research in health care. Assessing quality in qualitative research. *BMJ, 320*(7226), 50–52.
- Morse, J. M., & Richards, L. (2002). *README first for a user's guide to qualitative methods.* Thousand Oaks, CA: Sage.
- Onwuegbuzie, A. J., & Leech, N. L. (2007). Validity and qualitative research: An oxymoron. *Quality and Quantity, 41*(2), 233–249.
- Padgett, D. (2012). Strategies for rigor. In *Qualitative and mixed methods research in public health* (pp. 203–220). Thousand Oaks, CA: Sage.
- Patton, M. (2002). *Qualitative evaluation and research methods* (3rd ed.). Thousand Oaks, CA: Sage.

The question of quality becomes even more complicated when considering a mixed methods study. One position is that the philosophical underpinnings of qualitative and quantitative methods are wholly distinct and that independent criteria are needed to assess the respective qualitative and quantitative components of a mixed methods study. Others suggest that there are aspects of scientific investigation that are essentially analogous for qualitative and quantitative research, although they may be manifest differently in the research process (Bryman, 1988; Mays & Pope, 2000; Morse, 1999; Murphy, Dingwall, Greatbatch, Parker, & Watson, 1998). We agree with this view.

Accordingly, we endorse alignment of quantitative and qualitative methods across common standards in order to focus on the essential elements of quality in scientific investigations. To create the list of common standards of quality and appraisal criteria for qualitative and quantitative studies in Figure 6.2, we draw upon multiple sources (Bradley, 1997; Lincoln & Guba, 1985; Miles & Huberman, 1994; Polit & Beck, 2010; Sale & Brazil, 2004) to define core attributes, or common standards, of quality and to describe how these attributes are appraised in both qualitative and quantitative studies. In addition to distilling the standards to their essence and hence making them digestible, we believe this approach has the benefit of bringing us closer to a shared view of core standards that can unite (rather than divide) quantitative and qualitative researchers.

Figure 6.2   Common Standards of Quality and Appraisal Criteria for Qualitative and Quantitative Studies

STANDARD	QUALITATIVE Appraisal Criteria	QUANTITATIVE Appraisal Criteria
Veracity	**Credibility**–The degree to which the findings plausibly explain the phenomenon of interest or cohere with what is known; attention paid to alternative explanations; correspondence between the researcher's and respondent's portrayal of respondent experience	**Internal validity**–The degree to which the findings represent a "true" reflection of a causal relationship between the variables of interest in the population under study
Consistency	**Dependability**–The degree to which the researchers account for and describe the changing contexts and circumstances during the study	**Reliability**–The degree to which observations, measures or results can be replicated (for the same participant or in different studies)
Applicability	**Transferability**–The degree to which findings or research protocols can be transferred to other settings, contexts, or populations as determined by the reader	**Generalizability** (or external validity)–The degree to which the study results hold true for a population beyond the participants in the study or in other settings
Neutrality	**Confirmability**–The degree to which the findings of a study are shaped by respondents and not researcher bias, motivation, or interest	**Objectivity**–The degree to which researchers can remain distanced from what they study so findings reflect the nature of what was studied rather than researcher bias, motivation,or interest

SOURCES: Adapted from Bradley (1997); Lincoln and Guba (1985); Miles and Huberman (1994); Polit and Beck (2010); Sale and Brazil (2004).

Next we describe each of the common standards in detail and suggest techniques that can be used to address the appraisal criteria in study design, implementation, and data analysis. Reviewers of a mixed methods research proposal should look for whether and how these techniques will be employed to ensure quality in the study under consideration. Readers of peer-reviewed studies may find it difficult to assess adherence to these standards when the methods section of the article does not provide sufficient information, whether because of space constraints or the authors' lack of attention to the standards, or both. Experts have called for improved transparency and completeness of reporting in manuscripts for mixed methods studies (O'Cathain, Murphy, & Nicholl, 2008; Wisdom, Cavaleri, Onwuegbuzie, & Green, 2012).

▶ For more information on the transparency in reporting mixed methods studies, see Chapter 11: Publishing Mixed Methods Studies in the Health Sciences.

The first common standard is veracity, which refers to credibility in qualitative research and internal validity in quantitative research. Veracity is concerned with the "truth value" of the findings (Lincoln & Guba, 1985), or the degree to which the results accurately and precisely represent the phenomenon under study. In qualitative research, several questions can be asked to assess the credibility of findings: Are the findings plausible? Do they cohere with what is known? Do the researchers deliberately consider alternative explanations? Do they represent the respondents' experience accurately?

A key technique for enhancing credibility is triangulation (use of multiple methods, data sources, and researchers) (Campbell & Fiske, 1959; Cook, 1985; Denzin, 1978), which seeks convergence and corroboration across data sets. Several other techniques exist. A primary technique is sampling to the point of theoretical saturation (the point at which no new data emerge from subsequent data collection). Participant confirmation (or member checking) is a process of presenting findings to participants to assess whether the findings are consistent with their experience or the experiences of like others). Tactics to encourage participants to be candid and truthful can also enhance credibility, such as assigning interviewers who are concordant on a potentially salient characteristic such as gender (although the evidence on concordance is mixed) or reassuring participants of confidentiality protections. Finally, negative case analysis can increase credibility. This analysis involves deliberate examination of cases that present disconfirming or deviant evidence and developing modified analytic propositions to accommodate the data. Some also suggest that the iterative process of data collection and analysis in a qualitative study is a form of progressive validation of emergent constructs.

In quantitative methods, internal validity is concerned with the degree to which the findings represent a true reflection of a causal relationship between the variables of interest in the population under study. In evaluating internal validity, we want to know the following: Did the study measure what it was intended to measure? Were sources of bias and confounding addressed and minimized within the study conditions? Common techniques to enhance internal validity include randomizing study conditions, identifying and controlling for extraneous or confounding variables, comparing control versus intervention groups, and developing instruments through systematic processes such as cognitive interviews and factor analysis.

The second common standard is consistency and refers to dependability in qualitative research and reliability in quantitative research. In a qualitative study, dependability reflects the degree to which the researchers adequately document the research process in toto, from study conceptualization through to interpretation. Because qualitative research is carried out in naturalistic settings, with the researcher as a human instrument, unexpected and potentially relevant variables may emerge over the course of the study. Reviewers or readers might ask the following questions: Do the researchers provide enough detail about the context and process so that another researcher can repeat the study (if not find the same results)? Is variation in the phenomenon tracked or explained consistently, with possible sources of variability noted? The key technique for ensuring dependability in a study is an external audit. External audits involve having an independent researcher examine both the process and results of the study to evaluate whether the findings are supported by the data. There are differing views as to the value and feasibility of external audits. While they can help to assess the quality of a given study, there are many challenges to an outside researcher's ability to master the extensive amount of data and generate similar interpretations. Challenges include human research protection program (HRPP) policies and procedures that may preclude external parties accessing data, ensuring participant confidentiality, and encountering logistical impediments to data access.

▶ For more information on HRPPs as they relate to mixed methods, see Chapter 10: Implementation Issues in Mixed Methods Research.

In a quantitative study, reliability refers to the consistency, stability, and repeatability of observations or measures. In assessing reliability, one might ask the following: Can we repeat the measure with the same participant or in different participants and get the same results? Techniques to increase reliability of measures are using multiple measures of the same construct, cognitive testing and piloting of survey instruments, training of data collectors to ensure high inter-rater reliability, data cleaning, and using statistical procedures to adjust for measurement error.

The third common standard is applicability; it addresses what is known as transferability in qualitative research and generalizability (or external validity) in quantitative research. Applicability of a given study is the degree to which we can take what is learned in one study and use the findings in another setting or population. This concept is of critical importance in moving a body of knowledge forward. In qualitative studies, we assess transferability by asking the following: Can findings be applied in other similar contexts or settings? Transferability can be enhanced in several ways. Reports of findings should include a clear and explicit statement of research aims, including a compelling rationale for qualitative methods and appropriate citations. A thorough description of study context including aspects of the study setting that are most salient to the research question can also be useful. The intention is to provide readers of the research with information needed to evaluate the degree to which their own setting is similar to the study context. Finally, reports should include procedures for sampling, participants, data collection, and analysis including transcription and coding.

In quantitative studies, generalizability can be evaluated by asking the following questions: What is the degree to which similar results could be expected for others in the same population or in other populations? Techniques to enhance the generalizability of findings include random selection, clear definition of and rationale for inclusion and exclusion criteria, use of validated instruments, assessment of nonrespondent bias, and descriptions of statistical procedures including treatment of missing data and confidence intervals.

The final common standard, neutrality, refers to confirmability in qualitative research and objectivity in quantitative research. The concept of neutrality addresses whether the researchers have a priori assumptions that may bias implementation of the study or interpretation of results. A reviewer or reader might ask the following: Do the reported research findings accurately reflect the experiences and attitudes of participants, without bias from researchers? Those who have limited familiarity with qualitative methods may express concerns about bias. These concerns may be raised by several intrinsic features of qualitative methods, including the dynamic interpersonal nature of gathering data, the iterative process of collecting data and interpreting it, as well as the seemingly opaque methods of data analysis. For many researchers, however, theoretical sensitivity and deep prior experience with or knowledge of the research topic is considered an asset. Qualitative researchers seek to produce study findings that authentically capture the respondents' views or experience, without undue influence of researcher bias, motivation, or interest. Established techniques to facilitate confirmability include external audits (described previously). Bracketing is a process whereby the researcher holds in abeyance any biases, presuppositions, or previous experiences, which can be documented through memos or debriefs with an external party (Tufford & Newman, 2012). Finally, reflexivity involves acknowledging the effect of the researcher on every step of the research process, fostered by multiple investigators; journaling research reflections throughout the study; and reporting this information in manuscripts (Lincoln & Guba, 1985).

Neutrality may be less often perceived as a potential risk in quantitative research, which is typically regarded as protected from bias because studies use random selection, apply explicit protocols, and perform statistical computations. Yet our view is that quantitative studies are also vulnerable to biases. Biases may manifest themselves in the definition of the research question, the setting of inclusion and exclusion criteria, and decisions about measurement (what variables are included and how are they operationalized) and analytics (how models are built). Hence, neutrality is equally relevant for both qualitative and quantitative studies (Malterud, 2001) (see Box 6.2). As noted previously, transparency, or complete and detailed description of methods, is most often used as a standard for reporting qualitative studies. This should apply to quantitative studies as well. Sufficient detailed information should be provided to allow the reader to understand all key design and analysis decisions. Maximum transparency in reporting key decisions and processes for study implementation and analysis can go a fair way toward addressing concerns about neutrality.

Box 6.2   Neutrality as a Goal in Both Qualitative and Quantitative Research

A researcher's background and position will affect what they choose to investigate, the angle of investigation, the methods judged most adequate for this purpose, the findings considered most appropriate, and the framing and communication of conclusions. (Malterud, 2001, pp. 483–484)

ADDITIONAL STANDARDS FOR QUALITY IN DESIGNING AND CONDUCTING MIXED METHODS STUDIES

Simply appraising the rigor of the respective qualitative and quantitative components is not sufficient to ensure a high-quality mixed methods study. By definition, a mixed methods study is more than the sum of its parts, where data integration and generation of overarching (or meta) insights or inferences are essential characteristics. Experts have devoted substantial effort to the development of quality standards for mixed methods studies; there are over a dozen sets of standards currently available. Yet while there is an encouraging amount of consistency across these standards, there is also a fair amount of variability (Bryman, Becker, & Sempik, 2008; Caracelli & Riggin, 1994; Creswell & Plano Clark, 2011; Heyvaert, Hannes, Maes, & Onghena, 2013; Morse, Wolfe, & Niehaus, 2006; O'Cathain, 2010a; O'Cathain et al., 2008; Onwuegbuzie & Johnson, 2006; Pluye, Gagnon, Griffiths, & Johnson-Lafleur, 2009; Sale & Brazil, 2004; Teddlie & Tashakkori, 2009; Wisdom et al., 2012). Research funders have also become increasingly aware of criteria for rigor in qualitative and mixed methods studies. A senior official at the Commonwealth Fund describes the evolution of these approaches and the growing capacity of their reviewers in assessing quality in Box 6.3.

Box 6.3   Assessing Rigor in Mixed Methods Grant Applications

For a long time, study sections at NIH or other large funders did not recognize mixed and qualitative methods because there were just no criteria to evaluate them, but I think that's changed a lot now. There has been a lot of work to increase the awareness of some criteria that can be used . . . .At the Commonwealth Fund, because we're very small and may not have the expertise in house, we will reach out to experts that can help us evaluate the quality, validity, and soundness of a proposal. Over time we've really become aware that even if people put a lot of fancy words on the page, that doesn't mean that they really understand what these terms mean, and that's really what we want to know—whether there is a sound team behind those methods that can really deliver.

—Anne Marie Audet, MD, MSC, Vice President for
the Delivery System & Reform Breakthrough
Opportunities, The Commonwealth Fund

In an effort to make this extensive and somewhat disparate information more accessible for researchers new to mixed methods, we have attempted to distill current frameworks to a set of minimum essential elements. We fully appreciate that this is not an exhaustive list and recognize that experts will differ in the degree of depth of criteria within these broad domains. We also regard the existing more detailed standards as critical to advancing the broad field of mixed methods with regard to methods and quality. Nevertheless, in the pragmatic spirit of this book we sought to make the essential elements more accessible and therefore more likely to be understood and taken up by researchers in the health sciences. In addition to the common standards for qualitative and quantitative methods defined previously, we recommend the mixed methods appraisal framework outlined in Table 6.1. Note that while some of these standards must be applied retrospectively, reviewers of grant proposals can assess the degree to which the researchers describe their plans for adhering to them throughout the proposed study.

Table 6.1   Critical Appraisal Framework for Quality in Mixed Methods Studies in Health Sciences

Domain of Quality	Appraisal Criteria	References
Conceptualization and justification of the study as mixed methods	To what degree is there an explicit and sound rationale for using mixed methods? Are the strengths of each method used to minimize limitations of the other? Was there an a priori plan for ensuring yield (whole is more than sum of parts)?	1–7
Design quality	Is the design appropriate for addressing the overall question, and does it align with the reason for combining methods? Is a description of design from a known typology provided?	2–3, 5, 8, 9
Adherence to respective standards for qualitative and quantitative methods throughout the study	To what degree were established standards adhered to for each of the individual components with regard to sampling, data collection, and analysis?	2–3, 9–10
Adherence to standards for mixed methods data analysis		2–3, 5, 7–8

Domain of Quality	Appraisal Criteria	References
• Resolution of divergent findings	Have divergent findings from different components been adequately identified and plausibly explained?	
• Treatment of concordant findings	Has the possibility of shared bias between the methods been considered and addressed?	
• Rigor of data transformation	Is there a clear rationale for the data transformation? Have established procedures been described and followed?	
Quality of analytic integration		1–3, 4–8
• Statement of type of integration	Is there a clear a priori plan and technique for integration across data sets?	
• Type of integration is appropriate for the particular design	Is the integration plan appropriate given the particular study design? Is the plan designed with attention to sequencing, weighting of components?	
• Degree of yield	Do results from integration generate more comprehensive findings than either component would alone? Does the study produce publications that include findings from both components?	
Quality of interpretation		1–2, 5–9
• Interpretive transparency	Is it clear which findings have emerged from each method?	
• Interpretive efficacy	Do the overarching (meta) inferences adequately synthesize inferences from the qualitative and quantitative findings?	

References:
1. Bryman, Becker, and Sempik (2008).
2. Caracelli and Riggin (1994).
3. Creswell and Plano Clark (2011).
4. O'Cathain, Murphy, and Nicholl (2007).
5. Onwuegbuzie and Johnson (2006).
6. Pluye, Gagnon, Griffiths, and Johnson-Lafleur (2009).
7. Wisdom, Cavaleri, Onwuegbuzie, and Green (2012).
8. O'Cathain, Murphy, and Nicholl (2008).
9. Teddlie and Tashakkori (2009).
10. Morse (2010).

SOURCE: Adapted from O'Cathain (2010a).

Conceptualization and Justification
of the Study as Mixed Methods

The conceptualization and justification of the study as requiring a mixed methods approach is fundamental to assessing the quality of the research. While it may seem obvious, in our experience this initial stage is where many researchers who are new to mixed methods stumble. The researchers should make a convincing case that the phenomenon of interest is sufficiently complex and multifaceted as to require mixed methods (as opposed to simply being strategic by including a qualitative component because the funder has expressed interest, which we have seen in our grant reviewer and mentor roles). One review of published mixed methods health services studies found that only one third of reports provided justification for a mixed methods design (Wisdom et al., 2012). Not only is it necessary to make a compelling case that a mixed methods approach is warranted but the rationale for the specific design selected (e.g., explanatory sequential) must also be provided. Some common circumstances in which a mixed methods design might be appropriate are included in Box 6.4. As a reviewer, be sure to look for one of these or another justification early in the grant application or manuscript. Also pay attention to whether the stated justification carries throughout the conceptualization and presentation of methods and findings.

◄ For more information on justifications that many other researchers have used for employing mixed methods in health sciences, see Chapter 2: Applications and Illustrations of Mixed Methods Health Sciences Research.

Box 6.4   Examples of Justifications for Using Mixed Methods

- Pursuing a topic about which little is known and hence conducting both hypothesis generation and subsequent testing in one study
- Producing a comprehensive account of both the nature and magnitude of a phenomenon
- Seeking both in-depth detailed understanding and generalizable findings
- Aiming to describe context, process, and outcomes of a particular phenomenon
- Minimizing limitations inherent in each method through capitalizing on their respective complementary strengths

In addition to these circumstances that suggest a need for a mixed methods approach, there is also a broad range of potential focal topics that are well suited for mixed methods. In the health sciences, potential topics might include complex clinical or quality issues, health care organizational performance, behavioral interventions, processes of implementation of innovations, health care decision making, and measurement and development for complex constructs.

◄ Further discussion of topical areas that are well suited for mixed methods research is provided in Chapter 3: Determining the Appropriateness and Feasibility of Using Mixed Methods.

Design Quality

The second domain of quality relates the study design. Criteria for appraising the quality of a study design include how the study is conceived with regard to the aim and how it is described. As we have noted throughout the text, the overall research question drives the design decisions. It is essential that the chosen study design is well suited to generate quantitative, qualitative, and integrated data that are directly relevant to answering the study question. In addition, the design should align with the stated rationale for using a mixed methods approach. The rationale may either tie to the focal topic or to the needed methodology. For instance, if the rationale is to study a topic about which little is known and therefore to generate and test hypotheses, the design should be exploratory sequential.

In terms of describing the design, experts recommend using concepts, language, and formats from a known typology (Creswell & Plano Clark, 2011; Teddlie & Tashakkori, 2009). Typologies are intended to organize and simplify complex constructs through classification systems. The benefits of typologies in research are substantial, particularly in the earliest phases of development of a field. They can improve communication both within a professional community and externally through shared language and understanding. Typologies can facilitate comparisons across studies in order to allow for synthesis of evidence and the development of a body of knowledge. In a pragmatic sense, typologies can also serve as practical tools for researchers to guide the organization and implementation of a study. Importantly, they can also support efforts to legitimize a field of study. There are more than a dozen typologies of mixed methods studies available (Creswell, 1999; Creswell, Fetters, & Ivankova, 2004; Creswell, Plano Clark, Gutmann, & Hanson, 2003; Greene,

2007; Hannemann-Weber, Kessel, Budych, & Schultz, 2011; Morgan, 1998; Morse, 1991; Morse & Niehaus, 2009; Patton, 1990; Sandelowski, 2000; Steckler, McLeroy, Goodman, Bird, & McCormick, 1992; Tashakkori & Teddlie, 1998; Teddlie & Tashakkori, 2009); some are commonly used in the health sciences. However, existing typologies cannot fully accommodate the extraordinarily diverse forms of mixed methods studies—particularly large, complex projects that are iterative and dynamic. Guest (2013) has recently proposed an alternative approach that reduces the descriptive dimensions of a study to focus on points of interface. As there is no single correct or uniformly endorsed typology for mixed methods studies, researchers should identify one that captures and conveys the essential aspects of their study most effectively (Guest, 2013). Reviewers should assess the degree to which the design is a fit for the research question and also expect to see some form of study typology or recognized descriptors provided in a grant or manuscript.

Adherence to Respective Standards of Quality for Qualitative and Quantitative Research

As discussed at the beginning of this chapter, each component in a mixed methods study should comply with respective standards for qualitative and quantitative research. It is critical to follow the established methodological principles and practices of sampling, data collection, and analysis for each component to the greatest degree feasible.

Yet for multiple reasons (e.g., efficiency concerns, dominance of one orientation within the team, lack of awareness) it is not uncommon for threats to quality to appear in either the qualitative or quantitative components (or both).

◀ For more information on mixed methods sampling, data collection, and analysis, refer to Chapter 7: Sampling and Data Collection in Mixed Methods Studies and Chapter 8: Data Analysis and Integration in Mixed Methods Studies.

There are many existing resources that describe the standards of quality for qualitative and quantitative work, and as a result, this book will not describe these standards in detail. However, for a brief summary of guidelines to be used in assessing the rigor of each component of a mixed methods study, refer to Appendix C: Assessing Rigor in Quantitative Health Sciences Research and Appendix D: Assessing Rigor in Qualitative Health Sciences Research: Consolidated Criteria for Reporting Qualitative Research (COREQ).

In terms of sampling, a qualitative sample ought to be purposeful in nature (i.e., nonrandom), is typically smaller than sample sizes in quantitative studies and the size is not defined a priori. As such, a qualitative sampling frame is generally not suited to serve a quantitative purpose. A quantitative sample should be randomly drawn with attention to nonresponse bias and is typically larger than those in a qualitative design. Importantly, failure to adhere to principles of sampling for each method presents risks to the quality of findings generated in the respective components.

▶ See the Glossary of Key Terms and Definitions for more information on theoretical saturation.

Data collection in a qualitative study requires flexibility. The data collector must be nimble and able to pursue unanticipated directions during the observation or interview. In addition, the data collection instrument is dynamic and may be revised through the course of the study. The data collection period is not predefined; it continues until theoretical saturation is achieved through an iterative process of data collection and analysis. In a quantitative study, data collection is necessarily fixed, predetermined, and explicitly defined. The instruments are static and are not altered once the data collection begins. Standardization in administration is imperative, with careful training of interviewers including inter-rater reliability checks. Finally, deviations from the administration protocol are considered problematic.

Processes of data analysis differ in qualitative and quantitative methods. Qualitative data are typically analyzed with focus on narrative descriptions, using various techniques such as the constant comparative method (Glaser & Strauss, 1967; Lincoln & Guba, 1985) to generate themes, taxonomies, or conceptual frameworks (Bradley, Curry, & Devers, 2007). In some cases, researchers generate quantitative output from the qualitative data. We share the view of experts who note that quantifying qualitative data can present a threat to validity and should be thoroughly justified, approached with caution, and follow established procedures (Morse et al., 2006). In quantitative studies, hypotheses are precisely defined in advance, and data analysis is not performed until the data collection phase has closed. Output takes the form of numeric results from various forms of statistical modeling and testing. Analyses should be defined as exploratory or confirmatory in nature, as appropriate, at the outset.

In sum, qualitative and quantitative components in a mixed methods study must be implemented with deliberate attention to the key methodological assumptions, principles, and practices underpinning each. As researcher and mixed methods expert Jan Morse wisely cautioned, *"Mixed methods are not data soup!"* (Morse, 2010, p. 348). Several strategies for ensuring that the scientific integrity of each component remains intact exist. They include explicit valuing and supporting all methods by the principal investigator throughout the project; having sufficiently deep expertise on the team for both qualitative and quantitative methods; and developing an overall project budget that appropriately allocates adequate time and resources for each study component. As a reviewer, you will want to have sufficient information to be able to determine the degree to which respective standards for quality were adhered to in all aspects of the quantitative and qualitative study components (sampling, data collection, and analysis).

Adherence to Standards for Mixed Methods Data Analysis

A number of aspects of data analysis are unique to mixed methods studies: treatment of divergent data, treatment of convergent data, and procedures for data transformation.

First, it is possible that the qualitative and quantitative findings from a mixed methods study may be divergent or inconsistent. Simply putting aside or ignoring inconsistent findings is not an option. Points of divergence or inconsistency may highlight important areas of discovery. These points ought to be systematically examined and addressed through analysis. Insights and unanswered issues should be reflected in the final report of findings; readers should not be left to try to interpret or understand discrepancies on their own. Several strategies can help with divergence (Pluye, et al., 2009), including confirming the rigor of each study component, conducting additional data collection or analysis, and developing hypotheses about potential explanations.

▶ For more information on mixed methods data analysis, refer to Chapter 8: Data Analysis and Integration in Mixed Methods Studies.

Second, it is also possible that the two (or more) sources of convergent data may have a shared bias, which could mean that the results are converging toward a set of findings that does not reflect reality. One of the strengths of mixed methods research is that it can minimize the biases and weakness of individual methods; however, if the methods are subject to the same biases, then the use of multiple methods does not add to the strength of the study. For instance, if the data for both components were collected from similarly biased samples or if the researchers failed to control for confounders in the quantitative arm and the qualitative sample was derived from this group, then both methods could be pointing to the same results only because they suffer from the same weaknesses. These circumstances can be addressed in several ways, including having discussions throughout the planning process, keeping records of potential biases in different components, using caution when selecting a qualitative sample out of a quantitative sample, and collecting all of the data needed to adequately control for confounders in quantitative analyses.

The third form of analysis unique to mixed methods is data transformation (turning qualitative results into quantitative data or turning quantitative results into qualitative data). The most difficult challenges to rigor may arise in processes of data transformation, particularly when the implicit or explicit intention is to bring more validity to the qualitative data (Collingridge, 2013; Onwuegbuzie & Teddlie, 2003; Sandelowski, Voils, & Knafl, 2009).

In our view, researchers should use great care in carrying out data transformation; we recommend following established standards for transformation wherever possible (Onwuegbuzie & Teddlie, 2003; Sandelowski et al., 2009). We also note that this is an area of rapid development in the mixed methods field, with a steady emergence of novel approaches. This innovation is exciting in that it holds promise for advancing the field. At the same time, caution is advised since existing quality standards may not fully accommodate these techniques. The primary strategies for adhering to existing standards in mixed methods data analysis are to review the available resources and create a detailed written analytic plan, ensure relevant expertise is represented on the team, and build in sufficient time to allow for the analysis phase. Grant reviewers should look for evidence of these strategies in multiple parts of the application including the analysis section within methods, the biographical sketches of the team members, and the proposed timeline. Evaluating the quality of data analysis is more challenging for manuscript reviewers, as there is often limited information provided. At a minimum, the manuscript should describe treatment of divergent and convergent data in the analysis and perhaps findings and processes of data transformation, if applicable.

> ▶ Data transformation is discussed in Chapter 8: Data Analysis and Integration in Mixed Methods Studies.

Quality of Analytic Integration

The quality of analytic integration in a mixed methods study can be assessed with attention to several factors. First, as described in Chapter 1, there is general consensus in the field regarding the primary forms of data integration (e.g., connect, merge, build). The particular type of integration used in the analysis should be readily identified in the research proposal or manuscript, using established terminology and brief definitions if needed. Second, certain types of integration are suited for particular mixed methods study designs. The approach should be appropriate for the given design (for instance, a convergent design may not employ connected integration; an explanatory sequential design cannot use merged integration in data collection). Finally, reviewers should evaluate the yield of a mixed methods study (such that the whole is more than the sum of its parts). Key indicators of yield include the extent of integration in design, sampling, analysis, and interpretation and the types and content of publications from the study (O'Cathain, Murphy, & Nicholl, 2007). Ideally, the foundational publication from a mixed methods study will report findings from both qualitative and quantitative components. In our own work, we have sometimes experienced having the integration step glossed over or given superficial attention in an effort to publish findings in a timely way or in a particular disciplinary journal. A factor that cannot be underestimated in terms of its impact on publishing integrated results in mixed methods studies is word limits in journal articles. Space constraints may lead researchers to publish results separately, forgoing the opportunity for integration in reporting results. For instance, a manuscript may be published using data from only the initial component in a sequential design, without integrating the subsequent findings.

Reviewers should attempt to assess whether adequate resources (financial, technical, and intellectual) have been invested in the integration activities. Grant reviewers should look for evidence of plans for integration in the dissemination section of an application, where the applicants should explain the intended publications as well as how data will be integrated and reported in the publications. Reviewers of manuscripts can assess the quality of integration as described within the methods, findings, and discussion sections. In studies that have produced multiple publications, it can be useful for reviewers to assess whether linkages have been made across publications with respect to integration.

▶ For more discussion about challenges and strategies for publishing mixed methods studies, see Chapter 11: Publishing Mixed Methods Studies in the Health Sciences.

Quality of Interpretation

Finally, the quality of interpretation and inference is central to the rigor of a mixed methods study. Two considerations are particularly important elements of quality. First, as with the need for transparency in research methods generally, transparency of the interpretations derived from the respective qualitative and quantitative data sets is essential. Researchers should be deliberate in their interpretations from each data set and clearly identify which findings emerged from which data set.

Second, interpretive efficacy refers to the degree to which the researchers have leveraged the full potential of each data set in order to generate overarching inferences (referred to as "meta-inferences") (Teddlie & Tashakkori, 2006). In the process of generating meta-inferences, attention should be paid toward placing emphasis on particular components as appropriate given sampling and data collection strengths and limitations for each. The development of unique findings that adequately synthesize inferences from the qualitative and quantitative data is a signal of this important dimension of quality in mixed methods studies.

We have proposed a consolidated critical appraisal framework to assess the quality of mixed methods studies. The framework is recommended as an addition to existing standards of rigor for qualitative and quantitative research, which should apply to each respective component. This combination of traditional and alternative criteria has been recommended by several mixed methods experts (Bryman et al., 2008; O'Cathain, 2010a; Wisdom et al., 2012). These suggestions may be useful for reviewers of grants and manuscripts as well as readers of empirical papers reporting mixed methods studies.

EXAMPLES OF THREATS TO QUALITY IN THE DESIGN AND CONDUCT OF MIXED METHODS STUDIES

The risk of undermining quality standards is heightened in mixed methods studies, where team members with quantitative and quantitative orientations may disagree about specific design issues, such as approaches to sampling or data collection. They may also have very different views about data analysis and integration across data sets. These differences pose challenges for each aspect of the study—the qualitative component, the quantitative component, and the mixed methods elements. For example, qualitative researchers may regard a standardized closed-ended questionnaire as inadequate to capture the full range of respondent experience or views and may advocate for alternative or supplemental forms of data collection. An iterative process of data collection and analysis is contrary to quantitative methodological norms that data analysis cannot begin until data collection is complete. Quantitatively oriented members of the research team may question the validity of data collected with highly dynamic instruments and press for greater standardization. As one senior administrator for research reflects in Box 6.5, this heightened risk means that mixed methods researchers should set themselves a high bar for meeting quality standards.

Here we present several potential threats to quality that can occur in mixed methods studies. While this is far from an exhaustive inventory, these flaws are among the more common in our experience in the health sciences. We discuss threats to quality that arise from decisions related to sampling, data collection, analysis, interpretation, and presentation. For each topic, we present a potentially problematic design decision and then discuss the threats to quality that the decision may introduce into a mixed methods study.

Box 6.5   Setting a High Bar for Quality in Mixed Methods Research

Hold yourself and your team to the absolute highest standards possible. Don't do sloppy qualitative or quantitative research, and definitely don't just slap stuff together and call it mixed methods research because then that hurts the rest of the field.

—Dr. Jennifer Wisdom, MPH, PhD,
Associate Vice President for Research,
George Washington University

Design decision about sampling: *To conduct in-depth interviews with all members of a randomly selected, predefined sample of study participants enrolled in a large intervention trial*

> **Threats to quality:** This sampling approach poses at least three threats to quality. First, the proposed design violates the guiding principle of sample selection in qualitative studies, which is that the sample must be purposeful rather than random in nature. Second, the sample size was defined a priori according to power calculations. This approach violates the principle guiding sample size determinations in qualitative studies: theoretical saturation achieved during data analysis. Defining the sample size in advance is not appropriate for a qualitative study, where data

collection and analysis should be carried out iteratively and the decision to stop enrolling respondents is made when the analysis indicates that saturation is met. Finally, unless carefully designed, this extensive qualitative data collection activity may be expensive, disruptive, and intrusive and also interfere with the trial in unanticipated ways.

Design decision about data collection: *To gather qualitative data via an open-ended item at the end of a quantitative survey in order to maximize efficiency in data collection*

Threat to quality: This approach is inconsistent with established practices of data collection in qualitative research. Primary forms of qualitative data collection include interviews, focus groups, various forms of visual observations, and document analysis.

Underpinning these practices are the principles that qualitative data collection, particularly for interviews, is a dynamic interchange between respondent and interviewer (a "guided conversation"; Lofland & Lofland, 1984). The interviewer uses a discussion guide to elicit narrative, with probes for clarification or additional depth, letting the respondent shape the pace and direction of the interview. Intonation, gestures, and body language are also important sources of data (and may be less accessible if interviews are conducted by phone). In addition to these fundamental concerns, there is the pragmatic reality that open-ended items in questionnaires or surveys are more likely to have higher skip rates (resulting in a greater possibility for response bias) since they take more time and effort on the part of the respondent. For example, consider that those with negative attitudes may find it more cumbersome to describe their opinions, and are therefore more likely to leave the question blank than those with neutral or positive attitudes. In addition, this format tends to yield very thin or limited data (often a few sentences as compared to pages of free flowing narrative from an interview or focus group), which may leave many unanswered questions that could have been addressed in a dynamic interaction. There is also a risk that qualitative results generated in this fashion might be interpreted to be generalizable when reported with

> ▶ For more information on types of qualitative data collection, refer to Table 7.3 in Chapter 7: Sampling and Data Collection in Mixed Methods Studies.

findings from the forced choice items, which is not an appropriate inter-pretation. Finally, participants' qualitative responses might be biased by the quantitative items, limiting the range of discussable topics and thereby making the two sources less independent from one another.

Design decision about analysis: *Premature merging of quantitative and qualitative data sets in convergent studies*

Threats to quality: The question of when and how to combine qualita-tive and quantitative data sets is relevant across all mixed methods designs. However, the temptation to immediately merge data may be greatest in studies with a convergent design. In these studies, researchers collect both qualitative and quantitative data simultaneously with either overlapping or distinct participant groups. In contrast to working within a sequential design framework, investigators using a convergent design are not forced to wait and conduct preliminary analysis on the first study component before proceeding to the next phase of data collection. Therefore, the risk of merging data sets too soon is of particular concern. As noted previously, investigators sometimes will *transform* qualitative data into quantitative data (e.g., development of counts or scales or over-all scores) in order to facilitate merging with data from the quantitative component. Likewise, quantitative data may sometimes be transformed into qualitative data (e.g., profiling participants to create a verbal descrip-tion of them). However, data transformation should follow independent analysis of qualitative and quantitative data sets using the standards of rigor discussed earlier in this chapter. Because this is an essential step in mixed methods work, skipping this first part of the analytic process dilutes the mixed methods potential of the project. Whether data collec-tion occurs in a convergent or sequential manner, research teams should independently analyze qualitative and quantitative data initially prior to merging or connecting data sets for integrated analyses.

Design decision about interpretation: *Independent analysis of qualitative and quantitative data from different respondent groups yields divergent find-ings that are not addressed*

Threats to quality: Divergent results may emerge in multiple points—such as within and across respondent groups (patients and physicians), or methods (interviews and surveys)—and should be addressed in data interpretation. In mixed methods in particular, we focus on divergence across the qualitative and quantitative findings. For instance, survey results from physicians might identify language barriers as the primary contributor to poor communication between physicians and patients. Yet interviews with patients might describe insufficient time and poor interpersonal interactions as the primary barriers. Possible reasons for and implications of this difference in perspectives must be explored and reported. Approaches to explaining divergent findings include gathering additional data from the full sample or a subsample, reanalyzing current data and reviewing the study procedures to determine possible threats to data quality.

▶ For more information on addressing divergence, refer to Chapter 8: Data Analysis and Integration in Mixed Methods Studies.

Design decision about presentation: *In a sequential design, quantitative and qualitative data are interpreted and presented as merged data instead of as exploratory or explanatory*

Threats to quality: Space limitations in journals and a desire for health sciences researchers to succinctly communicate findings in a timely way are two reasons why researchers sometimes make this mistake. In a sequential design, one study component (qualitative or quantitative) builds upon the study component preceding it. Therefore, the link or relationship between the two components is predetermined; the second component is intended to extend the knowledge acquired in the first component. However, researchers sometimes compare these data sets as they interpret and present their findings. Comparison of data sets is appropriate in a convergent design when merging data is a key integration step. When interpreting and presenting merged data, researchers are answering this question: To what degree do the quantitative and qualitative findings converge? In contrast, data sets in a sequential design require interpretation and presentation that reflects the "follow-up" nature of the second component. Researchers are answering this question: How do the quantitative results generalize (or support transferability) the qualitative findings (explanatory designs)? or How do the qualitative results explain the quantitative findings (exploratory designs)?

Summary and Key Points

- Defining quality in mixed methods research is essential to maximizing the contribution of these methods to research in the health sciences.
- Common standards of quality of both the qualitative and quantitative components of mixed methods studies include veracity, consistency, applicability, and neutrality. Criteria for appraising the degree to which these standards are met differ for qualitative and quantitative research.
- In addition to the standards for quality that apply to qualitative and quantitative research, multiple frameworks exist for appraising quality in mixed methods studies.
- A comprehensive appraisal of the quality of mixed methods studies includes six core domains of quality: (1) justification for mixed methods, (2) design quality, (3) adherence to respective standards for qualitative and quantitative research, (4) adherence to standards for data analysis in mixed methods, (5) quality of analytic integration, and (6) quality of interpretation and inference.
- Several types of potentially problematic design decisions are common in the health sciences (related to sampling, data collection, analysis, interpretation, and presentation) and may introduce threats to quality in a mixed methods study.

Review Questions and Exercises

1. Select two mixed methods articles from journals in your discipline and review them with a focus on common standards of quality and appraisal criteria for qualitative and quantitative studies (Figure 6.2). What was done well? What could have been done better? How do the articles differ in terms of quality?

2. Using the two articles, refer to the appraisal framework for quality in mixed methods studies outlined in Table 6.1. To what degree does each study meet the domains of quality in the framework?

3. Researchers must be aware of potential threats to quality when they are designing a mixed methods study. Working in a group, discuss the threats to quality that may affect a study you would like to conduct. What are some ways you can avoid these threats?

4. Review the following case vignettes, and discuss threats to quality and strategies to address these threats for each.

Case #1

Dr. A sought to evaluate an innovative clinical decision support tool for physicians and residents treating diabetic ketoacidosis being implemented system-wide across three hospitals. She was interested in the impact of the tool on adherence to core clinical guidelines as measured by error rates in the electronic medical record (EMR) system. She was also interested in experiences of doctors and residents using the tool including overall attitudes as well as sources of user resistance, frustration, and implications for their workflow. She considered a convergent mixed methods design to assess effectiveness (quantitative data on error rates for guideline deviation), acceptability (quantitative survey and qualitative data), and user experiences (qualitative data). In addition to reviewing guideline error rates in the EMR system, she planned to administer a web-based survey to a random sample of doctors and residents on 10 shifts in the emergency department in each of the three hospitals to gather quantitative and qualitative data (five doctors and residents from each shift, 50 doctors and residents per hospital; 150 total). In addition to usability and attitudinal quantitative scales validated in previous evaluations of clinical decision support tools, he proposed to collect qualitative data by inserting an open-ended question at the end of the survey to be completed by all respondents. This design poses several threats to quality, primarily in terms of the qualitative component.

Discuss how to address these threats to quality. Are there others?
- Improper selection of qualitative sample
- Unsuitable determination of qualitative sample size
- Inadequate qualitative data collection strategy

Case #2

Dr. B was interested in understanding the impact of a novel peer-based intervention for breast cancer survivors in remission on mental health and health behaviors. The intervention was designed to support patients in remission transition out of intensive oncology care into follow-up care and to encourage patients to adhere to recommendations about diet and exercise. He proposed an intervention study with an embedded qualitative component to characterize attitudes about the usefulness of the support groups (qualitative focus groups) and to examine associations between support group participation and differences in mental health and health behaviors (standardized quantitative surveys, programmatic and clinical data). He planned to enroll 40 women total (20 in the intervention and 20 in the control group), based on feasibility issues given the number of patients available for recruitment at the hospitals in his network. The quantitative measures, to be gathered at three points during the six-month intervention, included standardized validated instruments to assess mental health and health behaviors in nutrition and exercise. In addition, he proposed focus groups (three groups with six participants in each for a total sample of 18), at the intervention midpoint (three months). For efficiency, he planned to administer the quantitative measures for the midpoint data collection at the conclusion of the focus groups since all participants would be onsite and available. This design poses several threats to quality in terms of both the quantitative and qualitative components.

Discuss how to address these threats to quality. Are there others?
- Inadequate and potentially biased quantitative sample
- Inappropriate qualitative data collection strategy

Case #3

Dr. C was interested in patient–provider communication in the context of primary care services for newly arrived refugees receiving care in refugee clinics. He wanted to understand the quality of communication from the perspectives of patients and providers, and because there was very little existing literature on this topic, he decided to conduct a mixed methods study that included a qualitative component that informed the development of a structured survey. He conducted in-depth interviews with patients and providers in several clinics in order to gain an understanding of range of experiences and attitudes regarding the quality of communication. He then used this information to develop questions and response options for a survey that aimed to measure patient and provider satisfaction with communication in the clinic setting. He was careful to adhere to the respective standards for sampling, data collection, and analysis for the qualitative and quantitative components of the study. However, this study did not achieve integration during analysis and interpretation. Dr. C set out with a plan for qualitative data collection that included a specific number of interviews in a specific time, and then the team did the qualitative analysis and survey development after the interviews ended. Although integration was possible given the sequential design, two separate teams analyzed the data from the qualitative and quantitative components and published the results separately in two articles.

Discuss how to address these threats to quality. Are there others?

- Lack of iterative qualitative data collection process
- Inadequate handling of divergent results

References

Aschengrau, A., & Seage, G. R. (2008). *Essentials of epidemiology in public health.* Sudbury, MA: Jones and Bartlett.

Bradley, C. (1997). Qualitative vs. quantitative research methods. In Y. Carter & C. Thomas (Eds.), *Research methods in primary care* (pp. 31–39). Abingdon, Oxon, UK: Radcliffe Medical Press Ltd.

Bradley, E. H., Curry, L. A., & Devers, K. J. (2007). Qualitative data analysis for health services research: Developing taxonomy, themes, and theory. *Health Services Research, 42*(4), 1758–1772.

Bryman, A. (1988). *Quantity and quality in social research.* London, UK: Unwin Hyman.

Bryman, A., Becker, S., & Sempik, J. (2008). Quality criteria for quantitative, qualitative and mixed methods research: a view from social policy. *International Journal of Social Research Methodology, 11*(4), 261–276.

Campbell, D. T., & Fiske, D. W. (1959). Convergent and discriminant validation by the multitrait-multimethod matrix. *Psychological Bulletin, 56*(2), 81–105.

Caracelli, V. J., & Riggin, L. J. C. (1994). Mixed method evaluation: Developing quality criteria through concept mapping. *Evaluation Practice, 15*(2), 139–152.

Collingridge, D. S. (2013). A primer on quantitized data analysis and permutation testing. *Journal of Mixed Methods Research, 7*(1), 81–97.

Cook, T. D. (1985). Postpositivist critical multiplism. In R. L. Shotland & M. M. Mark (Eds.), *Social science and social policy* (pp. 21–62). Beverly Hills, CA: Sage.

Cook, T. D., & Campbell, D. T. (1979). *Quasi-experimentation: Design & analysis issues for field settings.* Boston, MA: Houghton Mifflin.

Crabtree, B. F., & Miller, W. L. (1999). *Doing qualitative research* (2nd ed.). Thousand Oaks, CA: Sage.

Creswell, J. W. (1999). Mixed-method research: Introduction and application. In G. J. Cizek (Ed.), *Handbook of educational policy* (pp. 455–472). San Diego, CA: Academic Press.

Creswell, J. W., Fetters, M. D., & Ivankova, N. V. (2004). Designing a mixed methods study in primary care. *Annals of Family Medicine, 2*(1), 7–12.

Creswell, J. W., & Plano Clark, V. L. (2011). *Designing and conducting mixed methods research* (2nd ed.). Thousand Oaks, CA: Sage.

Creswell, J. W., Plano Clark, V. L., Gutmann, M., & Hanson, W. (2003). Advanced mixed methods research designs. In A. Tashakkori & C. Teddlie (Eds.), *Handbook of mixed methods in social and behavioral health* (pp. 209–240). Thousand Oaks, CA: Sage.

Denzin, N. K. (1978). *The research act: A theoretical introduction to sociological methods* (2nd ed.). New York, NY: McGraw-Hill.

Denzin, N. K., & Lincoln, Y. (Eds.). (2000). *Handbook of qualitative research* (2nd ed.). Thousand Oaks, CA: Sage.

Glaser, B. G., & Strauss, A. L. (1967). *The discovery of grounded theory: Strategies for qualitative research.* Chicago, IL: Aldine.

Gordis, L. (2009). *Epidemiology* (4th ed.). Philadelphia, PA: Elsevier/Saunders.

Greene, J. C. (2007). *Mixed methods in social inquiry* (1st ed.). San Francisco, CA: Jossey-Bass.

Guest, G. (2013). Describing mixed methods research: An alternative to typologies. *Journal of Mixed Methods Research, 7*(2), 141–151.

Hannemann-Weber, H., Kessel, M., Budych, K., & Schultz, C. (2011). Shared communication processes within healthcare teams for rare diseases and their influence on healthcare professionals' innovative behavior and patient satisfaction. *Implementation Science, 6,* 40. doi: 10.1186/1748–5908–6-40

Heyvaert, M., Hannes, K., Maes, B., & Onghena, P. (2013). Critical appraisal of mixed methods studies. *Journal of Mixed Methods Research, 7*(4), 302–327.

Horsburgh, D. (2003). Evaluation of qualitative research. *Journal of Clinical Nursing, 12*(2), 307–312.

Hulley, S. B., Cummings, S. R., Browner, W. S., Grady, D. G., & Newman, T. B. (2013). *Designing clinical research* (4th ed.). Philadelphia, PA: Wolters Kluwer/ Lippincott Williams & Wilkins.

Lincoln, Y. S., & Guba, E. G. (1985). *Naturalistic inquiry.* Beverly Hills, CA: Sage.

Lofland, J., & Lofland, L. H. (1984). *Analyzing social settings: A guide to qualitative observation and analysis.* Belmont, CA: Wadsworth Publishing Co.

Malterud, K. (2001). Qualitative research: Standards, challenges, and guidelines. *Lancet, 358*(9280), 483–488. doi: 10.1016/S0140–6736(01)05627–6

Mays, N., & Pope, C. (2000). Qualitative research in health care. Assessing quality in qualitative research. *BMJ, 320*(7226), 50–52.

Miles, M. B., & Huberman, A. M. (1994). *Qualitative data analysis: An expanded sourcebook* (2nd ed.). Thousand Oaks, CA: Sage.

Morgan, D. L. (1998). Practical strategies for combining qualitative and quantitative methods: Applications to health research. *Qualitative Health Research, 8*(3), 362–376.

Morse, J. M. (1991). Approaches to qualitative-quantitative methodological triangulation. *Nursing Research, 40*(2), 120–123.

Morse, J. M. (1999). Myth # 93: Reliability and validity are not relevant to qualitative inquiry. *Qualitative Health Research, 9*(6), 717–718.

Morse, J. M. (2010). Procedures and practice of mixed method design: maintaining control, rigor, and complexity. In A. Tashakkori & C. Teddlie (Eds.), *SAGE handbook of mixed methods in social and behavioral research* (pp. 348). Thousand Oaks, CA: Sage.

Morse, J. M., & Niehaus, L. (2009). *Mixed method design: Principles and procedures.* Walnut Creek, CA: Left Coast Press.

Morse, J. M., & Richards, L. (2002). *README first for a user's guide to qualitative methods.* Thousand Oaks, CA: Sage.

Morse, J. M., Wolfe, R. R., & Niehaus, L. (2006). Principles and procedures of maintaining validity for mixed-method design. In L. Curry, R. Shield, & T. T. Wetle (Eds.), *Improving aging and public health research: Qualitative and mixed methods* (pp. 65–78). Washington, DC: American Public Health Association.

Murphy, E., Dingwall, R., Greatbatch, D., Parker, S., & Watson, P. (1998). Qualitative research methods in health technology assessment: A review of the literature. *Health Technology Assessment, 2*(16), iii–ix, 1–274.

O'Cathain, A. (2010a). Assessing the quality of mixed methods research: Toward a comprehensive framework. In A. Tashakkori & C. Teddlie (Eds.), *SAGE handbook of mixed methods in social and behavioral research* (2nd ed., pp. 531–555). Thousand Oaks, CA: Sage.

O'Cathain, A. (2010b). Stakeholders relevant to the assessment of the quality of mixed methods research. In A. Tashakkori & C. Teddlie (Eds.), *SAGE handbook of mixed methods in social and behavioral research* (pp. 533). Thousand Oaks, CA: Sage.

O'Cathain, A., Murphy, E., & Nicholl, J. (2007). Integration and publications as indicators of "yield" from mixed methods studies. *Journal of Mixed Methods Research, 1*(2), 147–163.

O'Cathain, A., Murphy, E., & Nicholl, J. (2008). The quality of mixed methods studies in health services research. *Journal of Health Services Research and Policy, 13*(2), 92–98. doi: 10.1258/jhsrp.2007.007074

Onwuegbuzie, A. J., & Johnson, R. B. (2006). The validity issue in mixed research. *Research in the schools, 13*(1), 48–63.

Onwuegbuzie, A. J., & Leech, N. L. (2007). Validity and qualitative research: An oxymoron. *Quality and Quantity, 41*(2), 233–249.

Onwuegbuzie, A. J., & Teddlie, C. (2003). A framework for analyzing data in mixed methods research. In A. Tashakkori & C. Teddlie (Eds.), *Handbook of mixed methods in social and behavioral research* (pp. 351–384). Thousand Oaks, CA: Sage.

Padgett, D. (2012). Strategies for rigor. In *Qualitative and mixed methods research in public health* (pp. 203–220). Thousand Oaks, CA: Sage.

Patton, M. Q. (1990). *Quality evaluation and research methods* (2nd ed.). Newbury Park, CA: Sage.

Patton, M. Q. (2002). *Qualitative research & evaluation methods* (3rd ed.). Thousand Oaks, CA: Sage.

Pluye, P., Gagnon, M. P., Griffiths, F., & Johnson-Lafleur, J. (2009). A scoring system for appraising mixed methods research, and concomitantly appraising qualitative, quantitative and mixed methods primary studies in mixed studies reviews. *International Journal of Nursing Studies, 46*(4), 529–546. doi: 10.1016/j.ijnurstu.2009.01.009

Pluye, P., Grad, R. M., Levine, A., & Nicolau, B. (2009). Understanding divergence of quantitative and qualitative data (or results) in mixed methods studies. *International Journal of Multiple Research Approaches, 3*(1), 58–72.

Polit, D. F., & Beck, C. T. (2010). Generalization in quantitative and qualitative research: Myths and strategies. *International Journal of Nursing Studies, 47*(11), 1451–1458. doi: 10.1016/j.ijnurstu.2010.06.004

Sale, J. E. M., & Brazil, K. (2004). A strategy to identify critical appraisal for criteria for primary mixed-methods studies. *Quality and Quantity, 38*(4), 351–365.

Sandelowski, M. (2000). Combining qualitative and quantitative sampling, data collection, and analysis techniques in mixed-method studies. *Research in Nursing and Health, 23*(3), 246–255.

Sandelowski, M., Voils, C. I., & Knafl, G. (2009). On quantitizing. *Journal of Mixed Methods Research, 3*(3), 208–222. doi: 10.1177/1558689809334210

Steckler, A., McLeroy, K. R., Goodman, R. M., Bird, S. T., & McCormick, L. (1992). Toward integrating qualitative and quantitative methods: An introduction. *Health Education Quarterly, 19*(1), 1–8.

Strauss, A. L., & Corbin, J. M. (1998). *Basics of qualitative research: Techniques and procedures for developing grounded theory* (2nd ed.). Thousand Oaks, CA: Sage.

Tashakkori, A., & Teddlie, C. (1998). *Mixed methodology: Combining qualitative and quantitative approaches.* Thousand Oaks, CA: Sage.

Teddlie, C., & Tashakkori, A. (2006). A general typology of research designs featuring mixed methods. *Research in the Schools, 13,* 12–28.

Teddlie, C., & Tashakkori, A. (2009). *Foundations of mixed methods research: Integrating quantitative and qualitative approaches in the social and behavioral sciences.* Thousand Oaks, CA: Sage.

Tufford, L., & Newman, P. (2012). Bracketing in qualitative research. *Qualitative Social Work, 11*(1), 80–96.

Wisdom, J. P., Cavaleri, M. A., Onwuegbuzie, A. J., & Green, C. A. (2012). Methodological reporting in qualitative, quantitative, and mixed methods health services research articles. *Health Services Research, 47*(2), 721–745. doi: 10.1111/j.1475-6773.2011.01344.x

PART III

DESIGNING AND IMPLEMENTING A MIXED METHODS STUDY

In Part III, we address central issues related to designing and implementing mixed methods studies in health sciences. First, we describe how to design sampling and data collection strategies that adhere to the standards for each individual component while simultaneously supporting the integration of components. Next, we discuss the centrality of data integration and provide tips on strategies for achieving integration throughout the study. Because mixed methods work necessarily involves diversity in research team composition, we discuss key challenges and strategies for managing mixed methods teams. This section closes with a practical look at the challenges of carrying out a mixed methods study.

❧ SEVEN ❧

SAMPLING AND DATA COLLECTION
IN MIXED METHODS STUDIES

Information you will find in this chapter: This chapter addresses sampling and data collection in mixed methods studies. We highlight the importance of adhering to standards for each individual study component while simultaneously designing an overarching sampling plan to be applied across components. In the first section, you will find a brief overview of sampling approaches used in quantitative and qualitative research. The next section outlines the principles and practices of sampling in mixed methods in the health sciences, with illustrative examples. The remainder of the chapter addresses data collection. We describe the highly varied sources of data used in mixed methods studies, emphasizing the need for fitting the data collection instruments and procedures across components. Finally, we summarize the data collection capacities needed within the mixed methods research team.

Key features in this chapter:

- Brief quotations and reflections from mixed methods researchers
- Table summarizing purposeful and probability sampling techniques
- Table summarizing defining features of mixed methods sampling techniques
- Table describing fit of data collection and procedures in mixed methods studies
- Examples from published empirical literature using mixed methods
- Figure depicting an overarching mixed methods sampling algorithm

PRINCIPLES OF SOUND SAMPLING

A central challenge and strength of mixed methods is in the appropriate lever-aging of the breadth of data generated through the quantitative components and the depth of data generated through the qualitative components. The sampling approaches for each component largely determine the degree to which the over-all study design can achieve these complementary aims. This section reviews the principles of purposeful sampling for qualitative studies and probability sampling for quantitative studies, highlighting the differentiation along a num-ber of dimensions. These ideas are also summarized in Table 7.1.

A defining feature of qualitative methods is the use of purposeful sam-pling techniques, sometimes referred to as nonprobability sampling. These

Table 7.1   Comparisons Between Purposeful and Probability
Sampling Techniques

Dimension of Comparison	Purposeful Sampling	Probability Sampling
Issue of generalizability	A form of generalizability (transferability) sometimes sought	A form of generalizability (external validity) sought
Rationale for selecting cases or units	To select information-rich cases that can provide depth of information	To select representative units that can product generalizable results
Sample size	Typically small (usually 30 cases or fewer)	Large enough to establish representativeness (usually at least 50 units)
Depth and breadth of information per case or unit	Focus on depth of information generated by cases	Focus on breadth of information generated by sampling units
When the sample is selected	Before the study begins, during the study, or both	Before the study begins
Form of data generation	Focus on narrative data with potential for generating numeric data	Focus on numeric data with potential for generating narrative data

SOURCE: Adapted from Teddlie and Yu (2007).

techniques are primarily intended to generate depth of information (hence enhancing credibility) to address a defined research question. Transferability of findings may also be a goal of this approach. Transferability is the degree to which findings can be transferred to other settings, contexts, or populations as determined by the reader of the study.

▶ To read more about types of sampling in qualitative and quantitative methods, refer to the Glossary of Key Terms and Definitions or Appendix E: Quick Resource: A Short List of Readings and References.

The sample consists of cases (e.g., individuals, organizations, other entities) that are information rich, meaning they have experience with and knowledge of the phenomenon of interest. The size of the sample cannot be defined a priori but rather is determined by theoretical saturation, or the point at which no new information emerges during data collection. The sample can either be selected at the start of the study or at some predefined point during the course of the study, depending on the design. Examples of purposeful sampling techniques include deviant or confirming case sampling, sampling for maximum variation, and snowball sampling (Patton, 2002).

Quantitative methods rely on probability sampling techniques, sometimes referred to as random sampling techniques. These techniques aim to achieve high generalizability through representativeness so that inferences from the sample units can be made reliably to the larger population from which the sample was drawn. The size of sample must be large enough to achieve representativeness, and the focus is on generating breadth

◀ Credibility and transferability are further described in Chapter 6: Assessing Quality in Mixed Methods Studies.

of information. Sample sizes are determined at the outset of the study, based on power calculations that demonstrate the number of units required to detect statistically significant differences among groups. Examples of probability sampling techniques include simple random sampling, systematic random sampling, and stratified random sampling.

PRINCIPLES OF SAMPLING IN MIXED METHODS STUDIES

Sampling approaches in mixed methods studies capitalize on the complementarity of purposeful and probability approaches. The key defining characteristics of mixed methods sampling approaches are summarized in Table 7.2. In terms of generalizability, the quantitative component seeks maximum external validity, while the qualitative arm may or may not be concerned with transferability. The sample should be developed with attention toward both representativeness for the quantitative component (to enhance generalizability) as well as depth and richness of data for the qualitative component (to enhance credibility). The overall sampling plan should be defined at the outset of the study although sequential decisions regarding specific techniques may evolve during the course of the study. Most commonly, both narrative and numeric data are generated; in some instances data transformation may result in one or the other forms of data as the primary output.

Table 7.2 Characteristics of Mixed Methods Sampling Techniques

Dimension of Contrast	Mixed Methods Sampling
Issue of generalizability	For some components of a research design, there is a focus on external validity issues; for other components, the focus is on transferability.
Rationale for selecting cases or units	For some components of a research design, there is a focus on representativeness; for other components, the focus is on seeking out information rich cases.
Sample size	There can be multiple samples in the study; samples vary in size depending on the research component type and questions.
Depth and breadth of information per case or unit	The focus is on depth and breadth of information across the research components.
When the sample is selected	Most sampling decisions are made before the study starts, but qualitative questions may lead to the emergence of other samples during the study.
Form of data generation	Both numeric and narrative data are typically generated.

SOURCE: Adapted from Teddlie and Yu (2007).

PRACTICES OF SAMPLING
IN MIXED METHODS STUDIES

In creating the overarching sampling plan for a mixed methods study, the common practice is to apply probability and purposeful techniques either *interdependently* or *independently*. In the latter approach, the sampling plan includes two distinct samples, although the component samples may still be linked or connected even if the sampling frames are built independently. For example, in a sequential design, researchers may be interested in identifying a sample for the second component to answer questions developed based upon findings in the first component. Another option is that both independent and interdependent sampling approaches may be *combined* within the same mixed methods study. For instance, researchers might use an independent approach to develop a sampling frame for a quantitative questionnaire component through application of a probability technique and use an interdependent approach to develop the sampling frame for follow-up qualitative in-depth interviews through application of a joint probability and purposeful technique.

Informed by Teddlie's and Yu's (2007) typology for mixed methods sampling in the social and behavioral sciences, we present a streamlined and pragmatic framework for health sciences researchers which categorizes overarching mixed methods sampling plans as interdependent, independent, or combined as defined by the relationship between the chosen probability and purposeful sampling techniques. Each of the approaches allows for adjustment and modification as projects evolve, and none of the approaches is inherently more rigorous than the others. Similar to other key mixed methods design decisions such as timing of components and integration of data, deciding whether to pursue an interdependent, independent, or combined sampling approach is determined largely by the following: the research study objective (e.g., Is it hypothesis testing?), the stated rationale for using a mixed methods approach, and intended relevance of the findings (e.g., Is external validity–veracity or transferability–applicability the greater priority?)

◀ For more information on veracity and applicability, refer to Chapter 6: Assessing Quality in Mixed Methods Studies. For more information on rationale for using mixed methods, refer to Chapter 2: Applications and Illustrations of Mixed Methods Health Sciences Research and Chapter 8: Data Analysis and Integration in Mixed Methods Studies.

In the following section, we present examples from the peer-reviewed literature for interdependent, independent, and combined sampling strategies for some of the mixed methods designs most commonly used in the health sciences.

Interdependent Sampling

Interdependent mixed methods sampling frames are built through the joint use of probability and purposeful techniques to create one or more samples for a particular project. Researchers might decide to draw multiple samples from the defined sampling frame for participation in the different study components or to draw a single sample from the sampling frame that participates in both the quantitative and qualitative components of the project. Although the goal may be to have purposeful and probability influences contribute equally to the development of the sampling frame, the sampling decisions may "favor" one or the other. However, because principles of rigor must be upheld for each approach as feasible, we recommend against determining a single mixed methods study sample through the independent use of either a probability technique (e.g., simple random sample) or a purposeful technique (e.g., maximum variation). For example, a team conducting a study using a questionnaire may choose the simple random sample probability technique. In this situation, we would not recommend adding an open-ended question to the survey instrument administered to this random sample as the qualitative component of a mixed methods project (which would require a second sample identified using a purposeful or joint technique).

Although sometimes classified solely as a purposeful technique, the stratified purposeful sampling approach (sometimes referred to as quota sampling) fits within our framework of interdependent sampling in mixed methods. In a stratified purposeful approach, strata are created for salient subgroups of the population, and then cases are purposefully recruited into each cell (e.g., matrix with two dimensions of ownership status for profit or nonprofit and three dimensions of performance on a given quality metric). An interdependent sampling approach is often used when a purely probability-based sampling frame is not feasible for the

◀ For an example of a mixed methods study with challenges related to sampling, refer to Case #1 in the Review Questions and Exercises section of Chapter 6: Assessing Quality in Mixed Methods Studies.

quantitative component, such as when working with difficult-to-access populations. One relevant example of this method of targeted sampling, developed by Watters and Biernacki (1989), is where characteristics of a hidden population (e.g., intravenous drug users) are determined and used to create strata for purposeful recruitment. A variation of stratified purposeful sampling is purposeful random sampling in which a random sample is drawn from a large universe of available cases that satisfy specified criteria. Often this is done in a combined sampling plan when a large sample is being studied quantitatively and the qualitative data is intended to enrich the findings from the quantitative component.

In some cases, data collection within an interdependent sampling plan can be less resource intensive than other approaches. Study expenses may be reduced by recruiting one sample at one point in time. Time costs may be reduced by the ability to collect data for both components either simultaneously or in close time proximity in a convergent design. These savings may be offset by additional costs if the strata characteristics need to be identified and developed de novo. Also, working within an interdependent sampling plan may require greater mixed method expertise and skill among participant recruiters and data collectors as compared to other types of sampling plans (see Box 7.1).

Box 7.1   Abstract from a Study That Used Interdependent Sampling

Schwartz, R. P., Kelly, S. M., O'Grady, K. E., Mitchell, S. G., Peterson, J. A., Reisinger, H. S., Agar, M. H., & Brown, B. S. (2008). Attitudes toward buprenorphine and methadone among opioid-dependent individuals. *American Journal on Addictions, 17*(5), 396–401.

Abstract

Attitudes and beliefs about drug abuse treatment have long been known to shape response to that treatment. Two major pharmacological alternatives are available for opioid dependence: methadone, which has been available for the past 40 years, and

(Continued)

(Continued)

buprenorphine, a recently introduced medication. This mixed methods study examined the attitudes of opioid-dependent individuals toward methadone and buprenorphine. A total of 195 participants ($n = 140$ who were enrolling in one of six Baltimore area methadone programs and $n = 55$ who were out-of-treatment) were administered the Attitudes Toward Methadone and Toward Buprenorphine Scales and a subset ($n = 46$) received an ethnographic interview. The in-treatment group had significantly more positive attitudes toward methadone than did the out-of-treatment group ($p < .001$), while they did not differ in their attitudes toward buprenorphine. Both groups had significantly more positive attitudes toward buprenorphine than methadone. Addressing these attitudes may increase treatment entry and retention.

As described in Box 7.1, Schwartz and colleagues (2008) used a convergent parallel design to examine attitudes toward methadone and buprenorphine among opioid-dependent individuals. The mixed methods study featured in Box 7.1 is embedded within a large longitudinal mixed methods study that aims to learn why opioid-addicted individuals do or do not enter treatment and do or do not remain in treatment. Quantitative and qualitative data are collected simultaneously for each participant at baseline and at several follow-up points during a 12-month period following study enrollment. Two populations of opioid-dependent individuals are targeted: those in treatment and those out of treatment. In a separate paper describing the sampling methodology for this study, Peterson and colleagues (2008) detailed the step-by-step process of accessing and recruiting a sample of approximately 50 individuals from the target population of out-of-treatment opioid-addicted individuals. The research team used an interdependent sampling plan to define the samples for the qualitative and quantitative components of the parent and, therefore of the embedded, study. Informed by a formative ethnographic phase, the research team used a joint probability and purposeful technique—purposeful random sampling—to select 12 police patrol districts in Baltimore as recruitment sites and then to randomly recruit out-of-treatment opioid-using individuals from those sites. A priori, they established they would not recruit more than three participants per site nor would they recruit longer than one month at a site to protect randomization. All of the recruited out-of-treatment opioid-addicted individuals participated in the quantitative component that included completion of two assessment measures ("Attitudes Toward Methadone and Toward Buprenorphine Scales"). A subset of this sample ($n = 28$) was identified using another joint probability and purposeful technique stratified purposeful sampling to participate in the qualitative ethnographic component. The sample from the quantitative component was stratified by site and then further by race, gender, number of treatment episodes, and route of administration. The sample size of the quantitative–qualitative component was 195 and the sample size of the qualitative component was 46.

Independent Sampling

In an independent mixed methods sampling plan, a primary purposeful sampling technique is chosen for the qualitative component, and a primary probability sampling technique is chosen for the quantitative component. The selection of the specific techniques is determined separately based upon the research question developed for each component. Using an independent sampling plan in a mixed methods study commits the researchers to proposing at least two distinct samples, defined as having unique sampling frames but not requiring nonoverlapping participants. One potential advantage to using an independent sampling plan is to protect against generalizability critiques. Conversely, researchers using an independent sampling plan may need to defend against concerns they have simply used multiple methods to study a single research topic rather than conducting an integrated mixed methods study. Other considerations when using an independent sampling plan include the time and cost associated with recruiting and data collecting within two different sampling frames. However, an advantage to using an independent sampling plan is that participant recruiters and data collectors do not typically need advanced mixed methods expertise or skill (see Box 7.2).

As described in Box 7.2, McNulty and colleagues (2012) used an exploratory sequential design to understand public views on the appropriateness of physician visits and antibiotic utilization for respiratory illness in the wake of the H1N1 pandemic. Qualitative in-depth interviews ($n = 17$) examined participant views on the management of recent respiratory illness and subsequently informed the development of select items for inclusion on a population-based survey ($n = 1,767$), thereby connecting the study components.

Box 7.2   Abstract From a Study That Used Independent Sampling

McNulty, C., Joshi, P., Butler, C. C., Atkinson, L., Nichols, T., Hogan, A., & French, D. (2012). Have the public's expectations for antibiotics for acute uncomplicated respiratory tract infections changed since the H1N1 influenza pandemic? A qualitative interview and quantitative questionnaire study. *BMJ Open, 2*(2), e000674.

Abstract

Objective: To investigate the effect of the H1N1 influenza pandemic on the public's expectations for a general practice consultation and antibiotic for acute respiratory illness.

Design: Mixed methods.

Participants: Qualitative interviews: 17 participants with acute respiratory tract infection (RTI) visiting English pharmacies. Face-to-face survey: about 1,700 adults aged 15 years and older were recruited from households in England in January 2008, 2009, and 2011.

Results: The qualitative data indicated that the general public had either forgotten about the "swine flu" (H1N1 influenza) pandemic or it did not concern them as it had not affected them directly or affected their management of their current RTI illness. Between 2009 and 2011, we found that there was little or no change in people's expectations for antibiotics for runny nose, colds, sore throat or cough, but people's expectations for antibiotics for flu increased (26%–32%, $p = 0.004$). Of the 1,000 respondents in 2011 with an RTI in the previous 6 months, 13% reported that they took care of themselves without contacting their general practitioners and would not have done so before the pandemic, 9% reported that they had contacted their doctor's service and would not have done so before the pandemic and 0.6% stated that they had asked for antibiotics and would not have done so before the pandemic. In 2011, of 123 respondents with a young child (0–4 years) having an RTI in the previous 6 months, 7.4% requested antibiotics and would not have done so before the pandemic. Unprompted, 20% of respondents thought Tamiflu (oseltamivir) was a vaccine.

Conclusions: Expectations of the general public for a consultation or antibiotics with an RTI are similar now to before the H1N1 influenza pandemic; therefore, public antibiotic campaign messages and general practice advice to patients can remain unchanged. Parents with young children and those with personal experience of the H1N1 influenza are more likely to consult and will need more reassurance. The public need more education about Tamiflu.

The researchers used an independent sampling approach to define two separate sampling frames for the qualitative and quantitative components. For the qualitative interview component, they chose a primary purposeful sampling technique—typical case sampling—to capture information from adults with symptoms of acute respiratory illness who were self-managing or who were being treated by a physician. They chose to recruit from nine pharmacies in four geographic areas; the areas were selected based on normal or higher H1N1 influenza activity during the pandemic and their socioeconomic and ethnic diversity. Individuals were approached in the pharmacy and asked to agree to a telephone interview if eligible to participate. While 50 people agreed to an interview, the researchers concluded theoretical saturation had been achieved after analysis of 17 interviews.

For the quantitative survey component, they defined the target population as all adults (15 years of age and older) in England. They chose a primary probability sampling technique— stratified random sampling—to identify a representative sample of community dwellers ($n = 1,800$). Data were ultimately collected through in-home assessments with 1,767 respondents. The overall sample size for both components of this study was 1,784 (1,767 for the quantitative component and 17 for the qualitative component).

Combined Sampling

Combined mixed methods sampling plans are commonly used among published mixed methods studies in the health sciences. Typically, researchers will use an independent probability approach to determine the sample for the quantitative component and an interdependent approach to determine a subsample of the participants from the quantitative component for a subsequent qualitative component in an explanatory sequential design. Advantages to this approach include working with a single target population, creating opportunities to share recruitment and data collection resources across the study components. However, this sampling plan requires a wide range of expertise at all levels of the research team (see Box 7.3).

Box 7.3   Abstract From a Study That Used Combined Sampling

Krein, S. L., Kowalski, C. P., Damschroder, L., Forman, J., Kaufman, S. R., & Saint, S. (2008). Preventing ventilator-associated pneumonia in the United States: A multicenter mixed-methods study. *Infection Control and Hospital Epidemiology, 29*(10), 933–940.

Abstract

Objective: To determine what practices are used by hospitals to prevent ventilator-associated pneumonia (VAP) and, through qualitative methods, to understand more fully why hospitals use certain practices and not others.

Design: Mixed methods, sequential explanatory study.

Methods: We mailed a survey to the lead infection control professionals at 719 U.S. hospitals (119 Department of Veterans Affairs [VA] hospitals and 600 non-VA hospitals), to determine what practices are used to prevent VAP. We then selected 14 hospitals for an in-depth qualitative investigation, to ascertain why certain infection control practices are used and others not, interviewing 86 staff members and visiting 6 hospitals.

Results: The survey response rate was 72%; 83% of hospitals reported using semirecumbent positioning, and only 21% reported using subglottic secretion drainage. Multivariable analyses indicated collaborative initiatives were associated with the use of semirecumbent positioning but provided little guidance regarding the use of subglottic secretion drainage. Qualitative analysis, however, revealed 3 themes: (1) collaboratives strongly influence the use of semirecumbent positioning but have little effect on the use of subglottic secretion drainage; (2) nurses play a major role in the use of semirecumbent positioning, but they are only minimally involved with the use of subglottic secretion drainage; and (3) there is considerable debate about the evidence supporting subglottic secretion drainage, despite a meta-analysis of 5 randomized trials of subglottic secretion drainage that generally supported this preventive practice, compared with only 2 published randomized trials of semirecumbent positioning, one of which concluded that it was ineffective at preventing the development of VAP.

   Conclusion: Semirecumbent positioning is commonly used to prevent VAP, whereas subglottic secretion drainage is used far less often. We need to understand better how evidence related to prevention practices is identified, interpreted, and used to ensure that research findings are reliably translated into clinical practice.

As described in Box 7.3, Krein and colleagues (2008) used an explanatory sequential design to identify and understand hospital practice regarding the prevention of ventilator-associated pneumonia (VAP). Quantitative survey data ($n = 518$ hospitals) captured the frequency of use for specific infection control practices while qualitative semistructured interviews ($n = 14$ hospitals) described the perspectives of decision-making staff in different work roles.

   Their target population was defined as all hospitals in the United States. The researchers used an independent sampling approach to define the sample for the quantitative component. They included all Department of Veterans Affairs (VA) medical centers ($n = 119$), as they are part of the nation's largest centralized health care delivery system. In this case, they had the resources to include the entire subtarget population (VA hospitals) in the sampling frame. They used a probability sampling technique—stratified random sampling—to identify a sample of non-VA hospitals ($n = 600$) because they did not have the resources to include that entire population. They combined the two groups to create one sample for the quantitative component of the study ($n = 719$).

   They used an interdependent mixed methods sampling approach to identify a sample for follow-up semistructured interviews. Using a joint probability and purposeful sampling technique— stratified purposeful sampling—they stratified by hospital size and by results of the quantitative component that were used to create two dimensions of infection control practice frequency (typical or atypical) for a sampling matrix. They conducted a total of 86 interviews during telephonic interviews and site visits at 6 of the 14 hospitals. The overall sample size for this study was 719 as the 14 hospitals included in the qualitative component were identified from the larger universe of the 719 hospitals.

Sampling Considerations Unique to Mixed Methods

While attention to methodological principles for sound sampling is essential, sampling decisions are also inevitably informed by practical considerations. Health sciences researchers need to design a sampling strategy within the context of fixed resources and time. Because we are rarely able to access and evaluate entire target populations we must make strategic sampling choices that maximize both efficiency and veracity. In determining sampling approaches for mixed methods studies, it is helpful to develop a high degree of comfort with sampling plans that may evolve as the project progresses. Virtually every mixed methods study will involve careful balancing of the tenets and benefits of purposeful and probability sampling. However, thoughtful attention to maintaining rigor across study components can minimize threats to the overall study quality as a result.

We present a simplified four-step process to determine your sampling plan for a mixed methods study in the health sciences (see Figure 7.1). First, determine your overall sampling approach for the study. Will you take an interdependent, independent, or combined approach, as defined previously? Second, decide whether you intend to use the same sample for both study components or to use two different samples. A number of factors will shape this decision: (1) focus of the research questions (e.g., Would the same sample generate both information-rich and generalizable findings?); (2) timing of data collection (e.g., a convergent design might facilitate using one sample); (3) data collection protocols (e.g., an interviewer-administered questionnaire design can create the opportunity for the interviewer to collect qualitative and quantitative data in one sitting); (4) data analysis plans (e.g., Are you going to compare quantitative and qualitative responses for individual participants or compare aggregated data?); (5) integration strategy (e.g., Is the intent for the second component's sample to be built after the first component is completed?); and (6) ease of access to eligible participants (e.g., Is the population of interest small or difficult to recruit?).

The third step is to determine the sample size(s). If you decide to use the same sample across components, your team will still use both probability and purposeful techniques to propose an interdependent sampling strategy but will likely need to commit more strongly to one side of the "representation/saturation

Figure 7.1 Mixed Methods Sampling Algorithm

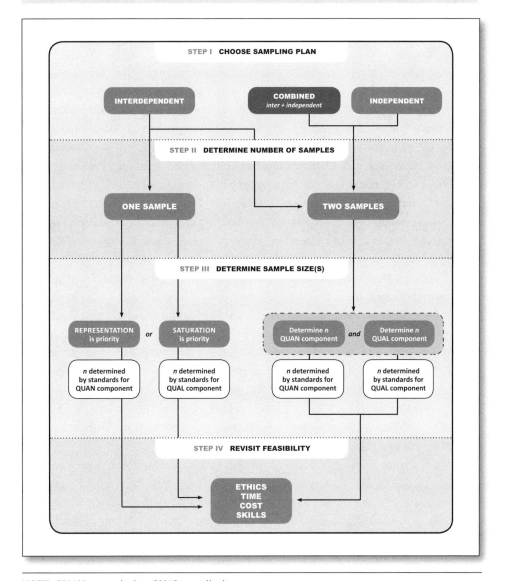

NOTE: QUAN = quantitative; QUAL = qualitative.

trade-off" (Teddlie & Tashakkori, 2009). This term captures the choice mixed methods researchers often have to make between prioritizing representation (e.g., the need for a random sample of a size that reflects the study population) or prioritizing saturation (e.g., the need for a purposeful sample of a depth that fully characterizes a phenomenon). If greater emphasis must be placed on the representativeness of the quantitative component, then the sample size will be determined by power calculations. In this situation, the number of participants in the qualitative component will be first determined by the number of eligible potential participants in the quantitative component and not by thematic saturation. Although limited by the criteria of entry for the quantitative component, you can still determine the "who" subset of participants for the qualitative study. Using a combined approach, you can create an independent probability frame for the quantitative component and use an interdependent frame (e.g., stratified purposeful sampling) for the qualitative component. Conversely, the project objective may require greater emphasis be placed on the qualitative component. In this case, sample size is primarily determined by thematic saturation and the minimum sample size requirements for qualitative research designs. However, it is important to make every attempt to avoid having a sample size that is too small for the quantitative component.

Although it is not possible to determine a sample size definitively, rough approximations for sample size minimums in qualitative designs common among health sciences research studies are 20 to 50 participants for in-depth or semistructured interviews, (Kuzel, 1999; Morse, 1994; Pope, van Royen, & Baker, 2002) four to five focus groups (Krueger & Casey, 2000; Morgan & Krueger, 1998) per targeted participant category (e.g., physicians, nurses, hospital administrators) with between six and nine participants per focus group. The number of cases included in case study designs can range widely from 1 to 20; case studies of individuals tend toward the higher end, and case studies of organizations tend toward smaller numbers.

If using one sample across components, be mindful about participant burden and fatigue when designing data collection tools. Although you can also conduct data collection with a single sample at two different snapshots in time, be cautious because of the risk of participant attrition. If you decide to recruit different samples across the qualitative and quantitative components, identify the primary probability technique (e.g., simple random sampling) and the primary purposeful technique (e.g., deviant cases) best suited for the designs of the quantitative (e.g., questionnaire) and qualitative (e.g., in-depth interviews) components. The process of sample size determination then can be separated for the qualitative and quantitative components regardless of whether the overall study's sampling frame is interdependent, independent, or combined.

The fourth and final step is to reconsider the sampling plan with feasibility in mind. This involves assessing whether time and other resources are available to recruit the desired number and type of participants. Estimating the costs associated with the sampling plan is a pivotal decision point in terms of moving forward or returning to the drawing board. Often overlooked, it is important to assess whether the necessary skills to conduct the sampling (and data collection) are represented on the research team.

▶ Issues related to working with human research protection programs (HRPPs) on mixed methods studies are further discussed in Chapter 10: Implementation Issues in Mixed Methods Research.

Once the sampling plan has been decided on and determined to be feasible, it is also important to consider any special ethical issues that may be raised by the mixed methods nature of the study. You may need to make special arrangements in your research protocol to account for confidentiality or consent issues arising from the use of participants in multiple components of the study.

APPROACHES TO DATA COLLECTION IN MIXED METHODS STUDIES

Once you have decided on a basic sampling design for your study, consider the specific data collection mechanisms and tools that will be used to gather information from participants. The sources of data in a mixed methods study are highly varied and, when thoughtfully aligned to serve complementary purposes, can generate a comprehensive and rich view of multifaceted phenomena in health and health care. Table 7.3 summarizes common sources of qualitative and quantitative data.

Qualitative data take many forms; within the health sciences data commonly come from three broad sources: (1) in-depth interviews (e.g., in person, phone, written correspondence such as e-mail; individual and group formats including focus groups); (2) observations and documents (e.g., observation notes, administrative and clinical records, organizational policies and protocols, Internet-based materials blogs); and (3) audiovisual materials (e.g., art, videos, photographs, audio recordings). Emerging forms of data are rapidly evolving given innovations in communication technology including social media (e.g., Twitter feeds, Internet-based focus groups). Qualitative data collection tools such as interview guides and observational protocols are

Table 7.3   Common Sources of Qualitative and Quantitative Data

Qualitative Data	Quantitative Data
Interviews • Unstructured or open-ended • In-depth • Individual and group formats, like focus groups • Oral and written formats	**Structured survey instruments** • Structured format • Closed-ended items • Forced-choice response categories
Observations and documents • Participant and nonparticipant observations with notes • Administrative and clinical records • Organizational policies and protocols • Journals, diaries, letters, blogs • News media • Archival material	**Administrative and clinical data** • Health care payers • Health care providers • Disease registries
Audiovisual materials • Art, photographs, film, audio recordings	**Census data** • At various government levels
Emerging forms • Social media content • Internet-based content	**Emerging forms** • Geospatial data • Big data collections

developed in advance with the understanding that they may evolve throughout the course of the iterative data collection and analysis that is central to qualitative methods. Audiotaping of the data collection and professional transcription is highly recommended.

▶ For more information on how to report data collection methods in manuscripts, refer to Chapter 11: Publishing Mixed Methods Studies in the Health Sciences.

Quantitative data include but are not limited to (1) primary survey instruments administered in multiple formats (interviewer in person or phone, self-administered, increasingly computer assisted); (2) clinical and administrative data from public and private payers, health care provider organizations, disease registries; and (3) census databases. Rapidly emerging forms of quantitative data include geospatial data and an astonishing array of big data collections. These collections are the next frontier in health sciences research and include large, complex, multidimensional data sets related to clinical care, population health, and health care performance.

"Fitting" Data Across Components

When creating an overall data collection strategy for a mixed methods study, be deliberate in deciding precisely how the quantitative and qualitative data collection instruments and procedures will fit together. Are they each measuring different aspects of a larger phenomenon (e.g., medication adherence in terms of the number of missed doses [quantitative] and patient strategies for reminders [qualitative])? Or are they measuring the same construct but in different ways (e.g., cognitive status in terms of Folstein Mini-Mental State Examination [quantitative] and individual's description of experiencing memory losses [qualitative])? Are the components interrelated such that one cannot be implemented until the other is complete, or are they relatively autonomous until integration in the final analysis phase of the project? In order to both define the conceptual linkages across study components and to anticipate logistical implications, consideration must be given to how the data fit together at each stage of the study, and the strategy for fit may be different in the various mixed methods design types (see Table 7.4).

In convergent designs, ask parallel questions to be sure data elicited are focusing on same focal topic to facilitate or support merging. Carefully bounding the focal topic will help in the qualitative component so that the emergent investigations do not stray too far afield from the primary research question. Of course, the setting of boundaries must be balanced with the importance of letting study participants direct the conversation to the greatest degree possible in order to allow unanticipated topics to emerge throughout the discussion.

In exploratory designs, the qualitative component is implemented first. Because the quantitative component is informed by the findings from the qualitative data, it cannot be fully developed until analyses on the qualitative data are complete. This can pose challenges in terms of approval by an HRPP review, since the quantitative survey instrument will not be finalized to be included with the submission. We recommend including a draft instrument that includes all boilerplate information that can be developed in advance (e.g., any consent language, instructions for completion) and potential conceptual domains and items. Be sure to explain the methodology, with citations, and

Table 7.4 Considerations for Fit of Study Components

Study Design	Considerations for Fit
Convergent	• Include data collection instruments that ask parallel or closely related questions. • Develop a qualitative data collection approach that emphasizes the focal topic while allowing for respondent direction.
Exploratory	• Approach analysis of qualitative data with the next phase in mind (e.g., create conceptual codes and subcodes with intentional goal of survey development). • Consider preparing draft instruments for the quantitative phase for submission to the HRPP.
Explanatory	• Approach analysis of quantitative data with the next phase in mind (e.g., focus on unexpected findings, inconsistencies, or salient characteristics) • Consider preparing draft instruments for the quantitative phase for submission to the HRPP.

indicate you will submit an addendum with the final instrument when it is complete. While some researchers opt to submit two separate HRPP applications, we do not recommend this because the project should be conceptualized and described as a single mixed methods study. In terms of the conceptual linkage from the qualitative data to the quantitative component, the data can be analyzed with the intentional goal of instrument development (e.g., broad conceptual codes domains become components of the survey, subcodes inform specific item content, and terminology can inform item writing and response categories).

In explanatory designs, the qualitative component is developed based on findings from the quantitative component. Consequently, data collection tools such as interview guides cannot be fully developed in advance. In terms of submission of the study protocol to the HRPP, we suggest following the process described previously. During quantitative analyses, the team will determine which results to follow up on with the qualitative component. The qualitative data collection might focus on unexpected findings, inconsistencies, statistically significant findings, or nonstatistically significant findings. It might also explore the role of characteristics of the sample that emerge as salient, such as hospital ownership or individual demographics.

Study designs that embed a qualitative component in a larger clinical trial are growing in popularity (Creswell & Plano Clark, 2011). There are a number of ways in which the qualitative data can fit with the quantitative data. Collecting qualitative data in advance of the intervention can inform the development of quantitative instruments. Qualitative data may be gathered throughout the intervention period to describe participant experiences, examine unanticipated events, identify reasons for attrition, document fidelity (or adaption) of the intervention, and uncover potential mediating and moderating factors. Qualitative data can also be collected at the conclusion of the trial to understand potential mechanisms or to help explain quantitative outcomes. An important consideration is whether the qualitative data collection will bias quantitative measures.

Case studies often include a wide range of both qualitative and quantitative data sources; data are typically collected longitudinally. The concept of fit of data may be slightly more complicated in case studies because of the sheer volume and diversity of data that might be collected. While primary data sources are defined at the outset, it is possible that additional sources may be identified once the data collection is underway. For instance, researchers may be observing a care team meeting in a nursing home in which the team discusses a change in their practice for advance care planning with residents; the researchers might decide to request a copy of the institutional policy in order to more fully understand how end-of-life conversations are managed in the facility.

Building Team Capacity for Data Collection

Typically in health sciences research teams, the capacity for quantitative data collection is well established, while the qualitative data collection skills may be more limited. A key decision is whether to assign different members of the team for each separate stream or to have team members working on both qualitative and quantitative data collection. Exposing quantitatively oriented researchers to qualitative data collection can have important benefits, such as contributing to collaborative dynamics and developing a coherent team (as described in Box 7.4). At the same time, the primary qualitative data collectors should be those with the

▶ Readers interested in guidance on developing qualitative data collection skills may refer to Appendix E: Quick Resource: A Short List of Readings and References.

greatest training and experience in these methods, as in-depth interviews and focus groups require particular training, skills, and experience.

Box 7.4   Involving Cross-Disciplinary Teams in Data Collection

I try to bring some of my quantitative colleagues on a limited number of site visits or interviews or focus groups. It's useful for colleagues who are coming from a different disciplinary background or have never collected and analyzed qualitative data to be exposed to the people who we're collecting data from, the process that we use to develop protocols, interview protocols . . . I've had situations where clinicians have sat in on focus groups on colon cancer screening. When they're with patients . . . physicians are being asked to give information, not necessarily to listen about why patients may not want to get certain kinds of screening for colon cancer . . . .I think it was very enlightening for [the clinician] to hear firsthand how patients thought about colon cancer screening.

—Kelly Devers, PhD, Senior Fellow in
the Health Policy Center, Urban Institute

When the qualitative data collection and analysis skills do not exist and training is not feasible (regrettably not uncommon currently in health sciences), the qualitative component may be outsourced to a consultant. Although they can be essential in certain circumstances, avoid reliance on external consultants if possible, as this can present challenges for team dynamics. There are some things you can do to minimize these challenges, as described in Chapter 3.

◀ To read more about tips for using consultants effectively, see Box 3.7 in Chapter 3: Determining the Appropriateness and Feasibility of Using Mixed Methods.

Engage consultants very early in the process (as described in Box 7.5). Develop explicit agreement on roles and deliverables in advance, and ensure the role of the consultant is clear to the team. It is also wise to address logistical issues for collaborative exchange and to plan a face-to-face meeting early in the project. Finally, be open to sharing data so the consultant might pursue her own interests in the context of the project.

Box 7.5   Engaging Consultants Early in the Process

I am a consultant for a lot of people, and a lot of times I need to really help advise people on how they develop relationships and communication within their teams . . . I try to involve people, everybody, early on—even in the conceptualization of a project. So it's not like you have a principal investigator that designs a project and then recruits people in it. You need people giving you insights right from the start.

—Benjamin Crabtree, PhD,
Professor and Director, Department of
Family Medicine and Community Health,
Rutgers Robert Wood Johnson Medical School

Logistics of Implementing Data Collection

Careful conceptual work of developing data collection strategies is critical to the success of a mixed methods study. Equally important, however, is attention to the logistical aspects of implementing the data collection. Develop precise timelines for data collection, considering how study components fit together. For instance, data collection for one component may require a substantial length of time or be longer than anticipated. Complex quantitative analyses may depend on securing and preparing administrative, clinical, or organizational performance data. Conversely, organizing and implementing focus groups may take longer than analysis of clinical data. These time considerations are relevant for sequential and convergent designs since delays have implications either way. Alignment of contemporary data so that time periods are synchronous across components can also present challenges. For example, quantitative data on organizational performance may be lagged (or delayed release for 12 months for instance), so that the qualitative data collection requires participants to reflect back to experiences from 12 months in the past.

Because mixed methods studies have many moving interrelated parts—and decisions are made throughout the course of the study—we recommend maintaining an audit trail (Miles & Huberman, 1994). Audit trails are tools primarily used in qualitative research yet are equally important in quantitative and mixed methods studies. An audit trail is a systematic, organized, comprehensive compilation of notes, files, data sources, audio recordings, coding manuals, and other procedures related to the project. The material can also be an important source of information for the research team. The documents are compiled at the inception of the project and maintained well after the study findings are published. This resource can assist the project manager and team by keeping a history of decisions on sampling, data collection, and analysis made over the course of the study and the rationale for these decisions. An audit trail also helps with the transparency of the research, which is a larger and equally important goal.

Summary and Key Points

- A central challenge and strength of mixed methods is in the appropriate leveraging of both breadth of data generated through the quantitative components) and depth of data generated through the qualitative components).
- The most common sampling practice in mixed methods health sciences research is to apply probability and purposeful techniques interdependently or to apply probability and purposeful techniques independently to create the overarching sampling plan.
- A sampling strategy for the study should be developed that identifies the sampling plan, specifies the number of distinct samples, approximates sample size(s), and addresses issues of feasibility.
- When creating an overall data collection strategy for a mixed methods study, be deliberate in deciding precisely how the quantitative and qualitative data collection instruments and procedures will fit together.

Review Questions and Exercises

1. Select an article from the *Journal of Mixed Methods Research,* and discuss the sampling approach. Is it interdependent, independent, or combined? Is this the optimal option given the research question?

2. Review the same paper, and discuss how the selected approach addresses the issue of representation/saturation trade-off.

3. Write a description of the data collection procedures you might use for an exploratory mixed methods design. How do your procedures differ if you used an explanatory mixed methods design?

4. Think about a mixed methods study of your choice. Specify the qualitative and quantitative data sources that might be utilized in this study. Discuss how you might integrate the components in this study.

5. Assume that you are planning who will be involved in conducting a mixed methods study. Discuss the important factors in building team capacity for the project.

References

Creswell, J. W., & Plano Clark, V. L. (2011). *Designing and conducting mixed methods research* (2nd ed.). Thousand Oaks, CA: Sage.

Krein, S. L., Kowalski, C. P., Damschroder, L., Forman, J., Kaufman, S. R., & Saint, S. (2008). Preventing ventilator-associated pneumonia in the United States: A multicenter mixed-methods study. *Infection Control and Hospital Epidemiology, 29*(10), 933–940. doi: 10.1086/591455

Krueger, R. A., & Casey, M. (2000). *Focus groups: A practical guide for applied research* (3rd ed.). Thousand Oaks, CA: Sage.

Kuzel, A. (1999). Sampling in qualitative inquiry. In B. Crabtree & W. L. Miller (Eds.), *Doing qualitative research* (pp. 33–45). Thousand Oaks, CA: Sage.

McNulty, C., Joshi, P., Butler, C. C., Atkinson, L., Nichols, T., Hogan, A., & French, D. (2012). Have the public's expectations for antibiotics for acute uncomplicated respiratory tract infections changed since the H1N1 influenza pandemic? A qualitative interview and quantitative questionnaire study. *BMJ Open, 2*(2), e000674. doi: 10.1136/bmjopen-2011–000674

Miles, M. B., & Huberman, A. M. (1994). *Qualitative data analysis: An expanded sourcebook* (2nd ed.). Thousand Oaks, CA: Sage.

Morgan, D. L., & Krueger, R. A. (1998). *The focus group kit.* Thousand Oaks, CA: Sage.

Morse, J. M. (1994). Designing funded qualitative research. In N. K. Denzin & Y. S. Lincoln (Eds.), *Handbook of qualitative research* (pp. 220–235). Thousand Oaks, CA: Sage.

Patton, M. (2002). *Qualitative evaluation and research methods* (3rd ed.). Thousand Oaks, CA: Sage.

Peterson, J. A., Reisinger, H. S., Schwartz, R. P., Mitchell, S. G., Kelly, S. M., Brown, B. S., & Agar, M. A. (2008). Targeted sampling in drug abuse research: A review and case study. *Field Methods, 20,* 155. DOI: 10.1177/152582XX08314988.

Pope, C., van Royen, P., & Baker, R. (2002). Qualitative methods in research on healthcare quality. *Quality and Safety in Health Care, 11*(2), 148–152.

Schwartz, R. P., Kelly, S. M., O'Grady, K. E., Mitchell, S. G., Peterson, J. A., Reisinger, H. S., . . . Brown, B. S. (2008). Attitudes toward buprenorphine and methadone among opioid-dependent individuals. *American Journal on Addictions, 17*(5), 396–401. doi: 10.1080/10550490802268835

Teddlie, C., & Tashakkori, A. (2009). *Foundations of mixed methods research: Integrating quantitative and qualitative approaches in the social and behavioral sciences.* Thousand Oaks, CA: Sage.

Teddlie, C., & Yu, F. (2007). Mixed methods sampling: A typology with examples. *Journal of Mixed Methods Research, 1*(77). doi: 10.1177/2345678906292430

Watters, J. K., & Biernacki, P. (1989). Targeted sampling: Options for the study of hidden populations. *Social Problems, 36*(4), 416–430.

∴ EIGHT ✢

DATA ANALYSIS AND INTEGRATION IN MIXED METHODS STUDIES

Information you will find in this chapter: This chapter discusses data analysis with a focus on integration as a unique and essential element of mixed methods research. We begin with key considerations in developing the analysis plan for a mixed methods study. Next, we review approaches to integration (e.g., connecting, merging, and embedding) in both the data collection and analysis phases of a study. We then turn to a summary of key issues in implementing integration, including how to address findings that are inconsistent across the data sets and how to use software to facilitate analysis. Finally, we present several common approaches for interpreting findings and presenting integrated data in peer-reviewed empirical research journal articles, with examples for each.

Key features in this chapter:

- Brief quotations and reflections from mixed methods researchers
- Figures to display major types of integration
- Table of key steps in data analysis by primary mixed methods study designs
- Table of general approaches to interpreting and presenting mixed methods findings
- Examples of common display formats for integrated results including narrative, joint, and data transformation displays

IMPORTANCE OF INTEGRATION OF MIXED METHODS DATA

The integration of qualitative and quantitative data is a unique and essential feature of mixed methods research (Bryman, 2006; Creswell & Plano Clark, 2011). As we have discussed throughout this book, effective integration of data can produce a more comprehensive set of insights than otherwise possible as well as enrich findings generated from the study's discrete components (O'Cathain, Murphy, & Nicholl, 2010). Qualitative inquiry can inform the development or enhancement of quantitative instruments or interventions, generate hypotheses for testing in the quantitative component, or help to explain unexpected or incomplete findings from the quantitative analysis. Quantitative inquiry can test hypotheses that are grounded in the qualitative data or generate questions to be explained with qualitative data. Fundamentally, each type of data addresses an aspect of the research question that the other cannot, such that the findings are "mutually illuminating" (Wooley, 2009, p. 7). But of course these advantages can only occur if the data are effectively integrated; failure to integrate in a project can produce essentially two independent studies, rather than a single, unified mixed methods study. In Box 8.1, an experienced health services researcher explains the dynamic interplay between the data as "conversations" that can occur across study components in a mixed methods design.

Box 8.1   Creating Conversations Between Study Components

You should constantly have conversations between the qualitative and quantitative components of the research . . . .[In my current study] I designed the study with the conversation built into it. I'm using ethnographic or qualitative residual analysis. You do a regression to try to explain variation in something and then you look at the cases where you've got large residuals, where really the predicted value is very different from the actual value. And then you go in and do some in-depth qualitative research to find out why that might be. And then return to your quantitative analysis to see if you can explain more of the variation in your variable based on the in-depth understanding you got from the qualitative research.

—Alicia O'Cathain, BSc, MSc, MA, PhD,
Professor of Health Services Research,
University of Sheffield

DEVELOPING A DATA ANALYSIS PLAN

In mixed methods studies, analyses are performed on the qualitative and quantitative data sets respectively, in accordance with established methods of analysis for each approach. Qualitative analysis is a systematic and iterative process of analyzing textual data inductively, generating conceptual categories or recurrent themes to describe or explain phenomena (Pope, Ziebland, & Mays, 2000). Quantitative analysis uses statistical approaches with numeric data to produce measures of statistical significance and association between variables (Best & Kahn, 2005; Hulley, Cummings, Browner, Grady, & Newman, 2013; Selvin, 2004). In this chapter, we do not review the extensive methodological guidance on independent qualitative and quantitative analysis for two reasons. First, our primary focus in this book is on elements of research that are unique to mixed methods per se, and second, there are extensive excellent resources on qualitative and quantitative analysis that provide comprehensive and detailed information and guidance.

▶ Readers interested in more detailed information about data analysis, particularly for qualitative research, may refer to Appendix E: Quick Resource: A Short List of Readings and References.

However, in keeping with our primary focus, this chapter will describe some of the key considerations at the analysis phase that are unique to mixed methods. Depending on the study design, the data analysis plan may be developed at different points during the project—either a priori or emergently. With convergent mixed methods designs, analysis plans for the qualitative and quantitative components are typically developed a priori and described in detail in the initial development of a study proposal. This is also the case with most sequential designs. On the other hand, some sequential or multiphase designs may use an emergent approach, where the data collection and analysis plan for a subsequent component is not defined until the findings from the prior component are available. In our experience, emergent approaches may be met with some skepticism by audiences who are unfamiliar with qualitative or mixed methods. If you choose an emergent approach, it is important to explicitly describe the interdependence across components and the rationale for developing the analysis plan after the initial phase, together with citations for the proposed methods.

In developing a data analysis plan for a mixed methods study, there are several key considerations to address: aligning the plan with study aims and design, determining the priority of study components, and defining the points of integration. Each of these issues is discussed briefly next.

Aligning the Overall Analysis Plan With the Study Aims and Design

The study aims and selected design are the primary drivers of the data analysis plan. For example, imagine a study in which the aim is to understand end-of-shift handoff protocols of in-patient units of hospitals, using interviews as the initial phase in an exploratory sequential design. The study must be structured so that the analysis of the qualitative data is completed by the end of the initial phase in order to produce insights to be operationalized as constructs in a quantitative survey. Subsequent analysis of the quantitative data can determine the prevalence of specific practices from a large and representative sample. In another example, if your aim is to assess psychosocial and clinical predictors of patients with hypertension who demonstrate high rates of adherence to a medication intervention, the process of qualitative data collection and analysis occurs throughout the course of the intervention period as well as through integration at the conclusion of the trial, together with quantitative measures of adherence.

In thinking about the overall analysis plan for a study, consider these key design elements: Will you use a convergent or sequential approach? How many and what types of sources of qualitative and quantitative data will you have? Are the data interconnected or independent? What data need to be analyzed in order to inform subsequent data collection? What parallel concepts can be the focus of the analysis in the two sets of data? What are plans for assessing divergence and convergence of data? A detailed analysis plan can be summarized in a grant application (and possibly included as an appendix). It can also be an excellent resource for internal use by the team. Detailed plans generally have at least three separate sections: one for the qualitative data, one for the quantitative data, and one for integration and interpretation across the data.

◀ For information on options for outlining study components and methods in a proposal or protocol, refer to Box 4.5 in Chapter 4: Writing a Scientifically Sound and Compelling Grant Proposal for a Mixed Methods Study.

Determining the Priority of Study Components

Although we do not consider relative weighting a defining feature of mixed methods designs, determining the priority of study components remains a consideration in the development of a data analysis plan.

◀ Relative weighting and our approach to this issue are further described in Chapter 1: Definition and Overview of Mixed Methods Designs.

The qualitative and quantitative components may or may not have equal weight in the overall study design. There are three possible scenarios: the qualitative and quantitative components are of equal priority; the qualitative component is emphasized more heavily than the quantitative component; or the quantitative component is emphasized more heavily than the qualitative component. For instance, a qualitative piece that is embedded in a randomized controlled trial may have a supplemental role (e.g., the quantitative piece is assigned higher priority in terms of addressing the study aims) and is defined as such from the outset. In other cases, the relative prioritization may not be defined in advance and will become apparent only as the findings begin to emerge. We agree strongly with experts who recommend that even if a component has a supplemental role, it must be carried out in accordance with standards for rigor to the maximum possible degree (Morse, 2010). In some cases, however, the supplemental component may be scaled more narrowly than the primary component or serve a pragmatic purpose in the context of the larger study (e.g., qualitative interviews with prospective participants in an intervention study to gather input on informed consent materials). Consequently, analyses may focus on a particular subset of qualitative data or may consist of basic statistical computations for quantitative data.

Defining the Points of Integration

The issue of timing of integration is relatively straightforward and in most cases can be defined during the design of the study. The point at which data are brought together depends on the intended interaction between qualitative and quantitative data, with regard to the samples for each, the data collection instruments, and analyses. When designing data collection tools for each component, planning for integration means that the various instruments must be both complementary and comprehensive. In some instances, the data will remain independent until the final phase of analysis, when an overarching inference is made to synthesize broadly across findings. In other cases, such as sequential designs where the samples are derived in stages, the data may be integrated early in the process.

Potential points of integration occur during sample selection, data collection, data analysis, and data interpretation. Integration during the sample selection involves either using the results of the first component to inform the selection of participants for subsequent components or designing a sampling strategy that accounts for both qualitative and quantitative needs during the initial recruitment strategy. Integration during data collection involves employing different components to answer unique questions or using the findings from the first research component to develop data collection tools or protocols for subsequent components. Integration during data analysis requires a deliberate attempt to create a single combined data set after initial independent analysis of each component. Integration during data interpretation is imperative in mixed methods research and is, in fact, a hallmark of mixed methods studies. Integration at this stage determines the conclusions that result from analyzing research findings across components. Importantly, the interpretation stage is the key point at which the unique assets of a mixed methods approach can be leveraged. For some research projects, this is the only point of integration in the study. We should note that increasing the number of integration points does not necessarily increase the quality of the study. In addition, the decision about the degree of component interdependence, or the number and types of points of integration, is shaped by the research questions and not from intrinsic properties of any mixed methods typology.

APPROACHES TO INTEGRATION IN DATA COLLECTION AND ANALYSIS

The question of how qualitative and quantitative data will fit together arises at the earliest point of developing a mixed methods study (e.g., when defining the aims) and remains relevant throughout the process, from choosing a design to sampling and conducting data collection and analysis (Yin, 2006). In this chapter, we focus specifically on integration during the data collection, analysis, interpretation, and reporting phases. There are a number of excellent resources that describe various methods for integration of qualitative and quantitative data (Castro, Kellison, Boyd, & Kopak, 2010; O'Cathain et al., 2010; Sandelowski, 2000). Here, we address approaches to integration in data collection and analysis currently most common in the heath sciences, including merging,

embedding, and connecting (or building) the
data sets (Creswell, 2013; Creswell & Plano
Clark, 2011; Fetters, Curry, & Creswell, 2013).

◀ These basic approaches
to integration are
introduced in Chapter
1: Definition and
Overview of Mixed
Methods Designs.

Data Integration Through Merging

Merging occurs after both the qualitative
and quantitative data collection and initial analyses are completed (see Figure
8.1). The findings are then interpreted in toto and can be compared in order to
identify complementarity, convergence, and divergence among data sets. The
approach to interpretation is to some degree influenced by the data collection
instruments, which gather data on particular dimensions of the phenomenon of
interest. The quantitative and qualitative data may be merged according to
domains developed a priori (e.g., patient–provider communication; clinic staff
capacity and expertise; safety protocols) and woven together to characterize
each domain. In cases where broad conceptual domains are defined in
advance, the data collection instruments will focus on very similar areas. For
example, in a study examining patient–provider communication, both quantitative and qualitative data might be collected from patient–provider dyads to
gather information on elements of communication hypothesized to be salient
(e.g., attentiveness, body language). Alternatively, the data may address
related but fairly discrete facets of a topic in which case the merging is more
like the fitting together of puzzle pieces. For instance, to understand patient
experiences of pain management in hospital intensive care units, quantitative
measures might include medication dose as well as frequency and timeliness
of administration, while a qualitative interview guide might explore patient
perceptions of how well the pain assessment reflects patients' needs and preferences. In this case, there is likely to be some overlap between the content
generated as well as some unique aspects of each.

There are several strategies for implementing merged data analysis
(Creswell & Plano Clark, 2011), including narrative side-by-side comparisons
of the quantitative and qualitative data, joint displays of data, and data transformation. Examples of how to display these forms of merged results when
reporting study findings are presented in the final section of this chapter.

One example of merging is a study of primary care practice transformation by Scammon and colleagues (2013) using a case study mixed methods
design. They merged extensive data from highly varied sources, including

Figure 8.1   Integration in Data Collection and Analysis Through Merging

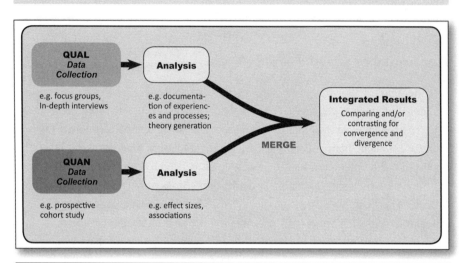

SOURCE: Adapted with permission from Michael D. Fetters.

NOTE: QUAL = qualitative; QUAN = quantitative.

archival documents, in-clinic observations, chart audits, interviews, focus groups, and multiple administrative claims databases in 10 primary care practice settings. The complementary data provided a simultaneously comprehensive and richly textured description of multiple facets of primary care practice redesign, including both the what and why of change processes in each clinic. For instance, a planned care element of the redesign included both reports of newly obtained lab results for use during a patient visit as well as an after-visit summary (AVS) including physician instructions. Quantitative data demonstrated variation of AVS implementation across clinics, while the qualitative data uncovered differences in providers' commitment to the vision for practice transformation.

Data Integration Through Embedding

Embedding occurs when data collection and analysis are linked at multiple points during the study (see Figure 8.2). This approach occurs typically in studies with both primary and secondary questions, in which different methods are employed to address each question. We view embedding as occurring

Figure 8.2   Integration in Data Collection and Analysis Through Embedding

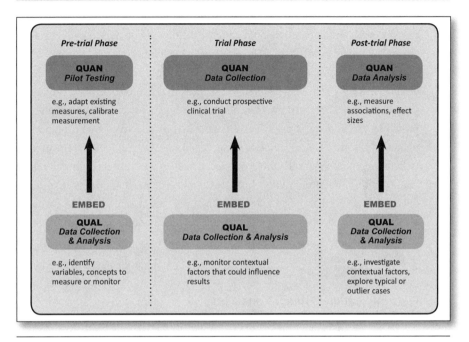

SOURCE: Adapted with permission from Michael D. Fetters.

NOTE: QUAL = qualitative; QUAN = quantitative.

when the secondary question (and method) is intended to support the work of the primary question (Greene, 2007) and therefore is nested or placed within the framework of the primary method (Creswell & Plano Clark, 2011). Experts have cautioned against the subsuming of one method by the other, particularly when it is the qualitative method that is in the supporting role (Morse & Niehaus, 2009). We agree with this caution and stress the need to ensure that each component is carried out with attention to rigor and that the qualitative data are adequately analyzed and interpreted in order to provide unique insights necessary for the quantitative component. The particular risk in these circumstances is that the qualitative component may be perceived as less rigorous or valuable than the quantitative component.

Embedding can occur in various designs, such as a case study in which some quantitative data are collected within a larger qualitative ethnographic or observational component. Most common in health sciences to date, however, is the embedding of one or more qualitative components within a randomized controlled trial. For example, Rycroft-Malone and colleagues (2012) conducted a cluster randomized controlled trial to evaluate the effectiveness of three strategies for the implementation of recommendations about perioperative fasting (Rycroft-Malone et al., 2012). Hospitals were randomized to one of three interventions, and average duration of fluid fast prior to induction of anesthesia among patients in each hospital was measured as the primary outcome. Interviews and focus groups were used to supplement quantitative results by providing richer data on patient experiences and perspectives regarding participation in the trial. In an embedded approach, the supplemental form of data (whether qualitative or quantitative) may be analyzed at various points along the continuum of the larger study. In the example just mentioned, the qualitative data were analyzed at the conclusion of the intervention and merged with quantitative data. In other cases, qualitative data might be analyzed either in advance of the initiation of a trial (to inform the intervention design) or at the conclusion of the trial (to complement or explain quantitative results).

Data Integration Through Connecting

Connecting occurs when one type of data builds upon the other (see Figure 8.3) (Creswell & Plano Clark, 2011). This can happen either in relation to the sampling or the content of the data collected. In the first type of connecting, the data set developed in one phase is used to define the sample for a later phase. For example, with an explanatory design, the quantitative findings may be analyzed in order to identify potential participants for follow up in the qualitative component. There are a number of ways to think about selecting a sample from a larger quantitative data set. You might be interested in locating typical or representative individuals of the larger group (e.g., individuals who purchased a long-term care insurance policy in the past six months) in order to learn more about their decision-making processes. In positive deviance designs for understanding health care organizational performance (Bradley et al., 2009) you might seek to identify outliers on a standard metric (e.g., hospitals at the top and bottom 5% of performance ranking) to be studied in depth. When studying individual behavior change, the quantitative analysis might reveal those who differ in terms of predictors or other patterns in the data (e.g., precontemplation scores in a stage of change model for individuals in a smoking cessation intervention). For instance, in an explanatory study seeking to understand strategies used by

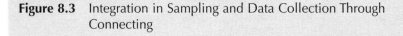

Figure 8.3   Integration in Sampling and Data Collection Through Connecting

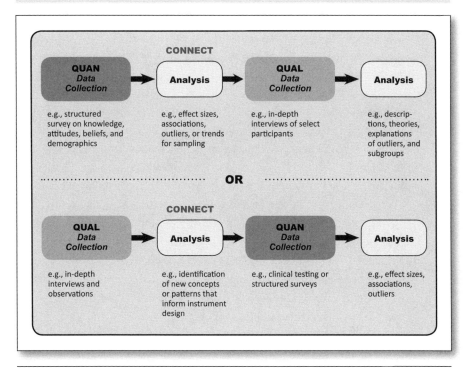

SOURCE: Adapted with permission from Michael D. Fetters.

NOTE: QUAN = quantitative; QUAL = qualitative.

individuals to maintain weight loss for at least 12 months after undergoing bariatric surgery, the qualitative component would connect to the quantitative component through the sampling frame. A purposeful sample of individuals who have maintained weight loss can be selected based on the quantitative measures gathered at a 12-month follow-up point.

In the second type of connecting, integration may occur when the first data collection procedure informs the second data collection procedure, such as a qualitative phase informing the development of a survey in a subsequent quantitative phase (also referred to as "building") (Onwuegbuzie, Bustamante, & Nelson, 2010). With this form of connecting, the qualitative data are analyzed with the aim of generating common conceptual domains or dimensions of the phenomenon under study. This output is sometimes referred to as *taxonomy,* or a framework for classifying multifaceted phenomenon (Patton, 2002). Taxonomies can both increase clarity in defining and comparing complex phenomena as well as provide a foundation for quantitative measurement development. Qualitative data can be analyzed in order to generate a taxonomy using conceptual codes to define key domains that characterize the phenomenon and conceptual subcodes to define common dimensions within those key domains (Bradley, Curry, & Devers, 2007).

For example, Keith, Hopp, Subramanian, Wiitala, and Lowery (2010) developed and tested a novel measure of fidelity of implementation, using interviews as a first phase to identify dimensions of staff perspectives regarding implementation of a nurse case management intervention for patients with congestive heart failure. The key dimensions were operationalized quantitatively as a standard measure of fidelity, which was then tested by examining the association between the measure and intervention effectiveness (Keith et al., 2010).

While most studies will use only one of these forms of integration, large-scale multistage studies may use several of these approaches. A multistage study by Krumholz, Curry, and Bradley (2011) used a positive deviance approach and exploratory sequential mixed methods design to discover hospital strategies associated with lower 30-day hospital risk-standardized mortality rates (RSMRs) for patients with acute myocardial infarction (AMI) (Bradley et al., 2012; Curry et al., 2011; Krumholz et al., 2011). This study sought to understand diverse and complex aspects of AMI care including hospital structures (e.g., emergency department space), processes (e.g., emergency response protocols, coordination within hospital units), and hospital internal environments (e.g., organizational culture). The qualitative stage included site visits and interviews of key staff at 11 purposefully selected high- and low-performing hospitals in the United States to characterize the organizational environment and to generate hypotheses. In the quantitative stage, hypotheses were tested using a survey of a nationally representative sample of acute care hospitals ($n = 537$). Integration was accomplished at multiple points, as indicated in Figure 8.4.

We have described common types of mixed methods data analysis presently in use. The field of mixed methods research is highly dynamic, with exciting and rapid developments in advanced analytic approaches. Many of these innovations hold great promise for expanding the range of techniques available to health sciences researchers. Examples of advanced approaches include Q methodology (combining qualitative and quantitative analytics to interpret subjectivity of individual perspectives using statistical methods), geographical information science (integrating qualitative and quantitative data including geographic data in

Figure 8.4 Integration at Multiple Points in Multistage Design

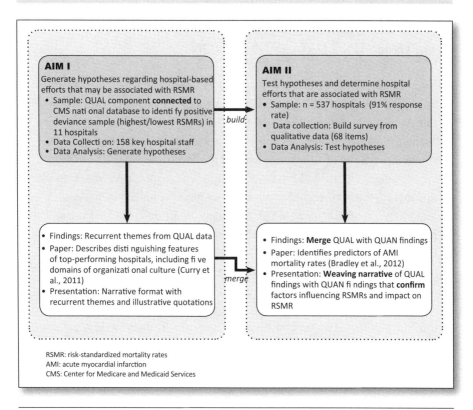

AIM I
Generate hypotheses regarding hospital-based efforts that may be associated with RSMR
- Sample: QUAL component **connected** to CMS national database to identify positive deviance sample (highest/lowest RSMRs) in 11 hospitals
- Data Collection: 158 key hospital staff
- Data Analysis: Generate hypotheses

build

AIM II
Test hypotheses and determine hospital efforts that are associated with RSMR
- Sample: n = 537 hospitals (91% response rate)
- Data collection: Build survey from qualitative data (68 items)
- Data Analysis: Test hypotheses

- Findings: Recurrent themes from QUAL data
- Paper: Describes distinguishing features of top-performing hospitals, including five domains of organizational culture (Curry et al., 2011)
- Presentation: Narrative format with recurrent themes and illustrative quotations

merge

- Findings: **Merge** QUAL with QUAN findings
- Paper: Identifies predictors of AMI mortality rates (Bradley et al., 2012)
- Presentation: **Weaving narrative** of QUAL findings with QUAN findings that **confirm** factors influencing RSMRs and impact on RSMR

RSMR: risk-standardized mortality rates
AMI: acute myocardial infarction
CMS: Center for Medicare and Medicaid Services

SOURCE: Adapted from Fetters et al. (2013).

NOTE: RSMR = risk-standardized mortality rate; QUAL = qualitative; CMS = Center for Medicare and Medicaid Services; QUAN = quantitative; AMI = acute myocardial infarction.

a visual representation), social network analyses (combining quantitative and qualitative data to characterize the connections between individuals, organizations, or other entities along multiple dimensions), and qualitative comparative analysis (using Boolean algebra to facilitate comparative analysis of qualitative data in small case sets). Because this text is primarily intended for those new to mixed methods, we focus on the basic, practical strategies for integration. Readers interested in learning more about these techniques and others are encouraged to explore comprehensive and excellent discussions of data analysis in mixed methods in a variety of sources (Newman & Ramlo, 2010;

Onwuegbuzie & Combs, 2010; Ragin, Shulman, Weinberg, & Gran, 2003; Tashakkori & Teddlie, 2010; Valenta & Wigger, 1997).

IMPLEMENTING DATA INTEGRATION

With this review of the primary approaches to integration as a foundation, we now turn to the practical aspects of implementing data integration. In this section, we describe the overall procedures for integration, discuss how to address findings that are inconsistent across the data sets ("divergent"), and briefly summarize the use of software to support analysis.

Although the particular type of study design determines the steps to be undertaken, there are several common procedures for implementing data integration in mixed methods studies that apply in all designs. These common procedures include analyzing qualitative and quantitative data using appropriate analytic approaches; integrating data through sampling, instrument development, or further analysis; interpreting (or inference generation); and obtaining a representation of findings. In addition to these common procedures, there are analytic activities that need to be performed for particular design types. For example, convergent designs require attention to divergence that might emerge across the data sets. The major steps for integration in each type of mixed methods design are presented in Table 8.1.

Addressing Divergence

The case for using multiple forms of quantitative measurement (also referred to as triangulation) to address limitations inherent in each method was first made by Campbell and Fiske in 1959, and this concept remains a core rationale for using mixed methods. However, while the qualitative and quantitative data will often be coherent or complementary, it is not uncommon for the data to be divergent in some respects. Divergence occurs when the qualitative and quantitative findings are dissimilar, inconsistent, or conflicting in some substantive way. This may initially be regarded as cause for concern; however, there is growing consensus that divergence is to be expected when using multiple methods and in fact can produce unique and important insights (Teddlie & Tashakkori, 2010). Moffatt, White, Mackintosh, and Howel (2006) suggest that divergence can be an asset in uncovering novel findings in complex phenomena (see Box 8.2).

Table 8.1   Major Steps for Integration in Data Analysis in Mixed Methods Study Designs

Type of Mixed Methods Design	Major Steps in Data Analysis
Convergent design	1. Collect the quantitative and qualitative data concurrently.
	2. Independently analyze the quantitative and qualitative data using appropriate analytic approaches.
	3. Decide how the two data sets will be compared, and specify the dimensions by which to compare the results.
	4. Specify what information will be compared across the dimensions.
	5. Complete refined quantitative and qualitative analyses to produce the needed comparison information (this may involve data transformation such as quantitizing qualitative data).
	6. Interpret how the combined results address the quantitative, qualitative, and mixed methods questions.
	7. Compare and contrast the quantitative and qualitative results, and determine whether further analysis is needed to address divergence that may emerge.
	8. Decide how to present the combined analyses and construct the schematic representation of comparisons (e.g., joint display if appropriate).
Exploratory sequential design	1. Collect the qualitative data.
	2. Analyze the qualitative data using appropriate analytic approaches.
	3. Design the quantitative component based on the qualitative results.
	4. Develop and pilot test the new survey instrument and/or intervention; assess psychometric properties.
	5. Collect the quantitative data.
	6. Analyze the quantitative data using appropriate analytic approaches.

(Continued)

Table 8.1   (Continued)

Type of Mixed Methods Design	Major Steps in Data Analysis
	7. Interpret how the connected results address the qualitative, quantitative, and mixed methods questions.
	8. Decide how to present the complete set of findings.
Explanatory sequential design	1. Collect the quantitative data.
	2. Analyze the quantitative data using appropriate analytic approaches.
	3. Design the qualitative component based on the quantitative results (e.g., sampling plan, topical focus for data collection).
	4. Collect the qualitative data.
	5. Analyze the qualitative data using appropriate analytic approaches.
	6. Interpret how the connected results address the quantitative, qualitative, and mixed methods questions.
	7. Decide how to present the complete set of findings.
Embedded design	1. Analyze the primary data set to answer the primary research questions.
	2. Analyze the secondary data set (quantitative or qualitative) where it is embedded within the primary design by merging or connecting using the steps involved in the other mixed methods study designs; determine how to incorporate the secondary results.
	3. Interpret how the primary and secondary results answer the qualitative, quantitative, and mixed methods questions.
	4. Decide how to present the complete set of findings.
Multistage design	1. Analyze the data for each project in the overall program; define the applicability of merged and connected data analysis or some combination for each phase in the project.
	2. Employ strategies for merged and connected analysis as the timing of projects dictates in order to address the overall research objective.
	3. Interpret how the results answer the project's research questions and contribute to the overall objective.
	4. Decide how to present the complete set of findings, whether in one publication or multiple publications over the course of the study.

SOURCE: Adapted from Creswell and Plano Clark (2011).

Box 8.2   Contributions of Divergent Findings

Not only [does divergence] enhance the robustness of the study, it may lead to different conclusions from those that would have been drawn through relying on one method alone and demonstrates the value of collecting both types of data within a single study. More widespread use of mixed methods in trials of complex interventions is likely to enhance the overall quality of the evidence base. (Moffatt et al., 2006, p. 1)

An example of a research team that faced divergent results is found in a study by Cox (2003) and colleagues, who examined patient experiences of participating in an anti-cancer drug trial. Participants completed quality of life questionnaires and baseline and follow-up and also completed in-depth interviews. While the quantitative data showed no statistically significant differences in scores over time, the qualitative data revealed important psychological, emotional, and social impacts of participation. Cox (2003) and colleagues hypothesized the following:

> One reason for the mismatch of quality of life scores with the interview data could be that the questionnaires asked patients to rate how they have been feeling over the last week, whereas the interviews allowed for a much broader coverage of time and also for a deeper description of the issue being discussed. Another reason could be that ratings were made before the interview and were based on what came to mind in that short rating interval. Ratings are often more accurate when made after a reflected or communicated exploration of the issue. (p. 931)

Addressing divergence is not a straightforward undertaking and can sometimes leave the research team with unresolved questions or perhaps even a lack of confidence in the study results. Nevertheless, there are several options for examining divergence across data sets (Morgan, 2013; Pluye, Grad, Levine, & Nicolau, 2009). The most commonly reported strategy is reconciliation, which refers to interpreting inconsistent results in a plausible manner. Begin by carefully examining all methodological assumptions and procedures within the study, including the rigor of each component and potential sources of bias. This examination can provide some reassurance as to the quality of the findings in each component and can demonstrate that both sets of findings have merit. As in all forms of research, inherent or unavoidable limitations should be reported, together with any strategies used to mitigate resulting threats to quality of the data. Once the rigor of each set of findings has been established, review and reanalyze the data with a deliberate focus on understanding any inconsistent findings and to consider further new analyses within existing data sets to explain results or validate the data. If warranted, additional data might be gathered (although this is often not feasible given available resources), or follow-up studies might be proposed to help uncover possible explanations for the conflicting data. Finally, consider developing hypotheses about the nature of the divergence and possible reasons it occurred, including challenging the validity of the underlying constructs in the findings. These kinds of reflections can be very valuable additions to the implications for future research in the discussion section of a manuscript. For more information on understanding divergence, including a detailed example, see a comprehensive review paper by Pluye and colleagues (2009).

Using Computer Software

Software is an essential tool for data management and analysis in mixed methods studies, given the sheer volume and diversity of forms of data to be analyzed (Maeitta, 2006). At the same time, we wholeheartedly agree with experts who caution that software does not "do" the analysis, nor does software automatically produce high-quality results (MacMillan & Keonig, 2004). That said, when used effectively and creatively, software can be very useful in facilitating comparative analyses within and across the data sets, developing targeted or focused analysis on segments of the data, and generating joint displays of data. As you might expect, data analysis software is a highly dynamic market, and we hesitated to be very specific given the risk this information will become quickly dated. Yet because we are asked about software regularly we include this brief overview.

While programs such as Excel or SPSS are familiar to most health sciences researchers, they lack key features found in qualitative and mixed methods software. Several software programs designed primarily for qualitative analysis are being used by mixed methods researchers. MAXQDA (www.maxqda .com) includes with MAXDictio an add-on module for data transformation.

NVivo (www.qsrinternational.com) and ATLAS.ti (www.atlasti.com) also have tools to support mixed methods designs. ATLAS.ti works in both Mac and PC. Some companies have integrated their qualitative and quantitative data analysis software tools into a mixed methods package, such as with QDA Miner, SimStat, and WordStat (www.provalisresearch.com).

Newer programs are emerging specifically designed for managing and analyzing mixed methods data. One example is Dedoose (www.dedoose.com), a web-based mixed methods platform that advertises its features as appropriate for research in the health sciences. Most programs have a free trial version (and check for student rates). While we recognize many statistical packages offering autocoding may be useful for some researchers, we confess to a bias against them for purposes of coding qualitative data. In our experience, the process of prolonged immersion in the data, together with deep coding and interpretation by a multidisciplinary team, generates richer, more contextualized findings. We recommend exploring programs and using a trial version before committing to investments in purchasing the software and any needed training. Important software features to consider are ability to work with qualitative and quantitative data, simultaneous access where multiple team members can be working in the data set at the same time, text and audio coding, and memo writing. Additional detail can be found in several excellent reviews in various mixed methods resources (Bazeley, 2009, 2010) or in Appendix F: Qualitative Analysis Software Comparison Table, where we provide a summary of common software packages and key features in a comparative matrix.

INTEGRATION IN INTERPRETING AND PRESENTING FINDINGS

After the data collection and initial analyses for each study component are complete, the final step is interpreting and presenting integrated data in various forms of research reports. Although novel techniques for reporting mixed methods findings are always being developed, there are three general approaches to data presentation in the health sciences literature. These approaches include narrative, joint displays, and data transformation (Fetters, Curry, & Creswell, 2013). Table 8.2 presents each of these general approaches, together with specific techniques and presentation formats for each.

Table 8.2   General Approaches for Interpreting and Presenting Integrated Data

General Approach to Data Presentations	Specific Technique	Presentation Format
Narrative approaches	Weaving	Present qualitative and quantitative data together within thematic or conceptual categories within a single manuscript.
	Contiguous	Present qualitative and quantitative data in separate findings sections of a single manuscript.
	Staged	Present findings from each step as they are available (typically large multistage studies).
Joint displays	Matrices	Include qualitative and quantitative data in tabular format with cells for each data type to facilitate comparisons across the data.
	Figures and graphs	Create schematic representations such as social network diagrams and plot charts.
Data transformation	Qualitative to quantitative	Convert narrative data into numeric data and merge with quantitative data.
	Quantitative to qualitative	Convert numeric data into qualitative data and merge with qualitative data.

SOURCE: Adapted with permission from Fetters et al. (2013).

Narrative Approaches

Narrative forms of integration are the most common approach in the health sciences. As reflected in Table 8.2, narrative forms of integration for reporting overall study findings include weaving, contiguous, and staged techniques. There is no optimal or preferred technique currently. The choice of presentation formats should be determined by the nature of the data and the needs and preferences of particular journal audiences. Weaving is accomplished through organizing the quantitative and qualitative findings according to unifying or recurrent themes or constructs. This technique is demonstrated in an article by Lim, Baik, and Ashing-Giwa (2012), who conducted a study on cultural health beliefs and health behaviors in Asian American breast cancer survivors. Using a convergent design, they gathered quantitative data through a culturally informed survey instrument consisting of standardized and new scales with 206 Asian American breast cancer survivors. They also conduced two focus groups ($n = 11$) with a key subset of women from the quantitative sample, Korean-American breast cancer survivors. In the findings section of the article, they weave the quantitative and qualitative data organized by pathways among variables that were significant in the quantitative analysis. An excerpt from one pathway ("doctor–patient relationship and stress management") appears in Box 8.3.

Box 8.3   Example of Weaving Qualitative and Quantitative Results in Narrative

In the quantitative analysis, the doctor–patient relationship showed a positive relationship with stress management ($b = 0.17$). The relationship with the doctor can be a major issue for patients with cancer, and that relationship may either cause or help resolve stress. Four themes were derived from the focus groups: the doctor's attitude and communication style, obtaining information from the doctor, emotional relief from the relationship with the doctor, and following the doctor's recommendations.

In the relationship with the doctor, many KABCS* mentioned trust, confidence, and the attitudes of doctors. Specifically, the doctor's attitudes and communication seemed to significantly influence KABCS level of stress.

"If you receive this, you will die today. Do you want to die today?" . . . How could a doctor speak this way to a cancer patient? I got so stressed.

A woman complained she did not obtain enough medical information because of an uncomfortable relationship with her doctor, the language barrier, and limited time.

"I had a few consultation sessions with a doctor before surgery. . . . It was a little regretful because I did not get any detailed information."

SOURCE: Excerpt taken from Lim et al. (2012, p. 394).

* Korean-American breast cancer survivors.

The contiguous technique presents the qualitative and quantitative findings in separate sections in a single manuscript. In this approach, the findings may be presented in either sequence, with narrative commentary linking major elements of each. Bradley and colleagues (2011) conducted a longitudinal mixed methods study to evaluate the impact of a systems-based approach to improving rural health care in Ethiopia. The quantitative component examined health services utilization at 10 primary health care centers, while the qualitative component gathered patient perspectives through 14 focus groups. The findings section of the article reports time trends in key indicators of service utilization, followed by thematic description of patient experiences of accessibility and quality of services. Results are integrated in the discussion section, where discordance is interpreted, noting the importance of both quantitative and qualitative measures of impact of systems reforms to improve health care access and quality.

Staged techniques present the qualitative and quantitative data in separate reports throughout the study period. They are more common in large-scale multiphase studies that typically span several years in duration, with a year or more transpiring between findings generated in each component. In these circumstances, it is necessary to assess the advantages and disadvantages of reporting data in stages in individual manuscripts versus holding all of the data for a single manuscript that integrates all findings. Possible reasons to pursue sequential reporting of components include concern for timeliness in sharing new knowledge, desire to be responsive to funders' desires for prompt reporting, and constraints on the scope of data that can be appropriately reported in most health sciences journals. The major risk associated with publishing independent papers is diluting the value of having conducted a mixed methods study through limited integration of findings.

▶ Further discussion of publication strategies is included in Chapter 11: Publishing Mixed Methods Studies in the Health Sciences.

Joint Displays

Joint displays present combined qualitative and quantitative data through visual means designed in order to provide additional insights into how the data fit together. As noted in Table 8.2, joint displays can take a number of forms, including matrices, figures, and graphs (Miles & Huberman, 1994; O'Cathain et al., 2010; Sandelowski, 2000; Wendler, 2001). Within a mixed methods matrix, the rows represent the cases (e.g., individual patients, clinics, quality improvement teams) or major constructs of the topic (e.g., teamwork, accountability, expertise) for which there are both qualitative and quantitative data, and the columns display different data collected on each case. This visual organization facilitates review of multifaceted data for each case and highlights patterns that may emerge across cases and are not easily identified through independent component analysis. The visual representation of related scale scores and individual narrative is of unique benefit in health sciences research and can serve as an aid in manuscript presentation of results.

Figures and graphs for visual display of integrated data are becoming more creative with advances in software and infographics technology. Meurer and colleagues (2012) conducted a convergent mixed methods study of stakeholder views of ethical advantages and disadvantages of adaptive clinical trials. Quantitative data included a 22-item survey assessing beliefs about ethical advantages and disadvantages from the patient, research, and societal perspectives. Qualitative data gathered through a free-text field and mini focus groups explored the reasons behind reported beliefs. The researchers developed a joint display of the results (see Figure 8.5). The left side of the figure reports participant views (n = 53 stakeholders) regarding ethical advantages using visual analog scales (0 = definitely do not agree, 100 = definitely agree) in a box plot format, while on the right appear illustrative data from the free-text responses on a survey and the mini focus groups. Using color codes for each type of data helps guide the viewer to match the data for each respondent group.

Data Transformation

Data transformation can take two forms, as indicated in Table 8.2 earlier. Qualitative data can be converted to quantitative data (also referred to as "quantitizing") and then integrated with illustrative examples from the original qualitative data set. Quantitative data can also be converted into a qualitative format (also referred to as "qualitizing"). For instance, results of a factor analysis of survey items might be assigned narrative labels representing conceptual domains (e.g., medication management practices, discharge and follow-up procedures, team-based leadership). Conversely, numerical results displayed in a table might be summarized in a narrative statement. We would note that data transformation is not a required aspect of mixed methods studies. We agree with experts (Driscoll, Appiah-Yeboah, Salib, & Rupert, 2007; Sandelowski,

Figure 8.5   Example of a Figure as a Joint Display

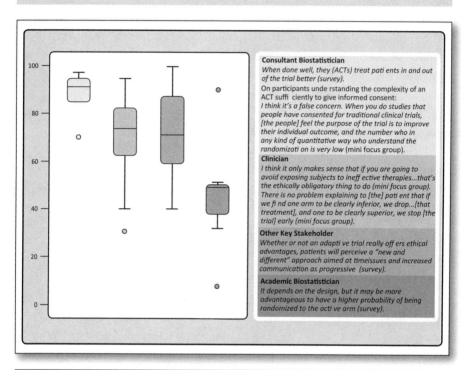

SOURCE: Adapted from Laurie J. Legocki, William J. Meurer, Shirley Frederiksen, and Michael D Fetters.

NOTE: ACTs = adaptive clinical trials.

Voils, & Knafl, 2009) who recognize the potential of data transformation yet suggest caution regarding both the converting qualitative into quantitative data and the substantial risks of sacrificing the richness and nuance of the qualitative data. Nevertheless, we also recognize that data transformation has the potential to contribute to advancement on both the methodological and empirical front. For instance, Zickmund and colleagues (2013) developed a novel measure ("view of self") among cancer patients using a convergent mixed methods design and the *quasi-statistical* approach (assigning textual data to categories and examining them statistically to uncover connections between them). Qualitative data from interviews with cancer patients ($n = 909$) included the following question: "As you go through this experience, have you begun to think of yourself differently?" Qualitative data were coded as "improved," "worse," or "unchanged." The view-of-self variable was an independent predictor of mortality among cancer patients, demonstrating the major potential of data transformation. In Table 8.3, the qualitatively derived view-of-self variable is reported as rows, with quantitative data on mortality in columns.

In this chapter we present the basic approaches and techniques for presenting mixed methods findings in health sciences literature. Creative techniques for data display are rapidly emerging, particularly with new technologies to support both integrated analysis and reporting. Various forms of data display will need to be tailored to fit the knowledge, interests, and orientations of primary audiences. Regardless of the specific technique used, the essential message is to ensure deliberate, early, and ongoing attention to integration of qualitative and quantitative data throughout the entire research project.

Table 8.3 Example of Data Transformation and Joint Display

a) Mortality Rate in Cancer Patients by Stage of Disease						
	Deceased		Alive			
Cancer Stage	$N = 480$	63%	$N = 278$	38%	x^2 test	p-value
1	36	39	56	61	94.38	<.001
2	53	41	76	59	3 df	
3	90	57	67	43		
4	301	79	79	21		
b) Mortality Rate in Cancer Patients by View of Self (measured through qualitative interviews and quantisized after coding)						
	Deceased		Alive			
View of Self	$N = 509$	62%	$N = 316$	38%	x^2 test	p-value
Improved	96	52	90	48	10.88	0.004
Unchanged	270	66	141	34	2 df	
Worse	143	63	85	37		

SOURCE: Zickmund et al. (2013).

Summary and Key Points

- Integration of qualitative and quantitative data at one or more points is a defining feature of mixed methods studies.
- Despite available guidance on integration in mixed methods, the extent to which integration is implemented in health sciences research is limited.
- The primary approaches to integration in data collection and analysis include merging, embedding, and connecting (or building) the data sets.
- Basic approaches for presenting integrated data are narrative, joint displays and data transformation, and innovative presentation formats are emerging.

Review Questions and Exercises

1. Think about a mixed methods project of interest to you where the qualitative component receives priority and quantitative data are embedded. Develop a figure to represent the data analysis plan. What are some of the implications for data integration and analysis?

2. Select three published mixed methods studies: one that integrates data by merging, another that uses embedding, and the third that integrates data by connecting. Develop a schematic representation of each, using the information in the article.

3. Select one of the software programs included in Appendix F: Qualitative Analysis Software Comparison Table that you find most interesting, and experiment with it. Discuss the key features of the program, especially as it relates to mixed analysis and integration.

References

Bazeley, P. (2009). Mixed methods data analysis. In S. Andrew & E. J. Halcomb (Eds.), *Mixed methods research for nursing and the health sciences* (pp. 84–118). Chichester, UK: Wiley-Blackwell.

Bazeley, P. (2010). Computer-assisted integration of mixed methods data sources and analyses. In A. Tashakkori & C. Teddlie (Eds.), *SAGE handbook of mixed methods in social & benavioral research* (2nd ed., pp. 431–468). Thousand Oaks, CA: Sage.

Best, J. W., & Kahn, J. V. (2005). *Research in education* (10th ed.). Portland, OR: Book News, Inc.

Bradley, E. H., Curry, L. A., & Devers, K. J. (2007). Qualitative data analysis for health services research: Developing taxonomy, themes, and theory. *Health Services Research, 42*(4), 1758–1772. doi: 10.1111/j.1475-6773.2006.00684.x

Bradley, E. H., Curry, L. A., Ramanadhan, S., Rowe, L., Nembhard, I. M., & Krumholz, H. M. (2009). Research in action: Using positive deviance to improve quality of health care. *Implementation Science, 4*, 25. doi: 10.1186/1748-5908-4-25

Bradley, E. H., Curry, L. A., Spatz, E. S., Herrin, J., Cherlin, E. J., Curtis, J. P., . . . Krumholz, H. M. (2012). Hospital strategies for reducing risk-standardized mortality rates in acute myocardial infarction. *Annals of Internal Medicine, 156*(9), 618–626.

Bradley, E. H., Thompson, J. W., Byam, P., Webster, T. R., Zerihun, A., Alpern, R., . . . Curry, L. (2011). Access and quality of rural healthcare: Ethiopian Millennium Rural Initiative. *International Journal for Quality in Health Care, 23*(3), 222–230. doi: 10.1093/intqhc/mzr013

Bryman, A. (2006). Integrating quantitative and qualitative research: How is it done? *Qualitative Research, 6*, 97–113.

Campbell, D. T., & Fiske, D. W. (1959). Convergent and discriminant validation by the multitrait-multimethod matrix. *Psychological Bulletin, 56*(2), 81–105.

Castro F. G., Kellison, J. G., Boyd, S. J., & Kopak, A. (2010). A methodology for conducting integrative mixed methods research and data analyses. *Journal of Mixed Methods Research, 4*(4), 342–360.

Cox, K. (2003). Assessing the quality of life of patients in phase I and II anti-cancer drug trials: Interviews versus questionnaires. *Social Science and Medicine, 56*(5), 921–934.

Creswell, J. W. (2013). *Research design: Qualitative, quantitative, and mixed methods approaches* (4th ed.). Thousand Oaks, CA: Sage.

Creswell, J. W., & Plano Clark, V. L. (2011). *Designing and conducting mixed methods research* (2nd ed.). Thousand Oaks, CA: Sage.

Curry, L. A., Spatz, E., Cherlin, E., Thompson, J. W., Berg, D., Ting, H. H., . . . Bradley, E. H. (2011). What distinguishes top-performing hospitals in acute myocardial infarction mortality rates? A qualitative study. *Annals of Internal Medicine, 154*(6), 384–390.

Driscoll, D. L., Appiah-Yeboah, A., Salib, P., & Rupert, D. J. (2007). Merging qualitative and quantitative data in mixed methods research: How to and why not? *Ecological and Environmental Anthropology, 3*(1), 19–28.

Fetters, M., Curry, L. A., & Creswell, J. (2013). Achieving integration in mixed methods designs: Principles and practices. *Health Services Research, 48* (6 Pt. 2), 2134–2156. doi: 2110.1111/1475-6773.12117.

Greene, J. C. (2007). *Mixed methods in social inquiry* (1st ed.). San Francisco, CA: Jossey-Bass.

Hulley, S. B., Cummings, S. R., Browner, W. S., Grady, D. G., & Newman, T. B. (2013). *Designing clinical research* (4th ed.). Philadelphia, PA: Wolters Kluwer.

Keith, R. E., Hopp, F. P., Subramanian, U., Wiitala, W., & Lowery, J. C. (2010). Fidelity of implementation: Development and testing of a measure. *Implementation Science, 5*, 99. doi: 10.1186/1748-5908-5-99

Krumholz, H. M., Curry, L. A., & Bradley, E. H. (2011). Survival after acute myocardial infarction (SAMI) study: The design and implementation of a positive deviance study. *American Heart Journal, 162*(6), 981–987. e989. doi: 10.1016/j.ahj.2011.09.004

Lim, J. W., Baik, O. M., & Ashing-Giwa, K. T. (2012). Cultural health beliefs and health behaviors in Asian American breast cancer survivors: A mixed-methods approach. *Oncology Nursing Forum, 39*(4), 388–397. doi: 10.1188/12.ONF.388-397

MacMillan, K., & Keonig, T. (2004). The Wow factor: Preconceptions and expectations for data analysis software in qualitative research. *Social Science Computer Review, 22*, 179–204.

Maeitta, R. (2006). State of the art: Integrating software with qualitative analysis. In L. Curry, R. Shield, & T. Wetle (Eds.), *Improving aging and public health research: Qualitative and mixed methods* (pp. 117–139). Washington, DC: American Public Health Association.

Meurer, W. J., Lewis, R. J., Tagle, D., Fetters, M. D., Legocki, L., Berry, S., . . . Barsan, W. G. (2012). An overview of the adaptive designs accelerating promising trials into treatments (ADAPT-IT) project. *Annals of Emergency Medicine, 60*(4), 451–457. doi: 10.1016/j.annemergmed.2012.01.020

Miles, M. B., & Huberman, A. M. (1994). *Qualitative data analysis: An expanded sourcebook* (2nd ed.). Thousand Oaks, CA: Sage.

Moffatt, S., White, M., Mackintosh, J., & Howel, D. (2006). Using quantitative and qualitative data in health services research—what happens when mixed method findings conflict? [ISRCTN61522618]. *BMC Health Services Research, 6*, 28. doi: 10.1186/1472-6963-6-28

Morgan, D. L. (2013). *Integrating qualitative and quantitative methods: A pragmatic approach.* Thousand Oaks, CA: Sage.

Morse, J. M. (2010). Procedures and practice of mixed method design: Maintaining control, rigor, and complexity. In A. Tashakkori & C. Teddlie (Eds.), *SAGE handbook of mixed methods in social and behavioral research* (2nd ed., pp. 339–352). Thousand Oaks, CA: Sage.

Morse, J. M., & Niehaus, L. (2009). *Mixed method design: Principles and procedures.* Walnut Creek, CA: Left Coast Press.

Newman, I., & Ramlo, S. (2010). Using Q methodology and Q factor analysis in mixed methods research. In A. Tashakkori & C. Teddlie (Eds.), *SAGE handbook of mixed methods in social & behavioral research* (2nd ed., pp. 505–530). Thousand Oaks, CA: Sage.

O'Cathain, A., Murphy, E., & Nicholl, J. (2010). Three techniques for integrating data in mixed methods studies. *BMJ, 341*, c4587. doi: 10.1136/bmj.c4587

Onwuegbuzie, A. J., Bustamante, R. M., & Nelson, J. A. (2010). Mixed research as a tool for developing quantitative instruments. *Journal of Mixed Methods Research, 4*(1), 56–78.

Onwuegbuzie, A. J., & Combs, J. P. (2010). Emergent data analysis techniques in mixed methods research: a synthesis. In A. Tashakkori & C. Teddlie (Eds.), *SAGE handbook of mixed methods in social & behavioral research* (2nd ed., pp. 397–430). Thousand Oaks, CA: Sage.

Patton, M. Q. (2002). *Qualitative research & evaluation methods* (3rd ed.). Thousand Oaks, CA: Sage.

Pluye, P., Grad, R. M., Levine, A., & Nicolau, B. (2009). Understanding divergence of quantitative and qualitative data (or results) in mixed methods studies. *International Journal of Multiple Research Approaches, 3*(1), 58–72.

Pope, C., Ziebland, S., & Mays, N. (2000). Qualitative research in health care. Analysing qualitative data. *BMJ, 320*(7227), 114–116.

Ragin, C. C., Shulman, D., Weinberg, A., & Gran, B. (2003). Complexity, generality, and qualitative comparative analysis. *Field Methods, 15*(4), 323–340.

Rycroft-Malone, J., Seers, K., Crichton, N., Chandler, J., Hawkes, C. A., Allen, C., . . . Strunin, L. (2012). A pragmatic cluster randomised trial evaluating three implementation interventions. *Implementation Science, 7*, 80. doi: 10.1186/1748-5908-7-80

Sandelowski, M. (2000). Combining qualitative and quantitative sampling, data collection, and analysis techniques in mixed-method studies. *Research in Nursing and Health, 23*(3), 246–255.

Sandelowski, M., Voils, C. I., & Knafl, G. (2009). On quantitizing. *Journal of Mixed Methods Research, 3*(3), 208–222. doi: 10.1177/1558689809334210

Scammon, D. L., Tomoaia-Cotisel, A., Day, R. L., Day, J., Kim, J., Waitzman, N. J., . . . Magill, M. K. (2013). Connecting the dots and merging meaning: Using mixed methods to study primary care delivery transformation. *Health Services Research, 48*(6 Pt. 2), 2181–2207. doi: 10.1111/1475-6773.12114

Selvin, S. (2004). *Statistical analysis of epidemiologic data* (3rd ed.). New York, NY: Oxford Press.

Tashakkori, A., & Teddlie, C. (2010). *SAGE handbook of mixed methods in social & behavioral research* (2nd ed.). Thousand Oaks, CA: Sage.

Teddlie, C., & Tashakkori, A. (2010). Overview of contemporary issues in mixed methods research. In A. Tashakkori & C. Teddlie (Eds.), *SAGE handbook of mixed methods in social & behavioral research* (2nd ed., pp. 1–44). Thousand Oaks, CA: Sage.

Valenta, A. L., & Wigger, U. (1997). Q-methodology: Definition and application in health care informatics. *Journal of the American Medical Informatics Association, 4*(6), 501–510.

Wendler, M. C. (2001). Triangulation using a meta-matrix. *Journal of Advanced Nursing, 35*(4), 521–525.

Wooley, C. M. (2009). Meeting the mixed methods challenge of integration in a socio-logical study of structure and agency. *Journal of Mixed Methods Research, 3*(1), 7–25.

Yin, R. K. (2006). Mixed methods research: Are the methods genuinely integrated or merely parallel? *Research in the Schools, 13*(1), 41–47.

Zickmund, S. L., Yang, S., Mulvey, E. P., Bost, J. E., Shinkunas, L. A., & Labrecque, D. R. (2013). Predicting cancer mortality: Developing a new cancer care variable using mixed methods and the quasi-statistical approach. *Health Services Research, 48*(6 Pt. 2), 2208–2223. doi: 10.1111/1475-6773.12116

✣ NINE ✣

MANAGING
MIXED METHODS TEAMS

Information you will find in this chapter: This chapter addresses the management of mixed methods research teams. In the first section, we present representational group theory as a framework for understanding teams and teamwork. We then identify potentially challenging dynamics that arise in mixed methods teams and suggest strategies for managing these dynamics. We include brief reflections "from the field" throughout to illustrate possible approaches to managing team dynamics in a research context, grounded in the experiences of mixed methods experts.

Key features in the chapter:

- Brief quotations and reflections from mixed methods researchers
- Schematic displays of representational groups
- Challenges in mixed methods health sciences research and suggested principles for addressing them
- A tool for mapping a mixed methods team as a representational group
- Checklist for enhancing success of mixed methods team

WHY THINK ABOUT MIXED METHODS TEAMS?

You might be wondering why we have dedicated an entire chapter to the topic of mixed methods teams. In our experience, the management of interdisciplinary mixed methods research teams is as challenging (or even more so) than the science and equally as important for the project outcome. Mixed methods teams can face unique challenges, stemming from the very qualities of diversity that also bring extraordinary strength to the research. These teams benefit from including members with varied professional backgrounds, such as sociology, psychology, statistics, economics, business, nursing, public health, and medicine. While this diversity can be a great asset to the team, it can also lead to both philosophical disagreements and practical challenges, including managing power differentials within the team and difficulties in communication. You may recall that in Chapter 3 (Table 3.4) we described potential pitfalls in mixed methods studies; a number of them had to do with team-based issues. Once you have designed your study, secured funding, assembled a strong team, and finally turn to implementation, managing the team becomes critically important to the project's success. Despite this reality, resource manuals for health sciences research typically focus exclusively on study design and methodology, with little to no attention to aspects of team leadership and team dynamics.

MIXED METHODS TEAMS AS REPRESENTATIONAL GROUPS

While there are many theories that help to explain human interaction in professional settings, we find one especially helpful in our work on mixed methods teams: representational group theory. Representational group theory was introduced to us by organizational psychologist Dr. David Berg, who is a regular member of mixed methods research teams in our institution. This theory suggests that the behaviors and perspectives of each individual within a group are not only formed by that individual's personality characteristics (e.g., reserved or extroverted) but also by organizational, professional, and identity "home group" memberships (e.g., scientific discipline or institution). Figure 9.1 illustrates the concept that each individual mixed methods team member belongs to multiple types of home groups and brings expertise and perspective from

Figure 9.1   Multiple Home Groups Represented by Each Mixed Methods Team Member

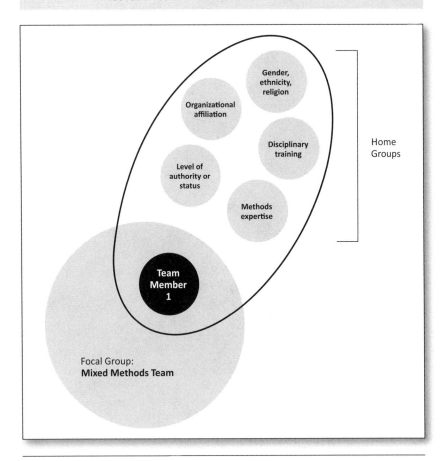

SOURCE: Adapted from Curry et al. (2012).

these home groups to their participation on the project. Figure 9.2 depicts the full mixed methods health sciences research team. Berg refers to this as a "kiwi" because it resembles a cross-section of a kiwi fruit with a core center and set of individual ovals surrounding the core (Berg, 1979; Rice, 1969; Wells, 1995). In this figure, black dots represent the individual and their personal characteristics. The black arrows represent the interactions between the individuals and their home groups (the gray dots). This may include, for

Figure 9.2   Multiple Dimensions of Interaction of Mixed Methods Health Sciences Research Team

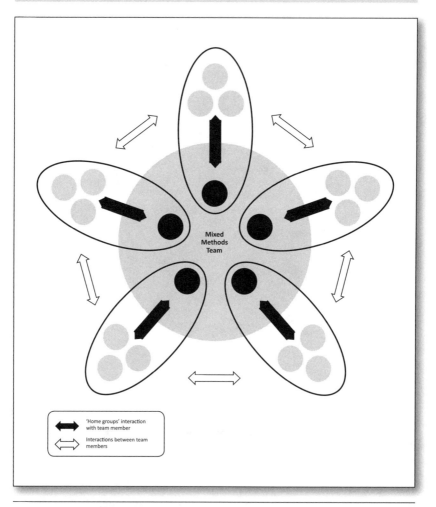

SOURCE: Adapted from Curry et al. (2012).

instance, how strongly they identify with this group and what norms are appropriate for professional collaboration. The white arrows represent the interactions between the various home groups. Finally, and perhaps most importantly, the gray circle in the background emphasizes the boundary of membership in the focal group, the mixed methods team.

Looking at mixed methods teams through the lens of representational group theory can help us be aware of some of the dynamics at work within our teams. For example, in health sciences research, the historical relationship between the professions of medicine and nursing may be very relevant. These histories influence the way team members interpret each other's words, react to each other's behavior, and feel about the relationships on the team. Likewise, histories between methodological "camps" can also influence mixed methods teams. Often, in mixed methods teams, we are recruited to the team because of expertise in a particular research methodology, for example as "the qualitative researcher" or, less frequently, "the mixed methods expert." Nevertheless, team members may also view us as representatives of other groups, such as women, physicians, or sociologists, regardless of whether we have been formally assigned this particular role. Some of these dynamics involve interpersonal histories, and past experiences, both positive and negative, between individuals (Kahn, 2008; Schein, 1969). Yet much of what affects the functioning of mixed methods teams is rooted in intergroup histories, or the past experiences among professional, organizational, and identity groups. Accordingly, the relationships between the groups on the team (e.g., their relative status on the project, their historical relations in this research area or institution) will influence how individual roles are assigned in the team. We also assume another critical role when we join a mixed methods project—that is, as a member of the mixed methods research team. From the first moment the team begins work, group dynamics are set into play.

CONSIDERATIONS AND GUIDING PRINCIPLES FOR MANAGING TEAMS

There is no question in our experience that the diversity inherent in working in mixed methods teams can be stimulating, rewarding, and fun. At the same time, this diversity can give rise to a number of challenges. Next, we describe five considerations common to mixed methods teams, together with suggested principles and strategies to guide the process of managing each. Table 9.1 presents a brief summary of these challenges. Much of the following discussion comes from a paper we wrote with a team of highly experienced mixed methods researchers, the product of an 18-month-long process of dialogue and exploration regarding our experiences in working in mixed methods health sciences research teams (Curry et al., 2012). We found that the nuanced and complex nature of challenges in mixed methods teams had not been well described in the literature, nor was there guidance regarding how to potentially manage such challenges. We synthesized our individual and collective reflections regarding teamwork in order to identify common challenges associated with teams conducting mixed methods research, and to suggest approaches for managing them, grounded in our collective experience.

Table 9.1   Challenges in Mixed Methods Health Sciences Research Teams and Suggested Guiding Principles for Addressing Them

Challenges	Suggested Guiding Principle for Addressing the Challenge
Dealing with differences	• Let people have their groups. • Foster and sustain respect among team members. • Ensure that all team members have a chance to speak up and explain their perspectives.
Trusting the other	• Make all group memberships discussable without penalty. • Encourage and support candor.
Creating a meaningful group	• Establish a minimum shared commitment to the project's overall goal. • Create a psychologically safe space. • Support members in sharing mixed methods team views with their home groups. • Develop a common language. • Ensure time and processes to enable information exchange.
Handling conflict and tension	• Normalize the essential tensions. • Recognize the temptation to withdraw. • Establish mechanisms for conflict resolution.
Enacting effective leadership roles within the team	• Treat leadership as a role rather than an individual characteristic. • Balance issues of relationship and task.

SOURCE: Adapted from Curry et al. (2012).

Dealing With Differences

Differences can bring both excitement and new ways of thinking to our work. Yet we typically tend to avoid differences, address them only superficially, or even silently wish they did not exist. Mixed methods team members may represent groups that have profoundly distinct beliefs about scientific discovery. Team members may have philosophical differences (Barbour, 1998; Richards, 1999; Sandelowski, 2000) or place different value on the various aspects of the research (Massey et al., 2006). These differences may be underscored by members' organizational contexts—for instance, a department of medicine or public health's norms for disseminating research through peer-reviewed publications. Or a researcher with a quantitative orientation may appropriately regard probabilistic sampling and large sample sizes as essential to rigorous science and question the sampling approach in the qualitative component. This view may lead to compromises over sample sizes, with the researcher responsible for the qualitative component to interview large numbers of participants that proves to be unmanageable in terms of recruitment, data collection, and analysis.

Guiding Principles for Dealing With Differences

Several guiding principles can be useful to teams as they struggle to manage differences among members. Recall that group memberships are always present on mixed methods teams; these memberships cannot and should not be ignored or minimized. Yet these groups are often characterized by deep disciplinary traditions in terms of methodologies that can create major challenges even in teams where positive, trusting, and respectful relationships exist (Hemming, Beckett, Kennerly, & Yap, 2013).

First, let people have their groups (Berg, 2005). Often in research teams, there is pressure to speak from a broad, almost generic, perspective rather than from the narrow perspective of one's professional background. For instance, a team discussing hospital organizational *culture* may use very general language interpreted differently by each member of the team rather than turning to an organizational behavior expert to invite a precise definition of this concept. Yet the fundamental reason that different types of researchers are on mixed methods teams is in order to represent their particular experience. If each member of the team speaks from their professional perspective first and explicitly, these diverse perspectives are available for discussion and debate.

This sharing also allows members of the team to refer back to the group interests being represented when a decision is being considered. This not only emphasizes that the opinion comes from a particular area of expertise, but also that the area of expertise, like all areas of expertise, has its limitations and needs reactions from other areas. The previous example regarding differences in sampling focused on the respective standards for quantitative and qualitative sampling, reinforcing the importance of respecting the expertise of each member. In Box 9.1, an expert in the mixed methods field shares how acknowledging the unique perspectives of each member on the team allowed them to resolve conflicts in data analysis.

Box 9.1   Discussing Biases to Build Stronger Teams

A challenge I've had is that people from different disciplines bring different expectations and different views of how qualitative methods should be applied. Anthropologists may view this process a little differently than a health services researcher. Certainly a physician who may have done clinical interviews may approach this kind of work quite differently . . . .One of the things that I do at the beginning of every project is to have the team sit around a table and have each person on the team talk about his or her perspective and the biases and relevant experiences that they bring to this particular research project. We get it out on the table. We discuss our views and biases, and this becomes very helpful when we get into the data analytic phase. We keep this discussion as a part of the audit trail of the study. We can refer back to that. So I'll give you an example: In working on one mixed methods study, I had a physician who, in reading the transcripts, kept saying, "Well that's a misdiagnosis, and they've got it all wrong. That's not what the illness is." And we would come back to our previous team discussion, noting, "The analysis here is of the transcript of the interview gathering the perspectives of the loved one of a person who died. We're not here to make a judgment on whether the diagnosis was correct."

—Terrie Wetle, PhD,
Professor of Health Services,
Policy and Practice, Brown University

We have found mapping the team members' home groups can help build an understanding among team members of the perspectives of others. A tool to facilitate this exercise is provided in Table 9.2.

Second, foster and sustain respect among team members. Respecting others' methodological expertise (and the expectations from their academic institutions or professional organizations) is a necessary but often difficult requirement for effective teamwork. Respect may be undermined in multiple ways. Individuals who do not value the expertise or input of others may acquiesce, act paternalistically, or act relatively uninterested in their suggestions. For instance, a qualitative methodologist on a mixed methods team may solicit input from team members on a discussion guide for in depth interviews yet dismiss the concerns of the statistician about its reliability. Individuals who disrespect other team members may exert control (subtly or not) or challenge them. In this same example, the statistician might question the qualitative methodologist, expressing skepticism about the utility of qualitative data and advocating for a standardized data collection instrument. If the statistician has greater credibility among team members, her opinion can provoke others to devalue the expertise of the qualitative researcher. In these cases, it is helpful to openly acknowledge each member's bias or assumptions about the other, since this dynamic cannot be managed unless it is made explicit in the group (see Box 9.1).

Table 9.2   Tool for Mapping Home Groups for Mixed Methods Team Members

Home Group	Team Member 1	Team Member 2	Team Member 3	Team Member 4	Team Member 5
Methods expertise					
Disciplinary training					
Status or level of authority					
Organizational affiliation					
Personal identity					

Third, ensure all team members have a chance to contribute their perspectives. As a leader of a mixed methods group or as a team member, it is also important to make efforts to ensure that all team members have a chance to speak up and explain their point of view. In teams where respect is fostered and sustained, sharing of information and expertise is enhanced, since members are more likely to feel safe in voicing concerns and in representing the view of one of their particular home groups.

Trusting the "Other"

Trust is a central issue in all work environments (Alderfer, 1977; Shaw, 1997). In mixed methods teams, trust can refer to the shared understanding that the different groups represented on the team will "fight fair" when inevitable conflicts arise over design, data collection, analysis, and writing. A fair fight is one that occurs in the open with all relevant thoughts and feelings, positive and negative, expressed (Alderfer, 1976; Rogers, 1961). Fights that erode trust among representatives are those that are avoided, handled "offline," or never get finished. These disagreements can lead to unilateral action (by one team member or a subgroup of the team) or withdrawal by one or more group members.

Guiding Principles for Trusting the "Other"

Two guiding principles can facilitate building trust among team members. First, make all group memberships discussable without penalty (Berg, 2005). When team members feel comfortable sharing the perspectives and concerns of their home groups, the dynamics associated with feelings of threat can often be softened. However, this comfort comes only when the members of the mixed method teams create a history of discussing their home groups, both at the inception of the project as well as throughout the course of work. Second, encourage and support candor among team members, including the simultaneous assertion of competence and limitations (Alderfer, 1977).This makes it possible to balance the role of group representative (e.g., bringing competence to the work) with the role of a mixed methods team member (e.g., bringing a limitation that requires the input of others). We have found this technique to be highly effective in facilitating communication and respect. For example, the team's qualitative expert might describe the procedures for identifying key informants in a purposeful sample, acknowledging the resulting lack of generalizability, and inviting the epidemiologist to discuss the implications in greater depth.

Creating a Meaningful Group

Meaningful teams must develop a common language and be able to approach the work from a mixed methods perspective, rather than a collection of individual quantitative or qualitative or disciplinary perspectives (Alderfer, 2011). If members cannot identify with the mixed methods team, they will persist in only representing their home groups and have difficulty acting on their mixed methods team membership. For example, individuals trained in different content areas (e.g., nursing and education) do not always share terminology (e.g., medical terms, drugs, learning approaches), which can get in the way of effective communication. In addition, individuals trained in different methods areas may have trouble differentiating important terms from what may be perceived as jargon, such as *purposeful sampling* or *mediating variable.* In Box 9.2, one expert with many years of mixed methods experience describes how she creates a group identity and supports relationship building in a team.

Box 9.2 Creating a Meaningful Group

We have a monthly management meeting where everybody gets together and discusses how the project is going. And the qualitative, quantitative, clinical, whatever expertise is sort of on our team gets together in those monthly meetings . . . .Sometimes [you] find in mixed methods studies that people don't really want to hear about the other type of method—they're only interested in their own . . . bit of it. I think it's the monthly meetings that are our key way of communicating and the key way of keeping the mixing there in the team.

—Alicia O'Cathain, BSc, MSc, MA, PhD,
Professor of Health Services Research,
University of Sheffield

Guiding Principles for Creating a Meaningful Group

Several guiding principles can be valuable in this regard. First, a minimum shared commitment to the project's overall content goal is a prerequisite for creating a meaningful group. Team members must have a common goal for the project and appreciation for the potential contribution of the others on the team. This shared vision is needed in order to realize the benefits of collaborating across groups and to hold the team together through the challenges that arise (Deutsch, 1973; Sherif & Sherif, 1969) (see Box 9.2). Second, create a safe space for members to voice the views of their groups to the mixed methods team. This requires managing the tension between maintaining the integrity of the boundaries around the group each member represents and around the mixed methods team as a whole, while also opening these boundaries up to allow the give and take across the groups. Third, support members in sharing mixed methods team views with their home groups. The representational dynamics of mixed methods teams work in two directions (recall double-headed black arrows in Figure 9.2). Not only is each team member a representative of her home group's expertise to the mixed methods team but she also represents the mixed methods team to her home group(s). If the home group (e.g., qualitative researchers) remains fixed in its narrow view of the other (e.g., quantitative researchers), then the qualitative members of the mixed methods team are more likely to remain fixed and narrow in their relationship to the quantitative members. Joint methodology papers in each other's respective professional groups or joint colloquia in each other's departments are examples of ways that team members can influence each of the team members' home groups. For instance, we have found it satisfying to write collaboratively across disciplines and publish papers introducing methods unfamiliar to new audiences (Curry et al., 2013; Curry, Nembhard, & Bradley, 2009). Fourth, develop a common language that can support team members in adopting a mixed methods perspective. The development of consistent terminology for mixed methods has been somewhat slow, which may be a reflection of the great diversity of disciplines that are applying these methods in their research and the fact that as a field mixed methods is relatively new to health sciences. One strategy is to develop a team glossary that provides collective understandings of key content and methodological terms.

▶ Refer to the Glossary of Key Terms and Definitions in the back of this book as a starting point for your own project's glossary of terms.

It is helpful when at least one team member can serve as a mediator, speaking a hybrid language that reflects and synthesizes the core terminology from different disciplines. Fifth, articulate roles, responsibilities, and processes. Explicit definition of roles and responsibilities in a formal document may be useful to the establishment and ongoing management of the team. It is worth noting that while these documents are potentially valuable they cannot prevent challenges from arising. Finally, ensure time and processes to enable information exchange. The importance of this is described by an expert in Box 9.3. Virtual communication is common in mixed methods teams since members are often geographically dispersed, yet face-to-face communication or teleconferencing is preferred in general and in some instances is required to minimize miscommunication. Communication via e-mail is never optimal and should be used primarily to share project documents and planning tools, to set up meetings, or to confirm agreed-upon information. Key discussions and decisions should be made in a format that supports dialogue and interchange to ensure all points of view are considered.

Box 9.3   Making Time to Collaborate

When you pursue a mixed methods research model, you have [to have] sufficient resources for people to not only collect the data that they need, but for people to really collaborate and learn from each other. When budgets get tight, people pull back . . . . There is less time for meetings, not extensive meetings, but meetings for people to really learn from each other about what they're learning, what data they're collecting and what to make of it and the implications for the other side, the other components or the team.

—Kelly Devers, PhD, Senior Fellow in
the Health Policy Center, Urban Institute

Handling Conflict and Tension

Tensions naturally spring from the extreme diversity among members of mixed methods teams as well as the potentially conflicting norms and expectations from team members' organizational and professional homes. Fragmentation within the team and incomplete information sharing are also sources of conflict and tension. Tensions may also develop over methodological decisions, such as using a representative or purposive sample. Conflicts can also spring from different clinical perspectives, such as viewing the issue from a physician or social worker perspective. A final source of tensions can be procedural decisions, such as the ordering of authors on manuscripts and selecting target publication outlets.

Guiding Principles for Handling Conflict and Tensions

Three guiding principles can be valuable in handling conflict and tensions. First, normalize the essential tensions. Accepting conflict as a natural consequence of working in highly diverse groups is an important premise (Blake, Shepard, & Mouton, 1964; Deutsch, 1973). Regular public acknowledgment of the need to work through these tensions is essential for any mixed methods team to be successful. Second, recognize the temptation to withdraw from the team in the face of these tensions, and take steps to help members remain engaged with each other. Box 9.4 describes the experience of one mixed methods researcher in a situation where the team did withdraw from tension, and unfortunately, this is all too common. As we will discuss, one of the responsibilities of the leadership role in mixed methods teams is to ensure that the team embraces rather than avoids any tensions that may be getting in the way of working together. For instance, discussion of emerging conflicts and tensions can be placed as a standing item on the team's agenda.

Box 9.4   Missing Opportunities by Withdrawing From Tension

An area where tensions come up is when you have methodological leads on a component who are not necessarily open to talking with each other, or having the qualitative lead be marginalized or pushed to the side because that part of the project is not viewed a most important . . . . On a project where I was the mixed methods and qualitative lead but not the overall lead, the statistician was not very open to qualitative methods and actually said, "You know, I don't really understand qualitative research. I don't understand why you are doing it and what you get out of it. When you look at it, isn't qualitative data just words?" So everyone in the meeting just kind of stopped and I'm thinking, "I don't know that this is such a good match to have this quantitative person as our quantitative lead, because they don't seem open to talking and playing ball." It wasn't just the question—which I think is a reasonable question for someone to ask—but it was really asked in a kind of way that denigrated the qualitative data. That situation ended up being resolved in a way that's not ideal, which was that the two parts were essentially separated and the PI was the go-between between the qualitative and the quantitative data, which required somewhat changing the research design to reduce the areas of integration because we did not have that support from the quantitative person. That was really unfortunate . . . . The PI decided that she didn't want to deal with it, she didn't want to confront it, she didn't want to use it as a learning opportunity; she just avoided it. Unfortunately I think that's pretty common. People don't want to have those hard conversations.

—Dr. Jennifer Wisdom, MPH, PhD,
Associate Vice President for Research,
George Washington University

Enacting Effective Leadership Roles Within the Team

Leadership has been identified as central to the success of mixed methods teams (O'Cathain, Murphy, & Nicholl, 2008). Representational group theory suggests that leadership requires constant attention to the relationships among groups. These relationships can create tension because home group affiliations are very deep, where one may have trained for decades as a qualitative researcher, or a statistician, or a cardiologist, or a nurse. This training creates a deeply embedded view of others. While these deep-seated views may pose challenges, these strong affiliations and resulting expertise are precisely the assets each member brings to the mixed methods team and are essential for the success of the effort. Team leadership that values integration of qualitative and quantitative study components can mitigate these challenges and potentially improve the quality of research outputs (O'Cathain et al., 2008). One model of leadership in mixed methods teams—"individual participatory leadership" (Galt, 2009)—suggests that fluidity in roles is central in such teams where individuals take action or lead the team at different points during a project, depending on the project needs.

Guiding Principles for Enacting Meaningful Leadership Roles

Two principles can guide teams in efforts to enact meaningful leadership roles. First, treat leadership as a role rather than an individual characteristic (Berg, 1998). On a mixed methods research team, there are often representatives of home groups at different levels of a traditional research hierarchy (e.g., tenured or non-tenured faculty, research assistants), and typically the principal investigator is seen as the sole leader of the team. However, while this individual may be an exceptionally skilled scientist, he or she may lack the strong organizational skills required to coordinate a large, complex research project. When leadership is viewed as a role (rather than an individual person), it is possible for the team to identify what functions it wants from this role throughout the project and determine which individuals could best provide these functions. To use the example from the preceding discussion of conflict and tension, the principal investigator may not be comfortable confronting the team with emerging conflicts that need to be addressed. If one thinks about leadership as a person, the team may feel stuck with an individual who is personally uncomfortable fulfilling this responsibility. The team can choose an individual more comfortable or skilled in dealing with conflict to perform this function. Second, balance issues of relationship and task that disrupt balance. In order for teams to work effectively, leaders need to attend to both task issues (such as getting a survey developed and administered) but also relationship issues among team members. At times of conflict, the team leader may need to assume a strong leadership role and focus on relationship issues to keep conflict from getting out of control. The commitment to inquire about the team's process—both intergroup and interpersonal—must be regularly built into the agenda of team meetings. As described in Box 9.5, there are ways in which a leader's handling of the task can support strong relationships.

This expert describes how she pays attention to how the project tasks can serve to meet the individual interests of each and every member in order to foster investment and ownership.

Box 9.5   Understanding the Needs of Each Team Member

An effective leader of a mixed methods team needs to be someone who is really skilled at pulling the rest of the team together when they are likely to be coming from very different places . . . . One of the things that I've found particularly helpful for mixed methods studies is to try to understand early on what is important to people. For example, is someone looking for preliminary data for another proposal? Is someone looking for a manuscript, and if so, what kind of manuscript? I try to solicit that information early so that I can then work with them to try to help them to get their needs met . . . . I always offer to the statistician on the study, who sometimes can be the person who's least committed . . . . I offer to that person that if there's any kind of methodological issue that you think could be explored using this data, please let me know. I'd like for you to get a quantitative only paper about that if that's what you want . . . . I think that a good leader does that—not just thinking about achieving this goal for this particular project but thinking about what are the individual goals for the other people on the team—to the extent that you can.

—Dr. Jennifer Wisdom, MPH, PhD,
Associate Vice President for Research,
George Washington University

In keeping with our goal of being pragmatic, we complement the prior review of guiding principles with a checklist to help you think through the major aspects of developing and managing mixed methods teams. We created this tool from work by Barbara Bowers, PhD, and her colleagues (2013) on a mixed methods project titled "The Research Initiative Valuing Eldercare." Based on their collective experiences in this project, the team identified strategies that can promote successful functioning in mixed methods teams. See Box 9.6.

Box 9.6   Checklist on Factors That Contribute to Success of Mixed Methods Teams

- Have you considered not only expertise but also interest, dedication, and personality when selecting team members?
- As the primary investigator, are you willing to both lead and follow others on the team?
- Are you comfortable with and committed to maintaining nonhierarchical and collaborative leadership responsible for not only organizational and logistical needs but also for identifying and promoting discussion of current substantive issues and future ones?
- Is there an explicit plan for maintaining frequent, regular, and multimodal communications (e.g., e-mail, phone, in person) throughout the collaboration?
- Have you put disciplinary and methodological differences on the table for discussion and regular revisiting?
- Has the dissemination plan been created collaboratively with input from all members?
- Are all team members aware that a mixed methods project will require more commitment, flexibility, time, and the ability and willingness to participate?

SOURCE: Adapted from Bowers et al. (2013).

SINGLE INVESTIGATOR RESEARCH

We have devoted this chapter to a discussion of teams and teamwork because the vast majority of mixed methods research is carried out by teams. Nevertheless, it is also important to acknowledge that some mixed methods studies are conducted by individual researchers—often in the context of a master's thesis or doctoral dissertation. While single investigator projects do not present the management and coordination challenges of team-based projects, other challenges may arise. For students, it may be difficult to arrange for input from colleagues from multiple disciplines. We advise students to try to find peers who may be interested in participating in data analysis; we find there is great interest in learning qualitative data analysis, and some students are willing to donate their time in return for this experience. Mentors should also caution students to understand the major time commitment required for a mixed methods study. As described in Box 9.7 by a researcher who recently completed a mixed methods dissertation, it is critical for students (as well as established investigators who may be working alone) to seek the advice and guidance of experts with specialized experience.

Box 9.7 Conducting Independent Research

For my dissertation I conducted all of the components myself. I went through the process of developing the survey, having reliability and validity checkpoints in place and pilot testing. Then I went to sites to collect data and analyzed the data myself. Upon completing the quantitative phase, I developed an interview protocol and pilot tested that, and then I chose participants to follow-up with based on the information they provided in the survey, and then I analyzed that data too. I had two methodologists in place to make sure I was following the correct steps. It's so important to always keep your advisors in the loop on the steps that you took and the decisions that you've made. This will reduce any errors and this is important for mixed methods because an error in one step can impact the outcomes in other parts of the study.

—Dr. Jennifer Cunningham, PhD,
Postdoctoral Fellow,
Meharry Medical College

Summary and Key Points

- The diversity of perspectives that brings value to mixed methods work can also present challenges when the dynamics within mixed methods teams are not fully appreciated and managed.
- It can be helpful to think about mixed methods teams within the framework of representational group theory, which acknowledges the organizational, professional, and identity "home groups" that each team member represents.

- The challenges confronted by mixed methods teams may be distinct from those of other types of teams; guiding principles for addressing these challenges include dealing with differences, trusting the other, creating meaningful groups, handling conflict and tension, and enacting effective leadership roles.

Review Questions and Exercises

1. Work together in a group, and discuss how representational group theory can be used to explain mixed methods teams. Report the ideas raised during this group discussion.

2. Imagine you are a member of a mixed methods team that is having difficulty making decisions due to different backgrounds of several team members. What approaches would you suggest to deal with these differences?

3. Refer to the home group tool in Table 9.2. Create a mock table for a mixed methods study of your choice.

4. Suppose you are serving in a leadership role on a mixed methods team. What do you think is most important to creating a meaningful group? Why?

References

Alderfer, C. P. (1976). Change processes in organizations. In M. D. Dunnette (Ed.), *Handbook of industrial and organizational psychology* (pp. 1591–1638). Chicago, IL: Rand McNally.

Alderfer, C. P. (1977). Improving organizational communication through long-term group intervention. *Journal of Applied Behavioral Science, 13,* 193–210.

Alderfer, C. P. (2011). *The practice of organizational diagnosis.* New York, NY: Oxford University Press.

Barbour, R. S. (1998). Mixing qualitative methods: Quality assurance or qualitative quagmire? *Qualitative Health Research, 8*(3), 352–361.

Berg, D. N. (1979). Intergroup relations: An abbreviated update. *Journal of Management Education, 4,* 48–51.

Berg, D. N. (1998). Resurrecting the muse: Followership in organizations. In E. Klein, F. Gabelnick, & P. Herr (Eds.), *The psychodynamics of leadership* (pp. 27–52). Madison, CT: Psychosocial Press.

Berg, D. N. (2005). Senior executive teams: Not what you think. *Consulting Psychology Journal: Practice and Research, 57*(2), 107–117.

Blake, R. R., Shepard, H. A., & Mouton, J. A. (1964). *Managing intergroup conflict in industry.* Houston, TX: Gulf Publishing.

Bowers, B., Cohen, L. W., Elliot, A. E., Grabowski, D. C., Fishman, N. W., Sharkey, S. S., . . . Kemper, P. (2013). Creating and supporting a mixed methods health services research team. *Health Services Research, 48*(6 Pt. 2), 2157–2180. doi: 10.1111/1475-6773.12118

Curry, L. A., Krumholz, H. M., O'Cathain, A., Plano Clark, V. L., Cherlin, E., & Bradley, E. H. (2013). Mixed methods in biomedical and health services research. *Circulation Cardiovascular Quality and Outcomes, 6*(1), 119–123. doi: 10.1161/CIRCOUTCOMES.112.967885

Curry, L. A., Nembhard, I. M., & Bradley, E. H. (2009). Qualitative and mixed methods provide unique contributions to outcomes research. *Circulation, 119*(10), 1442–1452. doi: 10.1161/CIRCULATIONAHA.107.742775

Curry, L. A., O'Cathain, A., Plano Clark, V. L., Aroni, R., Fetters, M., & Berg, D. (2012). The role of group dynamics in mixed methods in health sciences research teams. *Journal of Mixed Methods Research, 6,* 5–20. doi: 10.1177/1558689811416941

Deutsch, M. (1973). *The resolution of conflict; constructive and destructive processes.* New Haven, CT: Yale University Press.

Galt, K. A. (2009). *The process of participating in academic interdisciplinary health services team research: A grounded theory investigation* (Doctoral dissertation). Available from ProQuest Dissertations and Theses database. (UMI No. 3386837)

Hemming, A., Beckett, G., Kennerly, S., & Yap, T. (2013). Building a community of research practice: Intragroup team social dynamics in interdisciplinary mixed methods. *Journal of Mixed Methods Research, 7*(3), 261. doi: 10.1177/1558689813478468

Kahn, W. A. (2008). *A student's guide to successful project teams.* New York, NY: Routledge.

Massey, C., Alpass, F., Flett, R., Lewis, K., Morriss, S., & Sligo, F. (2006). Crossing fields: The case of a multi-disciplinary research team. *Qualitative Research, 6*(2), 131–149.

O'Cathain, A., Murphy, E., & Nicholl, J. (2008). Multidisciplinary, interdisciplinary, or dysfunctional? Team working in mixed-methods research. *Qualitative Health Research, 18*(11), 1574–1585. doi: 10.1177/1049732308325535

Rice, A. K. (1969). Individual, group and intergroup processes. *Human Relations, 22,* 565–584.

Richards, L. (1999). Qualitative teamwork: Making it work. *Qualitative Health Research, 9*(1), 7–10.

Rogers, C. R. (1961). *On becoming a person; a therapist's view of psychotherapy.* Boston, MA: Houghton Mifflin.

Sandelowski, M. (2000). Combining qualitative and quantitative sampling, data collection, and analysis techniques in mixed-method studies. *Research in Nursing and Health, 23*(3), 246–255.

Schein, E. H. (1969). *Process consultation: Its role in organization development.* Reading, MA: Addison-Wesley.

Shaw, R. B. (1997). *Trust in the balance: Building successful organizations on results, integrity, and concern* (1st ed.). San Francisco, CA: Jossey-Bass.

Sherif, M., & Sherif, C. W. (1969). *Social psychology.* New York, NY: Harper & Row.

Wells, L. (1995). The group as a whole: A systemic, socioanalytic perspective on interpersonal and group relations. In J. Gillette & M. McCollom (Eds.), *Groups in context* (pp. 49–85). Reading, MA: Addison-Wesley.

❧ TEN ❧

IMPLEMENTATION ISSUES IN MIXED METHODS RESEARCH

Information you will find in this chapter: In this chapter we address major issues that arise in implementing a mixed methods study, with a focus on technical and logistical procedures unique to these designs. The first section describes practical considerations for working with human research protection programs (HRPPs), including an overview of particular challenges with mixed methods research. In the next section, we present recommendations for preparing a strong application for HRPP review. We then turn to a discussion of key implementation issues for each major type of design, including emergent designs. The chapter concludes with analysis of real-world examples from the field, highlighting common challenges to doing mixed methods research.

Key features in this chapter:

- Brief quotations and reflections from mixed methods researchers
- Tips for working with HRPPs
- Sample informed consent form for mixed methods study
- Tips for communicating about emergent study designs

I n this chapter, we draw from our own experiences in conducting mixed methods studies, as well as the experiences of other researchers using mixed methods in the health sciences. Our goal is to move beyond the more theoretical and methodological aspects of mixed methods research to the highly practical, concrete realities of doing this type of research. In many ways, the practical issues in any given study will depend on the research question, population of interest, design, timeline, and other elements of the research. Nevertheless, in this chapter we have identified several issues that we believe are relevant for most mixed methods researchers, beginning with working with HRPPs and then turning to a number of aspects of study implementation. At the end of the chapter, we share experiences from the field to illustrate approaches to three common challenges, including prioritizing components and findings, developing team approaches to data analysis, and incorporating mixed methods expertise into the team.

WORKING WITH HUMAN RESEARCH PROTECTION PROGRAMS

In this section, we focus on key aspects of working with HRPPs for approval of studies using mixed methods. We open with a brief overview of the function and process of HRPPs, and then describe several important considerations when submitting mixed methods studies for review.

Human Research Protection Program Overview

HRPPs are charged with the protection of human subjects from mental or physical harm arising from participation in biomedical or behavioral research. We use the broadly inclusive term HRPP, which encompasses institutional review boards (IRBs) and research ethics committees and other human research protection activities. HRPPs review submitted protocols and approve, deny, or request revisions to the research plan. All research directly or indirectly supported through the U.S. Department of Health and Human Services, which includes the National Institutes of Health (NIH) and the U.S. Food and Drug Administration (FDA), must obtain approval from a federally recognized HRPP (U.S. Department of Health and Human Services, n.d.). These requirements also extend to research sponsored by a U.S. funding agency and being conducted internationally. In practice, all research involving human participants should be reviewed by an HRPP regardless of funding source (federal, foundation, institutional, or unfunded). In an effort to minimize risk and harm, hallmark requirements include maintaining participant confidentiality and obtaining participant consent. The current guidelines were largely developed to address prior ethical violations in biomedical research and do not always readily transfer to social or behavioral science research. In the past, ethics review committees were sometimes critiqued for not including members with an understanding of qualitative or mixed methods, for requiring unnecessary participant protections for behavioral research, and perhaps devaluing qualitative and mixed methodological approaches by considering them as exempt from review as nonresearch (Lincoln & Tierney, 2004; Oakes, 2002). As the adoption of mixed methods in health sciences research continues to grow, we are seeing positive developments, with increased interest and receptivity among review committees. With this as a brief foundation, we now describe HRPPs as they relate to mixed methods research. Although some of the content is specific to the United States, many of the principles and implications are transferrable across countries and research contexts.

Human Research Protection Program
Considerations Unique to Mixed Methods Research

There are several aspects of a mixed methods study protocol that merit careful consideration when preparing an application for an HRPP. First, your application may require review by several HRPP committees if the study will be conducted across multiple settings. Depending upon the scope of the project, you may need to seek approval by one or more committees at academic health centers in addition to committees based at clinical care delivery settings or from community-based review committees. For example, if you want to collect quantitative data through query of a hospital's electronic medical record and collect qualitative data with participants identified through an outpatient group practice, you may need to submit HRPP applications to your academic institution, to the hospital, and to the ambulatory practice. The onus is on the research team to identify all of the relevant bodies and to obtain approval prior to initiation of the research project. Most HRPPs require a local principal investigator to submit the application regardless of project risk or scope. Be sure to plan for any associated costs—time and financial—with recruiting site-specific principal investigators.

Whether you need to submit to one or to multiple HRPPs, we provide some tips later in this chapter to help your HRPP interactions be both efficient and beneficial (see Box 10.2 later in the chapter).

The second consideration is addressing the lack of familiarity of some HRPP members with qualitative and mixed methods designs. Review committee members may have a primary orientation toward quantitative methods (Lincoln & Tierney, 2004; Tol, Komproe, Jordans, Susanty, & de Jong, 2011). It is important to keep in mind that your audience may include members with a range of perspectives and levels of experience—from those who may not have mixed methods expertise or who may be skeptical of the methodology to those who are sophisticated qualitative and mixed methods researchers. Increasingly, review committees recognize the need for members with qualitative and mixed methods expertise.

A third consideration is the need for a thorough assessment of risk to research participants in mixed methods studies. The former director of the Yale University Human Subjects Committee, which is the group responsible for reviewing all social science, behavioral, and educational research at the university, provides perspective on the potential harms of qualitative methods in Box 10.1. Clinical researchers who are accustomed to considering the harm associated with clinical or biomedical research may underestimate risks and fail to safeguard against the potential harms associated with various methods. Be sure you address the potential risks associated with including qualitative methods in addition to those risks associated with the quantitative component. Although rarely directly life-threatening, the potential risks are real nonetheless and your application should identify specific types of harm and outline a mitigation plan as appropriate, especially when studying sensitive topics. Several resources exist for researchers interested in learning more on ethical considerations for mixed methods and qualitative research (Creswell, 2003; Holloway & Wheeler, 1995; Morse, 2007; Orb, Eisenhauer, & Wynaden, 2000).

Box 10.1   Addressing Potential Participant Harms Associated With Qualitative Methods

In many of the mixed method protocols that I was involved in reviewing, the qualitative portion appeared to be an afterthought that was added into the protocol without significant consideration of . . . potential harm. There was . . . a general lack of understanding of the potential harms that can arise in qualitative methods, as if the lack of physicality precludes significant harm. For example, has the protocol considered and developed response plans for participants who are upset by the line of questioning? For participants who provide sensitive or actionable information that was not the focus of the interview? In focus groups, does the anticipated make up of the groups create the potential for further distress or subsequent concern such as mixed genders in focus groups related to intimate partner violence or even awareness by peers that an individual was associated with a study on IPV?

—Susan Bouregy, PhD, CIP,
Chief HIPAA Privacy Officer,
Former Director of the Human
Subjects Committee (HSC), Yale University

RECOMMENDATIONS FOR PREPARING A STRONG MIXED METHODS APPLICATION FOR HUMAN RESEARCH PROTECTION PROGRAM REVIEW

Submitting a mixed methods application to your HRPP for the first time can be a daunting task. The good news is that a deliberate and thoughtful strategy can lead to a timely and successful outcome. In Box 10.2 we present a checklist of tips for working with HRPPs on an application for a mixed methods study. Each of these tips is described in more detail here.

Box 10.2 Tips for Working With Your Human Research Protection Program on Mixed Methods Applications

✓ Review application instructions thoroughly for requirements that may be unique for qualitative or mixed methods.
✓ Contact human research protection program (HRPP) staff before submission for guidance on mixed methods protocols.

(Continued)

> (Continued)
>
> ✓ Communicate clearly and effectively by reducing jargon, defining all terms that may be unfamiliar to reviewers, and using figures and schematics.
> ✓ Form a research team with the appropriate expertise, or ask colleagues with mixed methods expertise for advice and feedback.

SOURCE: Adapted from Labaree (2010).

Review Application Instructions Thoroughly

It may seem obvious, but we want to stress the importance of reading application instructions thoroughly in order to ensure the application is complete and correct. Application materials are typically available on HRPP websites (note that qualitative and mixed methods study guidelines and examples might be housed under a social or behavioral research link). As you review the information, pay attention to these key questions: Are there mandatory training sessions? Are there examples or templates for various components of the application? What are the particulars of the application and submission process? Carefully assess the criteria for an expedited or exempt review, and determine whether your study may qualify, as expedited or exempt reviews can save considerable time and effort. Allow for sufficient time to develop necessary informed consent forms, which may differ in some respects for qualitative or mixed methods studies. Fortunately, many review committees offer samples of consent forms (which must be signed by the participant) and information sheets (for which the signature requirement is waived) on their websites. See Box 10.3 for an example, and you might choose to view example documents at several HRPP websites across different institutions.

> ### Box 10.3   Sample Consent Form and Information Sheet for Mixed Methods Designs
>
> **Study Title:** *[Insert study title here.]*
>   This is a two-part research study about *[Insert short description about overall aim.].* We are *[Insert the methods (e.g., " . . . first interviewing a small group of people and then using that information to*

create a survey for a much larger group of people).]. The study researchers *[Insert names.]*, from the *[Insert academic affiliation.]*, will explain this study to you.

Research studies only include people who choose to participate. Please take your time to decide if you want to be part of this study, and discuss your decision with family and friends if you want to. Ask the researchers if you have questions.

You are being asked to take part in this study because you are/ have *[Specify the criteria used to identify participants.]*. This study has two parts, and we are describing the entire study to you. You may be asked to take part in one or both parts of the study.

Why is this study being done? The purpose of this study is to *[Explain in one to two sentences using lay language.]*.

Who is paying for this study? This study is being funded by *[List internal and external funding sources and role the funding source will play in the design and analysis. Include if the funders are providing equipment or other resources. Also include any investigator conflicts of interest.]*

How many people will take part in this study? We anticipate about *[State number.]* people will take place in part one of the study *[Insert the component (e.g., one-on-one interviews).]* and about *[State number.]* will take part in part two of the study *[Insert the component (e.g., surveys).]*. *[Include both local enrollment targets and whole study enrollment targets when presenting a multisite study.]*

What will happen next if I take part in this research study? *[List and describe all study data collection activities and their frequency under the following categories. Indicate the location where data will be collected.]*

[Insert method as title (e.g., one-on-one interviews).]

If you agree, this is the process *[Use bullets to list—example is next.]*:

- One of the researchers will interview you for about an hour in a private setting. *[Insert location.]*. The researcher will ask you to describe your experiences with . . .

(Continued)

(Continued)

- The researcher will record your conversation. After the interview, someone will type up the interview and will remove any information that ties the interview to you, such as the mention of names. At that point, the sound recording will then be destroyed.

[Insert method as title (e.g., surveys).]

If you agree, this is the process *[Use bullets to list.]*:

[Describe who on the team has access to data for management and analysis.]

Can I stop being in the study? *[Reinforce that participants can withdraw or be dropped at any time, and no reason for stoppage is necessary.]*

What risks can I expect from being in the study? *[List the risks. Typically, the risks in most mixed methods studies are limited to emotional or psychological effects such as feeling uncomfortable or upset by the topic of study or of having their privacy compromised.]*

Are there benefits to taking part in the study? *[Explain possible benefits or that the participant will not benefit directly. Remind the potential participant that choosing not to participate will not in any way affect that person's relationship with the academic institution, the study location/site, or any other relevant groups or organizations.]*

Will my information be private? *[Discuss the goal of maintaining privacy and anonymity in any dissemination forum such as presentations or papers. However, participants should be aware that researchers might be required to share original research records with oversight agencies such as the funder or the institutional review board (IRB).] [If conducting focus groups, include language about instructing participants to use only first names and not to discuss who participated but remind potential participants you cannot guarantee the latter. If collecting sensitive information, investigate a certificate of confidentiality.]*

Does it cost me anything to participate? *[Typically, the major cost is one of time for participants.]*

Will I be paid for taking part in this study? [*Indicate whether there is payment. If there is payment, specify the details for how and when payment occurs.*]

Who can answer my questions about the study? [*Include the researcher name and contact information as well as the information for contacting the relevant IRB. If there are others who might be contacted, include their role and contact information here as well*].

CONSENT [*This section is included if a signed consent is required for the study. Instructions on how to format the signature section are provided by your IRB. This section is omitted on information sheets, when signature is not required.*]

Contact Human Research Protection Program Staff Before Submission

Similar to the process of working with funding institutions on grant proposals, it can be helpful to communicate via e-mail or phone with HRPP staff to briefly discuss your study design and ask any questions that are not addressed in the application materials. In some cases, a mixed methods research application may be forwarded for review by a university social science committee rather than by biomedical reviewers at the academic health center. Also, state statutes or other local regulations about human subjects research design and informed consent may be relevant to your protocol. These types of details may not be specified in the instructions yet can be very helpful to know in advance as you prepare your application. Many review committees also host training sessions and other events for researchers. These sessions may provide an opportunity to interact with staff face-to-face and to ask specific questions about your application.

Communicate Clearly and Effectively

As is the case with health sciences journal editorial boards and funder review panels, expertise in mixed methods may be limited on ethics review committees. Keep in mind that some reviewers may be less familiar with your methods than others. There are several things you can do to communicate

◄ See Chapter 2: Applications and Illustrations of Mixed Methods Health Sciences Research or Chapter 5: Examples of Funded Grant Applications Using Mixed Methods for examples of how the components of a study can be presented in a table or figure.

clearly and effectively to a diverse audience. Be sure that you have a strong grasp of the terminology, use methodological jargon only when necessary, define concepts that may be unfamiliar to the reviewers, and provide citations for methodological approaches. Particularly for complex studies with multiple components, using figures and diagrams can also help to clarify the study design for reviewers. We recommend including these kinds of schematics wherever possible.

Form a Mixed Methods Team With Necessary Expertise

Building a strong team with mixed methods expertise is critical for developing a competitive grant proposal and executing a rigorous study. This is also a key factor in ensuring that the review process is smooth and that your study participants are afforded the necessary protections. An expert perspective on the importance of including relevant methodological expertise on your team is provided in Box 10.4. For teams that face challenges in recruiting mixed methods experts to join the team, it is important to solicit the perspective of a colleague, preferably at your institution, who has submitted a mixed methods application previously. HRPP staff may be able to provide you with the names of other researchers at your institution who have this experience. Although ethics review committees vary across institutions, it can also be useful to ask mixed methods researchers at other institutions to review your application and informed consent documents to offer suggestions for strengthening the application.

Box 10.4   Forming a Team With Appropriate Expertise

The best advice I have for clinical researchers considering including qualitative methodologies would be to include an individual experienced in these methodologies on the research team or at least to seek consultation. There is an art to conducting qualitative research, and when done properly it can significantly inform quality of life and other relevant questions associated with clinical research.

These are important questions and need to be addressed but it is also important that they be done properly, but inexperience with qualitative methods can result in some issues. For example, in my experience, it was not uncommon for protocols from quantitative clinical researchers to promise complete confidentiality of responses to participants in focus groups. While the researchers could take responsibility for ensuring that their handling of participant responses would be maintained confidentially, they cannot promise that the other focus group participants will not share what was said in the discussion.

—Susan Bouregy, PhD, CIP,
Chief HIPAA Privacy Officer,
Former Director of the Human Subjects
Committee (HSC), Yale University

Using the four tips in Box 10.2 as a starting point should help make your relationship with the HRPP committee both constructive and productive. The benefits can be many, and the interaction should not be viewed as a bothersome requirement. The process helps you to learn how to effectively communicate your research project to an external audience. As you prepare your application, you may also recognize ways in which the study can be improved and revise your research question or methods accordingly. If the review results in a request for resubmission, the committee's suggestions can also elevate the quality of your research in the same way that the peer-review process can improve manuscripts. The committee may help you identify alternative approaches and even outcomes that improve the efficiency and relevance of your science. Finally, there are also practical benefits, such as conveying to potential participants, colleagues, and journal editors that your study has been vetted and found to have benefit beyond any potential harm to participants.

KEY ISSUES FOR SPECIFIC MIXED METHODS DESIGN TYPES

With this overview of HRPP processes and broad recommendations for mixed methods protocols as a foundation, we now discuss in detail HRPP issues

◀ For more background information on these three design types, refer to Chapter 1: Definition and Overview of Mixed Methods Designs.

relevant for the three most common mixed methods designs used in health sciences research: convergent, exploratory sequential, and explanatory sequential designs.

We also address issues related to mixed methods studies where the aims or methods for a follow-up study component are emergent (e.g., arising after the first study component is underway or completed). We recognize there are several other mixed methods approaches (e.g., case studies and embedded designs are growing in popularity among health science research teams) that we do not explore here. The considerations for the major design types can often extend to these other approaches. Before we begin, we should note that while we offer general guidance based on our experiences at several universities, it is essential to check with your local HRPP for submission requirements specific to any particular research protocol.

Convergent Designs

In a convergent design, the qualitative and quantitative components are conducted in parallel, data from the individual components are analyzed separately, and then the databases are typically merged for interpretation. In convergent studies the research team finalizes sampling decisions and data collection instruments for both components at the same time, making critical decisions such as the order of data collection activities, whether there will be one or two samples, and sample size(s).

◀ For more information on how to approach sampling for mixed method designs, refer to Chapter 7: Sampling and Data Collection in Mixed Methods Studies.

Although the amount of time that must be initially invested in determining all of the design elements for a convergent approach is substantial, the HRPP application process is relatively straightforward. We often receive inquiries from other researchers on whether to submit two separate applications for convergent designs. We strongly suggest that you fully describe both the qualitative and quantitative components in a single application. Combining data from studies described in different HRPP applications frequently requires additional ethics approval and may even be prohibited at your institution. Initially including both components in a single application provides important context for reviewers by helping them to understand the overall design and the relationship between components. This approach also has the benefit of being more efficient, with a single review process and a single set of responses or revisions to complete.

Exploratory Sequential Designs

In an exploratory sequential design, the qualitative component comes before the quantitative component and serves to build a foundation for the sample or the research questions examined by the latter component. With this type of design (an initial qualitative component followed by a quantitative component), the application can be more complicated. There may be a number of critically important unknowns at the start that have implications for the science, the project resources, and the timetable: What are the follow-up research questions? What are the sample criteria for the second component? How large will that sample be, and where will it come from? Consequently, it may not be possible to describe key information needed to assess potential risks in an HRPP protocol. Given the nature of the design, you may be unable to articulate precise research questions or hypotheses, to present data collection instruments for the second or subsequent components, or to develop informed consent forms that describe in detail the entire study.

Three issues should be considered when preparing an application with an exploratory sequential design. First, this approach commonly requires the identification of two nonoverlapping samples. The sample for the qualitative component is determined by specified key informant characteristics and is purposeful in design. In contrast, a larger sample of random respondents is often required in the quantitative phase to allow the research team to conduct rigorous statistical analyses that are generalizable to a broad population. Second, at the study's outset it is not known precisely which qualitative findings will be developed as the foundation for the quantitative component. Third, exploratory sequential designs often give rise to the development of new questionnaire items that must undergo a process of psychometric testing as an intermediate step before full quantitative data collection. For these reasons, the qualitative component is the only study component that can be fully described at the time of the initial HRPP application. You may decide to present an application with provisional details about the quantitative component and submit an amendment after the quantitative data collection instrument is determined. Or you may choose to prepare two independent applications if sample selection, recruitment, and informed consent are distinct across components. Factors that influence this strategic decision include the timeliness of the institutional review process (How quickly are decisions made on amendments?), the urgency of getting started (Will presenting one well-defined component initially streamline the review process?), and the familiarity of the committee members with mixed methods design (How comfortable is the review committee with "to be determined" parts of the protocol?).

Explanatory Sequential Designs

In an explanatory sequential design, quantitative data are collected and analyzed before developing a follow-up qualitative component to provide insights about the quantitative findings. Like with an exploratory sequential design, there may be aspects of the project that are not fully defined at the HRPP protocol development stage, which can make this process difficult. Explanatory sequential designs require attention to several elements of the study when preparing an application for ethical review. First, the samples are typically overlapping. Because the follow-up component will explore a particular phenomenon generated within the quantitative component in greater depth and the qualitative sample targets "information rich" respondents, a subset of respondents to the questionnaire is typically selected to explain quantitative results. However, the sampling frame and the sample size are usually unknown at the time of initial submission. One exception to this rule occurs when the component samples are identical—that is, when the research team makes the design decision to collect follow-up qualitative data from all quantitative component participants. Another exception is when the sample size for the qualitative component is determined not by theoretical saturation but rather by purposive stratified sampling with prespecified participant criteria and numeric goals.

◄ For more information on sampling in mixed methods studies, see Chapter 7: Sampling and Data Collection in Mixed Methods Studies.

Regardless of approach, the application will need to include explicit language about the overlapping samples in the application, and the research consent forms should reflect that quantitative component participants may be contacted for a follow-up study and that they may be selected for invitation based upon their initial responses.

The application should include specific details about how confidentiality will be protected as individual responses are linked with contact information to create the samples. In some instances, you will not have access to participant identifiers from the quantitative component either because this information was not or could not be collected. In these cases, you can ask participants from the first component to volunteer if they would be interested in participating in the follow-up (e.g., by contacting the research team). Although the link between this self-selected sample and the quantitative results is not as strong as when particular individuals can be identified, this is an effective strategy to overcome the lack of initial participant contact information.

> ▶ An example of how a consent form might be created for a study with overlapping samples is provided in Box 10.3.

Another key consideration is that at the study's outset the research team is often unaware what quantitative findings will be used to develop the qualitative data collection tools. It is possible to create and submit a draft qualitative interview guide at the start of the study with an accompanying rationale that relevant broad content areas can be identified in advance. We generally recommend you delay identifying specific qualitative sample participants and developing the specific interview guide questions until after the quantitative data have been analyzed. This process facilitates the key mixed methods requirement of integration by enabling the research team to connect the components fully. However, this does not preclude the investigators from proposing broad topic domains as likely candidates for follow-up or anticipating the characteristics of the subsample that might be recruited for the qualitative component. It is critical to convey the strategy for how you will decide what quantitative results will be explored in the follow-up and how the sample for the qualitative component will be identified.

We suggest describing explanatory sequential designs in terms of four major steps in HRPP applications. The first step is to specify how the most important quantitative findings for subsequent exploration will be selected, most often defined as those results that are confusing, surprising, or incomplete. These results may or may not rise to the level of statistical significance, might emerge in subgroup analyses, or may be outliers. The second step is to determine and define the research questions for the qualitative component and identify the most appropriate qualitative research design if applicable.

▶ For tips on communicating about emergent designs, see Box 10.5.

The third step is to design the qualitative data collection instruments. Check with your HRPPs prior to developing draft data collection tools such as qualitative interview guides. Some committees will prefer researchers wait and begin version submission close to the time of data collection while others prefer to see iterations of the guide and expect a first draft be included with the initial application. The fourth and final step is to select the sample. Whenever possible, you should describe a systematic approach to sample selection such as using statistical cut points (e.g., those scoring above a set threshold on a scale). As with exploratory sequential designs, you have the option of submitting two separate applications for explanatory sequential designs. However, we caution against this approach because participant consent documents for the first component should indicate participants may be contacted again in the future. Instead, you can describe the overall study design at the outset and note these ethical considerations. Importantly, use language that conveys that the qualitative component design is preliminary and include a plan to submit an addendum when the sampling recruiting plan and the data collection tools are finalized.

Emergent Designs

Mixed methods studies may be described as either fixed or emergent in nature.

In a fixed design, the entire study design is conceptualized at the outset. The aims and methods for qualitative and quantitative components are explicitly defined a priori. In a pure emergent design, a second component is not planned at the start of the study; rather, the need for a mixed methods approach either arises or is confirmed once the project is underway. Once the need for an additional component becomes apparent, the researcher can then decide on either a convergent or sequential design (provided resources are sufficient to implement a new component). The key distinction between studies along the fixed to emergent spectrum is the degree to which the aims and methods of the second component are known at the start of the project. In practice, funded mixed methods projects may have both fixed and emergent elements in the design. For

◀ For more background information on emergent designs, refer to Chapter 1: Definition and Overview of Mixed Methods Designs.

example, researchers may decide on an explanatory sequential approach knowing in advance
they want a qualitative component to follow
initial quantitative data collection and analysis
but choose focus groups as the qualitative
method only after the first component is completed. However, pure emergent designs may be
on the increase within the health sciences—

◀ To read more about
CBPR in health sciences,
see Chapter 2:
Applications and
Illustrations of Mixed
Methods Health
Sciences Research.

especially with the mainstreaming of frameworks such as community-based
participatory research (CBPR) that require an academic and nonacademic
partnership to evolve together toward a research strategy.

As you might imagine, there are several types of challenges presented when
proposing pure emergent designs or any mixed methods design with a fair
degree of methodological uncertainty at the start. Reviewers may have questions
regarding the ethics of consenting participants for unknown risks and the potential for "creep" into new focal research areas because of the lack of clear a priori
definition of research questions. Concerns about emergent designs may extend
beyond the HRPP to funders who might be nervous about the feasibility of a
study that cannot be fully designed at the outset with accurate and complete
budgeting and resource estimates. They may also be uncomfortable with the
inability to fully specify deliverables and timelines at the start of the project. In
terms of project logistics, emergent designs by nature are dynamic and are likely
to require creative and flexible resource planning and management. For instance,
team members with specific expertise may need to be moved around on the
project to track with the workflow of evolving components, or unanticipated
needs for new expertise may surface. Implementing a new study component
may also have implications for existing workflow in terms of sampling, recruitment, data collection, and analysis. See Box 10.5 for tips on how to communicate effectively about emergent mixed methods designs.

Box 10.5 Tips for Communicating About Emergent Mixed Methods Designs

✓ Articulate the rationale for using an emergent design, with citations.
✓ Provide evidence that the planned methods are feasible.

(Continued)

(Continued)

✓ Provide preliminary draft research questions and data collection instruments, noting they will change during the course of the study.

✓ Propose to submit project update reports with addendum for new sampling protocol, instruments, and team members.

✓ Use consistent terminology to refer to central concepts throughout the entire document.

✓ Explicitly describe the process by which you expect methods and aims to emerge if possible.

IMPLEMENTATION CHALLENGES AND STRATEGIES FROM THE FIELD

In this section we turn to practical considerations related to implementing mixed methods studies in the health sciences. As we have done throughout the book, we feature the experiences of colleagues that illustrate insights helpful to researchers preparing to begin mixed methods projects. We asked several mixed methods researchers to share specific challenges they encountered as they implemented their mixed methods research components, promising them anonymity (hence, the quotes in Boxes 10.6, 10.7, and 10.9 are anonymous). We follow each example with observations and lessons learned from our own experiences and those of our mixed methods colleagues. In Box 10.6, one investigator describes challenges presented in a highly dynamic study:

Box 10.6   Implementation Experience: Evolving Study Designs

We ended up deciding to add a qualitative component over a year after the survey was already completed and initially analyzed . . . but then the question became which component would we emphasize in our dissemination? We ended up making the survey the core component for ease of publication and we decided, after the focus groups were conducted and analyzed, that we wanted to prioritize specific findings based on disagreement—focusing on where we were hearing different things in the focus group from in the survey. This was most relevant in the discussion section of the paper, more than even in the results, because we had to link the findings we decided to prioritize back to the conceptual model we presented in the introduction. But we could have focused on the findings that were similar, or more on the focus groups. The project maybe would have looked different if we started the survey part with a follow-up qualitative component in mind.

— Excerpt from original interview with a
health sciences researcher

Prioritizing Components and Findings

As described in Box 10.6, mixed methods studies require decisions about how to prioritize and represent the study components. Regardless of whether a supplemental component is planned in advance or emerges during analysis, assigning a supplementary role to one or more components presents several practical considerations at the interpretation and writing phases of a study. First is the question of how best to represent the contributions of the supplemental data to the overall study aims. Was the supplemental component defined at the outset, or did it emerge during the course of analysis? How do the data relate to the primary findings? In the example in Box 10.6, the team decided to prioritize focus group findings that were discordant with the survey results because they felt this approach would provide novel information within the relevant body of existing literature. In other situations, it may make sense to prioritize instead on concordant findings or on findings linked with a specific topic area or domain.

Second, the methods of the supplemental component should be described with sufficient information to convey rigor and yet not with a disproportionate level of detail. Were the data collected using a purely pragmatic and highly focused approach with an eye toward developing or informing the primary component? If so, what level of scientific rigor was applied and what trade-offs were made, with any resulting limitations? In this example, the plan to introduce a supplementary component over a year after the survey component meant that the people who completed the survey were lost to follow-up and had not consented to being recontacted. The team, therefore, conducted the focus groups with a completely distinct sample, viewed as less than ideal for their research question. Yet the team remained committed to a high level of rigor for the focus groups and secured additional funding to develop this new study component.

Third, the presentation and interpretation of findings should reflect the primary data, particularly in cases where a supplemental component was developed with the purpose of supporting the primary component. Care must be taken not to overreach or overstate the findings from a supplemental component.

As discussed in prior chapters, we do not regard the weighting or prioritization of quantitative and qualitative study components as a defining feature of mixed methods studies.

◄ Relative weighting and our approach to this issue are further described in Chapter 1: Definition and Overview of Mixed Methods Designs.

One reason for our view is that the particular contributions or strength of a given component may not be apparent until the analysis and interpretation stages, when decisions are made about which data to include or focus on in the preparation of a manuscript (Guest, 2013). Nevertheless, some experts do observe there are instances in which a supplementary role for one component can be a very deliberate decision early in the design process, commonly in sequential designs (Morgan, 2013; Morse & Niehaus, 2009). The decision to treat one component as supplementary might be determined by scientific factors, time and resource constraints, or both. It is important to be clear that the relative weighting or prioritization of a component does not necessarily equate to the size of the component (e.g., a large quantitative data set may still serve a supplemental role to a qualitative component; Morgan, 2013).

As the researcher mentions in this example, considerations such as preferences of the target journal might also inform prioritization decisions. This requires thinking early in the research process about target journals. Reaching out to journal editors as you begin to draft the manuscript can provide additional guidance on how to weight components and/or findings as you write.

► For more information on preparing manuscripts for peer-reviewed journals, see Chapter 11: Publishing Mixed Methods Studies in the Health Sciences.

It is also the case that one mixed methods project may yield many "products," and the emphasis on components or findings can shift in each piece. Ideas for these additional manuscripts may emerge after the study has ended. This is yet another reason to apply the highest standards of rigor to each component even when one may have a predetermined supplementary role.

Team Approaches to Data Analysis

The sheer volume and complexity of data generated in a mixed methods study requires a clear plan for how the team will approach the work of data analysis. In developing a plan, each of the moving parts must be mapped on a timeline in order to determine the interdependence of the components and to allocate time and human resources as needed. We find Gantt charts very useful for this purpose. There are multiple approaches to organizing data analyses; choose the one that works best for your team. In some cases, distinct subteams are formed and assigned to a given component and are responsible for the entire continuum of work, from instrument design to data collection and analysis. In others, the entire team may work on all aspects of all study components. In our experience, this is potentially very challenging, as roles and responsibilities can become muddled. One team's approach is described in Box 10.7. In this example, senior members of the team independently led the qualitative and quantitative analyses, regularly reporting out to the full team for input.

Box 10.7   Implementation Experience: Approaches to Collaboration on Data Analysis

We had a mountain of data. The group unanimously agreed [Person A] would take the lead on quantitative aspects of analysis given her wealth of experience with data analysis. We also had a biostatistician on our team with whom [Person A] would collaborate on some analyses. Additionally, a co-investigator, [Person B], who is a mixed methods expert, led the qualitative data analyses. A summary of the qualitative findings was generated for review and comment by the larger team prior to finalizing the results. All team members met monthly and communicated via electronic mail in between the monthly meetings when necessary to provide updates on study progress.

—Excerpt from original interview with health sciences researcher

Several considerations are relevant to the decision about how to organize data analysis activities. How large is the team? Are there enough team members to create small groups to work on distinct components? In this approach, it is essential to have a plan for collaboration and coordination across groups with an eye toward integration. What kinds of expertise exist on the team, and how is the best way to take the greatest advantage of that expertise? If there are senior members with a dominant strength in one method, you may want to have them lead those respective components, with a mixed methods expert involved in all components to facilitate integration. Is there an interest in expanding research capacity within the team? If so, assigning a statistician to work on qualitative analyses might help achieve this goal, provided there is adequate staff available to carry out the analysis while also training the statistician. The question of investing in expanding research capacity can be tricky because this can be extraordinarily time consuming, and the investment of time and effort needs to be balanced with the need to complete the funded research efficiently and within the constraints of the grant. In Box 10.8, an emergency medicine physician and health services researcher shared his experience with defining various roles and capacities within the team while keeping the project progressing. His strategy is to keep the goals of the analysis very clear and endorsed by the entire team (see Box 10.8).

Box 10.8   Fostering Positive Team Collaboration in Mixed Methods Research

Teamwork is the hardest part about this—engaging clinicians and qualitative experts together and different models of working in teams. And the data—there's so much data; it is so rich that it is possible to spend an enormous amount of time on the coding and the analysis. In my world, even in a multiyear grant, it's only one part of someone's day or week and so you don't have that much time. And so I think it's very important that the goals of the analysis by very clear and that they're agreed upon and that they are constantly thought about so that the project keeps moving along.

—Jeremiah Schuur, MD, MHS,
Assistant Professor of Medicine,
Brigham and Women's Hospital

How the team decides to approach data analysis also has implications for the tools used in the process. Software programs are useful assets to the mixed methods team. They can streamline management of a high volume of data, facilitate data analysis of each component, link quantitative and qualitative findings for interpretation, present a visual joint representation of the findings, and provide an audit trail of important research decisions made along the way. The team should preferentially identify one software program that can be used across components or software programs that are interoperable. When making decisions about software, consider the following: Are most team members already familiar with a particular software program? Is there money in the budget for new software purchase (including multiple licenses and/or subscriptions)? How much time do you have to train members in a new software program? Does everyone need to know the software or just a select few?

Box 10.9   Implementation Experience: Methodological Bilingualism

Although some members of our research team focused on particular methodological approaches, most of the team members had had some experience with both quantitative and qualitative techniques before we began designing this project. This methodological "bilingualism" facilitated design and implementation of our mixed methods project. We brought some mixed methods expertise to the project, but we continued to learn as the project unfolded. Although a division of labor in methodological expertise is a given in mixed methods designs, we believe that the overlap in both methodological skills and substantive interests facilitated communication and enhanced collaboration.

— Excerpt from original interview with
health sciences researcher

Incorporating Mixed Methods Expertise

In the example provided in Box 10.9, the majority of team members had experience with both qualitative and quantitative methods. This experience is a substantial asset in minimizing common challenges to collaboration that arise in many mixed methods teams. We see tremendous value in team members

▶ For resources on qualitative research refer to Appendix E: Quick Resource: A Short List of Readings and References.

having a shared foundation such as understanding basic terminology and concepts in both qualitative and quantitative methods (referred to as "methodological bilingualism") (Tashakkori & Teddlie, 2003). Because most contemporary health sciences researchers were trained either exclusively or predominantly in quantitative methods, team members are most likely to need a primer in qualitative research.

We encourage mixed methods team members unfamiliar with qualitative methods to explore these resources even if their individual responsibilities are exclusively quantitative in nature.

Bringing in an external consultant as the mixed methods expert for the team can be a solution when this expertise is not available on your team or at your institution. While this is commonly done, be aware that there are a number of risks with this approach.

◀ For tips on effectively using consultants, refer to Chapter 3: Determining the Appropriateness and Feasibility of Using Mixed Methods.

Whether or not the team includes consultants, the group must work hard at the start of the study to establish positive relationships and effective communication among team members.

The time, energy, and goodwill required for a consultant to educate and train and coach team members on mixed methods research should not be underestimated. In addition, during our interviews with researchers for this book, several commented on either publication delays or a decrease in the number of published products that resulted from having only one team member with sufficient expertise and experience in mixed methods to lead the writing efforts. Some funders will support a dissemination period within the project, and we strongly recommend requesting one in your grant application. In our experience, funders have supported the equivalent of between two and four calendar months for mixed methods dissemination. Finally, whether the team has internal mixed methods expertise or seeks support from an external consultant, we recommend the critical task of data integration be viewed as a shared responsibility of the group rather than the job of a single team member. We have found achieving

◀ For suggested principles and strategies to facilitate collaboration and communication, refer to Chapter 9: Managing Mixed Methods Teams.

team consensus on key integration decisions translates into smoother transitions in data sharing between subgroups or teams, improved team communication, and shared ownership and investment across team members.

Summary and Key Points

- Suggestions for communicating effectively when working with HRPPs on mixed methods studies include reducing jargon, defining core terminology, using figures and schematics wherever possible, contacting HRPP staff prior to submission, and utilizing expertise on team to be able to address ethics review committee concerns.
- The type of study design chosen has important implications for the information and materials included in the application for HRPP review.
- Emergent designs pose particular challenges in the health sciences, including HRPP review, funding agency concerns, and project management.
- Deciding how to prioritize study components or findings, approach data analysis as a team, and incorporate mixed methods expertise are key considerations in implementing mixed methods studies.

Review Questions and Exercises

1. Brainstorm a mixed methods study that addresses a potentially sensitive or difficult topic, and identify associated potential risks. Suggest possible strategies to minimize or address each of the risks.

2. Imagine you are proposing a study with an emergent design. What are some of the potential challenges you will face in describing the methods in the HRPP application? What might be some ways to address these challenges?

3. You are the lead investigator on a mixed methods project with a convergent design, with data being collected and analyzed accordingly. What are some key considerations in organizing data analysis, and how would you plan for those in terms of time and resources? Specify the key factors to facilitating integration, and draft a project management plan.

4. Choose an article from the mixed methods literature on a topic of interest to you. Try to determine the roles of each of the coauthors and their backgrounds. Imagine you are the mixed methods expert who had been asked to join this team at the beginning of the study. How might you approach your role? What strategies might you use to help the team gain a basic understanding of mixed methods and appreciation for the principles and processes of data analysis in mixed methods?

References

Creswell, J. (2003). *Research design: Qualitative, quantitative and mixed methods approaches* (2nd ed.). Thousand Oaks, CA: Sage.

Guest, G. (2013). Describing mixed methods research: An alternative to typologies. *Journal of Mixed Methods Research, 7*(2), 141–151.

Holloway, I., & Wheeler, S. (1995). Ethical issues in qualitative nursing research. *Nursing Ethics, 2*(3), 223–232.

Labaree, R. V. (2010). Working successfully with your institutional review board: Practical advice from academic librarians. *College Research Library News, 71,* 190–193.

Lincoln, Y. S., & Tierney, W. C. (2004). Qualitative research and institutional review boards. *Qualitative Inquiry, 10*(2), 219–234.

Morgan, D. L. (2013). *Integrating qualitative and quantitative methods: A pragmatic approach.* Thousand Oaks, CA: Sage.

Morse, J. M. (2007). Ethics in action: Ethical principles for doing qualitative health research. *Qualitative Health Research, 17*(8), 1003–1005. doi: 10.1177/1049732307308197

Morse, J. M., & Niehaus, L. (2009). *Mixed method design: Principles and procedures.* Walnut Creek, CA: Left Coast Press.

Oakes, J. M. (2002). Risks and wrongs in social science research: An evaluator's guide to the IRB. *Evaluation Review, 26*(5), 443–479.

Orb, A., Eisenhauer, L., & Wynaden, D. (2000). Ethics in qualitative research. *Journal of Nursing Scholarship, 33*(1), 93–96.

Tashakkori, A., & Teddlie, C. (2003). *Handbook of mixed methods in social & behavioral research.* Thousand Oaks, CA: Sage.

U.S. Department of Health and Human Services. (n.d.). *HHS regulations.* Retrieved January 19, 2014, from http://www.hhs.gov/ohrp/humansubjects/index.html

Tol, W. A., Komproe, I. H., Jordans, M. J., Susanty, D., & de Jong, J. T. (2011). Developing a function impairment measure for children affected by political violence: A mixed methods approach in Indonesia. *International Journal for Quality in Health Care, 23*(4), 375–383. doi: 10.1093/intqhc/mzr032

⸭ PART IV ⸭

DISSEMINATING FINDINGS

In this final section, we offer practical guidance on the dissemination of findings from mixed methods studies, with a focus on publication in peer-reviewed journals. We provide basic recommendations for what to include in manuscripts and present strategies for identifying target journals and working with editors. The chapter ends with a discussion on responding to peer reviews for mixed methods studies, including illustrative excerpts from a revision letter and brief commentary.

❊ ELEVEN ❊

PUBLISHING MIXED METHODS STUDIES IN THE HEALTH SCIENCES

Information you will find in this chapter: In this chapter we offer practical guidance on publishing mixed methods studies in peer-reviewed journals in the health sciences. We begin with describing the publication landscape for mixed methods research, including current challenges and opportunities for authors. Next, we discuss developing a publication strategy and plan, which should be done at the start of the project. In the third section, we address principles and practices for writing manuscripts for mixed methods studies. The chapter ends with suggestions for preparing an effective response to peer reviews for mixed methods studies, including an example from a published study.

Key features in the chapter:

- Brief quotations and reflections from mixed methods researchers
- List of selected journals that publish mixed methods
- Table for Good Reporting of a Mixed Methods Study (GRAMMS)
- Examples of published abstracts with brief commentary
- Example cover letter for a mixed methods study
- Flowchart and tips for preparing a response letter
- Excerpts from a response letter for a mixed methods study

CHALLENGES AND OPPORTUNITIES IN PUBLISHING
MIXED METHODS RESEARCH IN THE HEALTH SCIENCES

Despite a rapidly developing collection of excellent resources on conducting mixed methods studies, there are few practical guidelines for publishing this type of work, especially in health sciences (Leech, Onwuegbuzie, & Combs, 2011; O'Cathain, Murphy, & Nicholl, 2007; Stange, Crabtree, & Miller, 2006; Wisdom, Cavaleri, Onwuegbuzie, & Green, 2012). The path of mixed methods has an interesting parallel with qualitative methods as they have been introduced and integrated into health sciences research over the past two decades. The adoption of new research methods into a well-established field can be a slow process, particularly when those methods reflect orientations and traditions that differ from mainstream approaches. Facilitating the integration of new methods into a field requires efforts on three fronts: the development and general endorsement of robust methodological guidelines, training a cadre of researchers to compete successfully for extramural funding, and representation of empirical studies in respected peer-reviewed journals of the field. We have seen significant and exciting progress in the health sciences in recent years, with leading scientific journals increasingly welcoming qualitative studies (Devers, 1999; Krumholz, Bradley, & Curry, 2013; Schoenberg & McAuley, 2007; Shortell, 1999).

An important lesson from the growth of qualitative methods in health sciences is that guidelines for publishing qualitative studies were critical in both gaining credibility and supporting the aim of transparency in research methods. More than 22 guidelines have been synthesized to produce the Consolidated Criteria for Reporting Qualitative Research (Tong, Sainsbury, & Craig, 2007), which is similar in format and purpose to other reporting checklists for quantitative methods, such as the CONSORT standards for reporting trials (2012) and Preferred Reporting Items of Systematic Reviews and Meta-Analyses, or PRISMA (n.d.). As we describe later and previously in Chapter 6, widely endorsed standards for reporting mixed methods studies are not yet in place. Nevertheless, there is general consensus about key elements that should be included in manuscripts in the health sciences literature. In this chapter we focus primarily on considerations relevant for mixed methods, although much of the content also applies to writing manuscripts for qualitative or quantitative studies. Like any scientific research, regardless of method, the foundational principle is that researchers should conduct relevant, rigorous research with integrity and ensure that the research is fully transparent. In an era of widespread calls for greater openness in science, deliberate attention to accurate, thorough reporting is more important than ever.

Publishing mixed methods work presents several unique challenges, even for the most seasoned and prolific researchers. First, the lack of familiarity with mixed methods among journal editors and reviewers can present various impediments to the submission and review process and can also influence the quality of published manuscripts. Second, members of mixed methods teams, typically from a variety of backgrounds, may not agree on a publication strategy. Areas of potential disagreement include whether component findings are published independently or in a single manuscript, the timing and sequencing of papers, and choice of target journals (e.g., Do you aim for a journal that is receptive to mixed methods or one that reaches a particular professional audience?). Finally, space constraints in the top medical, nursing, and health sciences journals may be difficult to adhere to when attempting to report comprehensive findings from large mixed methods studies. In some cases the team may decide to publish component findings independently, although there are risks to this approach. As one leading mixed methods researcher observed, "different fields only come to know part of the research—reminiscent of the story of the 4 blind men each feeling a different part of the elephant and thus unable to develop a coherent idea of the whole" (Stange et al., 2006, p. 292).

Despite these challenges, there is unquestionably a growing interest in the use of mixed methods in health sciences research that presents excellent opportunities for researchers who conduct rigorous studies. The remainder of this chapter describes strategies and techniques for managing these challenges and increasing the quality of your mixed methods research publications. One analysis of trends in the use of mixed methods designs across a wide range of fields revealed that there were more publications using mixed methods in the health sciences than in any other and more than twice as many as the next most prominent field of education (Ivankova & Kawamura, 2010). Because mixed methods research is gaining significant traction in health sciences, well-done studies can gain visibility in high-impact peer-reviewed journals. For instance, a recent special issue of the journal *Health Services Research* was devoted to the topic of mixed methods (see Box 11.1).

Box 11.1   Growing Acceptance of Mixed Methods Research

The growing role of mixed methods in health services research is evident from the publication of hundreds of mixed methods studies and recent overviews of best practices in mixed methods research. This growing success reflects the capacity of mixed methods studies to capture the experiences, emotions, and motivations of people providing and receiving health care, as well as the objective conditions of care delivery. This wider use of mixed methods also reflects the ability of mixed methods to meet practical needs for assessing and understanding the complexity of health service delivery. (Miller, Crabtree, Harrison, & Fennell, 2013)

DEVELOPING A PUBLICATION STRATEGY AND PLAN

Plans for dissemination of research findings should be developed as part of the grant writing process, as many funders require this information as part of their applications. Peer-reviewed empirical scientific journals remain the primary mechanism for researchers to contribute new knowledge to their field. At the same time, funders are increasingly interested in innovative forms of dissemination that leverage the power of evolving technologies to reach diverse audiences, such as blogs, social media, brief reports, and other online forums accessed by health care policymakers and practitioners. Because mixed methods studies produce both quantitative and qualitative forms of information, findings can be very effectively translated for these diverse venues. In this section we describe how to develop a comprehensive publication strategy, including the overall approach to publications, target journals, author teams, and timelines.

Deciding on the Overall Approach to Publications

The first decision is whether the qualitative and quantitative findings from various components will be presented in a single manuscript or in multiple manuscripts. Several factors will influence this decision. Most importantly, the primary research aims determine the focal topics of the papers and primary intended audience. The study design determines when findings from each component are ready for publication. Finally, the characteristics of the journals in a given discipline need to be taken into consideration (e.g., space limits, availability of online appendices).

The emerging consensus in the field is that presenting fully integrated data in a single manuscript is optimal for maximizing the potential of mixed methods (O'Cathain et al., 2007). Unfortunately this approach is relatively uncommon in the health sciences, particularly for studies using sequential designs. Because the findings in sequential designs are typically available in stages, researchers may find it preferable to report findings in a series of articles rather than delay reporting data from the first stage. For instance, a sequential explanatory study on postoperative infections that includes discrete aims for the each component might produce three publications: identifying predictors of postoperative infections (quantitative), characterizing surgeon and nurse views on the incorporation of protocols to reduce postoperative infections (qualitative), and identifying best practices for improving adherence to protocols within and after surgeries (integrated data from both components). In these cases, if the decision is to publish sequentially, deliberate attention should be directed toward crosswalking from one publication to the next in the interpretation and reporting of findings. By crosswalking we mean making explicit and clear references to key elements of each publication, using consistent framing and terminology, and including sufficient information for the reader to identify linkages across the publications.

Health science journals are fairly consistent in their specifications and formats, although some are a better fit for reporting mixed methods studies. While space limits are a major challenge noted by mixed methods researchers, most authors—regardless of the methods they use—feel there is insufficient space to do their study justice. (See Box 11.2 for a reflection on space constraints from an editor of a prominent journal in the health sciences.) Nevertheless, mixed methods reports are typically longer than single method (especially quantitative) reports for two reasons. First, the methods section includes information regarding the design, sample, data collection, and analysis for multiple study components. Second, the results of purely quantitative studies are presented in tables that are usually excluded from the word count, while mixed methods publications typically present narrative data that are embedded in the manuscript text.

**Box 11.2   Adhering to Word Count Limitations for Health
           Journals**

Every author that I've ever worked with wants more space to describe what they've done. We report randomized controlled trials that go on in dozens of countries and last for years and years and involve extremely complex designs. They are at least as complicated as any mixed methods manuscript that I've ever read, and they are required to be described in the space limits we have in our journal, in ways that are appropriate and communicate well with our audience. In our world, brevity is a virtue that we insist on. Many people send us qualitative or mixed methods manuscripts from different backgrounds or traditions, and requiring them to adhere to our traditions may be a big burden, but I don't think we're asking more than we're asking of other authors.

—Sankey Williams, MD,
Deputy Editor,
Annals of Internal Medicine

There are a number of possible strategies to address space limitations (see Box 11.3). Requests for additional space are not likely to be met with success (but may be worth a try). Although reporting narrative data in tabular format can be a solution, we generally resist this approach. Presenting abbreviated quotes in isolation can sacrifice important context and lose the texture of qualitative data. Another option offered by a growing number of journals is online formats for appendices to provide additional information. While a potentially valuable tool, in our experience this material is rarely accessed, though this may change as the format becomes more widely adopted. Perhaps the most common approach is to publish the study components in separate articles, as noted previously. We strongly suggest making connections across the study components if they are reported separately. In the case of moderate- to large-sized studies, one very effective strategy can be to publish the study methods in detail as a research protocol; the subsequent empirical articles can conserve space by referring back to the previously reported methods (e.g., *Implementation Science, BMJ Open, Research in Nursing and Health,* and the

PLOS journals publish study protocols). The most obvious but often least palatable approach is to focus on presenting the most parsimonious selected findings in the most efficient format possible. Asking a colleague who is not associated with the project to suggest edits for length can be very helpful; the background and discussion sections are often good first stops for trimming.

Box 11.3   Engaging Diverse Strategies to Publish Mixed Methods Studies

There is the reality of word count . . . with mixed methods studies, particularly the bigger studies; it's really hard to tell the story briefly. I've used several strategies. Sometimes you can publish a few articles in the same journal. You can publish in a place that allows longer articles. Another strategy is online appendices—you can put a lot of stuff and refer to it in the article. You can also buy a journal supplement. A supplement is like you are basically buying a subissue that comes out all by itself, and you can try to get funding to do it. It usually costs $50,000 or $60,000 to do a supplement—which is different from a theme issue where you have three or four articles and you talk to the editors and they agree to include them.

—Benjamin Crabtree, PhD,
Professor and Director, Department of
Family Medicine and Community Health,
Rutgers Robert Wood Johnson Medical School

Choosing a Target Journal

Choosing a target journal for your manuscript is a strategic decision that is not always straightforward for mixed methods studies, since many health sciences journals are still relatively unfamiliar with these methods. Several important journals focus on mixed methods research per se (e.g., the *Journal of Mixed Methods Research* and the *International Journal of Multiple Research Approaches*). These journals fill an essential role, particularly in publishing editorials and methodological papers that are essential to moving the field of mixed methods forward. These journals also provide adequate space for fully integrated reports of mixed methods empirical studies and have highly qualified reviewers with relevant expertise. At the same time, we believe it is also critical for mixed methods studies to be published within the disciplinary journals in health sciences in order to ensure the findings contribute to the evidence base in clinical research, health services, and implementation science. This places the onus on researchers to advocate for mixed methods within their respective professional disciplines.

There are several ways to identify an appropriate primary target journal (we recommend also choosing Plan B and C journals at the outset). You can do a comprehensive search of the literature in your field and review several papers in specific journals in order to get a sense of their receptivity (see Box 11.4). Be aware that the term *mixed methods* is not consistently used in article titles or abstracts and therefore may not appear in searches. Alternative or additional search terms are *multiple methods, multi-methods,* and *qualitative and quantitative.* Another approach is to directly contact a journal's editorial office or board member to explore their interest in mixed methods submissions. As noted previously, a key journal in health sciences (*Health Services Research*) recently published a special issue on mixed methods, sponsored by the Agency for Healthcare Research and Quality (AHRQ). Some journals have made direct appeals for mixed methods, such as the following excerpt from an editorial in *Circulation: Quality of Cardiovascular Outcomes* (see Box 11.5). A list of selected journals that have published mixed methods previously appears in Box 11.6.

Box 11.4   Choosing a Target Journal

I will go through and read several articles that have been published in a journal to get a sense of how does this journal view this sort of work? Some journals won't list it in their guidance to authors but they have a policy of giving you a little more space if it's a qualitative or mixed methods study.

—Terrie Wetle, PhD,
Professor of Health Services, Policy and Practice,
Brown University

Box 11.5   Example of Journal-Led Calls for Mixed Methods Research

We want to signal the openness of our journal to publishing studies that use a range of designs optimally suited for a particular research question, provided that the research addresses important questions, is conducted in accordance with established standards, and is conveyed in high-quality, well-written contributions. We consider qualitative research designs and mixed methods research as a highly effective component of our research portfolio—and one that ought to be deployed to a greater extent. (Krumholz et al., 2013)

Box 11.6   Some Journals That Publish Mixed Methods Research

- *American Journal of Preventive Medicine*
- *American Journal of Public Health*
- *Annals of Family Medicine*
- *BMC Health Services Research*
- *BMC Public Health*
- *BMJ Open*
- *BMJ Quality and Safety*
- *The Gerontologist*
- *Health Education & Behavior*
- *Health Services Research*
- *Implementation Science*
- *International Journal of Multiple Research Approaches*
- *International Journal of Nursing Studies*
- *International Journal of Public Health*
- *Journal of Advanced Nursing*
- *Journal of General Internal Medicine*
- *Journal of Mixed Methods Research*
- *Journal of Palliative Medicine*
- *Midwifery*
- *Oncology Nursing Forum*
- *Qualitative Health Research*

Creating a Strong Author Team

Composing the author team for a given manuscript is a scientific, political, and strategic decision that can be tricky even for colleagues who have written collaboratively for years. As is true with any empirical paper, individuals in the author group must have made substantive and clearly defined contributions in accordance with established standards (e.g., International Committee of Medical Journal Editors, 2008). Authorship roles include contributions to the study conception and design; acquisition, analysis, or interpretation of data; a draft of the manuscript or edit with substantial intellectual content; and approval of the final manuscript.

◀ Many of the considerations for building a strong mixed methods research team are also relevant to a strong author team. For more information on building mixed methods research teams, see Chapter 3: Determining the Appropriateness and Feasibility of Using Mixed Methods.

What is unique (and challenging) in creating an author group for a mixed methods study is the need not only for mixed methods scientific expertise but also skill in representing mixed methods findings to audiences who are likely to be unfamiliar with the approach (see Box 11.7). This requires the capacity to communicate complex information about diverse methods while limiting language that might be perceived as jargon by readers with different backgrounds. Also perhaps more relevant to mixed methods is the importance of a multidisciplinary author group (although we feel strongly that author teams representing a range of disciplines and orientations is valuable regardless of method).

Box 11.7   Avoiding the Risks of Dividing Up Study Components for Publication

I think it's much easier to write a mixed methods article when you have an individual who has spanned across the different methods, understands what's there, and understands how the components interact with each other. I've worked on projects where individuals are responsible for different methods and then tend to write papers based on those individual methods and findings, but they don't know enough about what's gone on in different parts of the study to think about the interaction and the integration. This is one of the issues that researchers face—you can have all that team interaction, but sometimes what happens is the funding runs out, the team breaks up, and the papers get written after that, and so some of the integration that occurred within the team gets lost.

—Alicia O'Cathain, BSc, MSc, MA, PhD,
Professor of Health Services Research,
University of Sheffield

Principles and Practices for Writing a Mixed Methods Manuscript

The basic principles for effective writing of scientific manuscripts also apply to mixed methods: write accurately, clearly, and succinctly; edit for content and grammar; and review and revise the manuscript multiple times. In addition, there are several considerations especially relevant for writing mixed methods manuscripts. These include knowing the standards for reporting mixed methods studies, writing with the audience in mind, addressing data integration in methods, selecting the optimal presentation format for results, and ensuring the abstract and cover letter credibly convey the mixed methods design. In the following sections of this chapter, we synthesize suggestions from several useful general resources as well as those specific to publishing in the health sciences (Creswell, 2009; Creswell & Plano Clark, 2011; Dahlberg, Wittink, & Gallo, 2010; Leech et al., 2011; Stange et al., 2006).

Know the Standards for Reporting Mixed Methods Studies

A recent systematic review of mixed methods in health services journals found published articles notably lacking key information such as the rationale for a mixed methods approach, sampling and data collection strategies, methods of data analysis, procedures for integration of methods, and processes of generating inferences (Wisdom et al., 2012). A well-written manuscript will adequately address each of these areas. O'Cathain, Murphy, and Nicholl (2008) proposed a useful set of suggestions particularly developed for the health sciences, referred to as GRAMMS (see Box 11.8). GRAMMS identifies the core elements of a mixed methods study that should be included in a manuscript in order to facilitate transparent reporting: the rationale for a mixed methods approach and a description of the design, the methods of each component, the procedures for integration, the limitations of each method, and insights gained from mixing methods. A systematic review of 47 published mixed methods health services research articles in the United Kingdom revealed incomplete reporting on many of these elements, especially the description of qualitative methods (O'Cathain et al., 2008). While GRAMMS has been proposed as general guidance to authors rather than a formal checklist, we believe it can be a very valuable tool to ensure that manuscripts reporting mixed methods studies are sufficiently complete.

Box 11.8   Good Reporting of a Mixed Methods Study (GRAMMS)

- Describe the justification for using a mixed methods approach to the research question.
- Describe the design in terms of the purpose, priority, and sequence of methods.
- Describe each method in terms of sampling, data collection, and analysis.
- Describe where integration has occurred, how it has occurred, and who has participated in it.
- Describe any limitation of one method associated with the presence of the other method.
- Describe any insights gained from mixing or integrating methods.

SOURCE: O'Cathain et al. (2008).

Write With the Audience in Mind

The careful selection of a target journal for publication is critical to ensuring that research findings reach a specific desired audience. At the same time, it is safe to assume the audience may have little if any prior exposure or experience with mixed methods. In the health sciences literature, readers are typically most comfortable with terminology from quantitative methods and less likely to be familiar with terminology from qualitative or mixed methods. While being mindful to avoid jargon is the first rule, some terms are critical to describing study methods accurately (e.g., purposeful sampling, theoretical saturation, data integration), and excluding them will weaken the manuscript.

However, rather than simply using the term, define the word concisely and precisely in a clause or parenthesis, with an appropriate citation. Citations both enhance credibility of the concepts and also provide those interested with a resource for additional information. At the same time, busy readers may become frustrated with what may be perceived as superfluous information. A deputy editor of the *Annals of Internal Medicine* offers caution regarding the use of jargon in reporting mixed methods studies. He suggests translating key concepts into the language of your audience (see Box 11.9).

Box 11.9   Making Your Article Readable for Your Audience

Many people who send us mixed methods manuscripts are trained as social scientists, and the audience of our journal is largely clinicians who are not trained as social scientists. So we have experts in one field using the language that they use to communicate with one another and trying to communicate with people who are not comfortable with that language. What people sometimes do is use the jargon from their field, with definitions and citations, but that doesn't work. You're writing to an audience of people that have lots of other things to read, and if they come across materials that requires them to stop and have the jargon defined and go to another article to see what it really means, that's when they stop reading your material and move on to something else. It's a little like trying to explain what you did in one language to people who speak a different language. There will be some common words and there are some common roots you can use, but you can't get a complex message across unless you use the language of the audience you're trying to communicate with and in our case that's a clinical language.

—Sankey Williams, MD,
Deputy Editor,
Annals of Internal Medicine

As with any manuscript, it can be helpful to have a colleague from the same field as the journal audience review the paper and provide feedback. In a mixed methods manuscript reporting integrated qualitative and quantitative findings, it is particularly important to solicit input on the presentation format for the results.

Consider drafting a variety of possible types of data display for review. As discussed next, there are many ways to present integrated mixed methods results, and certain displays may resonate better with certain audiences.

Address Data Integration in Methods

As noted in the GRAMMS checklist (see Box 11.8 earlier), it is important to provide information in the methods section about data integration, including where it occurred, how it was done, and who participated in this aspect of the analytic process. This information can be included in the text, in the display of findings, or in both places. If space limitations are problematic, information about data integration should be prioritized. Informed reviewers and editors will be looking for this description, as noted in the following excerpt from our interview with a nurse researcher with extensive experience in editorial roles for nursing journals (see Box 11.10).

Box 11.10   Limitations of Current Publishing Practices

The other serious limitation of the literature is that there are very few publications where the triangulation is described so that the reader really understands how the different components were used together to produce the end interpretation. I think that has a lot to do with the page limit, but the lack of description of the triangulation process is a real limitation.

—Barbara Given, PhD, RN, FAAN,
Director of PhD Program,
College of Nursing Michigan State University
and Editorial Board Member,
*Journal of Oncology Nursing, Western
Journal of Nursing Research, Cancer Nursing,*
and *Research in Nursing* and *Health*

Select Optimal Presentation Format for Results

Approaches for presenting output from quantitative or qualitative data are well established and generally understood by researchers with an orientation to one or both methods. Presenting results for integrated data in mixed methods studies, especially for readers with limited prior exposure, is more challenging.

Journal space limits and word length requirements demand that the data displays be efficient, parsimonious, and effective in communicating multifaceted data. As you are thinking about presentation formats, remember that some journals allow for additional data to be reported in appendices posted on the journal's website, as noted previously. One health services researcher with substantial experience in mixed methods describes her strategy in Box 11.11.

◀ Options for presenting integrated mixed methods data are described in Chapter 8: Data Analysis and Integration in Mixed Methods Studies.

Box 11.11   Using Appendices to Present Comprehensive Results

More and more journals are allowing online appendices or links to project websites that allow you to see more how data was collected, analyzed, and richer results from the qualitative piece. It's never going to be as easy to present qualitative data, or summaries of it, as it is to present a table with coefficients or correlations or *p*-values for significance. It's just so much harder to reduce narrative text, words, behaviors, and summarize it and connect the two in mixed methods projects . . . . It's very hard but the good news is that more and more journals are open to qualitative and mixed methods papers.

—Kelly Devers, PhD,
Senior Fellow,
Health Policy Center, Urban Institute

Be Sure the Abstract and Cover Letter Credibly Convey Mixed Methods

It may seem reasonable to draft the study abstract as a first step in the writing process. However, we hold off on writing the abstract until the manuscript is fully developed. Seeing the entire arc and logic of the paper from primary findings and interpretation can help focus on the essential elements to be included in the abstract. Regardless of methods used, abstracts must be succinct yet convey sufficient information to be compelling to a potential reader. The selection of each word in the abstract, as well as the key words, should be deliberate and thoughtful, as these become search terms for electronic databases. The additional challenge for a mixed methods study is conveying the methods and design effectively. The question of whether to include *mixed methods* in the title depends on the particular journal and the author's preference. Including *mixed methods* in the abstract is universally recommended by leading mixed methods experts (Plano Clark, 2010), as greater consistency in classifying research as mixed methods is key to tracking its evolution. Reviewing the journal's prior published studies can generate ideas for style and approach. In some areas of the health sciences it can be beneficial to highlight the mixed methods design for your intended audience.

Various journals in the health sciences have their own standards and norms for abstract content and format; next we present several good examples. The first is an abstract from a mixed methods study published in a leading nursing journal that illustrates several key elements of a well-written abstract (see Box 11.12; Polovich & Clark, 2012). The title is a simple and clear declarative statement. It includes words that are appropriate search terms, increasing the likelihood that interested researchers will locate the article. The study design includes the descriptor *mixed methods*. The data analyses are described using precise terminology for each respective component (*hierarchical regression* and *content analysis*). The findings are summarized concisely and report both the quantitative and qualitative insights in a balanced and integrated way. The conclusions do not overstate the findings and have practical value for readers.

Box 11.12   Abstract That Illustrates Several Key Elements of a Well-Written Abstract

Polovich, M., & Clark P. C. (2012). Factors influencing oncology nurses' use of hazardous drug safe-handling precautions. *Oncology Nursing Forum, 39*(3), E299–309.

Abstract

Purpose/Objectives: To examine relationships among factors affecting nurses' use of hazardous drug (HD) safe-handling precautions, identify factors that promote or interfere with HD precaution use, and determine managers' perspectives on the use of HD safe-handling precautions.

Design: Cross-sectional, mixed methods; mailed survey to nurses who handle chemotherapy and telephone interviews with managers.

Setting: Mailed invitation to oncology centers across the United States.

Sample: 165 nurses who reported handling chemotherapy and 20 managers of nurses handling chemotherapy.

Methods: Instruments measured the use of HD precautions and individual and organizational factors believed to influence precaution use. Data analysis included descriptive statistics and hierarchical regression. Manager interview data were analyzed using content analysis.

Main Research Variables: Chemotherapy exposure knowledge, self-efficacy, perceived barriers, perceived risk, interpersonal influences, and workplace safety climate.

Findings: Nurses were well educated, experienced, and certified in oncology nursing. The majority worked in outpatient settings and administered chemotherapy to an average of 6.8 patients per day. Exposure knowledge, self-efficacy for using personal protective equipment, and perceived risk of harm from HD exposure were high; total precaution use was low. Nurse characteristics did not predict HD precaution use. Fewer barriers, better workplace safety climate, and fewer patients per day were independent predictors of higher HD precaution use. HD handling policies were present, but many did not reflect current recommendations. Few managers formally monitored nurses' HD precaution use.

Conclusions: Circumstances in the workplace interfere with nurses' use of HD precautions. Implications for Nursing: Interventions should include fostering a positive workplace safety climate, reducing barriers, and providing appropriate nurse-patient ratios.

As noted previously, one strategy to maximize efficiency and completeness in reporting larger mixed methods studies is to publish a foundational methods article early in the project. Subsequent empirical reports can then refer back to the protocol previously reported, reducing the length of the methods sections and making it easier to adhere to space limits. The next illustrative abstract indicates in the title that the article is a protocol description for a large-scale project and notes the specific design (although it does not indicate the mixed methods approach) (see Box 11.13; Kastner et al., 2011). The background section states the various components, describing them as "a series of mixed methods studies." In the methods section, the three study phases are clearly enumerated, with terminology for qualitative and quantitative components and linking each method to a specific aim. The discussion describes the contribution of this mixed method study to both the science of evaluating chronic disease interventions and to self-management of osteoporosis.

Box 11.13   Abstract for a Manuscript Reporting a Research Protocol for a Mixed Methods Study

Kastner, M., Sawka, A., Thorpe, K., Chignel, M., Marquez, C., Newton, D., & Straus, S. E. (2011). Evaluation of a clinical decision support tool for osteoporosis disease management: Protocol for an interrupted time series design. *Implementation Science, 6,* 77.

Abstract

Background: Osteoporosis affects over 200 million people worldwide at a high cost to healthcare systems. Although guidelines on assessing and managing osteoporosis are available, many patients are not receiving appropriate diagnostic testing or treatment. Findings from a systematic review of osteoporosis interventions, a series of mixed-methods studies, and advice from experts in osteoporosis and human-factors engineering were used collectively to develop a multi-component tool (targeted to family physicians and patients at risk for osteoporosis) that may support clinical decision making in osteoporosis disease management at the point of care.

Methods: A three-phased approach will be used to evaluate the osteoporosis tool. In phase 1, the tool will be implemented in three family practices. It will involve ensuring optimal functioning of the tool while minimizing disruption to usual practice. In phase 2, the tool will be pilot tested in a quasi-experimental interrupted time series (ITS) design to determine if it can improve osteoporosis disease management at the point of care. Phase 3 will involve conducting a qualitative postintervention follow-up study to better understand participants' experiences and perceived utility of the tool and readiness to adopt the tool at the point of care.

Discussion: The osteoporosis tool has the potential to make several contributions to the development and evaluation of complex, chronic disease interventions, such as the inclusion of an implementation strategy prior to conducting an evaluation study. Anticipated benefits of the tool may be to increase awareness for patients about osteoporosis and its associated risks and provide an opportunity to discuss a management plan with their physician, which may all facilitate patient self-management.

Cover Letter

While the cover letter may seem a perfunctory procedure, in the case of submitting a mixed methods manuscript, it can serve a strategic purpose. The letter is an opportunity to sell mixed methods to an editor who may be unfamiliar or uninterested in this approach. Because mixed methods is fairly (or entirely) new to many journals in the health sciences, the letter can appeal to an editor's instinct to introduce novel research methodology to the journal's readership. It can be useful to point to prior related work published by the author team, or by other researchers—especially in the target journal. Because there are currently insufficient numbers of editorial staff or reviewers with mixed methods training or expertise in the health sciences, editors may appreciate having several recommendations for qualified reviewers included in the letter. One senior editorial board member for a number of nursing journals provided some recommendations on this topic (see Box 11.14).

Box 11.14   Requesting a Mixed Methods Review

Authors can request mixed methods review. It would be the same thing if I submit a manuscript with an interesting methodology or a special statistics technique. I would put in my cover letter that we used this technique and that it would be helpful to have a reviewer with that knowledge—the same way I would do if I were submitting a grant.

—Barbara Given, PhD, RN, FAAN,
Director of PhD Program,
College of Nursing Michigan State University
and Editorial Board Member,
*Journal of Oncology Nursing, Western Journal of
Nursing Research, Cancer Nursing,* and
Research in Nursing and Health

If your manuscript exceeds the word limit, it is prudent to offer to shorten the length as needed, with the assistance of the editorial staff. You should note that you have made every effort to comply with the journal specifications and that you are open to reducing the length at the editor's suggestion, while not losing essential content. Box 11.15 presents a sample cover letter that reflects some of these strategies.

**Box 11.15   Sample Cover Letter for a Mixed Methods
Manuscript Submitted to a High-Impact Health
Sciences Journal**

Dear Editors,

Enclosed is a manuscript titled *<title>*. Our paper presents novel and timely data from a large mixed methods study funded by the Agency for Healthcare Research (AHRQ), Commonwealth Fund, and United Health Foundation and focused on understanding aspects of hospital performance in acute myocardial infarction care.

We recognize that *<journal>* rarely publishes mixed methods; however, *<journal>* did publish a prior study (*<title>*) that has been widely cited as a useful contribution to the literature. We have applied the same rigorous methodology with an equally skilled, multidisciplinary team with internationally recognized expertise in mixed methods research. We have made every effort to ensure the manuscript is as concise as possible; it is presently 837 words over limit for an original contribution. Although a growing number of journals extend longer word limits to allow for comprehensive presentation of mixed methods findings, we did not find information regarding this in the instructions for authors. Should the paper be determined to be suitable for the journal and space constraints exist, we would welcome the opportunity to work with the editorial staff to shorten the manuscript length as feasible without losing essential content. Finally, given the content area and methodology of the paper, we would suggest either of the following people who publish in *<journal>* as highly qualified reviewers:

<Reviewer 1>

<Reviewer 2>

We have no potential conflict of interest to report. We believe *<journal>* is the optimal forum for this work. We look forward to your review and comments.

RESPONDING TO PEER REVIEWS FOR MIXED METHODS STUDIES

The peer review process for empirical research articles in scientific publications is foundational to the advancement of science. Careful and constructive review by qualified peers can increase the quality, accessibility, and utility of empirical research articles. Nevertheless, peer review can sometimes be an anxiety-provoking or frustrating experience. There are several possible outcomes of the review process. The manuscript may be accepted immediately (although this has not happened to us in 20 years of writing), accepted with minor revisions, accepted with major revisions, rejected to varying degrees, or outright rejected. Rejection notifications may be difficult to interpret at times because each journal has their own specific terms and conditions of rejection. For example, a notification might say that an article requires substantial revision and would be considered as a new submission. In the case of an invitation to revise and resubmit, we encourage you to pause before abandoning the target journal outright. Persistence can pay off in multiple ways. Your manuscript may ultimately be accepted by your target journal. Increasing the publication of mixed methods studies in a particular discipline or field can also strengthen the evidence base. Greater representation of mixed methods studies is also the route to establishing credibility and a role for mixed methods in health sciences.

Key steps in preparing a revised manuscript are outlined in Figure 11.1. While perhaps an obvious point, the first step is to carefully read and interpret the reviews. If the comments are especially harsh or provocative, it may help to set the letter aside for a day or two or to share it with colleagues within or outside of the project team for an objective view. If you decide to move ahead, outline the major and minor comments received, particularly if there are sets of comments from multiple reviewers, which is the typical case. Reviewers of mixed methods manuscripts may be highly diverse in training, background, and discipline; consequently, their comments may be overlapping or inconsistent. Reviewers can also make erroneous observations or simply overlook content. In these instances, a polite correction and indication of the page number for the content is appropriate. Of particular relevance to mixed methods studies, reviewers may lack an understanding of the methods. In these instances, the response letter should provide all information and citations necessary to clarify or defend a given approach. Resubmissions should be completed as soon as possible, certainly before the deadline (our teams generally turn around revisions within three weeks). If you decide to submit the manuscript to a new journal, it is worthwhile to address or at least consider the initial reviews. There are relatively few health sciences mixed methods researchers in the health sciences, so it is possible that a manuscript may be assigned to the same reviewers at the new journal (and nothing makes an earnest reviewer more frustrated than to see their comments ignored).

In our view, the primary goal in a response letter is to make it as easy as possible for reviewers to have confidence that their comments were considered seriously and responded to as appropriate. We make every effort to avoid having reviewers go back into the manuscript if at all possible, as new concerns or questions may arise. The letter should be sufficiently complete, clearly written, and well organized so that the editor can follow the changes readily, and the reviewers can be assured that all of their comments were addressed in some manner. When introducing new text or making edits to the manuscript, include enough context surrounding each of the edits so that the

Figure 11.1 Steps in Preparing a Response Letter

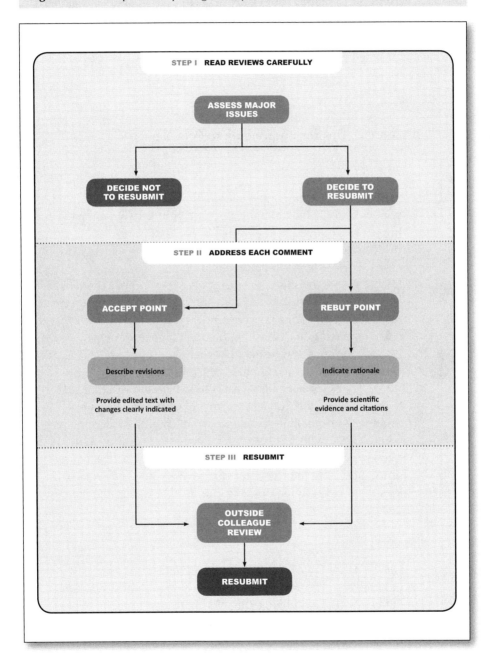

changes can be interpreted. Use formatting to clearly indicate where changes have been made within the surrounding text (e.g., using bold or underlined text). Finally, it can be helpful to have a colleague not connected to the study review the letter for coherence, clarity, and responsiveness. Tips for developing both the content and format of a response to peer reviews are presented in Box 11.16.

Box 11.16   Tips for Responding to Peer Reviews

Content

- ✓ Include an introductory paragraph thanking editors and reviewers for their time and perhaps very briefly summarizing major changes.
- ✓ Address all points raised by the editor and reviewers precisely, concisely, and completely.
- ✓ Describe the revisions to your manuscript with a narrative comment directed to reviewers, followed by the text from manuscript identifying new content or edits so that the reviewer does not need to refer back to the original manuscript.
- ✓ Use a courteous and respectful tone.
- ✓ Defer to the editor as much as possible.
- ✓ When reviewers contradict each other, take the recommendations of the one that you agree with and provide a rationale.
- ✓ Provide a compelling response to any points or comments you disagree with.
- ✓ Recognize that not all comments require edits to the manuscript; providing information to the reviewer may be sufficient.
- ✓ Reply as promptly as possible but always within the stated deadline.

Format

- ✓ Clearly label reviewer comments and your responses.
- ✓ Indicate major revisions in the text, either with underline, italics, or tracked changes (in line with any guidelines provided by the journal, if applicable).
- ✓ Itemize responses to each reviewer and editor comment.
- ✓ Provide page numbers for all edited text.

EXAMPLE OF LETTER FOR REVISION AND RESUBMISSION

In this section, we provide an example of two rounds of responses to reviews in order to illustrate the principles described previously (see Boxes 11.17 and 11.18). We present excerpts from a series of two revision letters from a manuscript published in the *Annals of Internal Medicine,* a high-impact journal in the health sciences (Bradley et al., 2012). We are grateful to Sankey Williams, MD, deputy editor of the *Annals of Internal Medicine,* for granting permission for us to include this material in the book. This manuscript was developed as part of a multistage study on hospital performance in care of patients with acute myocardial infarction (AMI).

◀ This study is also discussed in Chapter 8: Data Analysis and Integration in Mixed Methods Studies.

The study used a positive deviance approach and exploratory sequential mixed methods design to discover hospital strategies associated with lower 30-day hospital risk-standardized mortality rates (RSMRs) for patients with AMI. The aim was to understand diverse and complex aspects of care for patients with AMI including hospital structures (e.g., emergency department space), processes (e.g., emergency response protocols, coordination within hospital units), and hospital internal environments (e.g., organizational culture). The qualitative stage included site visits and interviews of key staff at 11 purposefully selected high- and low-performing hospitals in the United States to characterize the organizational environment and to generate hypotheses. In the quantitative stage, hypotheses were tested using a survey of a nationally representative sample of acute care hospitals ($n = 537$).

The methods for the overall study are reported in the *American Heart Journal* (Krumholz, Curry, & Bradley, 2011), and the qualitative data were reported in a separate article, also in the *Annals of Internal Medicine* (Curry et al., 2011). Here, we focus on the second empirical paper reporting findings from the quantitative component. We present excerpts that are relevant to the mixed methods aspects of the manuscript, including the editor and reviewer's comments as well as the author responses for each. Readers interested in understanding the broader study context may find it useful to review the published papers. The thorough and rigorous editorial process elevated the quality of the manuscript in general and the reporting of a mixed methods study in particular. In the first comment, the editor requests more explicit representation of the linkage between the qualitative findings and the items constructed for the quantitative survey, noting that the readership will be interested in this aspect of the mixed methods approach. The second comment raises a concern about the model building strategy. The strategy, driven by hypotheses from the qualitative study, had not been adequately described. Based on the editor and reviewer input, revisions to the text offer additional information and clarification of both item development and model building (see Boxes 11.17 and 11.18).

Box 11.17   Illustrative Excerpts From First Revision Letter

Dear XXX,

Thank you for your review of our manuscript, "Hospital Strategies for Reducing Risk-Standardized Mortality Rates in Acute Myocardial Infarction (M11–2034)." We very much appreciate the opportunity to submit a revised version for your consideration.

Enclosed is an itemized list of the comments and our response to each comment according to the specifications for the journal. We integrated some of the comments from reviewer #3 because our responses were similar. We have addressed each reviewer comment and believe the paper is substantially stronger due to the reviewers' comments.

Thanks reviewers and explains the format of the letter.

Reviewer Comment: I think readers will naturally ask how the domains in your qualitative article informed your choice of survey items. If you want readers to understand and accept what you've done, I think you need to map each survey item into one of the domains you describe in your qualitative study. In addition, I think you have to provide examples that illustrate how the qualitative domains led you to specific survey items.

Provides narrative response to reviewer and indicates in italics the next text added to the manuscript.

Author Response: We agree with the editor that it is important for readers to understand how the domains in our qualitative article (Curry et al., 2011) informed our choice of survey items. To address this comment, we retained Appendix A, which shows the final survey instrument, and we added a new appendix, Appendix B, which maps each survey item to the domains identified in our prior qualitative research (Curry et al., 2011). In addition, we edited the text of the methods as follows in italics

clearly label
reviewer
comment
and author
response.

(p. 6) and added a table (p. 21) with examples that illustrate how the qualitative domains informed the development of specific survey items, as requested.

The final survey (see Appendix A) measured use of strategies for patients with AMI using items that were designed to measure quantitatively the domains and concepts that emerged from our previous qualitative work (Curry et al., 2011). A crosswalk between the domains from the qualitative study and the survey items is available in Appendix B. Examples of the linking of qualitative data and quantitative items are displayed in Table 1.

Table   Examples of Linking of Qualitative Data to Quantitative Survey Items

Quotation in Curry et al., 2011	Corresponding survey item
BROAD STAFF PRESENCE AND EXPERTISE IN AMI CARE	
"I started writing my consult notes in the physician progress notes . . . over the years it's just become the standard . . . That was a way of my breaking into the culture saying, "This is my note; I want you to read it. It's not in the nurse's section. I have some ideas . . . and I'm open to talking about it." (Nurse Manager, ID #5)	Nurses are comfortable checking with physicians if they have concerns about patient care.
COMMUNICATION AND COORDINATION AMONG GROUPS	
"Everyone in this hospital from the housekeeper to the CEO plays a role . . . . The housekeeping needs to know why it's important for them to go out and do their job . . . . No one has an insignificant role in it . . . . So everybody needs to be educated. Everyone." (Director, Catheterization laboratory, ID #2)	Clinicians involved in the care of patients with AMI value each others' skills and talents (e.g., physicians' value nurses' skills and talents and vice-versa).

(Continued)

Table 1   (Continued)

Quotation in Curry et al., 2011	Corresponding survey item
PROBLEM SOLVING AND ORGANIZATIONAL LEARNING	
" . . . the performance improvement team . . . identifies action steps, the plan is put in place, and then we continue to measure to see if it's working or not working . . . you identify, you intervene, you improve, you monitor, you tweak and that's the model that they've been using for 10 years." (Director, Quality Management, ID #4)	After we make changes to improve AMI care, we fail to evaluate their effectiveness.

Reviewer Comment: In addition, we thought the model building strategy as described on p. 8 was driven too much by *p*-values and did not seem to take into account which variables might have been considered confounders a priori.

Concisely and precisely addresses reviewer comment.

Author Response: We understand the reviewer's concern and agree that it would not be appropriate to drive the model-building strategy on *p*-values. Our approach, in contrast, was driven by the hypotheses developed through our earlier qualitative study on this topic (Curry et al., 2011). We have described this effort more thoroughly in the revised manuscript and thank the reviewer for the opportunity to clarify our approach. We have revised the methods in two places to respond to this comment, in italics next. First, we added detail about the measure development process, which was based on hypotheses from our qualitative work (p. 6 and Table 1). Second, we revised our method for assessing possible collinearity, which was completed prior to model fitting (p. 8).

(p. 6) We designed a web-based survey to assess the use of specific strategies based on our qualitative study (Curry et al., 2011) and clinical experience. We developed closed-ended, multiple-choice questions for each strategy and field-tested the

instrument using cognitive interviews (Krause, 2002) with hospital quality improvement directors to assess clarity and comprehensiveness. We asked about strategies in place during the time that matched the most recent RSMR data available (January 2008–December 2009). The final survey (see Appendix A) measured use of strategies for patients with AMI using items that were designed to measure quantitatively the domains and concepts that emerged from our previous qualitative work (Curry et al., 2011). A crosswalk between the domains from the qualitative study and the survey items is available in Appendix B. Examples of how the qualitative data informed quantitative survey items are displayed in Table 1.

(p. 8) We considered as candidate independent variables those that were significant in the bivariate analysis and that were applicable for both hospitals that performed primary percutaneous coronary intervention for ST-segment elevation myocardial infarction and hospitals that did not. We excluded variables with less than 1% in a response category. We assessed multicollinearity among independent variables using the variance decomposition proportions with a conditional number cutoff of 30 as recommended (Belsley, Kuh, & Welsch, 1980) which was not apparent for any candidate variables.

Box 11.18   Illustrative Excerpts From the Second Revision Letter

After submission of the response letter and revised manuscript, a second round of revisions was requested. Excerpts from the letter related to the mixed methods aspects of the letter are next, with comments and responses for each. The first comment raises concerns regarding the nature of qualitative data analysis to operationalize constructs and processes of hypothesis generation and testing. The editor reminds the authors of the journal audience, which is

(Continued)

(Continued)

largely unfamiliar with (and perhaps skeptical of) qualitative research, and underscores the importance of explaining these methods with clarity and precision. In the third comment, the editor offers a recommendation to help readers appreciate the value of mixed methods by providing additional detail about the methods of hypothesis generation.

Reviewer Comment: In Table 3 of this manuscript you list five domains, but in Table 4 of your qualitative article you list six domains (the extra one in your qualitative article is "Organizational values and goals"). Also, some of the domain titles in Table 3 are slightly different from the domain titles in your qualitative article, for example, "Hospital Protocols and Practices" in this manuscript vs "Hospital practices and protocols to improve AMI care" in the qualitative article. In addition, the domains are listed in different orders in the two papers. All of these differences seem strange to me, because I thought you expended so much effort identifying domains in the qualitative study that they would be too important to change—perhaps almost sacred. For example, imagine the Israelites saying, "Once we got the 10 Commandments, we deleted one of them, rewrote a few of the others, and changed their rank order." I can understand why you consider the differences in titles and the differences in rank order unimportant, but what about the domain that was dropped? My concern here is that our readers who doubt that qualitative research can improve quantitative research will use these differences, including the minor ones, to confirm preconceived ideas. You can prevent this problem by eliminating differences when you can and explaining the others.

Author Response: Thank you for this careful reading of the paper. We have addressed the comments about (1) number of domains used, (2) labeling of domains, and (3) ordering of domains below. Additionally, we added a paragraph in the discussion to explicitly interpret the quantitative work in light of the qualitative domains (p. 14), as noted next.

ovides
mplete
sponse to
ch
ement of
e reviewer
mment.

es not
e
ggested
it,
vides
ionale,
d defers to
e editor.

Number of domains used. We agree it was important to analyze items in all six domains, as we did (see Appendix B). The reason that items in only five of the six domains appear in Table 3 is that none of the items within one domain, "Organizational Values and Goals," were significantly associated with RSMR. We have added the following in italics to p. 10 of the revised manuscript to clarify why Table 3 includes items in only five of the six domains.

A number of hospital strategies had significant unadjusted (bivariate) associations with RSMR (Table 3). These strategies corresponded to five of the six domains from our previous qualitative work (Curry et al., 2011); strategies in the organizational values and goals domain were not significant and therefore do not appear on Table 3.

Labeling of domains. We have also edited the labels to be consistent with the qualitative paper (Curry et al., 2011) as suggested; however, we have not written "in improving AMI care" at the end of the labels, in the interest of space and to limit redundancy. We defer to the editor if this is preferred to be added.

Ordering of domains. We agree with the editor that we changed the order of the domains, but this was to make the current paper more readable. We believe the order of the domains in the first paper was not central to the interpretation of the findings and therefore believe reordering this paper for readability is practical and appropriate; however, if the editor has a different perspective, we can discuss this approach further.

(p. 14) Added discussion. We have added the following to the discussion (in italics).

Our findings overall were largely consistent with our qualitative work (18), which identified five conceptual areas that were prominent in higher performing hospitals and less apparent in lower performing hospitals. This earlier work also suggested that higher performing hospitals were not distinguished by specific

(Continued)

(Continued)

practices and protocols but instead by organizational environments that could foster higher quality care. The present quantitative findings largely support this earlier qualitative work in that specific practices and protocols were not significantly related to RSMR once variables pertaining to the organizational environment were taken into account, in multivariable analysis. Furthermore, key aspects of the organizational environment including effective communication and collaboration among groups, broad staff presence and expertise, and a culture of problem solving and learning were apparent in the qualitative work and statistically associated with higher RSMRs in the quantitative work, providing evidence about the importance of these features in higher performing hospitals.

Reviewer Comment: Another way to help readers accept the idea that combining qualitative research with quantitative research adds value is to explain the process you used to convert the information from your qualitative study into the questions in Appendix A. This manuscript says you did it, but it doesn't tell us very much about how you did it.

Politely disagree and defer.

Author Response: We agree that more detail would be helpful about this process. Given space constraints, we have added the following (p. 6) with references for further reading. We believe that a more comprehensive discussion of survey design methodology is beyond the scope of this paper, but we defer to the editor if more detail is desired.

We designed a web-based survey to assess the use of specific strategies based on our qualitative study (Curry et al., 2011) and clinical experience. We examined concepts, wording, and specific descriptions of strategies from the text of our open-ended interviews to develop closed-ended, multiple-choice questions for each strategy, as recommended by experts in mixed methods (Creswell, 2009; Curry, Nembhard, & Bradley, 2009). Illustrations of how the qualitative data informed the quantitative survey items are displayed in Table 1. We field-tested the closed-ended items using cognitive interviews (Krause, 2002) with hospital quality improvement directors to assess clarity and comprehensiveness.

As we have described, publishing mixed methods research in mainstream health sciences journals is challenging in several ways. At the same time, the steadily growing interest in these methods presents important opportunities for mixed methods researchers. In this chapter, we draw on our own experience and those of colleagues to offer strategies and techniques for managing these challenges and increasing the quality of your mixed methods research publications.

Summary and Key Points

- Mixed methods researchers face challenges in publishing in health sciences journals, although mixed methods studies are increasingly accepted and even encouraged.
- Mixed methods teams should work together from the outset of a study to develop a dissemination plan, especially because team members from different backgrounds are likely to have varying expectations about optimal strategies for publication.
- Following suggestions for reporting mixed methods studies, such as GRAMMS, can greatly improve the quality of your manuscript.
- Keep the target journal audience in mind as you write; limit jargon but retain essential terminology with definitions and citations.
- In your response letter, provide thorough responses to concerns regarding methodology, with citations as appropriate. The primary goal in a response letter is to make it as easy as possible for reviewers to have confidence that their comments were considered seriously and responded to as appropriate.

Review Questions and Exercises

1. Search journals in your field, and develop a list of journals that publish mixed methods research articles.

2. Draft a cover letter, which is addressed to the editor of a journal of your choice, that you would use to submit a mixed methods study.

3. Select two mixed methods articles, and evaluate these articles according to GRAMMS.

4. Search the literature for a mixed methods study that is of interest to you, and read the entire article, except the abstract. After reading the article, draft an abstract for the article. Compare it to the abstract written by the authors.

References

Belsley, D. A., Kuh, E., & Welsch, R.E. (1980). *Regression diagnostics: Identifying influential data and sources of collinearity.* Hoboken, NJ: Wiley.

Bradley, E. H., Curry, L. A., Spatz, E. S., Herrin, J., Cherlin, E. J., Curtis, J. P., . . . Krumholz, H. M. (2012). Hospital strategies for reducing risk-standardized mortality rates in acute myocardial infarction. *Annals of Internal Medicine, 156*(9), 618–626.

CONSORT Transparent Reporting of Trials. (2012, January 20). *The CONSORT statement.* Retrieved February 28, 2014, from http://www.consort-statement.org/consort-statement

Creswell, J. W. (2009). Editorial: mapping the field of mixed methods research. *Journal of Mixed Methods Research, 3,* 95. DOI: 10.1177/1558689808330883.

Creswell, J. W., & Plano Clark, V. L. (2011). *Designing and conducting mixed methods research* (2nd ed.). Thousand Oaks, CA: Sage.

Curry, L. A., Nembhard, I. M., & Bradley, E. H. (2009). Qualitative and mixed methods provide unique contributions to outcomes research. *Circulation, 119*(10), 1442–1452. doi: 10.1161/CIRCULATIONAHA.107.742775

Curry, L. A., Spatz, E., Cherlin, E., Thompson, J. W., Berg, D., Ting, H. H., . . . Bradley, E. H. (2011). What distinguishes top-performing hospitals in acute myocardial infarction mortality rates? A qualitative study. *Annals of Internal Medicine, 154*(6), 384–390.

Dahlberg, B., Wittink, M. N., & Gallo, J. J. (2010). Funding and publishing integrated studies: Writing effective mixed methods manuscripts and grant proposals. In A. Tashakkori & C. Teddlie (Eds.), *SAGE handbook of mixed methods in social & behavioral research* (2nd ed., pp. 775–802). Thousand Oaks, CA: Sage.

Devers, K. J. (1999). How will we know "good" qualitative research when we see it? Beginning the dialogue in health services research. *Health Services Research, 34*(5 Pt. 2), 1153–1188.

International Committee of Medical Journal Editors. (2008, October 13). Ethical considerations in the conduct and reporting of research: Authorship and contributorship. *Uniform requirements for manuscripts submitted to biomedical journals.* Retrieved December 15, 2013, from http://www.icmje.org

Ivankova, N. V., & Kawamura, Y. (2010). Emerging trends in the utilization of integrated designs in the social, behavioral and health sciences. In A. Tashakkori & C. Teddlie (Eds.), *SAGE handbook of mixed methods in social & behavioral research* (2nd ed., pp. 581–612). Thousand Oaks, CA: Sage.

Kastner, M., Sawka, A., Thorpe, K., Chignel, M., Marquez, C., Newton, D., & Straus, S. E. (2011). Evaluation of a clinical decision support tool for osteoporosis disease management: Protocol for an interrupted time series design. *Implement Science, 6,* 77. doi: 10.1186/1748–5908–6-77

Krause, N. (2002). A comprehensive strategy for developing closed-ended survey items for use in studies of older adults. *Journals of Gerontology. Series B, Psychological Sciences and Social Sciences, 57*(5), S263–274.

Krumholz, H. M., Bradley, E. H., & Curry, L. A. (2013). Promoting publication of rigorous qualitative research. *Circulation Cardiovascular Quality and Outcomes, 6*(2), 133–134. doi: 10.1161/CIRCOUTCOMES.113.000186

Krumholz, H. M., Curry, L. A., & Bradley, E. H. (2011). Survival after acute myocardial infarction (SAMI) study: The design and implementation of a positive deviance study. *American Heart Journal, 162*(6), 981–987. e989. doi: 10.1016/j.ahj.2011.09.004

Leech, N. L., Onwuegbuzie, A. J., & Combs, J. P. (2011). Writing publishable mixed research articles: Guidelines for emerging scholars. *International Journal of Multiple Research Approaches, 5*(1), 7–24.

Miller, W. L., Crabtree, B. F., Harrison, M. I., & Fennell, M. L. (2013). Integrating mixed methods in health services and delivery system research. *Health Services Research, 48*(6 Pt. 2), 2126. doi: 10.1111/1475–6773.12123

O'Cathain, A., Murphy, E., & Nicholl, J. (2007). Integration and publications as indicators of "yield" from mixed methods studies. *Journal of Mixed Methods Research, 1*(2), 147–163.

O'Cathain, A., Murphy, E., & Nicholl, J. (2008). The quality of mixed methods studies in health services research. *Journal of Health Services Research and Policy, 13*(2), 92–98. doi: 10.1258/jhsrp.2007.007074

Plano Clark, V. L. (2010). The adoption and practice of mixed methods: U.S. trends in federally funded health-related research. *Qualitative Inquiry, 16*(6), 428–440.

Polovich, M., & Clark, P. C. (2012). Factors influencing oncology nurses' use of hazardous drug safe-handling precautions. *Oncology Nursing Forum, 39*(3), E299–309. doi: 10.1188/12.0NF.E299-E309

PRISMA. (n.d.). *Welcome to the PRISMA statement website.* Retrieved February 28, 2014, from http://www.prisma-statement.org

Schoenberg, N. E., & McAuley, W. J. (2007). Promoting qualitative research. *Gerontologist, 47*(5), 576–577.

Shortell, S. M. (1999). The emergence of qualitative methods in health services research. *Health Services Research, 34*(5 Pt. 2), 1083–1090.

Stange, K. C., Crabtree, B. F., & Miller, W. L. (2006). Publishing multimethod research. *Annals of Family Medicine, 4*(4), 292–294. doi: 10.1370/afm.615

Tong, A., Sainsbury, P., & Craig, J. (2007). Consolidated criteria for reporting qualitative research (COREQ): A 32-item checklist for interviews and focus groups. *International Journal for Quality in Health Care, 19*(6), 349–357. doi: 10.1093/intqhc/mzm042

Wisdom, J. P., Cavaleri, M. A., Onwuegbuzie, A. J., & Green, C. A. (2012). Methodological reporting in qualitative, quantitative, and mixed methods health services research articles. *Health Services Research, 47*(2), 721–745. doi: 10.1111/j.1475–6773.2011.01344.x

⚜ APPENDIX A ⚜

BIOGRAPHIES OF CONTRIBUTING EXPERTS

This book draws on the experiences and insights of experienced mixed methods researchers and senior representatives of funding agencies that support mixed methods research. This wisdom is reflected in the content of the chapter narrative, the practical tools, and in direct quotations. The quotations were derived from interviews conducted by phone during the development of this book. We are extraordinarily grateful to these busy individuals who, despite many competing demands, generously contributed their time and expertise to this effort. It does take a village.

Miriam Boeri, PhD

Dr. Boeri, a lecturer in sociology, has over 15 years of teaching at the university level. She is an associate professor emeritus at Kennesaw State University. Dr. Boeri's research has focused on ethnographic studies of drug user populations and alternatives to incarceration. Her recent studies have been funded through awards from the National Institute on Drug Abuse (NIDA). Through her research, Dr. Boeri aims to reduce the adverse effects associated with drug use, such as transmission of HIV/AIDS, hepatitis C virus (HCV), and sexually transmitted diseases, and address the harmful social effects of drug use, including incarceration, social isolation, unemployment, and violence.

Susan Bouregy, PhD, CIP

Dr. Bouregy is the chief HIPAA privacy officer at Yale University. She has served in this role since 2002 with responsibility for the HIPAA privacy program throughout the university, including both a health plan component and the health care providers in the faculty practice and University Health Services. From 2000 to 2013, Dr. Bouregy was responsible for oversight of the social and behavioral science institutional review board (IRB) at Yale, initially as IRB director and subsequently as vice chair. Dr. Bouregy also served as codirector of the university's successful human research protection program (HRPP) accreditation project. Dr. Bouregy holds a PhD in biology from Brandeis University.

Barbara Bowers, PhD, RN, FAAN

Dr. Bowers is professor and associate dean of research at the University of Wisconsin–Madison School of Nursing. She is recognized for her research and work in the field of long-term care and also in improving the quality of patient care in nursing homes. Dr. Bowers is an international expert in the retention for nursing home staff and the relationship between work practices and quality of care. She is the founding director of the University of Wisconsin–Madison School of Nursing Center for Aging Research and Education.

Giselle Corbie-Smith, MD, MSc

Dr. Corbie-Smith is professor of social medicine and medicine at the University of North Carolina School of Medicine and nationally recognized for her scholarly work on the practical and ethical issues regarding involvement of minorities in research. Her empirical work, using both qualitative and quantitative methods, has focused on the methodological, ethical, and practical issues faced by mandated inclusion of minorities in research and the need for this research to address racial disparities in health. She has built multidisciplinary research teams to conduct research and has been the principal investigator of grants funded through the National Heart Lung and Blood Institute, the Robert Wood Johnson Foundation, the National Center for Minority Health and Health Disparities, the National Institute of Nursing Research (NINR), and the National Human Genome Research Institute.

Benjamin Crabtree, PhD

Dr. Crabtree is a medical anthropologist and a professor and director of research in the Department of Family Medicine and Community Health at Rutgers Robert Wood Johnson Medical School. Dr. Crabtree has been a full-time primary care–health services researcher in family medicine for the past 25 years and has contributed to numerous articles and chapters on both qualitative and quantitative methods, covering topics ranging from time series analysis and log-linear models to in-depth interviews, case study research, and qualitative analysis strategies. Dr. Crabtree is known for his expertise in qualitative research and writes extensively in this area, including editing a book, *Doing Qualitative Research,* which is now in its second edition. He was also the lead editor on a book about developing collaborative research teams, *Exploring Collaborative Research in Primary Care.* Dr. Crabtree has been principal investigator on numerous National Institutes of Health (NIH)-funded grants.

Jennifer Cunningham, PhD

Dr. Cunningham is a postdoctoral fellow for the Meharry-Vanderbilt Alliance Community Engaged Research Core at Meharry Medical College in Nashville, Tennessee. Dr. Cunningham's current research interests are the human papillomavirus (HPV), cervical cancer, and community-engaged research. She received a master of arts and doctor of philosophy in health education and health promotion at the University of Alabama at Birmingham in 2013. Her dissertation work focused on factors associated with African American maternal intentions to vaccinate their daughters against HPV in Alabama to inform the development of interventions.

Neal V. Dawson, MD

Dr. Dawson is professor of medicine, epidemiology, and biostatistics at Case Western Reserve University and section head of the Medical Decision Making Division of the Center for Health Care Research and Policy at MetroHealth Medical Center (all in Cleveland, Ohio). His nationally funded research has covered a variety of topics (e.g., end-of-life decision making, alcohol-related issues in primary care, improving outcomes of patients with both diabetes and serious mental illness), which have been examined using methodologies from medical decision making, clinical epidemiology, and health services research. He has served as a manuscript reviewer for many clinical journals, is associate editor emeritus for the journal *Medical Decision Making,* and has served as a grant application reviewer for the National Institutes of Health (NIH), the National Science Foundation (NSF), national foundations, and international funding agencies. He currently serves in numerous capacities in a postgraduate multidisciplinary research training program (the NIH-funded Case Clinical Translational Science Award).

Kelly Devers, PhD

Dr. Devers is a senior fellow in the Health Policy Center at the Urban Institute. Her main areas of expertise are provider payment and competition; the organization and delivery of care; and their impacts on access, cost, and quality. She has used quantitative and qualitative methods to gather data and make recommendations on the implementation of national and state health policy reforms. She has published widely in major journals of health services research and policy, while also acting as a peer reviewer for federal and foundation grants, serving on editorial boards, editing a book and special journal issue, speaking widely, and in 2008 and 2009 advising the presidential transition team.

Jennifer Elston Lafata, PhD

Dr. Elston Lafata, PhD, is a professor in the Department of Social and Behavioral Health in the School of Medicine at Virginia Commonwealth University (VCU) where she is also coleader of the Cancer Prevention and Control Program at the National Cancer Institute (NCI)-designated Massey Cancer Center. She also has an appointment in the Center for Health Policy and Health Services Research at the Henry Ford Health System (HFHS) in Detroit, Michigan. Her training is in health services research, and her current research is focused on the use of mixed methods to study patient–physician decision making and its impact on health services use, primarily in the area of colorectal cancer (CRC) control and prevention. She has led a number of research projects, including a National Institutes of Health (NIH)-funded R01 that used direct observation and audio recordings of 500 patient–physician interactions during annual checkups, linked with patient survey and claims data, to evaluate CRC screening decision making in primary care. She has been involved with a number of practice-based trials, evaluating interventions designed to improve CRC screening decision making in primary care. Through these and other efforts, she has extensive experience working with delivery and financing organizations to develop, implement, and evaluate interventions designed to improve cancer control and routine chronic care management.

Michael Fetters, MD, MPH, MA

Dr. Fetters is a professor in the Department of Medicine at the University of Medicine and serves as director of the Japanese Family Health Program at

Dominos Farms Family Medicine. Dr. Fetters is a team leader on the University of Michigan Health System Adult Clinical Preventative Care Guideline Committee. Dr. Fetters focuses his research on the influence of culture on medical decision making; how to improve the delivery of preventative services, ethical issues involved in increasing understanding, and interest of underserved populations in clinical translational research; and the role of media for teaching ethics in medical education. He previously served on the National Institutes of Health (NIH) Mixed Methods Guidelines Committee sponsored by the Office of Behavioral and Social Sciences Research (OBSSR). Dr. Fetters has extensive experience in the application of mixed methods conducted in multiple settings and using multiple techniques in qualitative methods.

Jason Gerson, PhD

Dr. Gerson is the senior program officer for Comparative Effectiveness Research (CER) Methods and Infrastructure team at the Patient-Centered Outcomes Research Institute (PCORI). He is responsible for providing intellectual and organizational leadership in designing and implementing new CER methods and infrastructure initiatives, evaluating proposals, and monitoring programs and grants. Prior to joining PCORI, Dr. Gerson was a senior officer at the Pew Charitable Trusts, a commissioner's fellow at the U.S. Food and Drug Administration (FDA), and a faculty member in the Department of Epidemiology at the Johns Hopkins Bloomberg School of Public Health.

Barbara Given, PhD, RN, FAAN

Dr. Given is the director of the PhD Program for the College of Nursing at Michigan State University. Dr. Given's research has focused on functional outcomes, symptom management and control, medication adherence, patterns of care, utilization of care, and formal and informal cost of care for the chronically ill—especially those with cancer. Her work is supported by funding from the National Cancer Institute (NCI), National Institute of Mental Health (NIMH), National Institute of Nursing Research (NINR), National Institute on Aging, Walther Cancer Foundation, Michigan Department of Community Health, and the American Cancer Society. Dr. Given is also a reviewer for numerous professional journals and currently serves on the editorial board for research in *Nursing and Health, Cancer Nursing,* and the *European Journal of Cancer Nursing,* among others. She has served as a grant reviewer for the Agency for

Health Care Policy and Research (AHCPR) as well as a psychosocial researcher for the American Cancer Society and the Dissemination and Implementation Research and Health for the National Institutes of Health (NIH), National Cancer Institute (NCI), National Institute of Nursing Research (NINR), Department of Defense, National Institute of Aging, California Cancer Research Program, and the Alzheimer's Association of Canada.

Chanita Hughes-Halbert, PhD

Dr. Hughes-Halbert is professor and Endowed Chair in the Department of Psychiatry and Behavioral Sciences and the Hollings Cancer Center at the Medical University of South Carolina. Previously, she was founding director of the Center for Community-Based Research and Health Disparities and associate professor in the Department of Psychiatry at the University of Pennsylvania. The goal of Dr. Hughes-Halbert's research program is to identify sociocultural, psychological, and environmental determinants of minority health and health care and to translate this information into sustainable interventions in clinic and community-based settings to improve health outcomes in these populations. Dr. Hughes-Halbert is a nationally recognized expert in minority health and health disparities.

Holly Powell Kennedy, PhD, CNM, FACNM, FAAN

Dr. Kennedy is a specialist in maternal and child health care issues in the United States, and she has had broad experiences as a clinician, researcher, educator, policymaker and leader in a variety of settings. Collectively, these experiences have shaped her current vision of academic and clinical scholarship in U.S. maternal–child health care. Her research aims to understand the links between how care is provided during pregnancy and birth with clinical and social outcomes. She has employed mixed methods to examine the provision of care in complex settings and with various models. She is the past president of the American College of Nurse-Midwives (ACNM), the professional association representing certified nurse–midwives and certified midwives in the United States.

Helen Meissner, PhD, ScM

Dr. Meissner has 25 years of experience at the National Institutes of Health (NIH) and is currently the director of the Tobacco Regulatory Science Program. Formerly, she was senior advisor in the NIH Office of Behavioral and Social Sciences Research (OBSSR) from 2007 to 2013, where she was responsible for public health and population science research initiatives. In this role, Dr. Meissner commissioned the development of *Best Practices for Mixed Methods Research in the Health Sciences* and has been developing related resources for NIH investigators.

Janice M. Morse, PhD

Dr. Morse is a professor and presidential Endowed Chair at the University of Utah College of Nursing and professor emeritus at the University of Alberta. She was founding director and scientific director of the International Institute for Qualitative Methodology, University of Alberta. Dr. Morse is the founding editor for the *International Journal of Qualitative Methods*. She is the recipient of the Episteme Award and has received honorary doctorates from the University of Newcastle (Australia) and Athabasca University (Canada). Dr. Morse has authored over 300 articles and 15 books on qualitative research methods, suffering, comforting, and patient falls.

Alicia O'Cathain, PhD, MSc, MA

Dr. O'Cathain is a professor of health services research at the University of Sheffield in the United Kingdom. In her research, she has employed mixed methods designs to conduct evaluations of new health services, health systems, and patient views of health care. In particular, she has integrated qualitative data collection methods in randomized controlled trials. Dr. O'Cathain has published extensively on topics within mixed methods such as data integration, the role of qualitative data in randomized controlled trials, and assessing the rigor of mixed methods studies.

Robin Pollini, PhD, MPH

Dr. Pollini is a substance abuse and infectious disease epidemiologist with training in quantitative, qualitative, and mixed research methods. Her primary focus is on minimizing the public health impacts of injection drug use, including the transmission of HIV and other blood-borne infections. She is the principal investigator for numerous research grants through funders such as the National Institute on Drug Abuse (NIDA) and the Robert Wood Johnson Foundation. Dr. Pollini is currently a senior research scientist at the Pacific Institute for Research and Evaluation (PIRE).

Karen Schifferdecker, PhD, MPH

Dr. Schifferdecker is assistant professor of community and family medicine at the Geisel School of Medicine at Dartmouth and associate director of the Center for Program Design and Evaluation at Dartmouth. A medical anthropologist with public health expertise, she has extensive experience overseeing and conducting community- and practice-based research and medical education studies and evaluation using quantitative, qualitative, and mixed research methods. Her recent work involving mixed methods approaches includes an evaluation of the Multi-Specialty MOC Portfolio Approval Pilot Program, a study of the implementation of patient-reported measures in several clinical sites nationwide, and a randomized, matched-pairs study of child welfare offices in the state of New Hampshire to improve trauma screening and well-being for children and youth served by the system.

Jeremiah Schuur, MD, MHS

Dr. Schuur is a practicing emergency physician with a research focus on health care quality and policy. He is the chief of the Division of Health Policy Translation and the vice chair of patient safety and quality for the Department of Emergency Medicine of the Brigham and Women's Hospital and an assistant professor of medicine (emergency) at Harvard Medical School. Dr. Schuur's current research focuses on developing, implementing, and evaluating measures of quality of care and patient safety in emergency medicine. Dr. Schuur has received grant funding to study specialty consultation in the emergency department (ED) and quality of care for older adults in the ED.

Jonathan Singer, MD

Dr. Jonathan Singer is assistant professor of medicine in residence in the Division of Pulmonary, Critical Care, Allergy and Sleep Medicine at the University of California, San Francisco. He serves as an attending physician in the Lung Transplant Program, where he cares for patients with advanced lung disease before and after lung transplantation. Dr. Singer received his undergraduate degree from Stanford University and a master's in health and medical sciences from the University of California, Berkeley. He received his medical degree from the University of California, San Francisco School of Medicine and stayed there, where he completed a residency in internal medicine, a fellowship in pulmonary and critical care medicine and lung/heart–lung transplantation. Dr. Singer is board certified in internal medicine, pulmonary medicine, and critical care medicine. He is a member of the American Thoracic Society, International Society for Heart and Lung Transplantation, American College of Chest Physicians, and European Respiratory Society.

Dr. Eleanor Palo Stoller, PhD, AM

Dr. Stoller is research professor of sociology and gerontology at Wake Forest University, Winston-Salem, North Carolina. She was previously the Selah Chamberlain Professor of Sociology at Case Western Reserve University (Cleveland, Ohio) and professor of health policy at the University of Florida (Gainesville). Her research, which focuses on the ways older people and their families cope with health challenges, has been supported by the National Institute on Aging and the Administration on Aging. She served on the editorial boards of *The Gerontologist, Journal of Gerontology: Social Sciences, Research on Aging, Journal of Applied Gerontology,* the *Journal of Aging Studies,* and the *Journal of Family Issues.* She is a fellow of the Gerontological Society of America and has been a member of the Neuroscience, Behavior and Sociology of Aging Study Section of the National Institute on Aging.

Benita Weathers, MPH

Ms. Weathers has over 20 years of public health research experience with an emphasis on community-based participatory research (CBPR) and health disparities research and was the senior project manager at the Center for Community-Based Research and Health Disparities. She is currently a senior research project manager in the Department of Family Medicine at the University of Pennsylvania.

Terrie Wetle, PhD

Dr. Wetle is dean of the Brown University School of Public Health and professor of health services research, policy, and practice. Her research centers on the health and care of aging populations and the preferences and experiences of older persons and practices of health care professionals. She studies the influence of nursing home medical staff organization on processes of care and patient outcomes. She also is active in evaluation of services and educational programs, and she has published a book on qualitative and mixed methods research. Dr. Wetle has also worked in federal and local government positions and she is the past president of the Gerontological Society of America and past president of the American Federation for Aging Research.

She was awarded a docteur honoris causa by the University of Geneva and the Donald P. Kent Award by the Gerontological Society of America. She has served on the National Institutes of Health (NIH) National Advisory Council on Aging and the NIH Council on Councils.

Jonathan White, MD, PhD, FRCS, MSc

Dr. White was trained as a surgeon and is the University of Alberta's first Tom Williams Endowed Chair in Surgical Education. His research focuses on the development of professional identity in medical education, the use of qualitative methods to explore surgical practice, evaluation of innovative techniques to improve how surgery is taught and learned, the role of online education, and transformational leadership in medical education. His recent publications have focused on the use of team-based assessment of medical students and the use of podcasting in medical education.

Sankey Williams, PhD

Dr. Williams is a Sol Katz Professor of General Internal Medicine, senior fellow at the Lawrence Davis Institute of Health Economics, professor of health care management at the Wharton School, and associate scholar in the Center for Clinical Epidemiology and Biostatistics. He is a member of a committee that writes guidelines for the management of patients with chronic stable angina for the American College of Physicians, the American Heart Association, and the American College of Cardiology. He is associate editor at *Annals of Internal Medicine* for a series titled "Improving Patient Care" that describes new systems for better patient care for cardiac and other patients.

Jennifer Pelt Wisdom, PhD, MPH

Dr. Wisdom is a licensed clinical psychologist, professor of health policy, and associate vice president for research at the George Washington University. She studies the organization, delivery, and quality of behavioral health treatment for children and adolescents. Dr. Wisdom has received numerous federally funded grants, including for the following: (1) implementation of a measure to address alcohol use among veterans with mental health or substance abuse problems; (2) how family peer advocates work within publicly funded mental health systems to improve the quality of care for children and their families; and (3) a longitudinal study of lesbian, gay, bisexual, and transgender (LGBT) youths' experiences with substance abuse and obtaining treatment for substance abuse. She has also presented and published on the applicability of qualitative and mixed methods to health services research.

APPENDIX B

METHODOLOGY FOR NATIONAL INSTITUTES OF HEALTH REPORTER ANALYSIS OF TRENDS IN FUNDING FOR MIXED METHODS RESEARCH

As described in Chapter 4: Writing a Scientifically Sound and Compelling Grant Proposal for a Mixed Methods Study, we conducted a new analysis for this book of the trends in health-related mixed methods projects funded by the National Institutes of Health (NIH). We sought to replicate and extend a previous analysis that included grants up to U.S. fiscal year (FY) 2008 (Plano Clark, 2010) to include funding through FY 2013.

Our search was conducted using the NIH Research Portfolio Online Reporting Tools (RePORTER) Database. The NIH RePORTER Database is a public, searchable, and web-based system that provides information on NIH-funded research. The system satisfies the legislative mandate of the NIH Reform Act of 2006 and replaced the Computer Retrieval of Information on Scientific Projects (CRISP) system.

A search was performed to include all funded studies with the following terms in the title or abstract of the study: *mixed methods* or *mixed method* or *mixed methodology* or *multi-methods* or *multimethod* or *multimethods* or *multi-methodology*. One researcher reviewed each project abstract to determine whether the study met our definition of a mixed methods study, namely the following:

> the type of research in which a researcher or team of researchers combines elements of qualitative and quantitative research approaches (e.g., use of qualitative and quantitative viewpoints, data collection, analysis, inference techniques) for the broad purposes of breadth and depth of understanding and corroboration. (Johnson, Onwuegbuzie, & Turner, 2007, p. 123)

More simply put and in keeping with the original study upon which this analysis was based, we aimed to identify studies in which the "investigator indicated plans to collect, analyze, and integrate qualitative and quantitative data" (Plano Clark, 2010).

The search was conducted for all years beginning with 1997, which is the first year in which any of the search terms appear in grant abstracts or titles. The paper by Plano Clark (2010) includes results from FY 1997 through FY 2008. We replicated that study to ensure that we were employing a consistent defini- tion of mixed methods research. This replication was conducted in a blind man- ner, such that we did not have information about which studies were coded as mixed methods or not in the original study. After our independent coding, we checked to ensure that the total number of studies classified as mixed methods was the same as the original study results for that year. If there were any differ- ences, further review was conducted, and in some cases our operating definition for classifying studies was adjusted. For example, it was in this process that we determined that P Series grants should be excluded as described next. Next, we extended the analysis through FY 2013. Studies were classified based on the U.S. government FY, which runs from October 1 to September 30.

For the period from FY 2009 to FY 2013, there were 415 grants identified in the original search, and 378 were determined to meet the definition of mixed methods. The remaining 37 studies that did not meet the definition used multiple quantitative methods or multiple qualitative methods; represented funding for conferences, training, or other nonresearch activities; or mentioned other previ- ous evidence or separate planned mixed methods studies in their abstracts. Additionally, none of the P Series grants were included because these grants support research program projects and centers, and while they may provide small grants for research projects or training for researchers, any mixed methods work under such a grant would represent only part of the overall program.

References

Johnson, R. B., Onwuegbuzie, A. J., & Turner, L. A. (2007). Toward a definition of mixed methods research. *Journal of Mixed Methods Research, 1*(2), 112–133.

Plano Clark, V. L. (2010). The adoption and practice of mixed methods: U.S. trends in federally funded health-related research. *Qualitative Inquiry, 16*(6), 428–440.

✣ APPENDIX C ✣

ASSESSING RIGOR IN QUANTITATIVE HEALTH SCIENCES RESEARCH

Element	Questions
Domain 1: Research Team	
Experience, training, and credentials of researchers	What were the researchers' credentials? What experience or training did the researchers have with the methods and research topic of the study?
Gender	Were the researchers male or female?
Participant knowledge of the interviewer	What did the participants know about the researchers (e.g., personal goals, reasons for doing the research)?
Domain 2: Study Design	
Purpose	Is the purpose of the study or research problem clearly identified?
Literature review	Is the review clearly organized? Does it offer a critical analysis of the literature? Is the majority of literature recent and empirical?
Theoretical framework	Has a conceptual or theoretical framework been identified?
Objectives or research questions	What were the objectives of the study? Has a research question or hypothesis been identified?
Type of study	What type of study was done, and was the study design justified based on the research questions (e.g., cross-sectional, retrospective cohort, longitudinal)?

(Continued)

(Continued)

Element	Questions
Sample	Has the target population been clearly identified? How was the sample selected? Is it of adequate size and ratio of intervention to comparison subjects? Are inclusion and exclusion criteria clearly identified?
Ethical considerations	Were the participants fully informed about the nature of the research? Was the autonomy and confidentiality of the participants guaranteed? Was ethical permission granted for the study?
Operational definitions	Are all terms, theories, and concepts mentioned in the study clearly defined?
Domain 3: Data Collection	
Data collection protocol	Was the procedure for collecting data described? How was it developed?
Improving rigor	Were reliability and validity testing undertaken?
Domain 4: Data Analysis	
Statistical analyses	What type of data and statistical analyses were undertaken, and were the analyses appropriate?
Reducing bias	What methods were used to control confounding bias during the analysis?
Domain 5: Results and Reporting	
Results	What results were reported in the study? Did the results align with the goals and the methods of the study?
Discussion of bias	How is the interpretation of these results affected by information bias, selection bias, and confounding? Was the direction and magnitude of any bias considered?
Limitations	Did the discussion section adequately address the limitations of the study?
Conclusions	What were the authors' main conclusions? Were they justified based on the results?
Generalizations	To what larger population can the results be generalized?
Links with broader literature	Are the findings linked back to the literature review? Was a recommendation for further research made?
References	Were all the books, journals, and other citations alluded to in the text accurately referenced?

References

CONSORT Transparent Reporting of Trials. (2012, January 20). *The CONSORT statement*. Retrieved February 28, 2014, from http://www.consort-statement.org/consort-statment.

Couglan, M., Cronin, P., & Ryan, F. (2007). Step-by-step guide to critiquing research. Part 1: Quantitative research. *British Journal of Nursing, 16* (11), 658–663.

Monson, R. R. (1990). *Occupational epidemiology* (2nd ed.). Boca Raton, FL: CRC Press.

ASSESSING RIGOR IN QUALITATIVE HEALTH SCIENCES RESEARCH: CONSOLIDATED CRITERIA FOR REPORTING QUALITATIVE RESEARCH (COREQ)*

Element	Questions
Domain 1: Research Team	
Experience, training, and credentials of researchers	What are the credentials of the researchers? What experience or training did the researchers have with the methods and research topic of the study?
Interviewer or facilitator	Which researchers conducted the data collection? Were they matched by gender or other characteristics to the participants?
Participant knowledge of the interviewer	What did the participants know about the researchers (e.g., personal goals, reasons for doing the research)?
Interviewer characteristics	What characteristics were reported about the interviewer or facilitator (e.g., bias, assumptions, reasons and interests in the research topic)?
Domain 2: Study Design	
Methodology and theory	Was the methodological orientation to guide the study clarified (e.g., grounded theory, discourse analysis, ethnography, phenomenology, content analysis)?
Sampling	How were participants selected (purposive, convenience, consecutive, snowball)?

(Continued)

(Continued)

Element	Questions
Method of approach	How were participants contacted (e.g., face-to-face, telephone, mail, e-mail)?
Sample size	How many participants were in the study?
Nonparticipation	How many participants refused to participate or dropped out? Were the reasons described?
Setting of data collection	Where was the data collected (e.g., home, clinic, workplace)?
Presence of nonparticipants	Was anyone else present besides the participants and researchers?
Description of sample	What were the important characteristics of the sample (e.g., demographics, date of data collection)?
Ethical considerations	Were the participants fully informed about the nature of the research? Was the autonomy and confidentiality of the participants guaranteed? Was ethical permission granted for the study?
Domain 3: Data Collection	
Interview guide	Were questions, prompts, and guides provided by the authors? Was the guide pilot tested?
Repeat interviews	Were repeat interviews conducted? If yes, how many?
Audio/visual recording	Did the researcher use audio or visual recording to collect the data?
Field notes	Were field notes made during and/or after the interview or focus groups?
Duration	How long did the interviews or focus group last?
Data saturation	Was data saturation discussed?
Transcripts returned	Were transcripts returned to participants for comment and/or correction?
Domain 4: Data Analysis	
Number of data coders	How many data coders coded the data?
Description of the code structure	Did the authors provide a description of the code structure?

Element	Questions
Derivation of themes	Were themes clearly identified in advance or derived from the data?
Software	What software, if applicable, was used to manage the data (e.g., ATLAS.ti, NVivo, MAXQDA)?
Participant checking	Did participants provide feedback on the findings?
Domain 5: Results and Reporting	
Quotations presented	Were participant quotations presented to illustrate the themes or findings? Was each quotation identified (e.g., participant number or ID)?
Data and findings consistent	Was there consistency between the data presented and the findings?
Clarity of major themes	Were major themes clearly presented in the findings?
Clarity of minor themes	Is there a description of diverse cases or discussion of minor themes?
Links with broader literature	Are the findings linked back to the literature review? Was a recommendation for further research made?
References	Were all the books, journals, and other citations alluded to in the text accurately referenced?

* The COREQ represents a formal reporting checklist for in-depth interviews and focus groups, which represent the most common methods for data collection in qualitative health services research. The COREQ was developed following a comprehensive search of the literature of published checklists used to review qualitative studies.

Reference

Tong, A., Sainsbury, P., & Craig, J. (2007). Consolidated criteria for reporting qualitative research (COREQ): A 32-item checklist for interviews and focus groups. International *Journal for Quality in Health Care, 19*(6), 349–357.

⊰ APPENDIX E ⊱

QUICK RESOURCE: A SHORT LIST OF READINGS AND REFERENCES

People often ask us for recommendations for our top key readings on mixed methods. Here we provide this very brief list of readings and resources that we have found to be particularly useful in shaping our own thinking. Please note that this list is far from exhaustive, as there are many excellent textbooks and journals and web-based materials available; however, this is a useful starting place.

Resources on Qualitative and Mixed Methods

Creswell, J. W. (2013). *Research design: Qualitative, quantitative and mixed methods approaches* (4th ed.). Thousand Oaks, CA: Sage.

Creswell, J. W., & Plano Clark, V. L. (2010). *Designing and conducting mixed methods research* (2nd ed.). Thousand Oaks, CA: Sage.

Greene, J. C. (2007). *Mixed methods in social inquiry.* San Francisco, CA: Jossey-Bass.

Morse, J., & Niehaus, L. (2009). *Mixed method design: Principles and procedures.* Walnut Creek, CA: Left Coast Press.

Padgett, D. K. (2011). *Qualitative and mixed methods in public health.* Thousand Oaks, CA: Sage.

Patton, M. Q. (2001). *Qualitative research and evaluation methods* (3rd ed.). Thousand Oaks, CA: Sage.

Plano Clark, V. L., & Creswell, J. W. (Eds.). (2008). *The mixed methods reader.* Thousand Oaks, CA: Sage.

Tashakkori, A., & Teddlie, C. (Eds.). (2010). *SAGE handbook of mixed methods in social & behavioral research.* Thousand Oaks, CA: Sage.

Teddlie, C., & Tashakkori, A. (2008). *Foundations of mixed methods research.* Thousand Oaks, CA: Sage.

Yin, R. K. (2008). *Case study research: Design and methods* (4th ed.). Thousand Oaks, CA: Sage.

Additional Sources of Information

Collins, K., & O'Cathain, A. (2009). Ten points about mixed methods research to be considered by the novice researcher. *International Journal of Multiple Research Approaches, 3,* 2–7.

Cohen, D., & Crabtree, B. (2008). *Robert Wood Johnson, Qualitative research guidelines project.* Retrieved from http://www.qualres.org/

Creswell, J. W., Klassen, A. C., Plano Clark, V. L., & Smith, K. C. for the Office of Behavioral and Social Sciences Research. (2011). *Best practices for mixed methods research in the health sciences.* Bethesda, MD: National Institutes of Health. Retrieved from http://obssr.od.nih.gov/mixed_methods_research

Journal of Mixed Methods Research. Thousand Oaks, CA: Sage. Available from http://mmr.sagepub.com/

National Institutes of Health, Office of Behavioral and Social Sciences Research. (2001). *Qualitative methods in health research: Opportunities and considerations in application and review.* Washington DC: Author. Retrieved from obssr.od.nih.gov/pdf/qualitative.pdf

❈ APPENDIX F ❈

QUALITATIVE ANALYSIS SOFTWARE COMPARISON TABLE

	ATLAS.ti	Dedoose	Ethnograph	HyperRESEARCH	MAXQDA	NVivo	QDA Miner
Software location	Desktop	Web	Desktop	Desktop	Desktop	Desktop	Desktop
Supported OS	Windows XP, Windows Vista 7, 8; Parallels needed to run on Mac; mobile version available for iPad	—	Windows, Parallels needed to run on Mac	Windows XP, Windows Vista 7, 8; Mac OS X 10.39 or later	Windows XP, Windows Vista 7, 8; Mac OS X 10.7 or later; Max APP for mobile devices	Windows XP, S2, or later; Windows Vista 7, 8	Windows XP, 2000; Windows Vista 7, 8; Mac OS with virtual machine solution or Boot Camp
Cost	$$$$ (Student rates available)	$ (Monthly rates available for individuals or groups)	$$ (Student rates available)	$$$ (Student rates available)	$$$$ (Student rates available)	$$$$ (Student rates available)	$$$
Text coding	✓	✓	✓	✓	✓	✓	✓
PDF coding	✓	✓	✓	—	✓	✓	✓
Video coding	✓	✓	✓	✓	✓	✓	✓
Audio coding	✓	✓	✓	✓	✓	✓	✓
Image coding	✓	✓	✓	✓	✓	✓	✓
Memo writing	✓	✓	✓	✓	✓	✓	✓

	ATLAS.ti	Dedoose	Ethnograph	HyperRESEARCH	MAXQDA	NVivo	QDA Miner
Working with quantitative data	Can import quantitative data from spreadsheet or use manual entry Can export quantitative data to spreadsheet	Can import quantitative data from spreadsheet program or use manual entry Can export quantitative data to spreadsheet program	—	Will be coming out with a mixed methods importer tool in 2014 to import quantitative data from spreadsheet programs	Can import quantitative data from spreadsheet program or use manual entry Can export quantitative data to spreadsheet program	Can import quantitative data from spreadsheet program or use manual entry Can export quantitative data to spreadsheet program	Can import file formats such as Excel, Access, Paradox, dBase, SPSS
Teamwork: Simultaneous access	Projects cannot be accessed at the same time by different users	Simultaneous access in real time	—	Projects cannot be accessed at the same time by different users	Projects cannot be accessed at the same time by different users	Simultaneous access in real time (with the purchase of NVivo server)	Projects cannot be accessed at the same time by different users
Trial version available	✓	✓	✓	✓	✓	✓	✓
Website	http://www.atlasti .com/index.html	http://www .dedoose.com	http://www .qualisresearch .com/ ContactUs.htm	http://www .researchware.com/ products/ hyperresearch.html	http://www .maxqda.com/ great-reasons-to- use-maxqda	http://www .qsrinternational .com/products_ nvivo.aspx	http:// provalisresearch .com/products/ qualitative-data- analysis-software

371

GLOSSARY OF KEY TERMS AND DEFINITIONS

Key Term and Definition	Suggested Source(s) for Further Reading
Selected Health Sciences Terms	
Implementation science: Research that examines the level to which health interventions can fit within real-world public health and clinical service systems. A particular focus of this field is identifying barriers (e.g., social, behavioral, economic, management) that impede effective implementation or testing new approaches to improve health programming.	Damschroder, L. J., Aron, D. C., Keith, R. E., Kirsh, S. R., Alexander, J. A., & Lowery, J. C. (2009). Fostering implementation of health services research findings into practice: A consolidated framework for advancing implementation science. *Implementation Science, 4*(50). doi: 10.1186/1748–5908–4-50
	Madon, T., Hofman, K. J., Kupfer, L., & Glass, R. I. (2007). Public health. Implementation science. *Science, 318*(5857), 1728–1729.
Community-based participatory research (CBPR): Research arising from a partnership between academic researchers and community members to ensure integration of nonresearcher expertise into all stages of research in order to address health disparities and improve health outcomes	Horowitz, C. R., Robinson, M., & Seifer, S. (2009). Community-based participatory research from the margin to the mainstream: Are researchers prepared? *Circulation, 119*(19), 2633–2642.
	Israel, B. A., Schulz, A. J., Parker, E. A., & Becker, A. B. (1998). Review of community-based research: Assessing partnership approaches to improve public health. *Annual Review of Public Health, 19,* 173–202.
Patient-centered outcomes research (PCOR): Research that seeks to promote the effectiveness and value of health care with a results-based orientation by engaging patients as research partners and focusing on what matters to patients and the public	Selby J. V., Beal, A. C., & Frank, L. (2012). The Patient-Centered Outcomes Research Institute (PCORI) national priorities for research and initial research agenda. *JAMA, 307*(15), 1583–1584. doi: 10.1001/jama.2012.500.

(Continued)

(Continued)

Key Term and Definition	Suggested Source(s) for Further Reading
Mixed Methods Terms	
General terms	
Mixed methods: A type of research in which a researcher or team of researchers combines elements of qualitative and quantitative research approaches (e.g., use of qualitative and quantitative viewpoints, data collection, analysis, inference techniques) for the broad purposes of breadth and depth of understanding and corroboration	Johnson, R. B., Onwuegbuzie, A. J., & Turner, L. A. (2007). Toward a definition of mixed methods research. *Journal of Mixed Methods Research, 1*(2), 112–133.
Data integration: The interaction or conversation between the qualitative and quantitative components of a study; may be achieved through triangulation, following a thread, or a mixed methods matrix	O'Cathain, A., Murphy, E., & Nicholl, J. (2010). Three techniques for integrating data in mixed methods. *BMJ, 341,* c4587.
Yield: A criteria for judging the quality of mixed methods studies based on whether the output of a mixed methods study is greater than what could be achieved by individual single method studies. May be judged based on the extent of integration in design, sampling, analysis, and interpretation and the types and content of publications from the study	O'Cathain, A., Murphy, E., & Nicholl, J. (2007). Integration and publications as indicators of "yield" from mixed methods studies. *Journal of Mixed Methods Research, 1*(2), 147–163.
Triangulation: Process by which a single phenomenon is examined with multiple observers, theories, methods, or data sources to determine the degree of convergence across components	Campbell, D., & Fiske, D. (1959). Convergent and discriminant validation by the multitrait-multimethod matrix. *Psychological Bulletin, 56*(2), 81–105.
	Fielding, N. G. (2012). Triangulation and mixed methods designs: Data integration with new research technologies. *Journal of Mixed Methods Research, 6*(2), 124–136.
	Patton, M. Q. (1999). Enhancing the quality and credibility of qualitative analysis. *HSR, 34,* 189–208.
	Patton, M. Q. (2002). *Qualitative research and evaluation methods* (3rd ed.). Thousand Oaks, CA: Sage.

Key Term and Definition	Suggested Source(s) for Further Reading
Representational group theory: A theory of organizational psychology that can be applied to mixed methods research teams; this theory suggests that the behaviors and perspectives of each individual within a group are not only based on that individual's personality characteristics but also on organizational, professional, and identity "home group" memberships.	Berg, D. N. (1979). Intergroup relations: An abbreviated update. *Journal of Management Education, 4,* 48–51.
	Wells, L. (1995). The group as a whole: A systemic, socioanalytic perspective on interpersonal and group relations. In J. Gillette & M. McCollom (Eds.), *Groups in context* (pp. 49–85). Reading, MA: Addison-Wesley.
Research strategies and designs	
Explanatory sequential design: Mixed methods design that consists of a quantitative phase followed by a qualitative phase, such that the qualitative data and their analysis refine and explain the statistical results by exploring participants' views in more depth	Creswell, J. W., & Plano Clark, V. (2007). *Designing and conducting mixed methods research.* Thousand Oaks, CA: Sage.
	Ivankova, N. V., Creswell, J. W., & Stick, S. L. (2006). Using mixed-methods sequential explanatory design: From theory to practice. *Field Methods, 18,* 3–20.
Exploratory sequential design: Mixed methods design that consists of a qualitative phase followed by a quantitative phase, such that the qualitative data and their analysis help to inform the direction of the quantitative phase	Creswell, J. W., & Plano Clark, V. (2007). *Designing and conducting mixed methods research.* Thousand Oaks, CA: Sage.
Convergent design: Mixed methods design in which quantitative and qualitative data about the same phenomenon are collected and analyzed separately and then the results are converged during interpretation	Creswell, J. W., & Plano Clark, V. (2007). *Designing and conducting mixed methods research.* Thousand Oaks, CA: Sage.
Concurrent embedded design: Mixed methods design in which one data set provides a supportive, secondary role in a study based primarily on the other data type	Creswell, J. W., & Plano Clark, V. (2007). *Designing and conducting mixed methods research.* Thousand Oaks, CA: Sage.
	Lewin, S., Glenton, C., & Oxman, A. D. (2009). Use of qualitative methods alongside randomized controlled trials of complex healthcare interventions: methodological study. *BMJ, 339,* b3496.

(Continued)

Key Term and Definition	Suggested Source(s) for Further Reading
Case studies design: Mixed methods design in which there is a deliberate, intense focus on a single phenomenon while understanding its real-world, dynamic context; rigorous case studies often employ a range of qualitative and quantitative data collection methods	Yin, R. K. (1999). Enhancing the quality of case studies in health services research. *HSR,* 34(5 Pt. 2), 1209–1224.
Multistage design: Mixed methods design that combines more than one mixed methods design into a large and complex study in which many components build off of each other to address a cohesive set of research questions	Creswell, J. W., & Plano Clark, V. L. (2011). *Designing and conducting mixed methods research* (2nd ed.). Thousand Oaks, CA: Sage.
Sampling	
Independent mixed methods sampling: A sampling strategy for mixed methods studies that involves using completely separate sampling strategies for each study component based on the research aims of that component	
Interdependent mixed methods sampling: A sampling strategy for mixed methods studies that jointly uses probability and purposeful techniques to create one or more samples for a study	
Stratified purposeful sampling (or quota sampling): A type of interdependent mixed methods sampling approach in which strata are created for salient subgroups of the population and then cases are purposefully recruited from each strata	
Purposeful random sampling: A variation of stratified purposeful sampling in which a random sample is drawn from a large universe of available cases that satisfy specified criteria	

Key Term and Definition	Suggested Source(s) for Further Reading
Combined mixed methods sampling: A sampling strategy for mixed methods studies that involves selecting the sample for one study component independently and then selecting the sample for the second component in a way that is dependent on the first	
Data integration	
Merged integration: A type of integration in mixed methods studies in which findings are compared in order to identify complementarity, convergence and divergence among data sets; occurs after both types of data have been collected and analyzed	Creswell, J. W., & Plano Clark, V. L. (2011). *Designing and conducting mixed methods research* (2nd ed.). Thousand Oaks, CA: Sage.
Connected integration: A type of integration in mixed methods studies in which one data set is used to define the sample for the other, explain the other, or construct the research aims of a latter component of the study (this latter form of connected integration is also called "building")	Creswell, J. W., & Plano Clark, V. L. (2011). *Designing and conducting mixed methods research* (2nd ed.). Thousand Oaks, CA: Sage.
Embedded integration: A type of integration in mixed methods studies in which the secondary question (and method) is intended to support the work of the primary question and is therefore nested within the framework of the primary question; occurs through multiple points of integration throughout the study	Creswell, J. W., & Plano Clark, V. L. (2011). *Designing and conducting mixed methods research* (2nd ed.). Thousand Oaks, CA: Sage.

(Continued)

Key Term and Definition	Suggested Source(s) for Further Reading
Qualitative Research Terms	
General terms	
Grounded theory: Uses systematic procedures to generate theory or insights describing a phenomenon and is grounded in the views expressed by study participants; typically analyzed with constant comparative method	Creswell, J. (2003). *Research design: Qualitative, quantitative and mixed methods approaches* (2nd ed.). Thousand Oaks, CA: Sage.
	Glaser, B., & Strauss, A. (Eds.). (1967). *The discovery of grounded theory: Strategies for qualitative research.* Chicago, IL: Aldine.
	Patton, M. Q. (2002). *Qualitative research and evaluation methods* (3rd ed.). Thousand Oaks, CA: Sage.
Inductive reasoning: Reasoning from the particular to the general; involves the creation of meaningful and consistent explanations, understandings, conceptual frameworks, and/ or theories that are grounded in the data rather than being given a priori	Lincoln, Y. S., & Guba, E. G. (1985). *Naturalistic inquiry.* Beverly Hills, CA: Sage.
	Patton, M. Q. (2002). *Qualitative research and evaluation methods* (3rd ed.). Thousand Oaks, CA: Sage.
Sampling	
Purposeful sampling: Sampling strategy that seeks to include the full spectrum of cases and reflect the diversity within a given population by including extreme or negative cases; sample size varies depending on the breadth and complexity of the inquiry	Miles, M., & Huberman, A. M. (Eds.). (1994). *Qualitative data analysis: An expanded sourcebook.* Thousand Oaks, CA: Sage.
	Patton, M. Q. (2002). *Qualitative research and evaluation methods* (3rd ed.). Thousand Oaks, CA: Sage.
Information rich: Sampling strategy that seeks to include participants who have experience or knowledge of a given phenomenon and are willing and able to report on it; aims to select individuals from whom the most can be learned	Patton, M. Q. (2002). *Qualitative research and evaluation methods* (3rd ed.). Thousand Oaks, CA: Sage.
Theoretical sampling: Used in the grounded theory approach; the sample is developed and refined throughout the course of the study to explore insights that emerge from the data	Glaser, B., & Strauss, A. (Eds.). (1967). *The discovery of grounded theory: Strategies for qualitative research.* Chicago, IL: Aldine.
	Pope, C., & Mays, N. (1995). Reaching the parts other methods cannot reach: An introduction to qualitative methods in health and health services research. *BMJ, 311,* 42–45.

Key Term and Definition	Suggested Source(s) for Further Reading
Data collection	
Theoretical saturation: The point at which no new concepts emerge from the review of successive data from a sample that is diverse in pertinent characteristics and experiences; used to determine the adequacy of the sample size	Glaser, B., & Strauss, A. (Eds.). (1967). *The discovery of grounded theory: Strategies for qualitative research.* Chicago, IL: Aldine.
	Morse, J. (1995). The significance of saturation. *Qualitative Health Research 5,* 147–149.
	Strauss, A., & Corbin, J. (1998). *Basics of qualitative research: Techniques and procedures for developing grounded theory.* Thousand Oaks, CA: Sage.
Analysis	
Constant comparative method: Form of qualitative analysis that involves reviewing data line by line and coding sections as concepts become apparent, then comparing the text segments with segments previously assigned the same code to decide whether they represent the same concept; coding structure is redefined continuously	Glaser, B., & Strauss, A. (Eds.). (1967). *The discovery of grounded theory: Strategies for qualitative research.* Chicago, IL: Aldine.
	Miles, M., & Huberman, A. M. (Eds.). (1994). *Qualitative data analysis: An expanded sourcebook.* Thousand Oaks, CA: Sage.
	Strauss, A., & Corbin, J. (1998). *Basics of qualitative research: Techniques and procedures for developing grounded theory.* Thousand Oaks, CA: Sage.
Codes: Tags or labels that help catalogue key concepts while preserving the context in which these concepts occur	Miles, M., & Huberman, A. M. (Eds.). (1994). *Qualitative data analysis: An expanded sourcebook.* Thousand Oaks, CA: Sage.
Inter-rater reliability: The degree to which two or more coders agree in their independent assignment of codes to qualitative data	Miles, M., & Huberman, A. M. (Eds.). (1994). *Qualitative data analysis: An expanded sourcebook.* Thousand Oaks, CA: Sage.
Content analysis: The categorization and classification of data to make inferences about the antecedents of a communication, describe and make inferences about characteristics of a communication, and make inferences about the effects of a communication	Holsti, O. (1969). *Content analysis for the social sciences and humanities.* Reading, MA: Addison-Wesley.

(Continued)

(Continued)

Key Term and Definition	Suggested Source(s) for Further Reading
Audit trail: A transparent description of the research steps taken from the start of a research project to the development and reporting of findings; should include raw data, analysis products, synthesis product, process notes, etc.	Lincoln, Y., & Guba, E. (1985). *Naturalistic inquiry.* Beverly Hills, CA: Sage.
Output	
Taxonomies: Formal system for classifying multifaceted, complex phenomena according to a set of common conceptual domains and dimensions; used to increase clarity in defining and comparing complex phenomena	Bradley, E. H., Curry, L. A., & Devers, K. J. (2007). Qualitative data analysis for health services research: Developing taxonomy, themes, and theory. *HSR, 42,* 1758–1772.
	Sofaer, S. (1999). Qualitative methods: What are they and why use them? *HSR, 34,* 1101–1118.
Themes: Recurrent unifying concepts or statements about the subject of inquiry; used to characterize experiences of individual participants by the more general insights apparent from the whole of the data	Boyatzis, R. (1998). *Transforming qualitative information: Thematic and code development.* Thousand Oaks, CA: Sage.
	Bradley, E. H., Curry, L. A., & Devers, K. J. (2007). Qualitative data analysis for health services research: Developing taxonomy, themes, and theory. *HSR, 42,* 1758–1772.
Theory: A set of general propositions that help explain, predict, and interpret events or phenomena of interest; used to identify possible levels for affecting specific outcomes or to guide further empirical testing of explicit hypotheses derived from theory	Bradley, E. H., Curry, L. A., & Devers, K. J. (2007). Qualitative data analysis for health services research: Developing taxonomy, themes, and theory. *HSR, 42,* 1758–1772.
Standards of rigor	
Credibility: The degree to which the findings plausibly explain the phenomenon of interest, the extent to which findings cohere with what is already known, the attention paid to alternative or rival explanations or interpretations, and the correspondence between the researcher's and respondent's portrayal of respondent experience; analogous to validity in quantitative research	Lincoln, Y., & Guba, E. (1985). *Naturalistic inquiry.* Beverly Hills, CA: Sage.
	Patton, M. Q. (1993). Enhancing the quality and credibility of qualitative analysis. *HSR, 8,* 341–351.

Key Term and Definition	Suggested Source(s) for Further Reading
Dependability: The degree to which the researchers account for and/or describe the changing contexts and circumstances during the study; can be enhanced by altering the research design or data collection as new findings emerge during data collection, by using multiple coders who engage in multicoder agreement analysis, and by the establishment of a multidisciplinary research team; analogous to reliability in quantitative research	Lincoln, Y., & Guba, E. (1985). *Naturalistic inquiry.* Beverly Hills, CA: Sage.
	Patton, M. Q. (1999). Enhancing the quality and credibility of qualitative analysis. *HSR, 34,* 189–208.
Transferability: The degree to which themes or research protocols can be transferred or generalized to other settings, contexts, or populations; analogous to generalizability in quantitative research	Malterud, K. (2001). Qualitative research: Standards, challenges, and guidelines. *Lancet, 358,* 483–488.
Confirmability: The degree to which the findings of a study are shaped by respondents and not researcher bias, motivation, or interest	Lincoln, Y., & Guba, E. (1985). *Naturalistic inquiry.* Beverly Hills, CA: Sage.
Quantitative Research Terms	
General terms	
Prevalence: A measure of the proportion of a population found to have a condition (typically a disease or a risk factor)	Aschengrau, A., & Seage, G. R. (2008). *Essentials of epidemiology in public health* (2nd ed.). Sudbury, MA: Jones and Bartlett.
Incidence: A measure of the frequency of new cases of a disease or condition; always calculated for a specified period of time	Aschengrau, A., & Seage, G. R. (2008). *Essentials of epidemiology in public health* (2nd ed.). Sudbury, MA: Jones and Bartlett.
Effectiveness: The extent to which a specific intervention, procedure, regimen, or service, when deployed in the field in routine circumstances, does what it is intended to do for a specified population	Aschengrau, A., & Seage, G. R. (2008). *Essentials of epidemiology in public health* (2nd ed.). Sudbury, MA: Jones and Bartlett.
Efficacy: The extent to which a specific intervention, procedure, regimen, or service produces the intended result under ideal conditions	Aschengrau, A., & Seage, G. R. (2008). *Essentials of epidemiology in public health* (2nd ed.). Sudbury, MA: Jones and Bartlett.

(Continued)

(Continued)

Key Term and Definition	Suggested Source(s) for Further Reading
Meta-analysis: A statistical procedure that integrates the results of several independent studies considered to be combinable, allowing a more objective appraisal of the evidence than individual studies	Egger, M., Smith, G. D., & Phillips, A. N. (1997). Meta-analysis: Principles and procedures. *BMJ, 315,* 1533–1537.
Deductive reasoning: Reasoning from the general to the particular, or the application of general rules to specific cases; involves a hypothesis or theory that is established and tested in specific circumstances	Johnson, B., & Gray, R. (2010). A history of the philosophical and theoretical issues for mixed methods research. In A. Tashakkori & C. Teddlie (Eds.), *Handbook of mixed methods in social & behavioral research* (pp. 69–94). Thousand Oaks, CA: Sage.
Research strategies and designs	
Cross-sectional study: A type of descriptive study designed to estimate the prevalence of a disease or risk factor	Aschengrau, A., & Seage, G. R. (2008). *Essentials of epidemiology in public health* (2nd ed.). Sudbury, MA: Jones and Bartlett.
Randomized controlled trial: A type of experimental study where participants are randomly assigned to receive either an intervention or control treatment, allowing researchers to study the effect of the intervention; because of the comparability of the groups at baseline, any differences seen in the groups at the end can be attributed to the intervention.	Aschengrau, A., & Seage, G. R. (2008). *Essentials of epidemiology in public health* (2nd ed.). Sudbury, MA: Jones and Bartlett.
Case control studies: A type of observational study that compares individuals who have a disease with individuals who do not have the disease in order to examine differences in exposures or risk factors for the disease	Aschengrau, A., & Seage, G. R. (2008). *Essentials of epidemiology in public health* (2nd ed.). Sudbury, MA: Jones and Bartlett.
Longitudinal case study/Cohort study/ Prospective study: A type of observational study that collects data and follows a group of subjects who have received a specific exposure; the incidence of a specific disease or other outcome of interest is tracked over time and the incidence in the exposed group is compared with the incidence in groups that are not exposed	Aschengrau, A., & Seage, G. R. (2008). *Essentials of epidemiology in public health* (2nd ed.). Sudbury, MA: Jones and Bartlett.

Key Term and Definition	Suggested Source(s) for Further Reading
Retrospective study: A type of cohort study that uses historical data to determine exposure level at some time in the past and then follows up with cohort members to take measurements of occurrence of disease between baseline and the present	Aschengrau, A., & Seage, G. R. (2008). *Essentials of epidemiology in public health* (2nd ed.). Sudbury, MA: Jones and Bartlett.
Sampling	
Probability sampling: A sampling strategy in which each individual is chosen randomly and entirely by chance, such that each individual has the same probability of being chosen at any stage during the sampling process; aims to achieve high generalizability through representativeness	Daniel, J. (2012). *Sampling essentials: Practical guidelines for making sampling choices.* Thousand Oaks, CA: Sage.
	Friedman, L. M., Furberg, C. D., & DeMets, D. L. (2010). *Fundamentals of clinical trials* (4th ed.). New York, NY: Springer.
Standards of rigor	
Validity: The extent to which a measure actually represents what is intended to measure; analogous to credibility in qualitative research	Fowler, F. (1995). *Improving survey questions: Design and evaluation.* Thousand Oaks, CA: Sage.
Reliability: The degree to which observations or measures can be replicated; analogous to dependability in qualitative research	Last, J. M. (Ed.). (2001). *A dictionary of epidemiology* (4th ed.). New York, NY: Oxford University Press.
Generalizability/External validity: The degree to which the study results hold true for a population beyond the subjects in the study or in other settings; analogous to transferability in qualitative research	Fletcher, R. H., Fletcher, S. W., & Wagner, E. H. (1996). *Clinical epidemiology: The essentials* (3rd ed.). Baltimore, MD: Williams and Wilkins.
Objectivity: The degree to which researchers can remain distanced from what they study so findings reflect the nature of what was studied rather than researcher bias, motivation, or interest	Lincoln, Y., & Guba, E. (1985). *Naturalistic inquiry.* Beverly Hills, CA: Sage.

INDEX

Figures, boxes, and tables are indicated by f, b, or t following the page number.

ⓈSAGE research**methods**

The essential online tool for researchers from the world's leading methods publisher

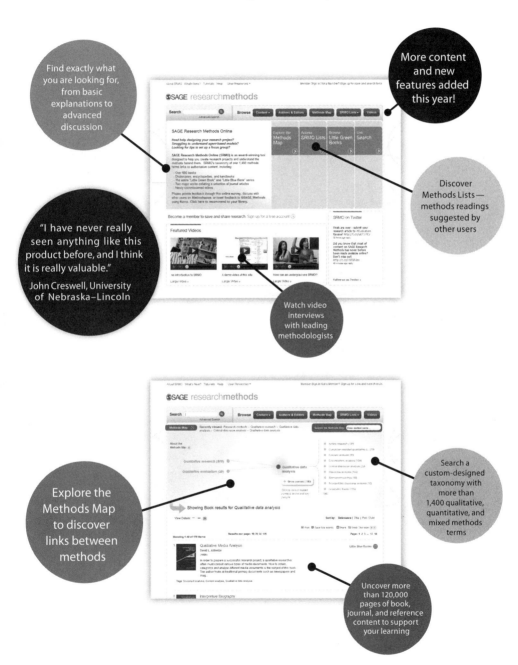

More content and new features added this year!

Find exactly what you are looking for, from basic explanations to advanced discussion

Discover Methods Lists— methods readings suggested by other users

"I have never really seen anything like this product before, and I think it is really valuable."
John Creswell, University of Nebraska–Lincoln

Watch video interviews with leading methodologists

Explore the Methods Map to discover links between methods

Search a custom-designed taxonomy with more than 1,400 qualitative, quantitative, and mixed methods terms

Uncover more than 120,000 pages of book, journal, and reference content to support your learning

Find out more at
www.sageresearchmethods.com